AI-Driven National Cyber Defense and Resilience Strategies

The acceleration of the digital transformation of critical infrastructure, government services, and military systems has profoundly changed the cyber threat landscape. Governments now face cyber risks of unprecedented scale and sophistication, ranging from advanced persistent threats (APTs) and AI-assisted cyber espionage to large-scale ransomware campaigns, hybrid cyber-physical attacks, and information influence operations. In this context, traditional and reactive approaches to cybersecurity are no longer sufficient to ensure effective national cyber defense and resilience.

AI-Driven National Cyber Defense and Resilience Strategies offers an in-depth, forward-looking analysis of how artificial intelligence—specifically, machine learning, deep learning, and generative AI—can be leveraged to strengthen national cyber defense capabilities. The book explores the role of AI in improving threat intelligence, intrusion detection, incident response, cyber deception, security orchestration, and large-scale decision support, while highlighting the new risks posed by adversaries themselves equipped with advanced AI capabilities.

Bringing together contributions from researchers, industry experts, and institutional decision-makers, this book presents cutting-edge methodologies, innovative architectural frameworks, and concrete use cases from national security operations centers (SOCs), incident response teams (CSIRTs), military cyber commands, and critical infrastructure operators. Particular attention is given to the concepts of AI-driven cyber resilience, including adaptive defense, autonomous response, cyber situational awareness, and collaborative intelligence sharing at the national and international levels.

Beyond technological advances, the book critically examines the issues of governance, ethics, trust, and regulation related to the deployment of artificial intelligence in contexts of digital sovereignty and national defense. By bringing together technical innovations, strategic considerations, and regulatory frameworks, this volume is a leading reference for researchers, practitioners, and decision-makers seeking to design resilient, secure, and trustworthy national cyber defense ecosystems in the age of artificial intelligence.

AI-Driven National Cyber Defense and Resilience Strategies

Edited by
Mounia Zaydi, Yassine Maleh,
Hayat Zaydi, and Youness Khourdifi

CRC Press
Taylor & Francis Group
Boca Raton London New York

CRC Press is an imprint of the
Taylor & Francis Group, an **informa** business

Designed cover image: Shutterstock ID: 2687501009

First edition published 2027
by CRC Press
2385 NW Executive Center Drive, Suite 320, Boca Raton FL 33431

and by CRC Press
4 Park Square, Milton Park, Abingdon, Oxon, OX14 4RN

CRC Press is an imprint of Taylor & Francis Group, LLC

ISBN: 9781041095071 (hbk)
ISBN: 9781041095101 (pbk)
ISBN: 9781003650478 (ebk)

DOI: 10.1201/9781003650478

Typeset in Sabon
by Deanta Global Publishing Services, Chennai, India

Contents

Preface

The current era imposes a strategic reality: national cybersecurity is no longer a purely technical issue but a prerequisite for state continuity, economic stability, and democratic trust. Critical infrastructure (energy, healthcare, finance, transportation, water), digital public services, software chains, industrial networks, and the IoT/IIoT constitute a highly interconnected "system of systems." In this context, a cyber incident is not just an IT event: it can become a systemic shock, spread through dependencies, and affect essential functions. This "systemic" view of security, where resilience becomes the central metric, runs throughout the book and structures the way the chapters articulate threats, architecture, governance, operational capabilities, and technological innovations.

At the same time, artificial intelligence is profoundly reshaping the cyber battlefield. On the defensive side, AI accelerates the analysis of massive volumes of logs, anomaly detection, multi-source correlation, alert prioritization, and response orchestration. On the offensive side, it increases the capacity for automation, persuasion, and polymorphism, while introducing specific attacks (poisoning, extraction, prompt injection, etc.). The integration of AI into national cyber defense is therefore not a simple technological "addition": it involves choices of sovereignty, compliance, social acceptability, and the security of the models themselves.

This is precisely the aim of this book: to offer a coherent, interdisciplinary, and actionable vision of national cyber defense and resilience strategies, covering the following:

- Conceptual foundations (interdependence, resilience, risk governance, regulatory frameworks);
- Operational architectures and frameworks for AI-augmented national SOCs and cross-sector coordination mechanisms;
- Advanced detection methods (OT/IoT anomalies, PR/AUPRC-centered assessment, security safeguards, physically informed approaches, digital twins); and

- Critical application areas where security takes on a cyber-physical and sectoral dimension (maritime/underwater, healthcare/medical imaging, robotic environments, etc.).

Readers will find here a deliberate balance between (i) strategic thinking at the national level, (ii) realistic technological architectures, and (iii) deployment-oriented research contributions: reproducibility, metrics, operational constraints, explainability, safeguards, and governance. The book also emphasizes a key idea: there is no resilience without governance, and there is no credible governance without measurable instruments (MTTD/MTTR, cost of false positives, governed thresholds, audits, compliance requirements).

Finally, this book has been designed to serve several audiences without dilution: national officials and regulators, critical infrastructure operators, SOC/SIEM/SOAR architects, researchers and doctoral students, as well as practitioners wishing to link architecture and public policy decisions to robust technical models. It is not just a matter of "defending," but of defending in a coordinated, measured, verifiable, and sustainable way, in a world where AI accelerates both attacks and countermeasures.

Editors

Mounia Zaydi is Associate Professor of Cybersecurity at JUNIA ISEN Engineering School and a researcher at the Interdisciplinary Laboratory of Transitions of the Catholic University of Lille, France. She is a member of IEEE and the International Association of Engineers (IAENG). Her research focuses on information security and privacy, network and IoT security, IT governance, risk management, and the application of artificial intelligence to cybersecurity operations, incident response, and digital transformation. Her work particularly addresses the role of AI in enhancing security agility, threat detection, and resilience within complex information systems. Prof. Zaydi has authored and co-authored numerous peer-reviewed publications, including journal articles and book chapters, and actively contributes to the academic community as a reviewer and member of executive and technical program committees for international conferences and journals.

Yassine Maleh is Associate Professor of Cybersecurity and IT Governance at Sultan Moulay Slimane University, Morocco. He is the founding chair of the IEEE Consultant Network Morocco and the founding president of the African Research Center of Information Technology & Cybersecurity. He is Senior Member of IEEE and a member of IAENG and the Machine Intelligence Research Labs. His research activities focus on information security and privacy, Internet of Things security, wireless and constrained networks, and IT governance. He has authored and edited numerous scholarly works, including journal articles, conference papers, and books, and is widely recognized for his contributions to cybersecurity research and knowledge dissemination. Prof. Maleh holds several key editorial roles, including Editor-in-Chief and Associate Editor positions in leading international journals, and serves as a series editor for academic book collections in cybersecurity management. He is actively involved in the organization of international conferences and regularly contributes as a reviewer and program committee member for high-impact journals and conferences. His academic leadership and service activities have significantly contributed to advancing cybersecurity research at both regional and international levels.

Hayat Zaydi is Professor of Computer Science at the National Superior School of Mines of Rabat (ENSMR), Morocco. She is a Cisco Academy Instructor and a member of the International Association of Engineers (IAENG). Her research spans the Internet of Things, with a particular emphasis on healthcare-oriented applications, as well as artificial intelligence and distributed computing paradigms such as edge, fog, and cloud computing. A central focus of her work lies in the design of secure and resilient data-driven architectures integrating machine learning and deep learning techniques, especially within Internet of Medical Things (IoMT) environments. Prof. Zaydi has published extensively in international journals, conferences, and edited volumes. She is actively engaged in the academic community through her participation in technical program committees and as a reviewer for numerous international scientific venues. Her work bridges advanced computing architectures, AI, and cybersecurity to address emerging challenges in smart and healthcare systems.

Youness Khourdifi is Professor and Researcher in Computer Science at Sultan Moulay Slimane University, Morocco, where he teaches at the Faculty of Polydisciplinary Studies of Khouribga. He is an active member of the Laboratory of Material Sciences, Mathematics, and Environment (LS2ME) and is affiliated with professional organizations, including IEEE, ACM, IAENG, and Fondation Maroc Numérique. His research interests lie at the intersection of artificial intelligence, data engineering, and healthcare technologies. His work includes database migration and interoperability, particularly the automation of relational-to-NoSQL transformations, as well as the application of deep learning techniques to medical data analysis. He also investigates issues related to information security, IoT security, big data, and intelligent systems. Prof. Khourdifi has authored numerous scientific publications and actively contributes to the research community as a reviewer and program committee member in the fields of artificial intelligence and data science. Through his academic and organizational activities, he promotes interdisciplinary collaboration and the practical application of advanced computational methods to real-world challenges.

Contributors

Qasem Abu Al-Haija
Cybersecurity Department
Jordan University of Science and Technology
Irbid, Jordan

Shahad Alnatsheh
Department of Cybersecurity
Jordan University of Science and Technology
Irbid, Jordan

Marya Alsaadi
Department of Cybersecurity
Jordan University of Science and Technology
Irbid, Jordan

Shahed A. Al-Tamimi
Cybersecurity Department
University of Doha for Science and Technology
Doha, Qatar

Sara Arabi
Laboratory of Innovation in Management and Engineering (LIMIE)
Edvantis Higher Education Group
ISGA
Rabat, Morocco

Zohra Bakkoury
Ecole Mohammedia d'Ingénieurs
Mohammed V University
Rabat, Morocco

Omar Er-Remyly
MISI Laboratory, Faculty of Sciences and Techniques
Hassan First University of Settat
Settat, Morocco

Esra'a F. Hader
Computer Information Systems Department
Jordan University of Science and Technology
Irbid, Jordan

Amal Hadri
Laboratory of Innovation in Management and Engineering (LIMIE)
Edvantis Higher Education Group
ISGA
Rabat, Morocco

Roa'a Hamudeh
Department of Cybersecurity
Jordan University of Science and Technology
Irbid, Jordan

Maya Iqtaish
Department of Cybersecurity
Jordan University of Science and Technology
Irbid, Jordan

Razan Khassawneh
Department of Cybersecurity
Jordan University of Science and Technology
Irbid, Jordan

Youness Khourdifi
Faculty of Polydisciplinary Studies of Khouribga (FPK)
Laboratory of Material Sciences, Mathematics, and Environment (LS2ME)
Sultan Moulay Slimane University
Beni Mellal, Morocco

Yassine Maleh
Department of Cybersecurity, Networks and Telecommunications
Sultan Moulay Slimane University
Khouribga, Morocco

Bouchaib Nassereddine
IT, Networks, Mobility and Modelling Laboratory
Faculty of Sciences and Techniques
Hassan 1st University
Settat, Morocco

Aysha Oqdeh
Department of Cybersecurity
Jordan University of Science and Technology
Irbid, Jordan

Yaqeen Qudah
Department of Cybersecurity
Jordan University of Science and Technology
Irbid, Jordan

Hadeel Rashaidah
Department of Cybersecurity
Jordan University of Science and Technology
Irbid, Jordan

Amine Riad
LM2I
ENSEM Hassan II of Casablanca
Casablanca, Morocco

Hayat Zaydi
National Higher School of Mines – ENSMR, Systems Engineering and Digital Transformation Laboratory – LISTD, Smart Systems and Digital Transformation Team – SSDT
Rabat, Morocco

Mounia Zaydi
ICL, Junia
université catholique de Lille
Laboratoire Interdisciplinaire des Transitions de Lille (LITL)
Lille, France

Introduction

0.1 WHY THIS BOOK NOW?

Contemporary crises (attacks on hospitals, OT incidents, hybrid campaigns, supply chain compromises) have highlighted a transformation: national cyber defense is no longer limited to perimeter hardening but requires the ability to anticipate, detect quickly, respond in a coordinated manner, and recover on a national scale. Interdependencies (cloud, suppliers, telecoms, software, data, industrial systems) amplify the impacts: a localized failure can produce cascading effects.

In this landscape, AI occupies an ambivalent position. It enables the industrialization of detection and response (weak signal analysis, multi-source correlation, playbook automation), but it also creates new vulnerabilities (adversarial attacks, bias, abuses, opacity), while accelerating offensive capabilities. Therefore, the question is not "should AI be integrated?" but how to integrate it in a governed, sovereign, verifiable, and resilient manner.

0.2 THE GUIDING PRINCIPLES OF THE BOOK

The book is structured around four complementary themes:

Theme 1: Foundations and national strategy
This involves establishing the foundation: industrialized threats, resilience logic, risk governance, regulatory frameworks and standards, cross-sector cooperation, crisis exercises, and steering indicators (MTTD, MTTR, dwell time, etc.).

Theme 2: AI architectures for national cyber defense
The chapters propose architectural frameworks (multi-layered, aligned with governance/detection/response/recovery functions) and address national coordination: SOC integration, intelligence sharing, compliance mechanisms, and conditions for scaling up.

DOI: 10.1201/9781003650478-1

Theme 3: Robust detection for OT/IoT and cyber-physical systems
The industrial world imposes significant constraints: multi-rate signals, extreme imbalance, latency, functional safety, and alert costs. The book emphasizes tailored assessments (AUPRC-first), safeguards, and physically informed approaches coupled with digital twins.

Theme 4: Sectorization, use cases, and critical verticals
Rather than remaining at a generic level, several chapters delve into verticals: underwater surveillance and data integrity, medical imaging and hybrid encryption, automated threat hunting, and more experimental systems (robotics/IDS).

0.3 ORGANIZATION OF THE BOOK

The book *AI-Driven National Cyber Defense and Resilience Strategies* is organized into ten complementary chapters, following a progressive structure from strategic foundations to advanced AI-driven and cyber-physical applications.

Chapter 1: National cyber defense in the era of AI: Foundations, evolution, and strategies—Establishes the strategic, regulatory, and conceptual foundations of national cyber defense in an AI-driven context.

Chapter 2: Exploiting wireless system vulnerabilities: A case study on remote hacking with robots—Illustrates how wireless systems can be exploited through an experimental setup combining robotic platforms and offensive techniques, highlighting emerging attack surfaces.

Chapter 3: Automated threat hunting using AI—Examines how AI enables proactive threat hunting through behavioral analysis and large-scale data processing, while addressing practical limitations.

Chapter 4: Securing medical imaging systems: A case study on hybrid cryptographic methodology—Presents a hybrid approach combining cryptography and AI to enhance the security and reliability of medical imaging systems.

Chapter 5: Hierarchical federated learning of large language models for national SOCs: A privacy-preserving architecture for nationwide cyber defense—Proposes a collaborative and privacy-preserving architecture for large-scale cyber defense using federated learning and LLMs.

Chapter 6: Tribology-aware AI for rotating equipment cyber integrity in oil and gas—Investigates AI-driven approaches for ensuring cyber-physical integrity in industrial systems, integrating physical constraints and operational data.

Chapter 7: Blockchain for secure underwater surveillance data—Explores how blockchain can enhance data integrity, traceability, and security in underwater surveillance systems.

Chapter 8: Defense-grade anomaly detection for OT/IoT: PR-centric ranking and safeguards—Develops a robust anomaly detection framework tailored to industrial environments, with a focus on evaluation metrics and operational safeguards.

Chapter 9: A comprehensive framework for modern threat mitigation—Introduces an integrated AI-driven framework to improve scalability, adaptability, and effectiveness in national threat mitigation strategies.

Chapter 10: Materials-aware cyber–physical anomaly detection using fiber Bragg gratings and NiTi shape memory alloys—Presents an innovative detection approach combining materials science, sensing technologies, and cyber-physical modeling for critical infrastructure protection.

Chapter 1

National cyber defense in the era of AI

Foundations, evolution, and strategies

Hayat Zaydi, Zohra Bakkoury, and Mounia Zaydi

1.1 INTRODUCTION

Twenty-first-century national security can no longer be reduced to the defense of territorial integrity. Financial, public health, climate, and digital crises demonstrate that a country's prosperity and vulnerability now hinge on interconnected networks of payments, cloud services, and data [9]. These interdependencies enable cascading effects: localized shocks (power outages, attacks on health systems, logistics disruptions) propagate through globalized supply chains [13], weakening critical sectors and generating systemic crises. Recent scholarship describes this dynamic as the "weaponization of interdependence," whereby hostile actors exploit cross-border dependencies to impose costs without crossing traditional thresholds of escalation.

In parallel, artificial intelligence is radically transforming both risks and responses [45]. It enables the analysis of massive data volumes, the detection of anomalies, and the correlation of weak signals in near real time [42]. Supervised, unsupervised, deep, and federated algorithms provide new capabilities to anticipate cyberattacks and orchestrate response actions. Yet AI also creates new attack surfaces (injections, data poisoning, model extraction) and raises ethical and regulatory challenges. Considering this duality, AI-driven national cyber defense requires the articulation of conceptual foundations, a historical memory of threats, appropriate AI technologies, robust governance frameworks, coherent national strategies, and a forward-looking analysis of future challenges.

1.2 CONCEPTUAL FOUNDATIONS

1.2.1 Interdependence and resilience

Contemporary national security rests on a convergence of military and civilian instruments: sensors, networks, and Security Operations Centers (SOCs) belong to hard security, while standards, regulations, and international

DOI: 10.1201/9781003650478-2

cooperation embody soft security, and the protection of fundamental liberties pertains to human security. This entanglement requires aligning public policy, private investment, and citizen behavior around a shared objective: ensuring the resilience of essential functions (healthcare, energy, transport, finance, water) under prolonged disruption. Indicators such as mean time to detect (MTTD), mean time to respond (MTTR), dwell time, and recovery objectives RTO/RPO derived from business impact analysis (BIA) help assess the capacity to absorb, adapt, and recover [29]. Complex-systems theory suggests that rising variance and autocorrelation in an indicator may signal the approach of a critical threshold, providing early-warning signals of crisis [62].

1.2.2 Integrated risk governance (GRC)

Risk governance integrates enterprise risk management and cybersecurity. The NISTIR 8286 series [52, 53] provides guidance for embedding cybersecurity risk management within ERM processes and aligning risk appetite, controls, and investments. ISO 22317 describes a business impact analysis (BIA) method to identify critical processes and determine tolerance windows; it complements ISO 22301 on business continuity. At the macro level, risk steering relies on a dynamic mapping of dependencies (supply chains, cloud providers, critical infrastructures) and on multi-domain stress tests coupled with crisis scenarios and regular exercises [62].

1.2.3 Responsibility architecture and contractualization

Intermediation between public and private actors is ensured through legal and economic instruments: compliance certifications, audit regimes, incident-notification obligations, and reversibility and data-portability clauses in cloud contracts. These mechanisms reduce information asymmetry and internalize security externalities. Governments should act as insurers of last resort by setting minimum standards and supporting investments, while operators of essential services must adopt a defense-in-depth posture and embed cybersecurity from the design phase (security by design). The adoption of indicators for social acceptability, transparency, and democratic oversight strengthens the legitimacy of this architecture [48, 65].

1.3 HISTORICAL EVOLUTION AND POLYCRISES

1.3.1 From territorial defense to holistic security

Historically, national security was primarily concerned with preserving territorial integrity. From the wars of religion through to the Cold War, sovereignty was asserted through defended borders, alliances, and deterrence signals. Since the late twentieth century, this concept has broadened into an extended notion of security that incorporates economic, social, and environmental dimensions. The September 2001 attacks, the massive cyberattacks WannaCry and NotPetya, and successive public health crises signaled a shift away from the pursuit of decisive victories toward the imperative of maintaining the continuity of essential functions, with resilience as the yardstick [9]. Polycrises, including terrorism, pandemics, and climate disruption, interact with the cyber domain: hospital networks are attacked at the height of a pandemic, electricity grids are disrupted by destructive software, and climate change is exploited to destabilize already fragile regions. This historical evolution underpins the argument that cyber defense is a complex public good requiring broad-based cooperation and ongoing innovation.

1.3.2 Transnational risks and multiplier effects

Transnational crises act as multipliers of instability. Terrorism is being reconfigured across transnational groups and lone actors radicalized online; the Global Terrorism Index reports a geographical diffusion of attacks and a diversification of operational methods. Pandemics have underscored global dependence on supply chains and health data; the 2024 amendments to the International Health Regulations strengthen early warning and information-sharing [10]. Climate change is increasing the frequency of extreme events [27, 28]; threatening water, food, and infrastructure; and driving the need for adaptive planning [16, 66, 67]. These dynamics require shared surveillance architectures, rigorously tested cross-sector continuity plans, and a coherent articulation of prevention, protection, response, and recovery.

1.3.3 Critical vulnerabilities and cross-sector interdependencies

Critical infrastructures (energy, health, transport, finance, water) concentrate systemic risk: a compromise of industrial control systems (ICS) can trigger production shutdowns, and the exfiltration of medical data can jeopardize continuity of care. Digital and physical dependencies must be mapped to diversify suppliers and embed contractual security clauses [33]. Dependence on space services (GNSS, observation, communications) is rising even as jamming and anti-satellite capabilities proliferate [14]; transparency and mutual trust are necessary to avoid escalation [36]. Finally, digital, software, and hardware supply chains constitute an expanded attack surface and require verification mechanisms (SBOM, supplier audits) and information-sharing [68, 69].

1.4 THREAT LANDSCAPE AND RESILIENCE CHALLENGES

Threats against states have both diversified and become industrialized [18], spanning state-sponsored operations, financially motivated cybercrime, hacktivism, and attacks on critical supply chains and industrial systems. The professionalization of tooling and services has lowered barriers to entry and accelerated campaign tempo, while hybrid tactics increasingly couple cyber effects with informational and physical impacts. In response, resilience must be conceived as a system-level property, linking prevention, detection, response, and recovery across sectors and jurisdictions.

1.4.1 Threat categories

Table 1.1 summarizes a typology of contemporary cyber threats, pairing concise operational descriptors with their likely impacts on essential functions, and frames the section's analysis of resilience.

Beyond these categories, denial-of-service (DoS) attacks, targeted espionage, exploitation of flaws in the manufacturing/production chain, influence operations, and sabotage of supply chains constitute major vectors [31, 39, 69, 70, 72]. Critical infrastructures are privileged targets for state, terrorist, or criminal adversaries, with motives ranging from espionage and extortion to political destabilization [39]. The growing integration of AI amplifies these threats: generative algorithms facilitate sophisticated phishing, deepfakes, and polymorphic malware, while autonomous agents accelerate the automation of campaigns.

1.4.2 Measuring and managing resilience

The objective is no longer solely to prevent attacks but to guarantee the continuity of essential services despite intrusions and to restore capabilities rapidly. Beyond MTTD and MTTR, the depth of redundancy, supplier diversity, and cloud exposure must be assessed. Critical slowing down can be used to anticipate a critical transition by detecting increases in a signal's variance and autocorrelation [62]. Cyber stress testing (TIBER, tabletop tests, and Locked Shields exercises) helps identify failure thresholds and calibrate continuity plans. States should institutionalize incident transparency and the publication of resilience indicators to strengthen public trust.

1.5 AI TECHNOLOGIES FOR CYBER DEFENSE

The integration of AI is central to the modernization of cyber defense [37, 38]. This section provides a structured overview of the principal families of

Table 1.1 Typology of contemporary cyber threats and their impacts on essential functions

Threat category	*Description*	*Potential impacts*
Ransomware and extortion	Data-encrypting malware demanding ransom; as-a-service models lowering barriers to entry; 2024 Verizon and IBM reports indicate ransomware remains a leading cause of major incidents [8, 19, 20].	Paralysis of hospitals/public services; financial losses; erosion of trust.
Supply-chain compromise	Malicious payloads injected into software/hardware components (e.g., SolarWinds, NotPetya), exposing high dependency risk and weak supply-chain management; NIST SP 800-82 outlines countermeasures for such environments [23, 68].	Cascade infections across customer organizations; sustained espionage; high remediation costs.
IoT/IIoT and industrial infrastructures	Exploitation of connected sensors/actuators (cameras, PLCs), often poorly secured; IIoT literature highlights limited standards, malicious node injection, and misconfiguration-driven vulnerabilities [69].	Production outages; physical sabotage; health and safety risks.
Generative threats (deepfakes, targeted phishing)	Generative AI used to craft credible synthetic content and targeted phishing; GANs and large language models enable deepfakes and polymorphic malicious code [72].	Large-scale fraud; opinion manipulation; psychological attack.
Stealth and fileless attacks (LOTL)	Abuse of legitimate tools/commands (PowerShell, WMI) to evade detection; studies show high evasion rates and call for in-memory detection; co-occurrence with DDoS and API intrusions [70].	Long dwell time; antivirus bypass; data compromise.

techniques, such as supervised and unsupervised learning, reinforcement and federated learning, and generative models, and outlines their operational applications in detection, triage, and prioritization, response automation, and intelligence fusion. The aim is to situate these methods within end-to-end defense workflows, clarifying where they complement human expertise and existing SOC processes.

1.5.1 Supervised and unsupervised learning

Supervised models (neural networks, support vector machines, random forests) learn from labeled data to distinguish normal from malicious behavior [44]. They are effective for detecting known malware and for alert classification. Unsupervised models (clustering, autoencoders) identify anomalies without prior labeling, which is useful for detecting previously unseen attacks. Their performance depends on the quality and diversity of the training data and on the ability to manage false positives and false negatives [49, 71].

1.5.2 Deep learning and anomaly detection

Deep learning leverages deep architectures (CNNs, RNNs, Transformers) to extract hierarchical data representations [40]. Recent work on security networks, such as DeepNetGuard, shows that combining multiple feature levels (sequence, flow, application) improves detection of complex threats and supports model interpretability [42, 43]. Hybrid architectures that couple CNNs with LSTMs are well suited to log and network-flow analysis, while Transformers facilitate the analysis of command and event sequences. For example, Chao and Xie propose DeepNetGuard, a threat-detection algorithm that fuses multiple feature levels, introduces a dynamic weight-adjustment mechanism, couples an autoencoder with a generative adversarial network, and applies attention to enhance interpretability; this approach detects both known and unknown threats with superior performance [61].

1.5.3 Reinforcement learning and automated orchestration

The DeepNetGuard algorithm is described in detail in a paper by Chao and Xie [61]. Reinforcement-learning techniques enable an agent to learn through interaction with an environment. In cyber defense, they are used to optimize response or containment strategies, for example, to automatically orchestrate security orchestration, automation, and response (SOAR) playbooks or to balance loads in a network under attack. These approaches require faithful modeling of the environment and human-in-the-loop control mechanisms to prevent unexpected decisions.

1.5.4 Federated learning and model sharing

Federated learning enables training models on data distributed across participants without centralizing the data. It is used to share threat intelligence among multiple organizations while preserving privacy and data sovereignty. This approach raises challenges of data heterogeneity, latency, and security (poisoning, model inversion). Recent work combines federated learning with secure aggregation and homomorphic encryption to strengthen protection. One example is the NIDS-FGPA algorithm: the scheme relies on gradient-similarity-based model aggregation, dynamically selects participants, and employs Paillier homomorphic encryption to improve accuracy while preserving the confidentiality of shared data [64].

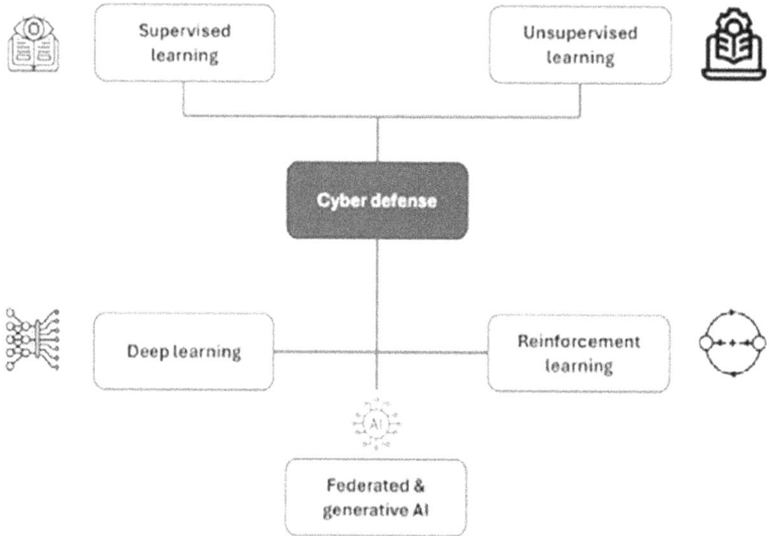

Figure 1.1 Classification of AI techniques for cyber defense.

1.5.5 Generative AI and simulation

The NIDS-FGPA algorithm, which combines gradient aggregation with Paillier encryption, is described in detail in a *PLOS ONE* publication [64]. Generative models (GANs, diffusion models, large language models) can be used defensively to simulate attacks, generate synthetic data for system testing, or create playbooks. However, the same models are weaponized to produce deepfakes, plausible phishing scenarios, or polymorphic malicious code. Generative AI therefore requires safeguards: responsible-use policies, human oversight, and misuse detection [54, 72]. Figure 1.1 illustrates the classification of the principal AI technique families used for cyber defense: supervised learning, unsupervised learning, deep learning, reinforcement learning, and federated and generative AI.

1.5.6 AI-driven reference architecture

To integrate these techniques effectively, an AI-driven reference architecture can be adopted. It is structured around the functions of Cybersecurity Framework 2.0 [32], Identify, Protect, Detect, Respond, Recover, and combines sensors, SIEM/SOAR, AI engines, and dashboards. The architecture rests on data collection (logs, flows, telemetry), normalization (STIX/TAXII formats), AI processing (anomaly detection, risk scoring), orchestration (automated playbooks) [77], and visualization (dashboards). It is accompanied by requirements for traceability, explainability, and human

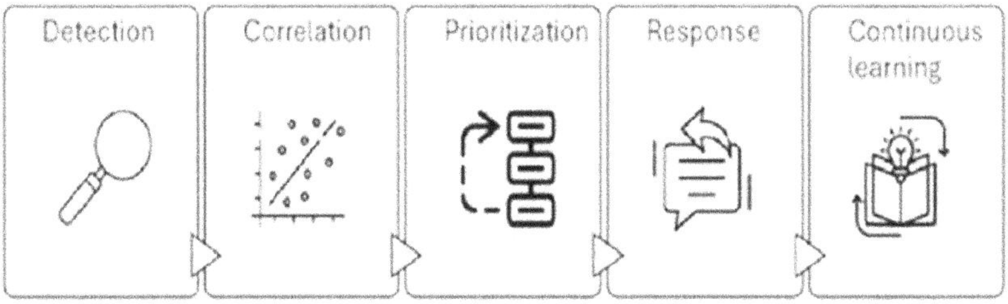

Figure 1.2 The five key stages of AI-driven cyber defense.

oversight [22, 46]. Figure 1.2 depicts the sequence (detection → correlation → prioritization → response → continuous learning), which represents the five key stages of AI-driven cyber defense. This representation synthesizes the architecture proposed in Cybersecurity Framework 2.0 and AI RMF 1.0.

1.6 GOVERNANCE, REGULATION, AND RISK MANAGEMENT

1.6.1 Legal and normative frameworks

Cybersecurity is governed by standards, laws, and reference frameworks. At the European level, the NIS 2 Directive imposes risk governance and mandatory incident reporting for essential entities; Regulation (EU) 2024/1689 (AI Act) adopts a risk-based approach with strengthened requirements for high-risk AI systems; the Digital Operational Resilience Act (DORA) [35] formalizes resilience testing (TIBER) and ICT third-party dependency management, while the Cyber Resilience Act establishes a security-by-design obligation for digital products. Internationally, the Budapest Convention [17] and its additional protocol frame cooperation against cybercrime, while international humanitarian law (IHL) applies to cyber operations in armed conflict [15, 73, 74].

ISO/IEC standards (ISO 27001, ISO 22301, IEC 62443) and NIST guidance (CSF 2.0, SP 800-53, SP 800-161, SP 800-82) provide operational frameworks to architect an information security management system (ISMS), define organizational resilience policies, and secure industrial infrastructures [24–26]. CISA's Cross-Sector Performance Goals (CPG 2.0) set baseline priorities to strengthen the security of essential services. Finally, ethical principles such as the OECD AI Principles and recommendations from the Global Partnership on AI call for transparency, fairness, and accountability [11, 12].

1.6.2 Integrated risk management and compliance

Integrated risk management aligns cybersecurity with enterprise risk management and data governance. Organizations should develop a risk-management strategy grounded in risk appetite, identify critical assets, map their supply chain, assess control maturity, and plan corrective measures [46, 47]. NIST AI RMF 1.0 provides a four-function framework, Govern, Map, Measure [21], and Manage, to address AI-specific risks [22]. Combining an ISMS (ISO 27001) with an AI management system (ISO/IEC 42001) enables integrated governance. ISO 31000 [51] offers general risk-management guidelines, while ISO 27036 covers security in supplier relationships [34]. The FIRST CSIRT Services Framework and STIX/TAXII agreements establish common foundations for threat-intelligence exchange.

1.6.3 Ethics, explainability, and human oversight

The adoption of AI in cybersecurity raises ethical concerns: bias, discrimination, hallucinations, and the risk of over-automation. The OECD principles, the AI Act, and ISO/IEC TR 24028 [60] emphasize the need to ensure reliability, explainability, robustness, and human oversight [30]. XAI (eXplainable AI) techniques enable understanding of model decisions [75]. Machine unlearning offers the possibility of removing data from a model when the legal basis no longer applies. Ex-ante and ex-post evaluation (algorithmic audits, red teaming) should be institutionalized. Finally, digital sovereignty requires control over value chains (data centers, hardware, talent) and avoidance of dependence on monopolistic vendors.

1.7 NATIONAL STRATEGIES AND INTERNATIONAL COOPERATION

1.7.1 Strategic vision and investments

States must articulate a strategic vision that brings together diplomacy, defense, the economy, and research to embed AI into national cyber defense [56]. This vision is structured around three pillars: (1) multi-domain deterrence, underpinned by credible attribution and proportional response; (2) the protection and resilience of both digital and physical supply chains, ensured through contractual transparency, audits, and stress testing; and (3) responsible innovation, combining secure-by-design AI with strong support for the surrounding ecosystem, including startups and universities [1–3]. Fostering a culture of resilience further requires comprehensive training programs, regular large-scale exercises, and targeted financial incentives (such as subsidies and tax credits) to strengthen the cybersecurity posture of SMEs [76].

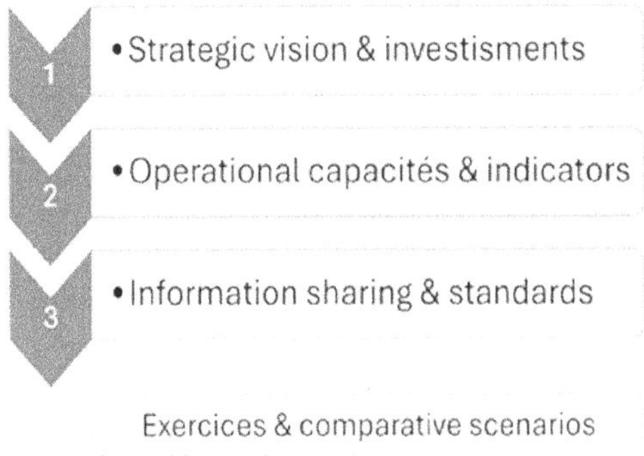

Figure 1.3 Overview of national strategies and cooperation.

1.7.2 Operational capabilities and indicators

Strengthening national capabilities requires the establishment or modernization of national Security Operations Centers (SOCs), the development of Computer Security Incident Response Teams (CSIRTs) [55] and sectoral Information Sharing and Analysis Centers (ISACs), the deployment of SIEM/SOAR platforms enhanced with AI-driven engines and explainability mechanisms, and continuous training for analysts [4]. Investments should be guided by performance indicators such as Mean Time to Detect (MTTD), Mean Time to Respond (MTTR), dwell time, sensor coverage rates, the percentage of alerts handled automatically, and the number of incidents reported to authorities. Public dashboards play a key role in reinforcing transparency and trust [6, 48, 76].

Figure 1.3 provides an overview of national strategies and cooperation for AI-driven cyber defense, showing four levels that progress from strategic vision and investments to operational capabilities and indicators, to information sharing and standards, and finally to exercises and comparative vignettes.

1.7.3 Information sharing and interoperability standards

Rapid and reliable intelligence sharing is essential to counter coordinated attacks. The OASIS STIX/TAXII standards [50] structure and automate the exchange of indicators of compromise and tactics; they are integrated into platforms such as MISP or OpenCTI. ISACs promote pooling within specific sectors (finance, healthcare, energy). Confidentiality and compliance with competition and data protection regulations must be ensured. Cooperation should extend to international allies (NATO, EU, Five Eyes) and multilateral initiatives (ITU, OECD, UNDRR) [78].

1.7.4 Exercises and comparative vignettes

Large-scale exercises test interagency coordination and resilience. Cyber Europe (ENISA), Locked Shields (NATO CCDCOE) [57], and Crossbow (CISA) simulate multi-domain crises to identify gaps and share lessons learned. Comparative vignettes highlight regional specificities: the EU emphasizes regulation and certification (NIS 2, DORA) and supports national CSIRTs via ENISA; the United States relies on CISA, the JCDC, and collaboration playbooks; OASIS focuses on standardizing intelligence exchange; NATO develops doctrines and joint exercises and contributes to legal analyses (Tallinn Manual 2.0). Lessons drawn from recent case studies (Ukraine 2015–2022, Colonial Pipeline 2021, NotPetya 2017, Volt Typhoon 2023–2024, ransomware attacks against the healthcare sector) underscore the importance of OT/IT segmentation, systematic MFA, rich telemetry, and rapid information sharing [76].

1.8 PERSPECTIVES AND CHALLENGES

1.8.1 Adversarial attacks and model robustness

AI models are vulnerable to adversarial attacks, including data poisoning (injection of toxic examples into training datasets), imperceptible input perturbations (adversarial examples), model extraction, and label inversion. Hardening mechanisms such as adversarial training, perturbation detection, model aggregation, and cross-validation can improve robustness. Certification frameworks (NIST AI Secure) and open-source initiatives (Adversarial Robustness Toolbox) provide tools to assess and strengthen models. A systematic review of the literature shows that deep learning–based intrusion detection systems are particularly vulnerable to adversarial examples; it classifies studies according to attack generation, robustness evaluation, and defense methods and identifies challenges and avenues for further research [62].

1.8.2 AI–IoT convergence and cyber-physical systems

The integration of AI into the sensors and actuators of the Internet of Things (IoT) and cyber-physical systems (CPS) offers promising prospects for local anomaly detection and adaptive control. Resource constraints (energy, memory) and vulnerabilities in wireless networks present significant challenges. Standardization (IEEE P2413 [59], ISA/IEC 62443) and the design of optimized edge AI models (TinyML, quantization, pruning) must be prioritized. Securing updates and managing identities (PUF, eSIM) are crucial to prevent large-scale compromises [5]. In the Internet of Medical

Things (IoMT) sector, an in-depth study highlights that the collection of physiological data through sensors exposes patients to privacy risks; medical devices face constraints that make cryptographic techniques difficult to apply, and machine learning methods are proposed to complement security. The survey describes the IoMT architecture, identifies threats, synthesizes ML methods and datasets, and underscores the challenges and future directions [63].

1.8.3 Post-quantum cryptography and quantum AI

The advent of quantum computing threatens classical cryptographic algorithms such as RSA and ECC. States must adopt post-quantum cryptography strategies, in line with NIST standards (algorithms selected in 2023), and plan a gradual migration of critical infrastructures. Quantum AI, which combines the power of qubits with machine learning, could deliver significant accelerations in detection and optimization but raises issues of sovereignty and control. International cooperation is required to define standards and prevent a quantum arms race [79].

1.8.4 Ethics, fairness, and data governance

Generative AI and autonomous systems heighten ethical concerns, including bias, discrimination, hallucinations, and privacy violations. The OECD AI Principles and the work of the Global Partnership on AI call for transparency, fairness, robustness, and accountability. Explainability techniques make it possible to understand decisions, while machine unlearning offers the possibility of removing data from models once the legal basis disappears. Algorithmic audits, black-box testing, and human oversight should become standard practice to ensure trust. Digital sovereignty requires control over value chains (data centers, hardware, expertise) and the adoption of reasoned openness policies to avoid dependency [7, 75].

1.9 DISCUSSION

Three structuring tensions emerge for policy and research. (1) Robustness vs. performance: balance operational gains (finer detection, faster orchestration) with safety assurances (explainability, human control, resistance to adversarial attacks) through shared metrics and realistic testbeds. (2) Sovereignty vs. interoperability: reduce strategic dependencies while adopting open standards (STIX/TAXII, ISA/IEC, IEEE) to facilitate CTI sharing and coordinated response. (3) Innovation vs. compliance: industrializing AI in SOCs requires rapid experimental cycles (including federated, sandboxed settings) while meeting regulatory and ethical requirements [58]. Priority work strands include public benchmarks for AI in SOC environments (data, scenarios, metrics); multilateral exercises incorporating adversarial agents and mixed OT/IT attacks; sector-specific PQC migration roadmaps; and integrated evaluation frameworks that link technical indicators (MTTD/MTTR/dwell time) with governance requirements (audits, transparency, oversight). Pursued jointly by states, operators, and the scientific community, these efforts condition the durable elevation of national resilience.

1.10 CONCLUSION

The integration of artificial intelligence into national cyber defense constitutes both a transformative opportunity and a vector of novel risks. This chapter sets out a coherent framework that articulates the conceptual foundations (interdependence, risk governance, contractualization), the historical evolution marked by polycrises and the "weaponization of interdependence," and an industrialized threat landscape. It then clarifies the role of AI technologies within end-to-end operational chains (anomaly detection, correlation, prioritization, automated response, continuous learning), before examining governance frameworks (reference frameworks, standards, ethics, explainability) and national strategies (capabilities, indicators, information sharing, and exercises). Finally, it identifies future challenges, adversarial attacks, AI–IoT and CPS convergence, post-quantum cryptography, fairness, and data governance, that compel a rethinking of robustness, resilience, and digital sovereignty.

For public policies to be both credible and effective, strategic vision must be tightly coupled with operational execution. This entails investing in national SOCs, CSIRTs, and sectoral ISACs; deploying SIEM/SOAR platforms augmented with explainable AI engines; and embedding capability uplift through continuous training. Steering should rely on shared indicators (MTTD, MTTR, dwell time, sensor-coverage rates, percentage of automated alerts, incidents notified) and on public dashboards that reinforce transparency and trust. Cooperation, domestic and international, gains effectiveness through exchange standards (STIX/TAXII) and large-scale exercises (e.g., *Locked Shields*, *Cyber Europe*) that test interagency coordination and failure thresholds. In parallel, compliance with frameworks (NIS 2, AI Act, DORA, NIST CSF/AI RMF, ISA/IEC 62443, IEEE P2413) and explainability (XAI, algorithmic audits, human oversight) provide essential safeguards for social acceptability and democratic legitimacy.

Resilience should be conceived as a system-level property: it links prevention, detection, response, and recovery, while incorporating the diversification of dependencies (suppliers, cloud, software supply chains), lifecycle security (updates, identity, PUF/eSIM), and edge optimization (edge AI/TinyML, quantization, pruning) for constrained environments (IoT/IIoT,

IoMT). Confronted with adversarial attacks (poisoning, adversarial examples, extraction), hardening strategies (adversarial training, perturbation detection, model aggregation, cross-validation), and evaluation frameworks (black-box testing, red teaming) become central. Post-quantum migration must be planned and prioritized for critical infrastructures, while digital sovereignty requires control over value chains (data centers, hardware, talent) without renouncing reasoned openness conducive to innovation.

REFERENCES

1. N. Tian, D. L. Da Silva, X. Liang, *et al.*, Trends in world military expenditure, 2023. Stockholm International Peace Research Institute, 2024.
2. NATO, *Strategic Concept*, Jun. 29, 2022. [Online]. Available: https://www.nato.int/nato_static_fl2014/assets/pdf/2022/6/pdf/290622-strategic-concept.pdf. Accessed: Sep. 10, 2025.
3. NATO, *Washington Summit Declaration*, Jul. 15, 2024. [Online]. Available: https://www.nato.int/cps/en/natohq/official_texts_227678.htm. Accessed: Sep. 10, 2025.
4. ENISA, *ENISA Threat Landscape 2024*, Sept. 19, 2024. [Online]. Available: https://www.enisa.europa.eu/publications/enisa-threat-landscape-2024. Accessed: Sep. 10, 2025.
5. ENISA, *Cybersecurity of Critical Sectors: Health*, 2024. [Online]. Available: https://www.enisa.europa.eu/topics/cybersecurity-of-critical-sectors/health. Accessed: Sep. 10, 2025.
6. IBM, *Cost of a Data Breach Report 2025*, 2025. [Online]. Available: https://www.ibm.com/reports/data-breach. Accessed: Sep. 10, 2025.
7. IBM Newsroom, "13% reported AI breaches; 97% lacked proper AI access controls," Jul. 30, 2025. [Online]. Available: https://newsroom.ibm.com/2025-07-30-ibm-report-13-of-organizations-reported-breaches-of-ai-models-or-applications,-97-of-which-reported-lacking-proper-ai-access-controls. Accessed: Sep. 10, 2025.
8. IBM, *X-Force Threat Intelligence Index 2025*, Apr. 16, 2025. [Online]. Available: https://www.ibm.com/thought-leadership/institute-business-value/en-us/report/2025-threat-intelligence-index. Accessed: Sep. 10, 2025.
9. World Economic Forum, *Global Risks Report 2025*, Jan. 15, 2025. [Online]. Available: https://www.weforum.org/publications/global-risks-report-2025/. Accessed: Sep. 10, 2025.
10. WHO/WHA, "Amendments to the International Health Regulations (2005)," 2024. [Online]. Available: https://apps.who.int/gb/ebwha/pdf_files/WHA77/A77(16)-en.pdf. Accessed: Sep. 10, 2025.
11. European Union, *Directive (EU) 2022/2555 (NIS 2)*, 2022. [Online]. Available: https://eur-lex.europa.eu/eli/dir/2022/2555/oj. Accessed: Sep. 10, 2025.
12. European Union, *Regulation (EU) 2024/1689 (AI Act)*, 2024. [Online]. Available: https://www.eur-lex.europa.eu/eli/reg/2024/1689/oj/eng. Accessed: Sep. 10, 2025.

13. OECD, "Promoting resilience and preparedness in supply chains," *Trade Policy Papers*, no. 286, Nov. 2024. [Online]. Available: https://www.oecd.org/en/publications/promoting-resilience-and-preparedness-in-supply-chains_be692d01-en.html. Accessed: Sep. 10, 2025.
14. Secure World Foundation, *Global Counterspace Capabilities Report 2025*, Jun. 12, 2025. [Online]. Available: https://www.swfound.org/publications-and-reports/2025-global-counterspace-capabilities-report. Accessed: Sep. 10, 2025.
15. ICRC, "International humanitarian law and cyber operations during armed conflicts," Nov. 2019. [Online]. Available: https://www.icrc.org/en/document/international-humanitarian-law-and-cyber-operations-during-armed-conflicts. Accessed: Sep. 10, 2025.
16. Institute for Economics and Peace, *Global Terrorism Index 2025*, 2025. [Online]. Available: https://www.visionofhumanity.org/resources/global-terrorism-index/. Accessed: Sep. 10, 2025.
17. Council of Europe, *Second Additional Protocol to the Convention on Cybercrime*, 2023. [Online]. Available: https://www.coe.int/en/web/cybercrime/second-additional-protocol. Accessed: Sep. 10, 2025.
18. Europol, *Internet Organised Crime Threat Assessment (IOCTA) 2024*, 2024. [Online]. Available: https://www.europol.europa.eu/publications-events/main-reports/internet-organised-crime-threat-assessment-iocta-2024. Accessed: Sep. 10, 2025.
19. Verizon, *Data Breach Investigations Report 2024*, 2024. [Online]. Available: https://www.verizon.com/business/resources/reports/dbir/. Accessed: Sep. 10, 2025.
20. Microsoft, *Digital Defense Report 2024*, 2024. [Online]. Available: https://www.microsoft.com/en-us/security/business/microsoft-digital-defense-report. Accessed: Sep. 10, 2025.
21. NIST, *AI Risk Management Framework 1.0*, 2023. [Online]. Available: https://www.nist.gov/itl/ai-risk-management-framework. Accessed: Sep. 10, 2025.
22. NIST, *SP 800-53 Rev. 5*, 2020 (updated 2023). [Online]. Available: https://csrc.nist.gov/publications/detail/sp/800-53/rev-5/final. Accessed: Sep. 10, 2025.
23. NIST, *SP 800-82 Rev. 3, ICS Security*, 2022. [Online]. Available: https://csrc.nist.gov/publications/detail/sp/800-82/rev-3/final. Accessed: Sep. 10, 2025.
24. ISO/IEC, *ISO/IEC 27001:2022*, 2022. [Online]. Available: https://www.iso.org/standard/82875.html. Accessed: Sep. 10, 2025.
25. ISO, *ISO 22301:2019, Business Continuity*, 2019. [Online]. Available: https://www.iso.org/standard/75106.html. Accessed: Sep. 10, 2025.
26. IEC, *IEC 62443-3-3*, 2020. [Online]. Available: https://webstore.iec.ch/publication/34421. Accessed: Sep. 10, 2025.
27. UNDRR, *Global Assessment Report 2023*, 2023. [Online]. Available: https://www.undrr.org/publication/global-assessment-report-disaster-risk-reduction-2023. Accessed: Sep. 10, 2025.
28. IPCC, *AR6 Synthesis Report*, 2023. [Online]. Available: https://www.ipcc.ch/report/ar6/syr/. Accessed: Sep. 10, 2025.

29. CISA, *Cross-Sector Cybersecurity Performance Goals (CPG 2.0)*, 2023. [Online]. Available: https://www.cisa.gov/resources-tools/resources/cross-sector-cybersecurity-performance-goals. Accessed: Sep. 10, 2025.
30. OECD, *OECD AI Principles*, 2019. [Online]. Available: https://oecd.ai/en/ai-principles. Accessed: Sep. 10, 2025.
31. Hybrid CoE, "Anticipating cognitive intrusions," Jul. 2023. [Online]. Available: https://www.hybridcoe.fi/publications/anticipating-cognitive-intrusions/. Accessed: Sep. 10, 2025.
32. NIST, *Cybersecurity Framework (CSF) 2.0*, 2024. [Online]. Available: https://www.nist.gov/cyberframework. Accessed: Sep. 10, 2025.
33. NIST, *SP 800-161 Rev. 1, Supply Chain Risk Management*, 2022. [Online]. Available: https://csrc.nist.gov/publications/detail/sp/800-161/rev-1/final. Accessed: Sep. 10, 2025.
34. ISO/IEC, *ISO/IEC 27036, Information Security for Supplier Relationships*, 2014–. [Online]. Available: https://www.iso.org/standard/59670.html. Accessed: Sep. 10, 2025.
35. European Union, *Regulation (EU) 2022/2554 (DORA)*, 2022. [Online]. Available: https://eur-lex.europa.eu/eli/reg/2022/2554/oj. Accessed: Sep. 10, 2025.
36. UN COPUOS, *Guidelines for the Long-term Sustainability of Outer Space Activities*, 2019. [Online]. Available: https://www.unoosa.org/oosa/en/ourwork/topics/long-term-sustainability-of-outer-space-activities.html. Accessed: Sep. 10, 2025.
37. N. Ben-Asher, "Cyber defense strategies: The role of artificial intelligence in mitigating national security threats," *Computers & Security*, vol. 85, pp. 312–327, 2019.
38. E. Bou-Harb, M. Debbabi, C. Assi, and R. Rabbat, "Cyber threat intelligence modeling for national security," *IEEE Trans. Inf. Forensics Secur.*, vol. 12, no. 5, pp. 1042–1053, 2017.
39. A. N. Kanellopoulos and A. Kanellopoulos, "Counterintelligence, Artificial Intelligence and National Security: Synergy and challenges in an era marked by rapid technological advancements and the increasing sophistication of security," *Journal of Politics and Ethics in New Technologies and AI*, vol. 3, no. 1, pp. 0–18, 2024, doi: 10.12681/jpentai.35617.
40. C. Badii, P. Bellini, D. Cenni, A. Difino, NesiP. , and M. Paolucci, "AI-based risk assessment in critical infrastructures: A comprehensive review," *IEEE Transactions on Industrial Informatics*, vol. 16, no. 4, pp. 2453–2467, 2020.
42. G. Pang, C. Shen, L. Cao, and A. Van den Hengel, "Deep learning for anomaly detection: A review," *ACM Computing Surveys*, vol. 1, no. 1, pp. 1–36, 2020.
43. W. Li, K. Wang, and X. Du, "AI-driven predictive modeling for risk assessment in critical infrastructure protection," *IEEE Transactions on Dependable and Secure Computing*, vol. 17, no. 2, pp. 235–248, 2020.
44. I. Goodfellow, Y. Bengio, and A. Courville, *Deep Learning*. Cambridge, MA, USA: MIT Press, 2016.
45. D. S. Hoadley, and N. J. Lucas, *Artificial Intelligence and National Security* (CRS Report R45178). Washington, DC: Congressional Research Service, 2018. *(Ajouter l'URL CRS officielle si souhaité.)*

46. M. H. Arif, H. R. Rabby, N. Y. Nadia, M. I. M. Tanvir, and A. A. Masum, "AI-driven risk assessment in national security projects: Investigating machine learning models to predict and mitigate risks in defense and critical infrastructure projects," *Journal of Computer Science and Technology Studies*, vol. 7, no. 2, pp. 71–85, 2025, doi: 10.32996/jcsts.2025.7.2.6.
47. K. Ruan, *Cybersecurity Risk Assessment: AI-driven Approaches for Predictive Analytics*. Cham, Switzerland: Springer, 2020.
48. S. Sharmin, and R. H. Chowdhury, "Digital transformation in governance: The impact of e-governance on public administration and transparency," Journal of Computer Science and Technology Studies, vol. 0, no. March 2025, pp. 362–379, 2023, doi: 10.32996/jcsts.2025.7.1.27.
49. R. H. Chowdhury, N. U. Prince, S. M. Abdullah, and L. A. Mim, "The role of predictive analytics in cybersecurity: Detecting and preventing threats," *World Journal of Advanced Research and Reviews*, vol. 23, no. 2, pp. 1615–1623, 2024, doi: 10.30574/wjarr.2024.23.2.2494.
50. OASIS, *STIX/TAXII 2.1 Specification*, 2021. [Online]. Available: https://docs.oasis-open.org/cti/stix/v2.1/os/stix-v2.1-os.html. Accessed: Sep. 10, 2025.
51. ISO, *ISO 31000:2018, Risk Management – Guidelines*, 2018.
52. NIST, *NISTIR 8286, Integrating Cybersecurity and Enterprise Risk Management*, 2020. [Online]. Available: https://csrc.nist.gov/publications/detail/nistir/8286/final. Accessed: Sep. 10, 2025.
53. NIST, *NISTIR 8286A, Identifying and Estimating Cybersecurity Risk for Enterprise Risk Management Systems*, 2020. [Online]. Available: https://csrc.nist.gov/publications/detail/nistir/8286a/final. Accessed: Sep. 10, 2025.
54. NIST, *Generative AI Profile (NIST.AI.600-1)*, 2024. [Online]. Available: https://nvlpubs.nist.gov/nistpubs/ai/NIST.AI.600-1.pdf. Accessed: Sep. 10, 2025.
55. FIRST, *CSIRT Services Framework v2.1*, 2023. [Online]. Available: https://www.first.org/standards/frameworks/csirt-services-framework/v21. Accessed: Sep. 10, 2025.
56. CISA, *JCDC AI Cybersecurity Collaboration Playbook*, 2024. [Online]. Available: https://www.cisa.gov/resources-tools/resources/jcdc-ai-cybersecurity-collaboration-playbook. Accessed: Sep. 10, 2025.
57. NATO CCDCOE, *Locked Shields, Exercise Overview*, 2023. [Online]. Available: https://ccdcoe.org/locked-shields/. Accessed: Sep. 10, 2025.
58. OECD, *AI in Science: Best Practices and Recommendations*, 2023. [Online]. Available: https://www.oecd.org/content/dam/oecd/en/publications/reports/2023/06/artificial-intelligence-in-science_4f3d6efd/a8d820bd-en.pdf. Accessed: Sep. 10, 2025.
59. IEEE, "IEEE standard for an architectural framework for the Internet of Things (IoT)," *IEEE Std 2413-2019*, 2019. [Online]. Available: https://standards.ieee.org/standard/2413-2019.html. Accessed: Sep. 10, 2025.
60. ISO, *ISO/IEC TR 24028:2020 – Information Technology – Artificial Intelligence – Overview of Trustworthiness in Artificial Intelligence*, 2020.
61. J. Chao and T. Xie, "Deep learning-based network security threat detection and defense," *Int. J. Adv. Comput. Sci. Appl.*, vol. 15, no. 11, pp. 669–678, 2024. [Online]. Available: https://thesai.org/Downloads/Volume15No11/Paper_64-Deep_Learning_Based_Network_Security_Threat_Detection.pdf. Accessed: Sep. 10, 2025.

62. H. A. Alatwi and C. Morisset, “Adversarial machine learning in network intrusion detection domain: A systematic review,” *arXiv preprint* arXiv:2112.03315, 2021, doi: 10.48550/arXiv.2112.03315.
63. A. Si-Ahmed, M. A. Al-Garadi, and N. Boustia, “Survey of machine learning based intrusion detection methods for Internet of Medical Things,” *arXiv preprint* arXiv:2202.09657, 2023, doi: 10.48550/arXiv.2202.09657.
64. JiaMing Wang, Kai Yang, and MinJing Li, “NIDS-FGPA: A federated learning network intrusion detection algorithm based on gradient similarity model aggregation,” *PLOS ONE*, vol. 18, no. 3, e0284030, 2023, doi: 10.1371/journal.pone.0308639.
65. NIST, *SP 800-161 Rev. 1, Supply Chain Risk Management Practices for Systems and Organizations*, 2022.
66. Kaiser Family Foundation, “The international health regulations and the U.S.: Implications of an amended agreement,” Jun. 18, 2024. [Online]. Available: https://www.kff.org/global-health-policy/the-international-health-regulations-and-the-u-s-implications-of-an-amended-agreement/. Accessed: Sep. 10, 2025.
67. World Meteorological Organization, *State of the Global Climate 2024*, 2025. [Online]. Available: https://public.wmo.int/en/resources/state-of-the-global-climate (PDF: https://library.wmo.int/idurl/4/80664). Accessed: Sep. 10, 2025.
68. NIST, *SP 800-82 Rev. 3, Guide to Operational Technology Security*, 2022.
69. L. L. Dhirani, E. Armstrong, and T. Newe, “Industrial IoT, cyber threats and standards landscape: Evaluation and roadmap,” *Sensors*, vol. 21, no. 11, art. 3901, 2021.
70. O. Khalid *et al.*, “An insight into the machine-learning-based fileless malware detection,” *Sensors*, vol. 23, no. 2, art. 612, 2023.
71. M. Alazab, S. P. RM, P. K. R. Maddikunta, T. R. Gadekallu, and Q.-V. Pham, “Federated learning for cybersecurity: Concepts, challenges, and future directions,” *IEEE Trans. Ind. Inform.*, vol. 18, no. 5, pp. 3501–3509, May 2022, doi: 10.1109/TII.2021.3119038.
72. J. Zhou, Y. Liu, and S. Chen, “A survey on the application of generative adversarial networks in cybersecurity,” *arXiv preprint* arXiv:2107.10338, 2021.
73. RAND Corporation, *Risk-Based AI Regulation: A Primer on the Artificial Intelligence Act of the European Union*, 2024. [Online]. Available: https://www.rand.org/pubs/research_reports/RRA3243-3.html. Accessed: Sep. 10, 2025.
74. European Commission, “NIS2 directive: Securing network and information systems across the EU,” 2024. [Online]. Available: https://digital-strategy.ec.europa.eu/en/policies/nis2-directive. Accessed: Sep. 10, 2025.
75. V. Z. Mohale, and I. C. Obagbuwa, “A systematic review on the integration of explainable artificial intelligence in intrusion detection systems to enhancing transparency and interpretability in cybersecurity,” *Frontiers in Artificial Intelligence*, vol. 8, Article 1526221, 2025, doi: 10.3389/frai.2025.1526221.
76. TDI, “CISA cross-sector cybersecurity performance goals: Baseline, benchmark and recommended practices,” 2024. [Online]. Available: https://tdisecurity.com/resources/cisa-cross-sector-cybersecurity-performance-goals/. Accessed: Sep. 10, 2025.

77. K. Smith, L. Brown, and J. Reyes, "Hyper-automation and large language models for security operations centers: A new SOAR architecture," *Preprints*, 2024.
78. OASIS, "Introduction to STIX," 2021; "Introduction to TAXII," 2021. [Online]. Available: https://oasis-open.github.io/cti-documentation/stix/intro.html; https://oasis-open.github.io/cti-documentation/taxii/intro.html. Accessed: Sep. 10, 2025.
79. NIST, "NIST releases the first three quantum-resistant cryptography standards," Aug. 15, 2024. [Online]. Available: https://csrc.nist.gov/news/2024/first-post-quantum-cryptography-standards-published. Accessed: Sep. 10, 2025.

Chapter 2

Exploiting wireless system vulnerabilities

A case study on remote hacking with robots

Aysha Oqdeh, Roa'a Hamudeh, Shahad Alnatsheh, Razan Khassawneh, and Qasem Abu Al-Haija[1]

2.1 INTRODUCTION

The advent of wireless communication has revolutionized the way devices communicate with each other. Their existence helped shape the path for modern technology and laid the groundwork for further advancements in the field. This made them vulnerable to malicious actors, as their appeal for attack also increased. Our work presents an approach to wireless security issues and real-life attacks that threaten our systems [1]. This work involves the creation of a remotely controlled robot that exploits wireless vulnerable systems. In our scope, we have included especially important attacks, such as Wi-Fi Pineapple, Bluetooth exploits like BlueBorne, and RF proprietary protocol attacks like MouseJack. We want to highlight security issues in the 2.4 GHz ISM band, where laptops, PCs, and IoT devices typically operate.

The 2.4 GHz ISM band is especially important because of its widespread availability and common use in electronics and IoT devices. This frequency band is shared globally with other unlicensed communication applications, making it a perfect option for protocols such as Wi-Fi (802.11b/g/n), Bluetooth, and RF technologies. Although the 2.4 GHz band is cost-effective and a reliable communication channel, it also proves to be an attractive target for attacks. As a result, any vulnerability found within this band will expose millions of users to danger that may eventually result in stolen sensitive information or compromised operational flow. Ironically, the advantages of the 2.4 GHz band, such as extended range and superior penetration through various obstacles compared to higher-frequency bands, made it an appealing target. The high reliance on this band, combined with the lack of implemented security measures, such as encryption, presents critical vulnerabilities. If these vulnerabilities remain unnoticed, they can result in major breaches affecting personal, corporate, and IoT systems.

The traditional way of testing wireless vulnerabilities manually is often inefficient and inconsistent and has a limited scope. Implementing a robot-based approach provides an automated and scalable solution that facilitates easier testing while enhancing overall performance through precise control, repeatability, and the ability to simulate complex attack scenarios in real

DOI: 10.1201/9781003650478-3

time. This work covers both sides of wireless security, the offensive and defensive. We aim to achieve that by developing an Intrusion Detection System (IDS) as part of our work. The IDS will monitor, analyze, and detect malicious activities in wireless networks in real time to help mitigate the risk. By automating both offensive and defensive security operations, our work not only enhances testing efficiency and covers a wider range of wireless threats but also helps mitigate them.

With technology, our daily lives have undergone significant changes; our way of living, working, and even thinking has evolved. Contrarily, the absence of proper protective measures makes it prone to various types of hacking. This work, therefore, covers Bluetooth and Wi-Fi vulnerabilities, focusing on identifying ways to protect against potential security threats. This decision makes the work all the more meaningful, as the number of high-tech wireless attacks on consumer and enterprise devices continues to rise. Understanding how each attack works will help us design more efficient defensive strategies. Additionally, utilizing a robot in this work provides significant advantages over traditional manual testing methods. The robot conducts automated scans, emulates the attacker's behavior, and moves through the physical environment. This robot may test wireless communications vulnerabilities in a dynamic, real-world setting. In tasks that require high proximity to devices, robots are deployed, which can be positioned correctly to take advantage of signal weaknesses or to test multiple security protocols across various locations. This increases efficiency, accuracy, and scalability compared to manual methods, which are limited by human scope, effort, and potential for error.

2.1.1 Underlying challenges and research gaps

Over the last few years, with the widespread adoption of wireless applications worldwide, the demand for 2.4 GHz in the license-free non-ISM band has increased due to its features that match the needs of wireless communications [2] like Wi-Fi, Bluetooth, and other 2.4 GHz protocols. This band is not licensed, and it's poor in terms of regulations because the original (ISM band) is regulated to be used in scientific, medical, and industrial applications [2]. Therefore, any non-ISM band communication should be able to tolerate harmful interferences [2]. This is considered a complex vulnerability, and it is a key reason why wireless attacks are possible. The lack of awareness of this vulnerability, combined with poor encryption mechanisms and weak interference protection in wireless communication, creates vulnerabilities that enable many severe attacks.

We focus on three main attack scenarios in our work: MouseJack, BlueBorne, and Wi-Fi Pineapple. These attacks can be executed remotely, often without the victim's knowledge, leading to unauthorized access, data breaches, and malware infections. The lack of effective solutions to detect and prevent these attacks in real time makes them attractive targets for attackers and a major threat point to most systems. Our work aims to develop a remotely controlled robot capable of simulating real-world wireless attacks on Wi-Fi, Bluetooth, and RF proprietary protocols. By understanding the attack vector and its impact on our systems, we can design a robust IDS solution to protect against these threats. We focus on testing the feasibility of these attacks and raising awareness among PC and laptop users, as well as cybersecurity professionals, about the potential risks to pave the way for more effective defense mechanisms. Our contribution to this work is to address various vulnerabilities within a range of widely used wireless protocols, which significantly impact wireless network systems. The work represented a remotely controlled robot designed to autonomously perform attack scenarios. This robot is capable of simulating multiple attack scenarios across different protocols. On the other hand, the IDS is designed to perform real-time detection of these attacks, featuring a scalable defense mechanism against multiple attack vectors. The IDS is designed to monitor and analyze traffic from various protocols, providing security protection at the physical and link layers of devices. Figure 2.1 illustrates the problem definition of this work.

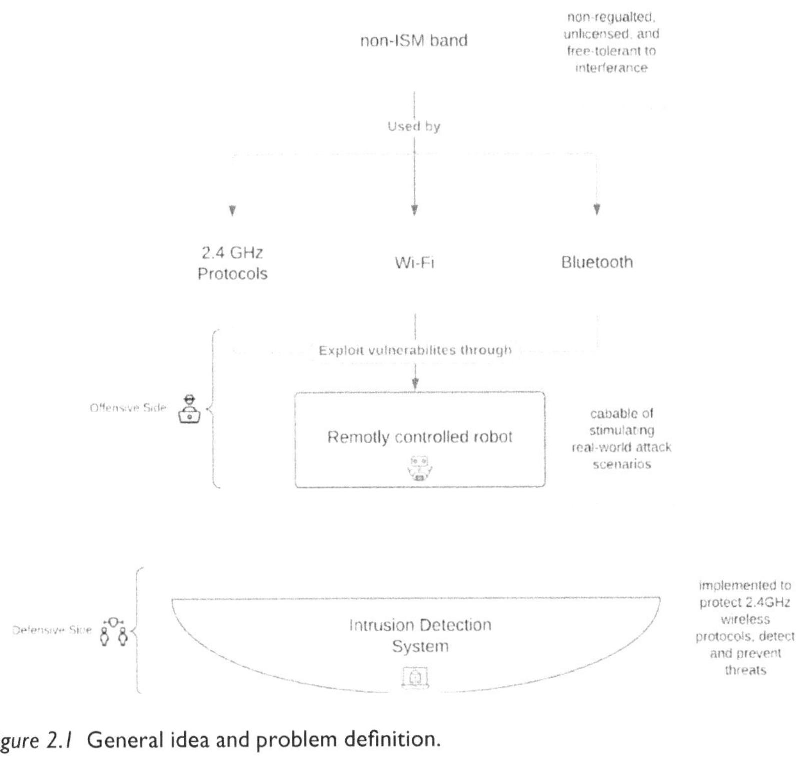

Figure 2.1 General idea and problem definition.

2.1.2 Research significance and impact

This work is significant in its approach to wireless security, as it addresses both offensive exploitation techniques and defensive detection mechanisms. The combination of automated wireless attacks and a responsive IDS solution demonstrates a comprehensive understanding of wireless vulnerabilities and the need for proactive defense. The current challenges include:

- Insecure Wireless Communications: Over 1.5 billion IoT devices are estimated to be vulnerable due to outdated security protocols or a lack of encryption. High-profile attacks like MouseJack and BlueBorne continue to highlight these weaknesses [3].
- IoT Adoption increase: By 2025, the number of IoT devices is expected to exceed 18.8 billion, significantly expanding attack surfaces for Bluetooth, Wi-Fi, and other communication protocols [4].
- Lack of Real-Time Detection: Traditional security measures often fail to detect wireless attacks in real time. Our work addresses this gap by integrating an IDS capable of detecting anomalies as they occur.

By demonstrating how automated attacks on wireless devices can severely compromise their security and privacy, this work represents a significant step forward in the field of cybersecurity. The framework it provides allows for the real-time detection of these wireless attacks using Intrusion Detection Systems (IDS). Thus, cybersecurity training is augmented with a practical, hands-on method for comprehending wireless vulnerabilities. Regarding real-world applications and advantages, the work's conclusions can be applied in network security audits to protect wireless networks by identifying and addressing potential weaknesses. Additionally, this work can serve as a source of guidance for designing security policies that can be implemented to protect wireless communication channels, particularly in IoT environments. Moreover, the work aligns with industry trends that underscore the importance of securing wireless communications, particularly in an era where remote work and IoT adoption are increasing.

2.1.3 Research objectives

In this section, we'll discuss the main goal of the work and justify the development of each part. Our primary objective in developing this work is to implement an intrusion detection system that detects and prevents 2.4 GHz communication attacks, while also highlighting the need for robust security mechanisms in protocols that operate over the 2.4 GHz band. Moving to smaller objectives will help us reach the primary reason. We need to implement an offensive component of the work to demonstrate the importance of enhancing the defensive part, which is our primary objective. Minor objectives can be summarized as follows:

- Deep Understanding of the Theoretical Background of This Work: Including signals and electromagnetic waves, 2.4 GHz radiofrequency, and communication protocols using 2.4 GHz bands like Wi-Fi and Bluetooth. The reason for the existence of vulnerabilities in wireless systems and how vulnerabilities in wireless systems can be exploited.
- Design and Implement a Remote-Controlled Robot: Create a Wi-Fi-enabled robot with a live camera feed for real-time navigation and attack execution.
- Automate Wireless Attacks: Implement MouseJack, BlueBorne, and Wi-Fi Pineapple attacks to demonstrate vulnerabilities in wireless protocols.
- Target 2.4 GHz Devices: Focus attacks on devices using 2.4 GHz protocols (Wi-Fi, Bluetooth).
- Automate Attack Execution: Ensure the robot autonomously identifies vulnerabilities and executes attacks from a distance.
- Gain Full Access to the Attached Devices: Develop techniques to attain full access and install malware on the victim's device.
- Real-Time Data Collection: Log attack actions and target responses with high accuracy during operations.

2.1.4 Scientific and practical contributions

Our work addresses the various risks associated with wireless attacks, aiming to raise awareness of the overlooked aspect of our day-to-day technology use and how people often underestimate the dangers related to wireless security. It highlights how easily someone can hack into our communication channels without detection. This approach to understanding where hackers stand will help us understand on a deeper level how to build an effective countermeasure to these attacks. While many gadgets are available nowadays that focus on wireless security and penetration testing, our work is unique because it tackles both the offensive and defensive aspects of wireless security. We also aim to combine automation, portability, and versatility with our work by covering multiple attacks that target different wireless protocols within a single module rather than focusing solely on a single protocol. Additionally, using a robot also enhances the stealth of the attack by reducing human presence and lowering the chances of detection. It can also be precisely navigated to the victim's location, ensuring the attacker stays at a safe distance and making it easier to close the proximity gap needed to execute chosen attacks without being detected.

Scalability is a key strength of our work. At the same time, the initial focus is on protocols affecting the 2.4 GHz ISM band; the framework is designed to be flexible and adaptable to other wireless technologies. The robot is a future solution for wireless penetration testing because it can be modified or upgraded to target different protocols or additional wireless attack scenarios, such as Wi-Fi 6 security flaws, ZigBee and Z-Wave exploits, or Bluetooth Low Energy (BLE) vulnerabilities, among many others. The robot operates smoothly in various environments, ranging from small lab experiments to full-scale penetration tests on large corporate networks. Portability and flexibility make it easy to bring it on-site, making it the perfect solution for organizations looking to assess their wireless security. Our primary audience is cybersecurity professionals, penetration testers, or anyone interested in wireless security and understanding the attack vector that affects our current communication methods. The diversity of attacks we cover makes this work relevant to any security enthusiast or IoT specialist looking to secure modern wireless technologies. In our work, we focus on designing a custom-built model that follows a straightforward yet effective process of scanning, discovery, attack, and feedback. This rhythm mirrors the normal behavior of an attacker. The automation of the process makes it easier for the user to test wireless security, while the feedback helps maintain the hands-on approach of a penetration tester.

2.2 SCIENTIFIC AND TECHNICAL BACKGROUND

The technical background needed for this work includes: (1) Wi-Fi (IEEE 802.11) [5] Vulnerabilities, focusing on unencrypted management frames that can be exploited through de-authentication and Evil Twin attacks; (2) Bluetooth vulnerabilities, particularly the BlueBorne attack, which allows remote code execution without user interaction; and (3) RF security issues, including MouseJack attacks that exploit unencrypted 2.4 GHz connections in wireless mice and keyboards.

2.2.1 Wi-Fi Pineapple attack scenario

- Reconnaissance and Environment Scanning: We start our attack model by scanning the environment to define accessible wireless networks and devices through Wi-Fi, Bluetooth, and RF transceivers and adapters. After this essential step, vulnerabilities are detected by exploiting the lack of encryption in Wi-Fi management frames and Bluetooth's device discovery protocol, allowing access to sensitive information such as MAC addresses, SSIDs, and device types, which can be used to identify vulnerable targets [6].
- Wi-Fi Pineapple Attack (Evil Twin): After identifying possible targets, the robot executes a Wi-Fi Pineapple attack by generating a fake access point (AP) that mimics the authorized network's SSID and lures victims into linking to it. This exploit utilizes frequently used devices to reconnect to familiar networks automatically. The rogue AP can entice these devices away from their initial network by sending

a more powerful signal [7]. This process exploits the lack of Protected Management Frames (PMFs) in numerous Wi-Fi setups, allowing hackers to mimic valid networks and capture confidential information, potentially resulting in a Man-in-the-Middle (MITM) scenario [7].

- De-authentication Attack: In this step, we force devices to connect to the rogue AP, and the robot sends de-authentication frames, leading to their disconnection from their current network. These packets are unencrypted, allowing attackers to kick users off their networks without verification. The devices are then forced to reconnect to the most available network, which is the rogue AP. This step exploits a vulnerability in the Wi-Fi protocol, where management frames like de-authentication packets are not encrypted, making them easy to spoof and use for denial-of-service (DoS) attacks or network redirection [8].
- Perform SSL Stripping: SSL stripping aims to address the lack of security settings on some websites and user devices. This attack targets secure HTTPS connections, reducing them to unencrypted HTTP connections. Once the connection is disrupted, the attacker can intercept and capture sensitive data, such as login credentials and personal information, that is protected by encryption. This attack exploits the initial connection handshake, redirecting users to an insecure version of the website and exposing their data to eavesdropping. The vulnerability exploited in this step takes advantage of the user's trust in automatic HTTPS connections and the lack of their enforcement, allowing attackers to execute Man-in-the-Middle (MitM) attacks on supposedly secure communications [9].
- Inject Malicious Redirects (DNS Spoofing): The robot utilizes DNS spoofing to alter DNS responses and deceive users into obtaining fraudulent websites through malicious redirects. When a user attempts to visit a valid website, the attacker hijacks the DNS request and sends a fake response, leading the victim to a phishing page or a malicious domain under the attacker's control. This technique exploits weaknesses in the DNS, specifically in systems without DNS Security Extensions (DNSSEC), enabling hackers to conduct Man-in-the-Middle (MitM) attacks, steal confidential information such as login credentials, or spread malicious software by masquerading as legitimate websites [10].

Figure 2.2 illustrates the comprehensive attack sequence, which begins with reconnaissance and environment scanning, and culminates in DNS spoofing and data exfiltration. It visually links the steps.

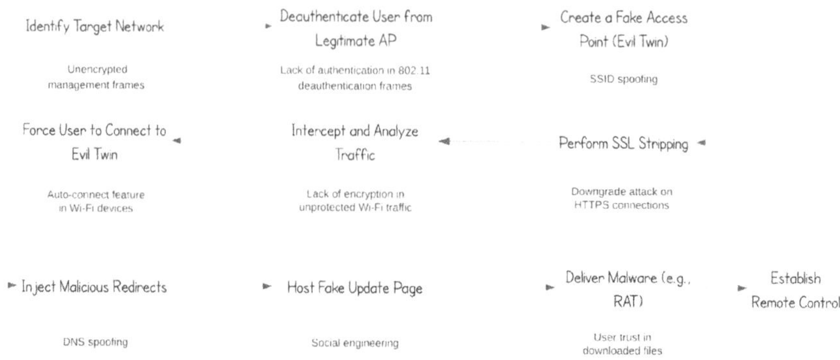

Figure 2.2 Wi-Fi Pineapple attack scenario.

2.2.2 BlueBorne attack on bluetooth devices

The robot also targets Bluetooth-enabled devices by exploiting the BlueBorne vulnerability, with a particular focus on Windows systems. This attack exploits vulnerabilities within the Bluetooth protocol stack to bypass authentication protocols, allowing unauthorized access without requiring user interaction or pairing. Once a vulnerable Windows Bluetooth device is identified, the robot exploits these protocol vulnerabilities to gain unauthorized access, potentially exposing sensitive data or enabling remote control. The attack exploits weaknesses in how the Bluetooth stack handles incoming connections, particularly on Windows devices, which can be silently compromised within range. By bypassing security protocols, the robot can exploit these vulnerabilities to establish a foothold on the target system, opening the door for further attacks or data extraction without raising immediate alarms [11]. Figure 2.3 illustrates the BlueBorne attack process, highlighting the steps from identifying the vulnerability to executing unauthorized access.

2.2.3 MouseJack attack on wireless peripherals

For devices using wireless peripherals, the robot executes a MouseJack attack. It uses an RF transceiver to inject malicious keystrokes into the communication channel between a wireless keyboard/mouse and its receiver. As shown in Figure 2.4, many devices communicate over unencrypted channels, allowing attackers to send unauthorized commands that the computer interprets as legitimate input. This attack exploits the lack of encryption in the 2.4 GHz communication used by many wireless mice and keyboards, allowing for the hijacking of control over the victim's system [12].

Figure 2.5 illustrates the exploitation of unencrypted RF communication between a wireless mouse and its USB receiver.

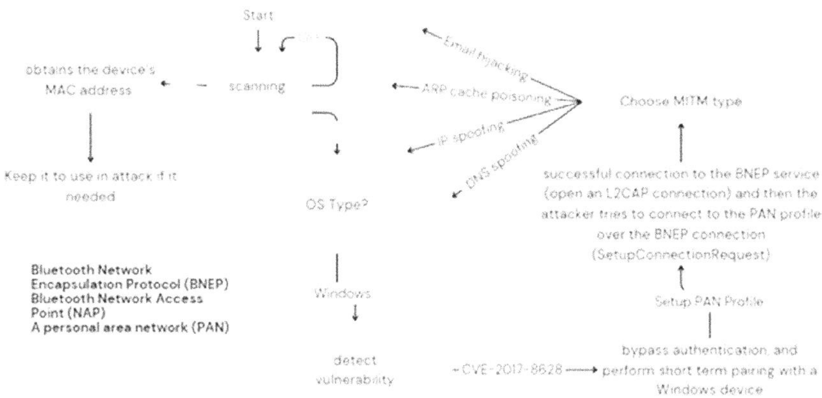

Figure 2.3 BlueBorne attack scenario.

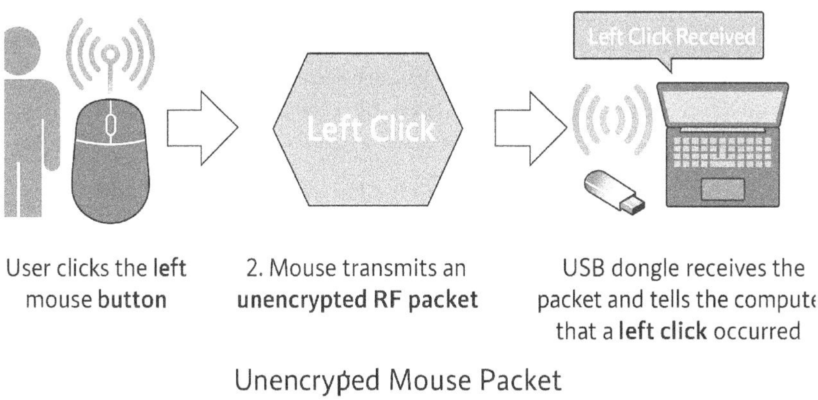

Figure 2.4 Unencrypted RF communication [12].

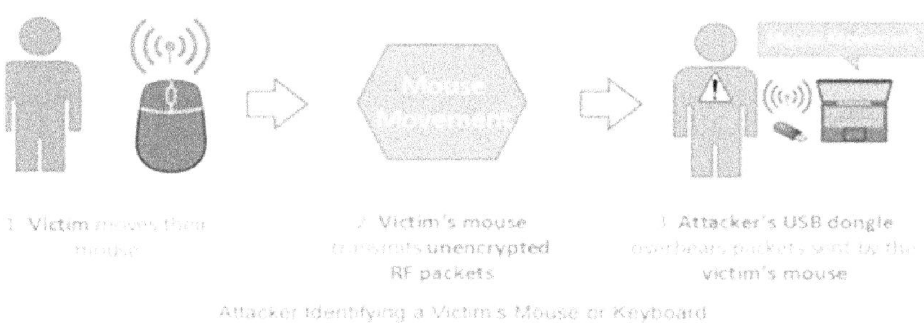

Figure 2.5 MouseJack attack [12].

2.2.4 Malware deployment and persistence

After exploiting the target device, the robot uses social engineering techniques to convince users to download malicious files disguised as legitimate software updates or tools. Once the malware is executed, attackers gain remote access using tools such as Remote Access Trojans (RATs), allowing them to exert full control over the victim's system and employ persistence techniques to maintain their access. One way to maintain continuous access is for attackers to deploy persistence techniques even after the system reboots [13]. This includes installing rootkits or configuring scripts that establish a persistent backdoor, ensuring the exploited system remains accessible over the long term. These techniques help attackers gain control, steal data, and execute additional commands remotely.

2.2.5 Intrusion Detection System (IDS)

The work includes an Intrusion Detection System (IDS) to prevent and monitor wireless traffic in real time against these attacks. The IDS uses machine learning algorithms, which are signature-based and anomaly-based techniques, to learn and detect suspicious activities like rogue APs, unusual Bluetooth connections, or unauthorized RF communication. This defense layer addresses vulnerabilities by providing active detection and alerts, thereby helping mitigate the risks associated with wireless attacks.

2.3 RESEARCH PLAN AND DELIVERABLES

2.3.1 Main deliverables

- **Intrusion Detection System (IDS):** Pre-configured IDS rule sets are designed to detect specific wireless threats, including MouseJack, BlueBorne, and Wi-Fi Pineapple attacks. Comprehensive documentation for configuring and deploying the IDS to monitor, analyze, and identify malicious activities in real time exists. Datasets and logs capturing IDS alerts during simulated attacks validate the effectiveness of detection mechanisms.
  - Milestones include: The IDS rule sets, configuring and deploying the system, and generating comprehensive documentation for setup and usage.
  - The system will be evaluated based on: Detection accuracy: Targeting $\geq$ 90% under typical conditions; False positive rate: Aiming for $\leq$ 10%; and Response time: Ideally $\leq$ 3 seconds per alert.
- **Attack Module:** Custom scripts for executing wireless exploits, including MouseJack, BlueBorne, and Wi-Fi Pineapple attacks, to

demonstrate real-world vulnerabilities in wireless protocols. Detailed guides on replicating these attacks in controlled environments, ensuring an educational and practical approach to cybersecurity training. Traffic datasets showcasing the impact of the attacks, enabling analysis and fine-tuning of detection systems.

- Milestones include: Written exploit scripts for MouseJack, BlueBorne, and Wi-Fi Pineapple attacks; control scripts for redoing attacks and the flow of each scenario; and a detailed guide and documentation.
- Evaluation will focus on: Attack success rate: Aiming for $\geq 80\%$ across various environments; Execution time: Ideally ≤ 7 seconds per exploit; Compatibility: Ensuring integration with the robot's hardware and software; Stability: Striving for $\leq 10\%$ error rate during automated scanning and attack execution.

- **The Robot:** A remotely controlled robot equipped with wireless modules (Wi-Fi, Bluetooth, RF) to perform automated scanning and attack execution. The robot simulates a mobile attacker capable of exploiting vulnerabilities in target environments, providing realistic scenarios for testing and analysis. Demonstration videos showcasing the robot's functionality, attack execution, and integration with the IDS, offering a visual and hands-on learning resource.
  - Milestones include: Assembling and configuring the robot; Integrating wireless modules (Wi-Fi, Bluetooth, RF); Developing its scanning and attack execution capabilities and making sure it works; and Demonstration videos that showcase the functionality of the robot.
  - Performance will be assessed based on: Navigation Accuracy: Controls work nicely; Execution Speed: Targeting ≤ 5 seconds to initiate an attack once in range; and Battery Life: Aiming for at least 1.5–2 hours of continuous operation.

2.3.2 Risk assessment

Our work involves robotics, hardware, and cybersecurity, inherently carrying several risks that can impact timeline, outcomes, and safety. The most critical risks likely to affect the work's flow are human errors (R2), time constraints (R3), and component malfunctions or failures (R1). Both human errors and time constraints have the highest risk levels, as they can lead to significant delays and reduced quality if not addressed early. Mitigating these risks is essential to ensure smooth work progress and the achievement of critical milestones. Table 2.1 presents the detailed risk analysis and mitigation plan. In Table 2.2, we present the risk matrix [14].

Table 2.1 Risk evaluation and mitigation plan

Risk ID	*Risk name*	*Risk likelihood (1–5)*	*Risk impact (1–5)*	*Risk level (1–5)*	*Risk description*	*Mitigation plan*
R1	Component Malfunction or Failure	Low -1-	High -4-	Moderate -3-	This risk poses a major threat due to a lack of sufficient experience in hardware, which can lead to both financial and medical risks to team members if the disruption results in a fire, for example.	Before starting implementation, training must be provided to team members, whether through practical training, videos of others who have implemented the robot in the industry, or requesting supervision from a specialist.
R2	Human Errors	Moderate -3-	High -4-	High -5-	Mistakes made by team members during work, such as misconfigurations, incorrect coding, or mishandling of hardware, can lead to delays, malfunctions, or unexpected outcomes.	Provide hands-on training to all team members on handling hardware, software, and tools used in their work; share best practices and lessons learned from similar projects.
R3	Time Constraints	Moderate -3-	High -4-	High -5-	When there isn't enough time to complete the work, tasks might be rushed, leading to lower-quality work or even leaving some parts unfinished.	Focus on the most important parts of the work first to ensure critical goals are met. Distribute tasks evenly among team members to prevent bottlenecks and ensure the team addresses any challenges promptly, thereby avoiding misalignment and ensuring a cohesive approach.

R4	Disagreement or Misunderstanding between Team Members	Low -1-	High -4-	Moderate -3-	Disagreements or misunderstandings between team members can occur, especially during periods of pressure and fatigue, which may affect teamwork and hinder the work from being completed as effectively as possible.	It's important to encourage immediate apologies when mistakes occur. The team leader plays a crucial role in managing conflicts, addressing issues promptly, and ensuring tasks are distributed fairly, especially when a team member faces personal challenges. This approach helps maintain harmony and keeps the team focused on achieving goals.
R5	Malware Mismanagement	Low -1-	High -4-	Moderate-3-	Since we are working with malware, there's always a chance we could make a mistake during testing or implementation, which might cause the malware to behave unexpectedly. This could result in damage to our equipment or loss of control of the situation.	Always test malware in isolated and secure environments, such as virtual machines and sandboxed networks, to prevent unintended spread or damage. Train all team members on handling malware safely, including understanding its behavior, risks, and containment strategies.
R6	Battery Depletion	Low -1-	High -4-	Moderate -3-	The robot's battery could run out unexpectedly or fail during operation, leading to the robot losing power and becoming inoperable. This could occur due to insufficient battery capacity, prolonged use without recharging	Ensure the battery is fully charged before starting implementation, and have an additional power bank available in case the battery dies simultaneously.

(*Continued*)

Table 2.1 (Continued) Risk evaluation and mitigation plan

Risk ID	*Risk name*	*Risk likelihood (1–5)*	*Risk impact (1–5)*	*Risk level (1–5)*	*Risk description*	*Mitigation plan*
R7	Violation of Cybersecurity Laws	Low -1-	High -4-	Moderate -3-	Since our work involves conducting a cyberattack and downloading malware, it may lead to legal liability if not used properly and responsibly.	Ensure that cybersecurity laws are followed, as the work is implemented solely for awareness and educational purposes, and on individuals' devices after obtaining their consent.
R8	Incomplete Threat Detection by IDS	Low -1-	High -4-	Moderate -3-	Failure to address all vulnerabilities can lead to significant danger, especially from malicious or unethical attackers.	Focus on identifying and addressing the most critical vulnerabilities first, particularly those that could result in high-impact consequences. Manual Intervention: Establish a protocol for manual log reviews and system audits by cybersecurity professionals when IDS performance is suspected to be inadequate. Review and integrate findings from peer-reviewed papers and industry reports for addressing secondary risks.

Table 2.2 Work risk heat map

Impact/Likelihood	*Low*	*Moderate*	*High*
Low	Low -1-	Low -2-	Medium -3- #R1 #R4 #R5 #R6 #R7 #R8
Moderate	Low -2-	Medium -4-	High -6- #R2 #R3
High	Medium -3-	High -6-	High -9-

2.4 LITERATURE REVIEW

This section presents a literature review that examines the major security challenges faced by wireless technologies, with a focus on attacks related to peripheral devices, protocol vulnerabilities, and wireless penetration methods. It also discusses defensive mechanisms and recent advancements in threat detection and mitigation. By analyzing existing studies, this review aims to provide a comprehensive overview of the security landscape of wireless networks and contribute to the development of more efficient solutions to address the growing threats.

Our work was motivated by two main technical papers that deepened our understanding of the attack mechanisms used in wireless and Bluetooth devices, forming a foundational framework for our attack module. In [12], researchers discovered a collection of vulnerabilities known as "MouseJack," affecting a wide range of non-Bluetooth wireless keyboards and mice from major companies. Wireless peripherals communicate using proprietary protocols over radio frequency, which sometimes lack the necessary security because there is no industry standard to follow. The methodology researchers followed involves identifying vulnerable devices, using RF modules (e.g., NRF24L01+), and sending rogue inputs to compromise systems, exploiting the lack of encryption. During their tests, Bastille experts identified three categories of vulnerabilities: keystroke injection, spoofing a keyboard or a mouse, and forced pairing, which allowed attackers to control the victim's device. MouseJack is a prime example of how vulnerabilities in wireless devices can be exploited to bypass security defenses. Owners of vulnerable devices should update the firmware or replace the device to stay safe. Further extending the scope of MouseJack. In [11], the paper highlights one of the famous attacks that affects Bluetooth technology, known as BlueBorne. This vulnerability enables attackers to infiltrate and control devices without requiring user interaction, targeting billions of devices worldwide. The research demonstrates how attackers can utilize weaknesses in the Bluetooth protocol to carry out man-in-the-middle attacks, steal sensitive data, and even gain full control over devices. The BlueBorne attack involves scanning for Bluetooth-enabled devices and exploiting vulnerabilities in the protocol stack. Researchers at Armis utilized penetration testing and reverse engineering to identify these weaknesses. Armis identified eight zero-day vulnerabilities that posed risks to billions of devices. The impact of these vulnerabilities varied depending on the platform but underscored the potential for malware to spread between devices without user involvement. Patching affected devices is critical, and Armis's disclosure pushes manufacturers and users to prioritize security over convenience in Bluetooth technology. Governments and organizations must promote awareness and establish frameworks for rapid response to vulnerabilities.

Building on this foundation, we examined studies that highlight the overall security landscape of wireless systems and identify key areas where advanced security measures are necessary. For instance, in [15], the paper comprehensively analyzes the fundamental vulnerabilities in wireless networks and different attack techniques to exploit these vulnerabilities. Wireless communication techniques have become the backbone of various applications across multiple industries, presenting significant security challenges. This research presents six key findings and six mitigation techniques, ranging from encryption to physical security, addressing each problem from multiple angles. The paper states that security is a constantly evolving challenge, so we must focus on researching, developing, and implementing best practices to protect the future of wireless communication systems. In [16], the research shows that online security threats have increased, which has led many security companies to research protection methods regarding keyboard-entered data. Keyboard security issues have arisen due to the production of new malicious codes by attackers who have combined existing attack techniques with novel ones. The researchers analyzed attack techniques, implemented sample attacks, and confirmed the exposure of the keyboard scan code input by the user while running the secure keyboard software. The experimental results showed a 70% success rate for the attacks. In the case of secure keyboard programs, which are used on many websites, this result indicates that these attack techniques can cause significant damage. The research motivation is to provide more secure user authentication methods. Anti-virus programs do not detect sample attack programs, so a new countermeasure for this problem is needed quickly.

Focusing more on Bluetooth-specific security concerns. In [17], the authors report that Bluetooth technology, particularly Bluetooth Low Energy (BLE), has become the backbone of short-range wireless communication in IoT applications. The lack of a centralized security infrastructure leaves it vulnerable to significant security risks. Vulnerabilities in the Bluetooth protocol, including weak encryption and insecure pairing processes, enable attacks such as BlueBorne, Bluebugging, and MAC spoofing. The study analyzed various Bluetooth attacks through the lens of their protocol weaknesses, categorized by device classes and connection modes. Common exploits such as BlueSnarfing, PIN cracking, and man-in-the-middle attacks were studied alongside mitigation strategies. The analysis revealed that vulnerabilities in older Bluetooth versions persist in modern environments due to outdated devices and insufficient security measures in commercial devices, such as default passwords and unencrypted communications, exacerbating risks. Recommended measures include enforcing Secure Simple Pairing (SSP) for modern devices, integrating encryption, and utilizing adaptive frequency hopping to avoid interference. Regular software updates and user education on best practices for Bluetooth are necessary. The study [18] examines Bluetooth Media Access Control Scanner (BMAS) technology, which is widely used in transportation systems for real-time data collection. It captures MAC IDs from Bluetooth devices to estimate travel times and monitor traffic. Challenges like multiple devices from buses biasing travel time estimates and instances of cloned MAC IDs compromise its accuracy. For example, a bus carrying several Bluetooth-enabled devices can appear as multiple vehicles, skewing travel time calculations. The study used real-world BMS data focusing on two key concerns: the overrepresentation of buses and the uniqueness of MAC IDs. Bus Overrepresentation: Analysis revealed that buses accounted for up to 20% of Bluetooth travel time points during peak periods. MAC ID Uniqueness: Cloning of MAC IDs was minimal, with duplications constituting less than 0.025% of total daily observations. Cloned MAC IDs currently pose negligible risks. However, the authors recommend ongoing monitoring of non-unique MAC IDs to prevent future challenges.

After that, we reviewed more targeted research focusing on specific attack scenarios and mitigation techniques, offering valuable insights into system-level defense. In [19], experts examine the vulnerabilities of battlefield IoT systems, with a specific focus on Crazyflie drones. It demonstrates how the MouseJack attack, previously targeting wireless keyboards and mice, can be repurposed to compromise drones by sniffing unencrypted wireless network channels and injecting malicious packets. IoT-enabled military systems, such as the Internet of Battlefield Things (IoBT), often lack robust security. Adversaries can exploit unencrypted communication protocols to hijack devices, compromising operational effectiveness and risking sensitive data. The researchers exploited the Crazy Real-Time Protocol (CRTP), which Crazyflie drones utilize, by combining the MouseJack attack with packet reverse engineering. The attack involved sniffing wireless traffic, identifying vulnerable devices, and injecting custom payloads using modified Crazyradio PA dongles and Python libraries. The MouseJack-based attack successfully disrupted drone operations, allowing adversaries to hijack control. The study exploited a serious flaw in the unencrypted CRTP communication protocol. The paper highlights the urgent need for encryption in drone communication protocols. It recommends using secure key exchange mechanisms and encrypted payloads to prevent similar attacks. In [20], the study addresses the challenge of defending operating systems from malicious peripherals. As we know, computer peripherals such as USB and Bluetooth devices have virtually unrestricted functionality, presenting a threat of malicious devices that can compromise computer systems in numerous ways. Launching attacks can be done in one of two ways: sending unexpected packets to active extra functionality or crafting specially formed packets to exploit vulnerabilities within the stack. Methods used to analyze how USB privileges granted by operating systems can be escalated, along with a detailed examination of USB interfaces, protocols, and Bluetooth vulnerabilities, to build multi-layered solutions. The results include a security solution within operating systems, such as Linux (e)BPF Modules, USB Type-C Authentication protocols, formal verification of USB protocols, and defining good USB practices. The research has enabled further research on hardening operating systems and building trusted peripherals. It is recommended to investigate how to combine different solutions on multiple layers. In [21], the paper focuses on Man-in-the-Middle (MITM) attacks, which affect all wireless technologies, including Bluetooth. Bluetooth is a relatively new technology that enables wireless communication and data transfer between electronic devices operating at the 2.4 GHz frequency within the free Industrial, Scientific, and Medical (ISM) band. However, Bluetooth security remains a growing concern among users of mobile devices and gadgets. The research explores vulnerabilities in the Secure Simple Pairing (SSP) mode that allow MITM attacks, discusses different existing solutions, and what they lack, and suggests two novel scenarios using ESP along with two novel countermeasures. While some countermeasures offer security and seem promising, none can prevent intrusions without compromising the practicality and ease of use of Bluetooth. This study highlights the need for future research to focus more on a radical change to the existing Bluetooth structure, taking a different, non-traditional approach.

Active detection methods also play a crucial role in mitigating wireless threats. In [22], the study suggests wireless packet forwarding detection (WPFD) as a new solution for users to detect Evil Twin APs. These fake APs, posing as authentic, can enable man-in-the-middle (MITM) and phishing attacks. WPFD addresses the limitations of existing solutions that require administrator assistance or specialized hardware. Problem Statement: Traditional methods for detecting Evil Twin APs are costly, dependent on network administrators, or easily bypassed by attackers. Users lack effective tools to autonomously detect these threats. WPFD uses the retransmission mechanism of TCP/IP protocols to identify packet-forwarding behavior indicative of an Evil Twin. The system forwards SYN packets to websites and monitors retransmissions using a wireless network interface card (WNIC) in monitor mode. This detection requires no exterior data, such as trusted IP lists or machine learning models. WPFD proved high accuracy in detecting Evil Twins, achieving a true positive rate and a true negative rate of 100%. The system was forceful across varying traffic levels and resistant to attempts at evasion by attackers. WPFD is a practical and profitable solution for detecting Evil Twin attacks in public and private Wi-Fi networks. It is recommended that WPFD be able to address limitations, such as detecting rogue APs using alternate internet connections like 3G/4G, and discover optimizations for faster detection across multiple Wi-Fi channels.

Furthermore, research on wireless penetration testing offers practical insights into simulating real-world attack scenarios. The paper [23] investigates the current state of drone security and demonstrates a set of Wi-Fi-enabled drone vulnerabilities. Drone security within IoT systems has become a growing concern. Drones are becoming increasingly popular in both commercial/non-commercial markets. The increased usage of drones means they will become common targets for malicious attackers. As with IoT devices, security is often an afterthought, leaving drones vulnerable to hackers. The methodology followed includes a series of attacks: DoS, De-authentication, MITM, and Wi-Fi disablement. The Parrot AR will be investigated to see whether it is possible to gain unauthorized access. The access points lack any form of security. This means that any user within the Wi-Fi range can connect to the drones without a password or knowledge of the legitimate owner. The investigations successfully reveal the drone vulnerabilities that are vital security and privacy concerns for the public and smart city IoT applications. In [24], wireless networks are similarly exposed; they have become the prime target for many attacks since you can get into any wireless network as long as you're close to its range. This work aims to secure these networks and identify their vulnerabilities by building a remote-controlled car robot and programming it to demonstrate wireless penetration testing by attempting to hack surrounding Wi-Fi connections using various tools (e.g., Aircrack-ng suite, Kali Linux, etc.). The robot demonstrated potential for scanning networks and proved to be an ideal solution for securing wireless networks. With increased processing power, the robot can be scaled up to four networks simultaneously. In [25], this study further explores the security threats associated with IoT-capable drones and highlights their susceptibility to Wi-Fi attacks. The proposal recommends using Raspberry Pi devices to protect drones from hacking techniques, like de-authentication attempts, unauthorized entry, and man-in-the-middle attacks. The use of drones powered by technology is growing across various industries, making them a key target for cyberattacks. Weak encryption and poor security configurations exacerbate risks such as Wi-Fi hijacking and unauthorized access. The authors employed a step-by-step attack simulation using Raspberry Pi, Ubuntu Parrot OS, and Wi-Fi Pineapple to demonstrate vulnerabilities in drone communication. Data security was improved by implementing the RSA cryptographic algorithm. The investigation was efficient in identifying significant threats, including de-authentication attacks and illegitimate access. By introducing a secure channel of communication between drones and their operators, the RSA-based encryption technique significantly reduced most identified threats. To defend drones against cyberattacks, the study highlights the significance of robust encryption and secure Wi-Fi connection protocols. For dynamic threat management, real-time intrusion detection technologies should be investigated in future research. In [26], a wireless auditing tool called Wi-Fi Auditor is proposed, built on the Raspberry Pi platform. It's designed to perform penetration tests, reconnaissance, and security assessments effectively and affordably. Wi-Fi Pineapple has restrictions that hinder accessibility and flexibility for penetration testers and researchers. There is a pressing need for an affordable, customizable, and user-friendly penetration testing tool to address these vulnerabilities. The proposed Wi-Fi Auditor uses Raspberry Pi and open-source tools to conduct wireless security testing, including reconnaissance, targeted attacks, and reporting. Key features include monitoring devices, jamming, and man-in-the-middle attacks. Wi-Fi Auditor demonstrated a robust capability to simulate and detect common wireless security threats, including unauthorized access and data interception. Its modular design and affordability make it an accessible option for small businesses and researchers. The study highlights the potential of low-cost platforms, such as Raspberry Pi, for wireless penetration testing and security auditing. Wi-Fi Auditor offers a user-friendly, flexible, and efficient solution for securing wireless networks against emerging threats.

After that, we examined research related to intrusion detection systems and their importance, and we expanded our selection to include studies that cover multiple aspects of this topic. Study [27] focuses on the Evil Twin attack, which involves creating a rogue access point that mimics a legitimate one, deceiving users into connecting to a malicious network. The lack of unique signatures renders these systems ineffective in identifying such attacks, necessitating alternative approaches that consider variations in signal strength and environmental factors. The k-nearest neighbor (KNN) algorithm was used to classify signal strength data collected from sensors. The data includes minimum, maximum, average, and mode signal strengths. The KNN model successfully identified Evil Twin attacks by detecting deviations in signal strength. The study demonstrated that this is possible even when legitimate and illegitimate signal ranges overlap. We can use machine learning and signal strength analysis to detect Evil Twin attacks. Practical deployment in real-world environments requires fine-tuning models and addressing limitations such as the need for extensive legitimate access point data during initial setup. This study [28] focuses on

Physical Layer Security (PLS), a major concern that modern IoT networks face, as wireless channels, being open, are susceptible to eavesdropping. However, IoT devices often operate in environments with low signal-to-noise ratios, and the detection of active eavesdropping attacks during communication is rarely studied. This paper proposes a novel methodology for detecting active eavesdropping using deep learning. Focusing on signal classification performance, the method employs a BP neural network model to learn and classify the structured eigenvectors of signals, and various parameters in the detection task are optimized to enhance the performance of the active detection algorithm. The results show that the model exhibits stronger robustness and accuracy and can be significantly improved by up to 19.58% compared to other approaches.

Going to a deeper level, we explored the two main systems in IDS: host-based intrusion detection (HIDS), which monitors individual devices, and network-based intrusion detection, which examines and monitors network traffic. Both are compatible and can work together to create strong security systems. Study [29] examines the vulnerability of Wi-Fi (802.11) networks to de-authentication attacks, WPA handshake cracking, and captive portal exploits. It introduces Wi-Fi-NID, an automated detection tool that identifies and analyzes Wi-Fi-specific threats and subsequent network intrusions. Wi-Fi networks remain vulnerable to attacks. Current detection systems often lack specificity for Wi-Fi attacks and fail to automate PCAP file analysis effectively. The researchers designed a penetration testing methodology targeting Wi-Fi-specific attacks, including DoS, Evil Twin, and WPS attacks. Wi-Fi-NID was implemented to detect attack traces and subsequent malicious network behavior using tools like TShark, Python, and Bash scripts. Wi-Fi-NID successfully identified various Wi-Fi attacks in real-time, including de-authentication and WPS attacks, with minimal false positives for generic network intrusions. Testing revealed that the tool is effective across various Wi-Fi setups, achieving high detection accuracy. The paper highlights that Wi-Fi-NID offers a robust layer of security by identifying and evaluating Wi-Fi-specific attacks. Future work will enhance the tool's functionality for active prevention and refine methods beyond MAC address detection. In [30], the study refines Network-Based Intrusion Detection Systems (NIDS), highlighting the challenges of detecting threats in these systems and the transition from traditional IDS to advanced techniques, such as machine learning and hybrid tactics. Industrial and robotic systems face increasing threats, including Advanced Persistent Threats (APTs) and zero-day vulnerabilities, which traditional systems often struggle to control effectively. The lack of specialized datasets for industrial environments exacerbates these challenges. The authors reviewed multiple NIDS methodologies, including signature-based, anomaly-based, and machine learning-based methodologies. They assessed their application to industrial control systems (ICS) and robotics, highlighting the need for adaptive, real-time solutions. Emerging technologies like blockchain, federated learning, and digital twins show potential for enhancing NIDS. However, datasets such as UNSW-NB15 and SWaT are insufficient for training models tailored to industrial-specific traffic. The paper calls for robust dataset creation, real-time monitoring solutions, and lightweight ML algorithms. It also emphasizes the importance of leveraging emerging technologies to mitigate risks in industrial systems. Study [31] focuses on IDS in IoT systems. IoT is introduced as one of the technology applications that relies heavily on wireless communications. The research indicates that IoT technology is experiencing rapid growth due to its benefits in automation and improvements to the quality of life. However, many IoT devices have several vulnerabilities that make IoT networks susceptible to attacks. This study presents a comparative analysis of recent machine learning-based network intrusion detection systems (NIDSs) by evaluating different learning models to determine the optimal performance. Shallow learning models were separately tested and compared alongside deep learning models. In addition to these models, ensemble models of different learning approaches were also tested. The results showed that deep learning techniques achieved better results than shallow learning, with the highest mean accuracy belonging to the Deep Neural Network (DNN) (95.86%). This shows the potential effectiveness of deep learning models implementing NIDS. At the same time, ensembles outperformed all the other models, with the best model, RF/DNN, achieving an accuracy of 95.91% and representing the top model overall.

On the other hand, the study [32] indicates that IoT devices have limited resources and are vulnerable to various attacks, including denial-of-service (DoS) and man-in-the-middle (MITM) attacks. While intrusion detection systems are designed to detect these types of attacks, they are typically deployed at gateways or in the cloud. However, in the absence of a gateway, IDSs must be embedded directly in the nodes themselves. In this work, the researchers embedded a tree-based IDS trained on a custom dataset, named Intrusion Detection in the Smart Homes (IDSH), in a small thermostat. The system was designed to work with IoT devices that communicate with the cloud, and the results showed a high accuracy rate of 98.71% for binary classification and 97.51% for multi-classification. The IDS successfully detected both DoS and MITM attacks.

Finally, the study [33] illustrates some obstacles that face the IDS in detecting potential threats and how to improve detection systems. In [33], the research presents a technique for setting up cybersecurity networks that entails using evolutionary computation to enhance multi-layer perceptrons (MLPs). The primary concern is navigating obstacles in detecting cybersecurity risks, including APTs, ransomware attacks, and unknown vulnerabilities. Conventional approaches to training neural networks struggle with optimizing noisy datasets and high-dimensional spaces, resulting in subpar intrusion detection performance. Adaptive and robust optimization approaches are critical for improving model accuracy in cybersecurity contexts. The authors propose the Cybersecurity Optimizer (CSO), which uses adaptive differential evolution for optimizing ML parameters. CSO dynamically tunes weights and biases while integrating features such as hybrid mutation, crossover, and an archive mechanism to retain promising solutions. Using datasets such as NSL-KDD, CICIDS2017, UNSW-NB15, Bot-IoT, and CSE-CIC-IDS2018, the proposed optimizer achieved superior classification accuracy, with results of 99.5% on Bot-IoT and 98.8% on CSE-CIC-IDS2018, outperforming traditional methods like Genetic Algorithms and Particle Swarm Optimization. The CSO significantly enhances MLP training efficiency and robustness in threat detection. Future research should focus on integrating the optimizer into real-time detection systems and extending its applications to other cybersecurity domains. Finally, we summarize the related works in Table 2.3.

2.4.1 Knowledge gap

The literature surrounding security vulnerabilities in IoT devices and wireless communication protocols highlights significant gaps that need further exploration. Some studies have addressed the limitations of existing detection and mitigation systems; however, they have not provided a robust solution to address these problems directly. On the other hand, some other researchers suggest using an IDS as a mitigation technique. However, general datasets are commonly used, thus limiting the generalizability of the proposed machine learning models. Similarly, while tools like Wi-Fi-NID have effectively detected basic Wi-Fi threats, such as de-authentication attacks, these systems struggle with real-world deployment, especially in dynamic environments with interference and high device density, revealing a gap in scalability and performance in complex, real-world network conditions.

Moreover, applying deep learning models to cybersecurity threats remains hindered by challenges such as computational overhead and the lack of real-time adaptation. While deep learning models, including DNNs, demonstrate high accuracy in laboratory settings, their efficiency in real-time systems, particularly in resource-constrained IoT environments, remains largely unexplored. Additionally, despite improvements in the security of IoT devices, such as drones and Bluetooth devices, there is an insufficient focus on more sophisticated threats, including GPS spoofing and advanced persistent threats (APTs) in drones, as well as the evolving vulnerabilities in newer Bluetooth protocols, like BLE (Bluetooth Low Energy), used in IoT networks. These gaps underscore the need for a comprehensive approach to real-time detection and proactive defense strategies, ensuring that emerging technologies are addressed before they become widespread vulnerabilities.

Table 2.3 Research summary table

REF#	*Year*	*Solution*	*Attacks*	*Advantages*	*Limitation*
[12]	2016	Details vulnerabilities in non-Bluetooth wireless peripherals	MouseJack	Highlights vulnerabilities in unencrypted communications	Focuses on specific peripheral types
[11]	2024	Demonstrates the BlueBorne attack vector for Bluetooth	BlueBorne, information leaks, RCE vulnerabilities	Reveals critical vulnerabilities in widespread Bluetooth stacks	Focuses only on Bluetooth-related vulnerabilities
[15]	2022	Explores AI-based solutions for wireless security	Eavesdropping, DoS, unauthorized access	Diverse security measures	High overhead for resource-limited devices
[16]	2023	Analyzes vulnerabilities in keyboard software for the PS/2 interface	Keylogging, RESEND command utilization	Detailed assessment of keyboard vulnerabilities	Focuses on specific keyboard types and scenarios
[17]	2024	Bluetooth vulnerabilities analysis in IoT	BlueJacking, BlueBorne, BlueBugging	Detailed investigation of Bluetooth security weak spots	Focuses on Bluetooth, not other IoT protocols
[18]	2024	Analyzes Bluetooth MAC scanner data and its implications	N/A	Provides insights into the overrepresentation of buses in scanning	It does not explore implications beyond transportation systems
[19]	2024	Simulates drone hijacking using MouseJack and packet injection	Drone hijacking, packet injection, DoS	Highlights critical security flaws in IoT systems	Limited to specific drone models and open-source protocols
[20]	2019	Proposes defenses for USB-based malicious peripherals	HID spoofing, malicious USB device attacks	Innovative defense mechanisms	Implementation challenges in diverse environments

[21]	2017	Proposes novel countermeasures to Bluetooth MITM attacks	MITM attacks including two novel scenarios	Addresses limitations in existing solutions and proposes two novel countermeasures	The proposed solutions may not be practically applicable
[22]	2024	Introduces a user-side detection system for Evil Twin APs (WPFD)	Evil Twin APs, MITM	There is no need for network admin support or special devices with 100% accuracy.	Requires an initial connection
[23]	2019	Explores hacking techniques and mitigation for drones	DoS, MITM, Root access, Packet spoofing	Comprehensive analysis of vulnerabilities	Focuses only on two commercial drone models
[24]	2024	Develops an IoT-based car prototype for pen-testing	MITM, De-authentication, Spoofing	A practical tool for wireless network security evaluation	Focuses on a specific case
[25]	2023	Wi-Fi-based drone security using Raspberry Pi	MITM, Service Refusal, De-authentication, Unauthorized Source Access	Enhanced drone data security and real-time protection	Limited to specific IoT drone models
[26]	2019	Describes Wi-Fi Auditor for wireless penetration testing	MITM, WPA cracking, Rogue AP setups	Portable and versatile testing platform	It relies on specific hardware (Wi-Fi Pineapple).
[27]	2024	Develops a hardware-software system to detect Evil Twin attacks	Evil Twin attacks in Wi-Fi networks	Accurate detection using signal strength variations	Environment-dependent accuracy simulation-based results
[28]	2024	Uses a BP neural network to detect active eavesdropping attacks	Active eavesdropping, spoofing attacks	Higher detection rate compared to traditional approaches	Focus on simulation data, and it may not work as well in real-world environments

(Continued)

Table 2.3 (Continued) Research summary table

REF#	*Year*	*Solution*	*Attacks*	*Advantages*	*Limitation*
[29]	2023	Introduces Wi-Fi-NID for intrusion detection on 802.11 networks	De-authentication, WPA/WPA2 cracking, captive portal attacks	Real-time analysis and automated detection	Requires specific configurations for optimal performance
[30]	2024	Intrusion detection assessment in industrial/robotic systems	Advanced Persistent Threats (APTs), insider threats	Highlights real-time detection in complex environments	Dataset limitations with legacy systems
[31]	2024	Compares different ML-based NIDs for cyber-attack detection	IoT-related attacks, DDoS	Compares different models for performance comparison	Generalized datasets, not industrial-specific
[32]	2024	Suggests embedding tree-based IDS in smart thermostats	DoS, MITM	High accuracy and fast prediction capability without relying on gateways or cloud computing	Limited to specific IoT devices
[33]	2024	Presents Cybersecurity Optimizer (CYO) for training neural networks	Network intrusion, phishing, malware, ransomware	High accuracy (up to 99.5%) in detecting diverse cyber threats; robust against complex datasets	Computationally intensive; dependency on dataset quality

Another notable gap is the lack of integration across different wireless communication protocols, such as Bluetooth and Wi-Fi. Many existing tools are limited to a specific protocol and do not account for other communication standards. By addressing this limitation, our work aims to develop a comprehensive security solution that detects attacks across various protocols. We also noticed that most studies focus on either the offensive or defensive side, without addressing both simultaneously, which affects the practicality and applicability of the suggested solution. We aim to fill this gap by working on both sides of the equation. Doing so will improve the effectiveness and real-world applicability of our solution.

2.4.2 Main contributions and outcomes

Our work aims to address some of the knowledge gaps directly. Our goal is to detect a wide range of vulnerabilities by combining different data collections from Wi-Fi, Bluetooth, and RF protocols, which collectively reflect the diversity of communication standards found in modern systems around us. The work utilizes a remotely controlled robot and attack module capable of autonomously scanning, identifying, and attacking vulnerable wireless devices. Our robot is capable of applying and mimicking real-world attack scenarios, where multiple communication protocols usually interact in the same space. Furthermore, the addition of an Intrusion Detection System (IDS) to the work offers real-time detection of these attacks, demonstrating an adaptive defense system that reacts to attacks in real time. This IDS is designed to simultaneously offer a cross-protocol detection solution that helps mitigate the threats faced by them. The IDS's ability to detect attacks in a dynamic environment with high interference addresses one of the scalability and deployment challenges in existing systems. Ultimately, the integration of attack simulation and real-time defense offers a comprehensive framework that can serve as a foundation for future research on enhancing detection and mitigation techniques for various vulnerabilities across diverse wireless protocols. We summarize the key gaps in Table 2.4.

2.5 TECHNICAL REQUIREMENTS OVERVIEW

2.5.1 Involved parties and their interests

We divided our stakeholders into five categories: penetration testers and ethical hackers, the defense community and blue teams, vendors and companies, students and universities, and researchers. In Table 2.5, we will provide a description, interaction with our system, and the role and importance of each stakeholder.

Table 2.4 Knowledge gaps summary table

Identified gap	*Existing tool limitation*	*How our work addresses it*
Real-world deployment failures of IDS systems	Tools like Wi-Fi-NID fail in dynamic environments with high device density and interference.	Our IDS is designed for scalability and adaptability, enabling it to address dynamic environments effectively.
Limited integration across multiple wireless protocols	Many tools focus solely on Wi-Fi or Bluetooth, neglecting cross-protocol vulnerabilities.	Our work integrates Wi-Fi, Bluetooth, and RF for cross-protocol detection and defense.
Computational overhead in deep learning models	DNNs demonstrate high accuracy in lab conditions but struggle with real-time IoT adaptation.	Our system optimizes lightweight models suitable for IoT devices in real-time environments.
Lack of simultaneous offensive and defensive approaches	Most research focuses on either attacks or defense, not both simultaneously.	Our work combines attack simulations with IDS in a unified framework for comprehensive testing and mitigation.

2.5.2 Platform requirements

The platform requirements for the system encompass the necessary hardware and software components to ensure the successful operation of the robot and its subsystems. The system is divided into three subsystems: (A) Robot (server-side): Performs scanning and exploitation tasks while navigating the physical environment, (B) Control Application (client-side): Provides remote guidance, real-time monitoring, and system management capabilities, and (C) Intrusion Detection System (IDS): Enhances security by monitoring network activities, detecting potential threats, and alerting the user to anomalies. Below are the detailed requirements for each subsystem, categorized as essential (must-have) and recommended.

(A) **Robot Subsystem (Server-Side):** The robot subsystem is considered the core of our work and is responsible for vulnerability scanning, exploitation, video streaming, and movement control. It requires specifically selected hardware components to perform its job flawlessly, including the Raspberry Pi 5 and wireless communication modules, as well as other essential software libraries and tools to facilitate scanning, motion, and camera operations. Table 2.6 outlines the hardware and software requirements for the robot subsystem.

(B) **Control Application Subsystem (Client-Side):** The control application subsystem acts as an interface for the user to interact with the robot system. It enables the user to control the robot remotely, drive it to a specific location based on the user's command, and access the

Table 2.5 Stakeholder roles and interactions with the system

Stakeholder	*Description*	*Interaction*	*Role importance*
Vendors and companies	Integrate the system into their security infrastructure.	Be aware of vulnerabilities that the robot system exploits. Develop the IDS system to be involved in their defense system.	High. They will help to improve the IDS system to meet real-world security needs.
Researchers	Estimating the validity of the entire system and improving it.	Testing the system to enhance it. Conducting future research on it.	High. Their interventions will develop the system and make it a dependable source.
penetration testers and ethical hackers	Utilize the robot system to simulate real-world wireless attacks and enhance their understanding of these threats.	Interact with the robot to help penetrate wireless systems in multiple scenarios.	High. They are the main intended users of the attack module. Using the robot system ensures that it's valid.
Defense community and blue teams	Use the IDS to mitigate multiple systems' threats.	Involving the IDS as part of their mitigation plan to ensure that the system is secure at the physical and network layer levels.	High. They are the main intended users. Using the IDS ensures that it's valid.
Students and universities	The system's diversity in fields can be used as a learning tool and resource for future work.	Using the system as a source of learning in multiple majors.	Medium. Their contribution will reach part of the system's goals, and the system can inspire them in their studies and research.

robot's live video streaming capability to assist in navigating it to the target location. The requirements for the control application subsystem primarily focus on ensuring smooth interactions and ease of use, with minimal hardware requirements and essential software tools (see Table 2.7).

(C) **IDS Subsystem:** The IDS subsystem helps enhance system security by monitoring network activities, identifying potential threats, and responding to any anomalies. It operates independently of the robot and control application subsystems but integrates seamlessly to enhance overall security, which is the primary goal of this work (see Table 2.8).

Table 2.6 Robot subsystem requirements

Requirement type	*Details*	*Priority*
Hardware	Raspberry Pi 5 (minimum 4GB RAM) with compatible power supply	Essential
	Wireless communication modules (Bluetooth, Wi-Fi, and RF receivers)	Essential
	Camera module (e.g., OV2640 2MP Wi-Fi+ Bluetooth)	Essential
	SD card (minimum 16GB storage for OS and system logs)	Essential
	Robot chassis with motor control module (DC/ servo motors)	Essential
	Optional external battery pack (for extended operation time)	Recommended
	Raspberry Pi 5 Case Acrylic Case	Recommended
	Raspberry Pi Active Cooler Official	Recommended
Software	Raspberry Pi OS (64-bit version)	Essential
	Python 3.x with libraries: scapy, pywifi, Bluetooth, RPi.GPIO, pigpio, OpenCV	Essential
	SSH server for secure communication with the robot	Essential
	Motion control libraries for motor operation	Essential

Table 2.7 Control application subsystem requirements

Requirement type	*Details*	*Priority*
Hardware	Mobile device with internet/Wi-Fi connectivity	Essential
Software	Prebuilt Application designed to interface seamlessly with the robot for navigation and monitoring	Essential
	Python Flask-based application or Node.js runtime for GUI control	Essential
	Real-time communication protocols (e.g., MQTT) for robot interaction	Essential
	Encrypted communication channels to secure data exchange	Recommended

2.5.3 Functional requirements

This section outlines the functional requirements that determine the system's primary functions, as listed in Table 2.9, to ensure it operates as intended. For each requirement, we identified the inputs, outputs, processes, and any constraints that affect it. We have also categorized each requirement as either essential for the system or recommended, making it easier to prioritize tasks.

Table 2.8 IDS subsystem requirements

Requirement type	*Details*	*Priority*
Hardware	Minimum 2.0 GHz multi-core processor for real-time data processing and analysis	Essential
	At least 8 GB of RAM (16 GB recommended) to support large datasets used for training and real-time analysis of network traffic, and 512 GB SSD storage	Essential
	Wi-Fi and Bluetooth-compatible adapters for monitoring and analyzing wireless network traffic	Essential
Software	Logging and alerting system	Essential
	IDS tool (e.g., Snort, Suricata) for detecting and analyzing suspicious activities	Essential

2.5.4 Non-functional requirements

This section outlines the non-functional requirements, specifying the attributes we aim to achieve in our system. These requirements outline how well our system operates and act as a criterion to judge our system's success. We primarily focused on performance, reliability, and scalability in our system, without underestimating other important factors such as security, portability, and many others.

1. Performance: The IDS must detect malicious wireless activity (e.g., MouseJack, BlueBorne, Wi-Fi Pineapple) within 5–7 seconds of occurrence.
2. Security: All stored and transmitted logs should be encrypted by the system using the AES-256 encryption algorithm, confirming data to be safe and secure. Also, the system should adhere to cybersecurity standards.
3. Reliability: IDS must provide stable and consistent outputs and be available most of the time, with an uptime of ($\geq$ 95%).
4. Scalability: IDS and robot modules should handle up to 20 to 30 concurrent devices without any major degradation in performance.
5. Portability: The system must be willing to navigate and perform attacks in multiple environments and must be easy to move and use in various locations.
6. Usability and Accessibility: The system should be user-friendly and deliver a well-defined and easy-to-navigate interface.
7. Data Efficiency: 10 GB is the maximum limit of logs used in datasets & IDS, ensuring no exhaustion of resources.
8. Development Standards: scripts and IDS configurations should be followed by industry standards.

Table 2.9 Key functional requirements for system operations

#	*Requirement*	*Input*	*Output*	*Processes*	*Constraint*	*Classification*
Intrusion Detection System						
1	Threat Detection (AI Model)	Wireless Packets	Logs and alerts for potential threats	Real-time packet monitoring and analysis of threats	1. High accuracy (> 90%) 2. Low latency in processing packets	Essential
2	Model Training	A labeled dataset that contains normal and malicious wireless traffic	An AI model that can detect wireless threats	Data preprocessing, model training, and model tuning	1. Storage requirement (<10GB)	Essential
Attack Module						
3	Automated Wireless Scanning	Wireless signal parameters, specification of different protocols	List of detected wireless devices and protocols	Wireless signal scanning, device discovery, and protocol identification	1. Limited range (<100 meters) 2. Discover most devices	Essential
4	Automated Wireless Analysis	Detected List of wireless devices after scanning, attack specifications	List of detected vulnerable devices and the suitable attack	Traffic analysis, vulnerability scanning, and determining attacks	1. Analysis time must be within 5 seconds to maintain the real-time aspect	Essential
5	Exploit Execution	Exploit scripts, identified targets	Exploitation of the target	Execution of MouseJack, BlueBorne, Wi-Fi Pineapple exploits	1. Requires proximity to target device (<10 meters)	Essential

The Robot Module						
6	Remote Control and Navigation	User commands via Wi-Fi	Robot movement	Interpreting commands, controlling motors	1. Environmental obstacles 2. Robot must operate within the 2.4 GHz ISM band	Essential
7	Power Management	Battery status	Power usage alerts	Monitoring power levels	1. Robot must run for ≥1 hour on a single charge	Recommended
User Interface						
8	Movement and Command Input	User commands via clicks	Command signals to the robot	Interpreting movement commands	1. No delay for movement (<1 second)	Essential
9	Attack Status Feedback	Attack execution status (success or failure)	Visual prompts indicating the success or failure	Displaying real-time feedback and error messages if attacks fail	1. Feedback within 3 seconds	Essential
10	Traffic Simulation	Simulation parameters (e.g., attack type, duration, intensity)	Network traffic patterns to replicate the attacks	Visual representation of traffic to simulate the attacks	Traffic must be accurate compared with real-world attacks	Recommended

9. Documentation: The work must contain inclusive, easy-to-use guides for using the IDS and attack module.

2.5.5 Other requirements

Excluding the functional and non-functional requirements, the work has further requirements associated with technical requirements and implementation preferences. These include:

1. Protocol Requirements: The robot must be able to communicate over Wi-Fi (802.11) protocol so it can be controlled remotely and be able to interchange data and feedback with the user interface.
2. Data Storage Format: Attack data, IDS logs, and robot feedback must be stored in an easy-to-process format such as JSON or CSV to make processing easier, which eventually increases performance.
3. Performance Constraints: The AI model used for threat detection should be able to handle at least 100 wireless packets per second without much delay or resource usage.
4. Logging and Data Retention: IDS logs and attack module logs should be stored for a minimum of 30 days and must comply with industry standards for logging formats, such as Syslog or ELK (Elasticsearch, Logstash, and Kibana).

2.6 TECHNICAL ARCHITECTURE AND DESIGN PRINCIPLES

The design phase of our work, covered in this chapter, bridges the gap between planning and implementing our system. Our system's structural blueprint comprises the designs discussed in this chapter. The system comprises three main modules: the Robot Module, the Attack Module, and the Intrusion Detection System (IDS). We used detailed diagrams and well-designed models to illustrate how each module communicates with the others and how they process data to achieve their objectives successfully. We focused on efficiency, scalability, and modularity when designing these systems. Additionally, to ensure transparency in our designs and make our goals visible through our diagrams, we paid special attention to making these designs clear and easy to understand. The resulting designs will help us in the future implementation phase by providing a clear picture of the system.

We present a high-level outline of our system in the following chapter. We primarily focus on each component separately, explaining the logic behind it while also clarifying how all these elements work together to form the full picture. This architecture focuses on the Robot Module, Attack Module,

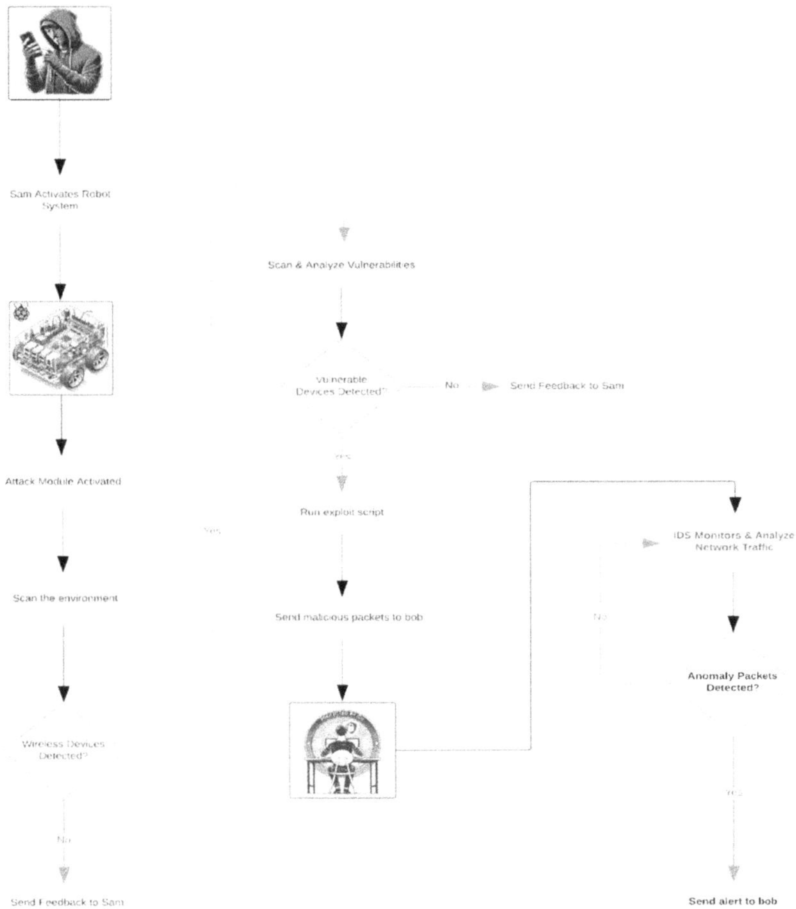

Figure 2.6 Overall system design.

and Intrusion Detection System (IDS). The design details how user commands and interactions are integrated. We used data flow diagrams (DFDs) to draw our designs because they are efficient in demonstrating complex workflows and representing step-by-step processes. Figure 2.6 illustrates a top-level diagram of the overall system, highlighting how its components connect in a real-world scenario and focusing on the flow of interactions for each part.

Figure 2.7 illustrates the workflow of the User Interaction and Robot Movement module, demonstrating how user commands via a mobile application influence the attack's progression and the robot's movement,

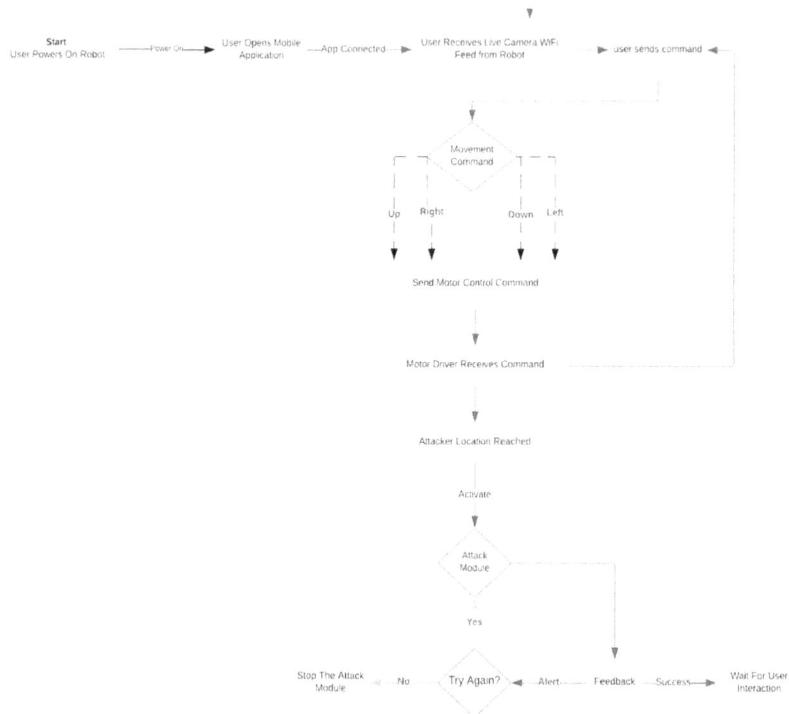

Figure 2.7 User Interaction and Robot Movement module design.

enabling it to reach the target location and provide the user with feedback during the attack's execution.

Figure 2.8 illustrates the Attack Module, showing the sequential processes it follows, beginning with wireless scanning and signal analysis, and continuing through the identification of vulnerabilities across various communication protocols, including Wi-Fi, RF (Radio Frequency), and Bluetooth. The module begins by actively scanning the surrounding environment to detect available wireless devices and their associated metadata, such as SSIDs, MAC addresses, signal strength, and protocol types. It then proceeds to analyze this data using pre-defined fingerprinting techniques and known vulnerability signatures. Once potential weak points are identified, the system maps them to specific attack vectors—such as rogue access points for Wi-Fi (e.g., Wi-Fi Pineapple), spoofing and injection techniques for RF, or protocol-based exploits for Bluetooth (e.g., BlueBorne, MouseJack). This automated workflow enables the robot to simulate real-world cyber threats in a controlled and repeatable manner, enhancing the overall realism and applicability of the testing environment.

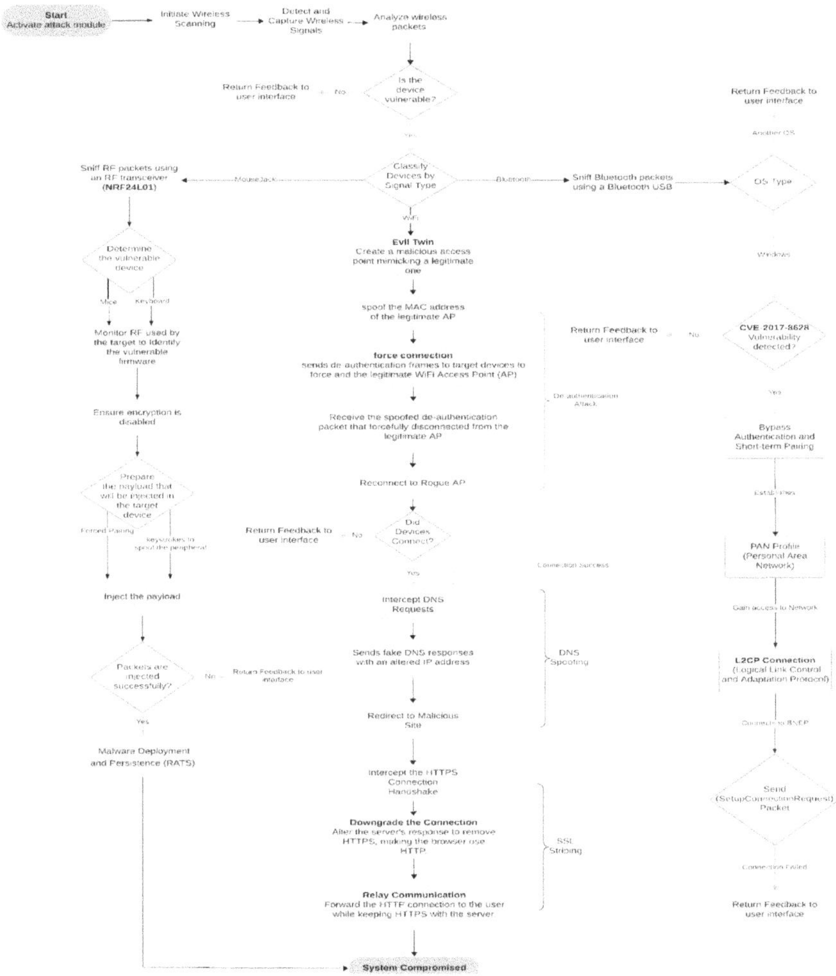

Figure 2.8 Attack Module design.

Figure 2.9 outlines the workflow of the Intrusion Detection System (IDS), detailing how it processes incoming wireless traffic and identifies malicious packet sequences. The workflow begins with data acquisition, where the IDS continuously monitors wireless communication channels (e.g., Wi-Fi, RF, Bluetooth) to capture live traffic in real time. This raw data is then passed through a pre-processing stage, which involves filtering noise, normalizing packet structures, and extracting relevant features such as protocol types, payload sizes, and timing patterns. Once pre-processed, the data is fed into the detection engine, which employs rule-based, anomaly-based, or machine learning techniques to analyze packet behavior and flag suspicious

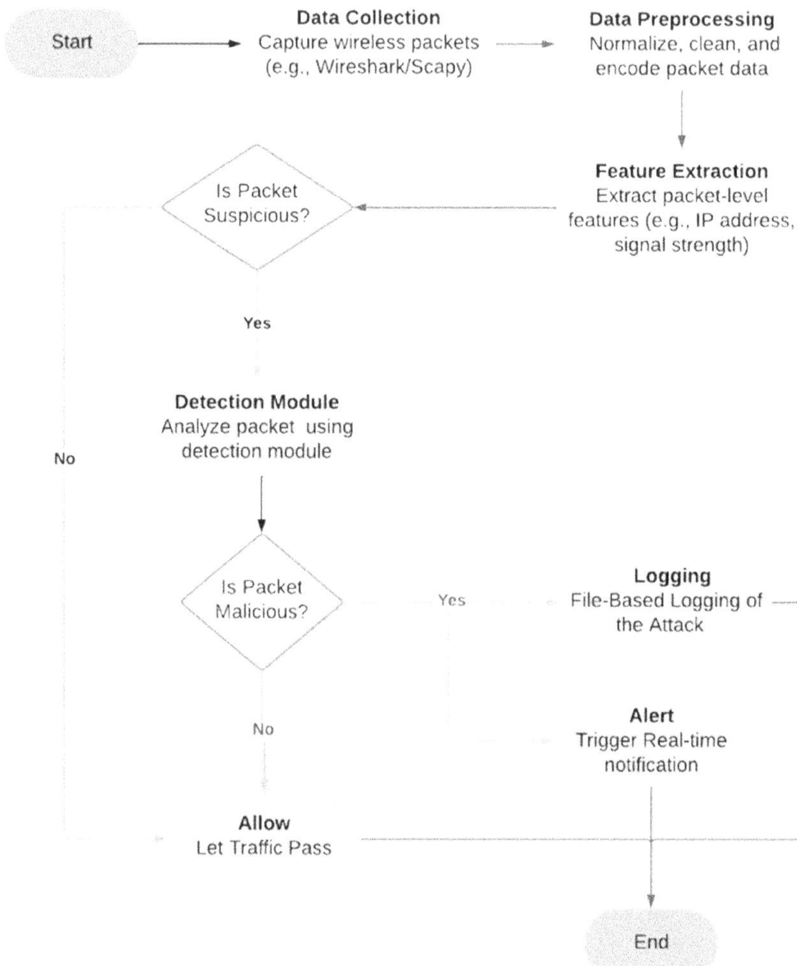

Figure 2.9 Intrusion Detection System design.

activity. The system correlates sequences of packets to detect complex intrusion patterns—such as spoofing, injection, or replay attacks—rather than isolated anomalies. Upon identifying a threat, the IDS triggers an alert generation module, which logs the incident and optionally interfaces with defensive mechanisms for response or mitigation. This structured workflow ensures that the IDS can adapt to diverse wireless environments while maintaining accuracy and efficiency in detecting evolving attack strategies.

2.7 CONCLUSIONS AND REMARKS

This work aims to design and develop a comprehensive scenario that incorporates a Raspberry Pi-based robot, an attack module, and a standalone Intrusion Detection System (IDS). The primary goal is to replicate real-world wireless attacks, such as MouseJack, BlueBorne (CVE-2017-8628), and Wi-Fi Pineapple, to develop effective mitigation strategies that can detect and prevent these attacks from occurring. The attack module is designed to exploit common vulnerabilities in different protocols (Wi-Fi, Bluetooth, and wireless peripherals), demonstrating how easily these communication channels can be exploited if sufficient security measures aren't in place. Meanwhile, the IDS will serve as our line of defense by analyzing network behavior, identifying anomalies, and stopping malicious activity. While the system is still in its theoretical stage, detailed analysis, architectural design diagrams, and thorough study of the concept have proven the work to be feasible. The proposed designs enable clear communications, modular architecture, and scalable components, providing a solid foundation for future implementation. The work addresses significant cybersecurity issues and highlights the importance of integrating both offensive and defensive measures in modern security frameworks.

2.8 WORK LIMITATIONS

This work faced many challenges and limitations, for example:

- The battery life during operation on the Raspberry Pi is low and may inevitably affect the work; another limitation is the SD memory storage space. Given that the malware that we want to download at the end of the attack module may be large and heavy, this may lead to slowdowns. One of the most important challenges to focus on is the range of wireless signals, so the robot must be positioned very close to the victim's location. Additionally, broadcasting the camera to guide the robot poses a significant challenge, as it must be both fast and of high quality.
- For IDS, the false positive rate may be high if training is not done on a large dataset, and this leads us to another challenge, which is the lack of datasets that suits our needs. The IDS of our work can only detect the vulnerabilities that we want to exploit in the attack module, MouseJack, BlueBorne, and Wi-Fi Pineapple, so this poses restrictions that lead to non-detection of other types of vulnerabilities. It is one of the reasons for false negatives, which lead to undetected breaches. Excessive logs can overwhelm storage systems and slow down analysis.

2.9 FUTURE WORK

Expanding the scope of this work is one of our future intentions. The planned directions for future work can be summarized as follows:

1. Advanced machine learning models: Enhance the IDS by integrating advanced machine learning and deep learning algorithms for improved anomaly detection and predictive analysis.
2. Include GPS in robot navigation: Add a GPS feature to the robot to assist in tracking the robot's movement and improve navigation control. This feature will enable the robot to follow a predetermined path accurately and expand its navigation range further.
3. Include additional wireless protocols: Add testing capabilities for a couple of extra protocols that are becoming more and more used and relied on, such as ZigBee, Z-Wave, and 5G, to address vulnerabilities within these standards.
4. Boost robot battery: Add a power bank to the robot module so it can last longer and stay powered on for extended periods without any problem.
5. Replace the robot with a drone: A drone can cover larger areas, which helps improve the range of locations we can reach and allows us to reach more difficult environments. It's more portable, which makes it ideal for remote attack simulations.
6. Integrate the robot into a penetration testing work environment, which helps specialists with their work and offers a touch of innovation to the job process.
7. Expand scalability: Build the same system using different components and make it compatible with multiple operating systems.
8. Use a custom-made dataset: Create a custom dataset with wireless packets that simulate real-world attacks to be used in training the IDS for more flexibility and increased accuracy in detecting and analyzing malicious activities.

NOTE

1. Corresponding author.

REFERENCES

1. C. Foo, "How does technology influence our lives?" *Sogolytics*, Jun. 28, 2024. [Online]. Available: https://www.sogolytics.com/blog/how-technology-influences-us. Accessed: Nov. 29, 2024.

2. Wikipedia, "ISM radio band," Nov. 19, 2022. [Online]. Available: https://en.wikipedia.org/wiki/ISM_radio_band. Accessed: Nov. 11, 2024.
3. Business Wire, "Smart commercial buildings IoT devices market report," May 18, 2023. [Online]. Available: https://www.businesswire.com/news/home/20230518005470/en/. Accessed: Dec. 15, 2024.
4. IoT Analytics, "The number of connected IoT devices," Sep. 3, 2024. [Online]. Available: https://iot-analytics.com/number-connected-iot-devices/. Accessed: Dec. 5, 2024.
5. IEEE Standards Association, "Wi-Fi (IEEE 802.11) standards," Oct. 3, 2023. [Online]. Available: https://standards.ieee.org/beyond-standards/the-evolution-of-wi-fi-technology-and-standards/. Accessed: Nov. 17, 2024.
6. N. Handy, "Penetration testing introduction: Scanning & reconnaissance," *Medium*, Aug. 18, 2024. [Online]. Available: https://medium.com/@nickhandy/penetration-testing-introduction-scanning-reconnaissance-f865af0761f. Accessed: Nov. 16, 2024.
7. Avast, "Wi-Fi Pineapple attack (evil twin)," *Avast Security Blog*, Oct. 12, 2023. [Online]. Available: https://www.avast.com/c-evil-twin-attack. Accessed: Nov. 15, 2024.
8. Wikipedia, "Wi-Fi deauthentication attack," Oct. 11, 2017. [Online]. Available: https://en.wikipedia.org/wiki/Wi-Fi_deauthentication_attack. Accessed: Nov. 16, 2024.
9. A. Chiarelli, "Perform SSL stripping," Sep. 22, 2023. [Online]. Available: https://www.andreachiarelli.net/ssl-stripping/. Accessed: Nov. 16, 2024.
10. KeyCDN, "DNS spoofing (inject malicious redirects)," Sep. 5, 2023. [Online]. Available: https://www.keycdn.com/support/dns-spoofing. Accessed: Nov. 15, 2024.
11. Armis Labs, "BlueBorne: Attack on Bluetooth devices," Sep. 12, 2017. [Online]. Available: https://www.armis.com/research/blueborne/. Accessed: Nov. 17, 2024.
12. Bastille Networks, "MouseJack vulnerabilities: Technical details," Feb. 23, 2016. [Online]. Available: https://bastille.net/research/vulnerabilities-mouse-jack-technical-details/. Accessed: Nov. 17, 2024.
13. Imperva, "What is a remote access Trojan (RAT)?" 2024. [Online]. Available: https://www.imperva.com/learn/application-security/remote-access-trojan-rat/. Accessed: Nov. 16, 2024.
14. Vector Solutions, "Levels of a risk matrix," Jun. 25, 2019. [Online]. Available: https://www.vectorsolutions.com/resources/blogs/levels-of-a-risk-matrix/. Accessed: Nov. 18, 2025.
15. A. Alabi, "Security challenges and solutions in wireless networks: A computer science perspective," Sep. 9, 2024. [Online]. Available: https://www.researchgate.net/publication/383908002. Accessed: Nov. 21, 2024.
16. A. K. L. Al-Khatib and K. Yim, "Vulnerability analysis and security assessment of secure keyboard software to prevent PS/2 interface keyboard sniffing," 2023. [Online]. Available: https://www.proquest.com/docview/2799748892. Accessed: Nov. 23, 2024.
17. S. Patil, "Security vulnerabilities in Bluetooth technology as used in IoT," *Future Internet*, vol. 7, no. 3, Jul. 2018. [Online]. Available: https://www.mdpi.com/2224-2708/7/3/28. Accessed: Nov. 25, 2025.

18. A. Bhaskar *et al.*, "Is bus overrepresented in Bluetooth MAC scanner data? Is MAC-ID really unique?" May 2014. [Online]. Available: https://www.researchgate.net/publication/271914061. Accessed: Nov. 29, 2024.
19. S. McMahon *et al.*, "Bewitching the battlefield: Repurposing the MouseJack attack for Crazyflie drones," in *Proc. IEEE Conf.*, 2022. [Online]. Available: https://ieeexplore.ieee.org/document/10225819. Accessed: Nov. 29, 2024.
20. A. J. Tian, "Defending operating systems from malicious peripherals," Ph.D. dissertation, 2019. [Online]. Available: https://www.proquest.com/docview/3044057009. Accessed: Nov. 21, 2024.
21. M. Albahar, K. Haataja, and P. Toivanen, "Bluetooth MITM vulnerabilities: A literature review," Dec. 2016. [Online]. Available: https://www.researchgate.net/publication/323846712. Accessed: Nov. 24, 2024.
22. F.-H. Hsu *et al.*, "Active user-side detection of evil twins," *Applied Sciences*, vol. 12, no. 16, Aug. 2022. [Online]. Available: https://www.mdpi.com/2076-3417/12/16/8088. Accessed: Nov. 29, 2024.
23. M. S. Alam *et al.*, "Drone hacking with raspberry Pi 3 and WiFi pineapple," in *Proc. IEEE Conf.*, Mar. 2019. [Online]. Available: https://ieeexplore.ieee.org/document/8658279. Accessed: Nov. 29, 2024.
24. J. D. Mukhopadhyay *et al.*, "Prototype of IoT-based remote-controlled car for pentesting wireless networks," Oct. 2019. [Online]. Available: https://ieeexplore.ieee.org/document/8658279. Accessed: Nov. 23, 2024.
25. P. M. Sekar and S. K. Sekar, "Security of drone hacking with Raspberry Pi using IoT," Apr. 2024. [Online]. Available: https://www.researchgate.net/publication/363859626. Accessed: Nov. 29, 2024.
26. P. Shinde *et al.*, "Wireless security audit penetration test using Raspberry Pi," Nov. 2018. [Online]. Available: https://ieeexplore.ieee.org/document/8537246. Accessed: Nov. 20, 2024.
27. R. Banakh *et al.*, "Data mining approach for evil twin attack identification in Wi-Fi networks," Oct. 2024. [Online]. Available: https://www.researchgate.net/publication/384923873. Accessed: Nov. 23, 2024.
28. D. Jovanović *et al.*, "Active eavesdropping detection: A novel physical layer security in wireless IoT," Nov. 2023. [Online]. Available: https://www.researchgate.net/publication/375831513. Accessed: Nov. 24, 2024.
29. J. N. Patel *et al.*, "Automated Wi-Fi incident detection attack tool on IEEE 802.11 networks," Aug. 28, 2023. [Online]. Available: https://ieeexplore.ieee.org/document/10218077. Accessed: Nov. 29, 2024.
30. R. Holdbrook *et al.*, "Network-based intrusion detection for industrial and robotics systems: A comprehensive survey," *Electronics*, 2024. [Online]. Available: https://www.mdpi.com/2079-9292/13/22/4440. Accessed: Nov. 23, 2024.
31. F. Genuario *et al.*, "Machine learning-based methodologies for cyber-attacks and network traffic monitoring: A review and insights," *Information*, Nov. 2024. doi: 10.3390/info15110741.
32. J. Javed *et al.*, "Embedding tree-based intrusion detection systems in smart thermostats for enhanced IoT security," *Sensors*, vol. 24, no. 22, Nov. 2024. [Online]. Available: https://www.mdpi.com/1424-8220/24/22/7320.
33. A. A. Salem and M. A. Salem, "Adaptive cybersecurity neural networks: An evolutionary approach for enhanced attack detection and classification," *Applied Sciences*, vol. 14, no. 19, Oct. 2024. [Online]. Available: https://www.mdpi.com/2076-3417/14/19/9142.

Chapter 3

Automated threat hunting using AI

Esra'a F. Hader and Qasem Abu Al-Haija[1]

3.1 INTRODUCTION

Cybersecurity threats are constantly shifting, often faster than defenses can adapt. This reality exposes the limits of reactive approaches, which rely on matching known patterns and issuing alerts only after an attack vector is identified. Passive methods like these can overlook novel tactics or subtle breaches. Because of this, many organizations are turning to proactive threat hunting, an effort to detect compromise before serious harm occurs. The rise of artificial intelligence (AI), especially machine learning (ML), is driving this shift, offering ways to process massive security datasets and highlight risks that might otherwise go unnoticed [1].

Unlike traditional incident response, which kicks in after something goes wrong, threat hunting is a forward-looking activity. Analysts start with a hypothesis, perhaps based on past attack behavior, odd system behavior, or threat intelligence. From there, they comb through logs, events, and patterns to uncover threats that haven't triggered alarms yet. It's not automated detection, it's inquiry-driven, requiring familiarity with the system environment, attacker behavior, and subtle deviations from the norm. The manual version of this process comes with real challenges. Today's enterprises produce enormous volumes of data from network logs to telemetry feeds that are difficult to sift through without automation. Human-driven analysis struggles to keep up. Add in the global shortage of trained cybersecurity professionals, and it's no surprise that threats are missed or discovered too late [2, 3].

This is where AI enters with practical impact. Machine learning models can examine user behavior, event flows, and traffic anomalies in real time, flagging unusual patterns for review. These systems assist human analysts, not by replacing them but by helping them focus on signals that matter most [4, 5]. They also uncover correlations across data sources, allowing defenders to see attacks as connected chains, not isolated events.

Figure 3.1 offers a visual comparison between two mindsets: proactive and reactive threat hunting. On the proactive side are measures like real-time monitoring and predictive modeling strategies to anticipate breaches.

DOI: 10.1201/9781003650478-4

Figure 3.1 Proactive vs. reactive threat hunting timeline.

Reactive techniques, by contrast, focus on what to do after something has happened: post-mortems, manual investigations, and response protocols. The point is not that one replaces the other but that AI is helping to shift emphasis toward earlier detection, where damage can still be prevented.

In AI-assisted threat hunting, machine learning plays a key role in uncovering subtle indicators of compromise within massive, complex datasets. These datasets typically include network logs, endpoint activity, and user behavior records, which must be preprocessed, aggregated, cleaned, and normalized before analysis. Different models are used depending on the goal: unsupervised learning is common for anomaly detection when labels aren't available; supervised classifiers are trained on known attack signatures; and in some experimental settings, reinforcement learning is being explored to respond to changing environments adaptively. Natural Language Processing (NLP) also helps analysts make sense of textual threat reports, dark web chatter, and unstructured log data that might otherwise go unused [6]. Its ability to scale automated threat hunting is valuable beyond just efficiency. A single analyst cannot feasibly monitor thousands of endpoints or parse terabytes of logs in real time, but automated systems can. They continuously evaluate system events without the fatigue, delay, or bottlenecks that limit human capacity [7].

Another key strength of automation is speed. Traditional detection methods often lag, requiring hours or days to respond to unusual activity. In contrast, AI-driven systems can surface anomalies as they occur or within minutes, giving defenders a critical time advantage [8]. These systems also tend to improve accuracy over time. Machine learning models refine their understanding of what constitutes a real threat by learning from historical data and observing behavioral context. False positive is an enduring challenge in Security Operations Centers (SOCs); they can be reduced significantly as models better distinguish between noise and true malicious activity [9, 10].

Automation also brings consistency. While human analysts are skilled, their judgments may vary depending on workload, fatigue, or unconscious bias. An AI system, by design, applies the same detection criteria every time, ensuring standardized evaluation across environments [11]. By combining the speed and scale of machine learning with intelligent analysis of large-scale security data, organizations are moving toward a more adaptive and robust cyber defense posture that evolves as threats evolve.

While AI and automation bring clear advantages to threat detection, they also introduce some limitations. Much depends on the training data. The resulting models can behave unpredictably or miss important signals if they lack diversity or quality. This issue is particularly serious in cybersecurity, where data from one environment might not generalize well to another. On top of that, adversarial attacks where inputs are carefully manipulated to deceive models pose an emerging threat to the reliability of AI systems [12].

Another difficulty is that some AI models, especially deep learning ones, are hard to interpret. Analysts may struggle to explain why a system flagged something as suspicious or didn't in fields like security, where accountability and traceability matter; this can be a deal breaker. Questions about data privacy, algorithmic fairness, and legal compliance only add to the hesitation around deploying AI in regulated environments [13].

This chapter explores both theory and practice around AI-enabled threat hunting. That includes how detection strategies have changed over time, how machine learning is used in security operations, and what scalable frameworks look like in practice. Case studies and implementation examples are used to illustrate both the power and the limitations of these techniques.

3.2 BACKGROUND: THREAT HUNTING AND CYBER THREATS

3.2.1 Overview of the cyber threat landscape

The scale and complexity of the current cyber threat landscape have increased. Attackers have turned to progressively advanced techniques like Advanced Persistent Threats (APTs), fileless malware, and ransomware-as-a-service (RaaS), while traditional threats like viruses and worms still exist. These attacks frequently use zero-day vulnerabilities, avoid traditional file-based signatures, and operate in stealthy, multi-phase campaigns to escape detection [14]. For example, APTs allow for long-term data theft or espionage infiltration, whereas fileless malware runs directly in memory and avoids antivirus software [15]. RaaS has even made it easier for non-technical criminals to launch ransomware attacks using pre-built tools purchased on the dark web [16]. Even more concerning are supply chain attacks, where hackers infiltrate a third-party software update or a trusted vendor rather than targeting an organization directly, converting legitimate software into an attacking tool, as was the case with the infamous SolarWinds breach [17].

As cyber attackers become more advanced, defenders must also improve their strategies. Traditional security tools are no longer enough to protect against today's fast-changing and highly sophisticated threats. Recent reports show a sharp rise in cyberattacks, with over 38% growth in 2023 alone, particularly against high-stakes industries including government services, healthcare, and energy [18]. Many of these threats result from organized cybercriminals and state-sponsored organizations taking advantage of long-standing system vulnerabilities. Adding to the difficulty, malware driven by artificial intelligence (AI) that can instantly adapt to network activity is fast emerging as one of the most alarming trends for security teams [19].

3.2.2 Types of cyber threats

Cyber threats can take many forms, and each one causes difficulties for businesses attempting to protect their systems. Defenders must know the full spectrum of risks they might face as attackers become more resourceful and inventive.

Ransomware and malware remain the most common types of cyberattacks. Malware includes trojans, spyware, and viruses, but ransomware encrypts user data and requests payment for the decryption keys. Recent trends include polymorphic malware, which alters its code to evade detection, and double extortion ransomware, where attackers encrypt and exfiltrate sensitive data [20].

Advanced Persistent Threats (APTs) are stealthy, long-duration attacks frequently implemented by highly organized groups or nation-states. To stay undetected for long periods, APT campaigns usually use a variety of strategies, such as initial compromise, lateral movement, persistence, and data exfiltration. These attacks are frequently observed in defense, finance, and energy [21].

Insider threats are another serious concern. Sometimes, the greatest risk comes from people already inside the organization. These insiders may actively leak private information, abuse their access rights, or accidentally provide attackers with opportunities through phishing or inadequate security procedures. The challenge lies in detecting abnormal behavior from otherwise legitimate accounts [22].

Supply chain attacks adopt the use of third-party hardware or software requirements. One of the best examples is the SolarWinds Orion breach, in which hundreds of companies, including federal agencies in the United States, were impacted by compromised software upgrades [23]. Supply chain compromises are difficult to detect because they come from trusted sources, often bypassing traditional defense perimeters [24].

Fileless attacks are especially tricky to detect. These threats do not install software on a machine, in contrast to conventional malware. Instead, they operate entirely in memory and often abuse legitimate system tools like PowerShell, WMI, or PsExec. These kinds of attacks frequently evade conventional security measures because there is no file to scan [25].

Zero-day exploits focus on vulnerabilities unknown to the software vendor and thus lack patches. These vulnerabilities are frequently employed in targeted attacks by nation-state actors and are highly valuable on the black market. The lack of predefined signatures or defensive guidelines increases their influence [26].

This dynamic and multifaceted nature highlights the limitations of static defense mechanisms. A proactive, AI-driven threat hunting strategy is now indispensable for identifying and mitigating such evolving threats before they cause widespread damage.

3.2.3 Traditional threat hunting methodologies

Before the rise of AI, the solutions for threat hunting were predominantly manual and analyst-driven activities. This traditional model relies heavily on human expertise to proactively search for signs of compromise within organizational systems. A search usually starts with a hypothesis developed from threat intelligence reports, abnormalities noticed, or known attack patterns. It then moves on to thoroughly examine system logs, endpoint telemetry, and network traffic [27]. The Cyber Kill Chain, developed by Lockheed Martin, is still a go-to model for breaking down how attacks unfold, starting from initial reconnaissance and ending with exfiltration. It helps analysts visualize what stage an attack might be in. Alongside that, MITRE's ATT&CK framework has become central for mapping out the specific tactics and techniques real threat actors use. By lining up observed behaviors with known patterns, analysts can better understand what they're facing [28].

In actual practice, threat hunting based on these models involves digging through SIEM data logs, alerts, and events, looking for signs like lateral movement, privilege escalation, or command-and-control communication. This process usually depends on manual queries, custom detection scripts, and experience-driven rule sets [29]. While these methods can be effective, they don't always keep up with the scale of modern environments. The flood of data generated today makes relying purely on manual techniques tough. Scalability is one of the biggest challenges security teams now face. Modern IT environments generate petabytes of data daily, making it impossible for human analysts to keep up without automation. Second, timeliness is critical to respond quickly, since manual threat hunts can span days or weeks, during which an attacker may continue operating undetected. Third, there is the problem of inconsistent and biased analysis. Depending on the analyst's experience, human intuition might vary widely, resulting in inconsistent detection quality [30]. Lastly, many traditional methods rely on static rules and predefined signatures, which fail to detect emerging or unknown threats, particularly those using polymorphic or fileless techniques [25].

To enhance prioritization in manual hunts, analysts often refer to frameworks like the Pyramid of Pain (Figure 3.2), introduced by David Bianco, which classifies threat indicators based on how difficult they are for an adversary to change. Hunting for high-value indicators such as TTPs (Tactics, Techniques, Procedures) provides more durable and effective detection.

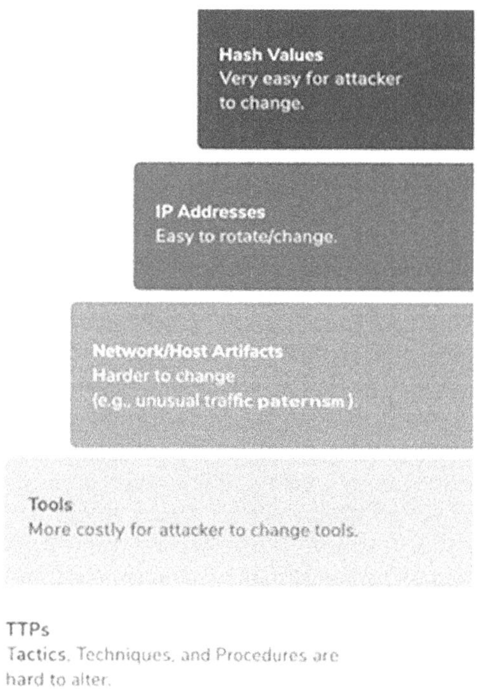

Figure 3.2 The Pyramid of Pain based on difficulty.

3.2.4 Gaps and pain points in existing approaches

Traditional threat hunting faces key limitations. Massive telemetry data makes manual analysis unscalable [31]. SOC teams have alert fatigue due to high false positive rates: fragmented tools and a lack of qualified analysts further slow investigations. Most strategies continue to be reactive, depending on established signs following breaches. Furthermore, traditional techniques frequently overlook insider or stealthy threats due to a lack of behavioral context [32]. These difficulties show how important AI-driven threat hunting is for scalable, proactive, and ongoing detection.

3.3 FUNDAMENTALS OF AI AND MACHINE LEARNING IN SECURITY

3.3.1 Key AI/ML concepts relevant to cybersecurity

AI and ML are transforming cybersecurity by giving systems the capacity to recognize and react to threats instantly. As cyberattacks become more sophisticated and widespread, traditional rule-based approaches are finding it increasingly difficult to keep up. The gaps are filled by AI and ML, which learn from enormous datasets, spot hidden patterns, identify hidden patterns, and adapt to evolving attack techniques without human intervention. Security teams may focus on high-priority tasks according to these technologies, which improve threat detection, automate response processes, and lower false positives [33, 34].

The most important part of artificial intelligence (AI), machine learning (ML), enables systems to automatically learn from data and improve over time without explicit programming. In contrast, artificial intelligence (AI) seeks to mimic human cognitive processes, including learning, reasoning, and decision-making [35]. Machine learning is key in helping security teams detect threats as they happen. It can spot unusual patterns in network traffic, flag suspicious login attempts, and even recognize known attack types like phishing or DDoS based on past data [10]. Some models are trained to group similar events, which helps uncover coordinated attack campaigns that might not be obvious initially. Several techniques are commonly used in day-to-day situations. Clustering is useful for grouping related malicious activities; classification helps identify malware; and anomaly detection highlights rare or unexpected behavior like failed logins from unusual locations. Natural Language Processing (NLP) also comes into play, especially for scanning messages or documents for signs of phishing. Sometimes, time-series analysis monitors gradual behavioral shifts that could indicate a slow-moving threat [36].

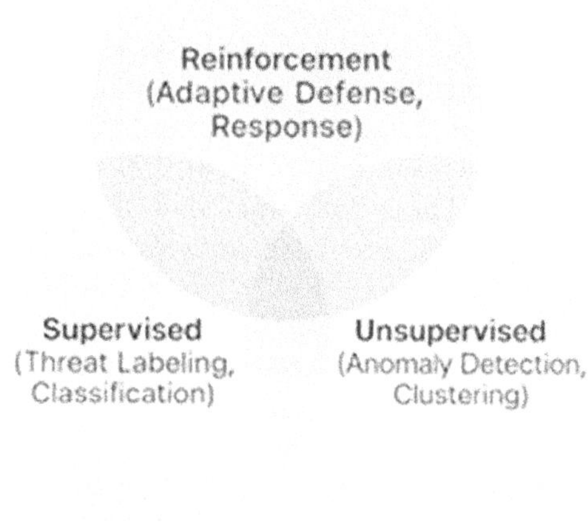

Figure 3.3 Types of machine learning in cybersecurity.

3.3.2 Types of learning in cybersecurity

There are many machine learning (ML) approaches, including supervised, unsupervised, and reinforcement learning, and each has particular strengths for cybersecurity applications [37]. In Figure 3.3, how each machine learning technique relates to security features like threat classification, adaptive protection, and anomaly detection is conceptually illustrated.

Supervised Learning: This approach trains models on labeled datasets where inputs are paired with known outputs. It's commonly used when historical data of known threats is available. Some practical applications include spotting phishing in emails, recognizing malware based on its code signature, or evaluating whether a login seems legitimate based on prior user behavior. Algorithms like Random Forests, Support Vector Machines (SVM), Decision Trees, and Deep Neural Networks are common in this context [38].

Unsupervised Learning: There is no need for labeled data in this approach. Instead, it finds hidden structures and patterns in the dataset, which makes it perfect for spotting unknown threats. It deals with cases like detecting anomalies in system logs, clustering similar attack behaviors, and spotting zero-day vulnerabilities. Common methods include K-Means Clustering, DBSCAN, Isolation Forests, and Autoencoders. It is also used in deep learning for high-dimensional security data [39].

Reinforcement Learning (RL): This approach is more dynamic, where agents learn optimal behaviors through trial and error by interacting with an environment. Despite its less developed implementation, RL is being explored for firewall rule tuning, honeypot configuration, and adaptive intrusion response. By learning how to defend a network in actual or simulated settings, the agent is rewarded or penalized according to its actions [40].

These types of learning work together to build smart cybersecurity systems that can understand the context of threats, adapt to new attack patterns, and scale to effectively protect large, complex networks.

3.3.3 Role of AI in threat detection, analysis, and prediction

Artificial intelligence is essential for improving cybersecurity because it makes decision-making faster, more intelligent, and more flexible. Three primary categories include its capabilities:

1. **Threat Detection:** AI-powered systems can monitor data from devices, networks, and cloud platforms in real time to identify known and unknown cyber threats. Unlike traditional techniques that depend on fixed rules, machine learning can adapt when attackers modify their strategies. For example, it can identify strange login behavior, such as a large number of unsuccessful tries in a short period, which could be a sign of a brute-force or stolen password attack [39].
2. **Threat Analysis:** AI assists cybersecurity teams in handling the deluge of security warnings they get daily. AI can automatically examine logs, security events, and background data to identify patterns in each alert rather than manually reviewing each one. This enables analysts to focus their efforts on where they are most needed by identifying trends and highlighting the most significant threats. For example, an AI-powered system can combine data from endpoint protection tools, security monitoring platforms (SIEM), and external threat intelligence sources to detect if different warning signs are part of the same coordinated cyberattack, saving time and improving accuracy [34].
3. **Threat Prediction:** Predictive models estimate which systems are most likely to be targeted in the future based on historical attack data and behavioral trends. This helps security teams act before an attack, rather than waiting to respond afterward. For example, an AI system can examine past hacking attempts, system weaknesses, and cloud resource usage. Based on that information, it can predict which servers or applications might be at risk next. This early warning gives cybersecurity teams time to fix issues, update defenses, and protect sensitive systems before attackers can exploit them [10].

3.3.4 Data requirements and challenges

The effectiveness of AI and ML in cybersecurity depends mainly on the data they are trained on to ensure they offer strong capabilities. The following major issues need to be addressed to make sure these systems operate reliably:

1. **Data Quality and Labeling:** Supervised learning requires high-quality labeled data, which is challenging to obtain. Many organizations lack annotated datasets, and raw security logs often contain noise and inconsistencies that hinder performance [8].
2. **Imbalanced Datasets:** The majority of cybersecurity data is biased because normal events outnumber true attacks. Models may ignore infrequent but significant risks (true attacks) due to this imbalance. The problem persists despite the use of specialized methods such as anomaly detection and oversampling [24].
3. **Data Privacy and Compliance:** Sensitive infrastructure details or personally identifiable information (PII) may be included in security datasets. Models must comply with data protection regulations like GDPR, HIPAA, and CCPA, requiring strong governance over data access and usage [41].
4. **Concept Drift:** Threats are constantly shifting. A model developed on attack data from the previous year might not be able to identify modern tactics. To keep AI systems up to date and functional, ongoing retraining and monitoring are essential [39].
5. **Adversarial Machine Learning:** Adversarial machine learning happens when attackers tamper with data on purpose to confuse an ML system. For instance, someone might insert fake log entries that seem normal, just to slip past an anomaly detection model without being noticed [42].

3.4 THE EVOLUTION OF THREAT HUNTING: MANUAL TO AUTOMATED

The way cybersecurity teams handle threats has changed a lot over the years. What used to be a mostly passive game, waiting for alerts and reacting, has turned into something more active. That's because modern threats are faster, more complex, and harder to pin down. So instead of just responding, organizations now try to hunt down threats before they do damage. This approach, threat hunting, was originally a fully manual job. Analysts would sift through logs, looking for anomalies, testing ideas, and connecting dots. These days, AI and automation are stepping in to speed things up. They help teams catch more threats, cover more ground, and respond faster. In this section, we'll look at how this shift happened and why it matters.

3.4.1 Manual threat hunting techniques

Back when automation wasn't available, analysts handled everything by hand. They'd use tools like Wireshark, Sysmon, or Splunk to trace odd behaviors in system logs. They'd compare patterns, look up IPs, check file hashes, and anything that might offer a clue. The MITRE ATT and CK framework helped guide these efforts [7].

Manual hunting had its strengths. Skilled analysts could find things that automated tools often missed. But it was slow. Really slow. Investigations could take days, especially when dealing with terabytes of log data. And it required a high level of experience, which meant not every team could do it effectively. Also, it is not scalable because analysts can only process a certain amount of data at a time. Additionally, it is a reactive process, which means the hunt starts only when the attack has already occurred. Furthermore, it is expertise-dependent, meaning it highly depends on the analyst's abilities, which can differ. This approach may still be helpful, but it struggles to work successfully due to the complexity and speed of current cyber threat developments [39].

3.4.2 Transition to semi-automated and automated processes

Organizations have increasingly used automation in their hunting workflows to address these challenges:

1. **Scripting and Rule Automation:** Analysts began using YARA, Sigma, and Python scripts to automate repetitive searches, like identifying known malware patterns.
2. **SIEM and SOAR Platforms:** Semi-automated investigations are supported by advanced systems like Microsoft Sentinel, Splunk, and QRadar. "Playbooks" for automatically reacting to threats, such as deactivating a user account or isolating an endpoint, were introduced by Security Orchestration, Automation, and Response (SOAR) systems [43].
3. **AI-Powered Detection:** ML models trained on behavioral patterns are now able to identify anomalies in real time, such as unexpected data transfers or strange user activity. These systems continuously improve as they ingest new data.
4. **Adaptive Learning Systems:** Innovative approaches like Vectra AI, Darktrace, and Microsoft Defender ATP use self-learning algorithms

that evolve as threats evolve, allowing for proactive and autonomous threat detection [44].

3.4.3 Comparative analysis: human vs. AI-driven approaches

Table 3.1 shows that both human and AI-driven hunting offer distinct advantages. A comparison table reflects an assessment that evaluates the trade-offs between human expertise and AI capabilities in cybersecurity, especially in the context of threat hunting.

Human Strengths: When it comes to cybersecurity, human analysts have special advantages. They have a thorough awareness of the internal environment of their company, including system architecture, business procedures, and normal user behaviors. This allows them to interpret threats not just by the data, but also by understanding how an attacker might be taking certain actions. Their flexibility and intuition help when dealing with ambiguous or incomplete information, something machines can struggle with.

AI Strengths: On the other hand, AI has distinct advantages. It can process and analyze vast amounts of data at a speed that is significantly faster than human ability. AI systems also provide continuous, around-the-clock monitoring across complex, distributed environments.

Table 3.1 Human vs. AI-driven threat hunting

Criteria	*Human-driven approach*	*AI-driven approach*
Speed	Humans take time in investigation.	AI can analyze massive data in seconds, providing near real-time detection.
Scalability	Limited by the number of analysts and their capacity.	Easily scale across entire networks, cloud, and hybrid environments.
Consistency	Results can vary, because different analysts may interpret things differently.	Always apply the same logic, ensuring uniform analysis every time.
Accuracy	Good at spotting complex or contextual threats but can miss small patterns.	Great at identifying subtle data anomalies but may generate false positives if not trained well.
Context Awareness	Understands the business, systems, and user behaviors that add rich context to decisions.	Lacks full situational awareness unless paired with detailed, structured input data.
Explainability	Easy to explain conclusions to others, especially important for reports and audits.	Often a "black box," that means hard to explain how deep models make decisions without interpretability tools.

Their ability to identify small patterns and abnormalities that would be practically hard for a person to discover manually is perhaps their greatest strength, which makes them an effective addition to human threat hunters.

Limitations: While AI lacks transparency (particularly in deep learning models) and requires high-quality data for training, humans can be prone to bias or fatigue. The most successful strategy is frequently a hybrid one that combines human judgment with computer speed [35, 45].

3.4.4 Benefits and limitations of automation

Benefits: Modern cybersecurity operations can greatly benefit from automated threat hunting. It dramatically improves efficiency by scanning terabytes of security data in just minutes, significantly reducing the time it takes to detect potential threats. Security teams can respond quickly through real-time alerting, often stopping attacks before they can cause serious damage. Automation is perfect for businesses with growing infrastructures in on-premises, cloud, and hybrid settings since it is extremely scalable and doesn't require a corresponding increase in workforce. Furthermore, AI systems apply consistent detection rules that eliminate the variability and errors that come with manual analysis.

Limitations: Automation can have limitations, though. Excessive false positives from poorly trained models might overwhelm analysts with irrelevant alerts. On the other hand, clever attacks that mimic typical behavior may slip through undetected and cause false negative results. Deep learning models also lack transparency, making it difficult for analysts to understand or trust their decisions. Finally, an overreliance on automation may result in a lower investment in human expertise, making businesses more susceptible to the limitations of automated tools. Therefore, even while automation is strong, it functions best when carefully integrated into a larger cybersecurity framework [45]. Automation is not a silver bullet but a powerful tool when integrated thoughtfully into a larger cybersecurity strategy.

3.5 AI-DRIVEN THREAT HUNTING FRAMEWORKS

Organizations are implementing AI-enhanced threat hunting systems to transition from defense-only postures to proactive security as cyber threats become more widespread. These frameworks automate reactions in a variety of situations, detect anomalies, and continuously monitor data. This section presents the architecture and operational flow of an AI-driven threat hunting system, including its key components such as data ingestion, normalization, threat intelligence fusion, automated analysis, and response orchestration.

3.5.1 Core components of an automated framework

An AI-driven threat hunting framework typically consists of the following modular components:

1. **Data Sources:** Input comes from Endpoint Detection and Response (EDR) logs, network telemetry (NetFlow, packet captures), application logs, identity and access data (e.g., Active Directory, IAM), and cloud telemetry (e.g., AWS CloudTrail, Azure Monitor) [47].
2. **Data Aggregation and Normalization:** It is necessary to gather, interpret, and convert raw data from various sources into a common format. This step ensures consistency and allows for effective correlation across telemetry sources.
3. **Threat Intelligence Integration:** Internal data is enhanced with actionable context by the integration of external threat feeds, adversary profiles, vulnerability databases (such as CVEs), and behavioral indicators (TTPs) [33].
4. **AI/ML Threat Detection Engine:** The core analytical module includes supervised models for known threat classification, unsupervised algorithms for anomaly detection, Natural Language Processing (NLP) to interpret log messages or threat reports, and time-series models for detecting behavioral shifts over time [35].
5. **Orchestration and Automated Response:** Based on risk scores and detection confidence, automated playbooks can trigger actions such as quarantining a host, blocking an IP or domain, notifying analysts, and enriching alerts with additional context.
6. **Security Analyst Dashboard:** Human analysts interact with visual dashboards that display prioritized alerts, reasoning behind AI decisions, and investigation tools.

Figure 3.4 illustrates the architecture of an AI-driven threat-hunting framework, showing the data flow and integration points of key components in an automated system.

3.5.2 Data collection, aggregation, and normalization

For AI models to accurately detect malicious behavior, they need access to high-quality, diverse data. An advanced platform uses agents, log connectors, and cloud APIs to gather information from every part of the company. However, raw logs often differ in structure and semantics. Therefore, a

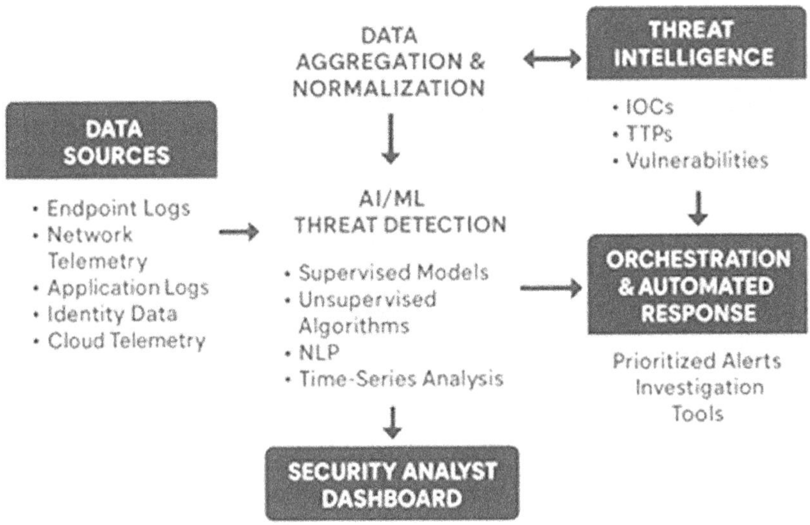

Figure 3.4 Architecture of an AI-driven threat hunting framework.

normalization layer transforms incoming data into a common schema using ETL (Extract, Transform, Load) techniques. For example, the representation of unsuccessful login events may change across Windows, Linux, and AWS platforms. Without standardization, it is impossible to detect suspicious login patterns across all systems.

Additionally, the framework uses stream processing engines (like Spark Streaming and Apache Kafka) to handle data in batch and real-time modes. This makes time-series correlation and event sequencing possible, which are essential for comprehending the length of an attacker's stay and the evolution of the kill chain [30].

3.5.3 Threat intelligence integration

AI-driven hunting has several advantages over conventional techniques, one of which is the direct integration of external threat knowledge into the detection and correlation process. That includes:

1. **Indicators of Compromise (IOCs)**: Known malicious IPs, domains, malware hashes.
2. **Tactics, Techniques, and Procedures (TTPs)**: Behavioral insights derived from MITRE ATT and CK or similar frameworks.
3. **Exploit feeds**: Real-time updates about new vulnerabilities or zero-day campaigns.

The ML models can contextualize raw behaviors by applying threat intelligence. For instance, the detection engine could determine a higher threat confidence score if an anomalous DNS request resolves to a domain that is known to be connected to a phishing campaign. Modern platforms use STIX/TAXII protocols for real-time, automated ingestion of threat intelligence, ensuring that the framework is always aligned with the latest threat landscape [44].

3.5.4 Orchestration and response automation

Detection is only the first step. Timely response is crucial to minimizing damage from an incident. AI-driven frameworks are integrated with SOAR (Security Orchestration, Automation, and Response) platforms that execute automated actions based on predefined logic trees or machine learning-driven decisions.

Examples of how AI-driven systems can respond automatically to threats include actions like immediately disconnecting a compromised computer from the network to prevent further spread, requesting that users use multi-factor authentication to confirm their identity if a login seems questionable, or modifying firewall and proxy settings to prevent connectivity with known dangerous sites. In some cases, the system can even open a support ticket with all the relevant threat information so that human analysts can investigate further. There is no one-size-fits-all approach to these automatic reactions; instead, they are typically structured into playbooks that trigger specific actions based on how severe or risky the threat appears to be. This ensures prompt control of significant risks while preventing unnecessary disruptions. The ability to learn from input is what gives these systems even greater strength. The AI needs human analyst confirmation, for example, to determine if a flagged warning was a false alarm or a valid one. This helps the AI make better judgments in the future, making it more reliable and accurate over time [46].

3.5.5 Architecture workflow and integration

In order to identify and address cyber threats, an AI-powered threat hunting system usually follows an organized, planned procedure. This is how it works in practice:

1. **Data Ingestion:** The system constantly gathers raw data from various sources, including network logs, cloud services, and endpoint devices. Consider this a real-time collection of all the digital "footprints" across the organization.

2. **Preprocessing:** Clean and organize raw data. The system removes duplicate data, timestamps events, and structures the data into a structured format, making the analysis more effective.
3. **Threat Intelligence Fusion:** In this stage, it collects known threat indicators from threat feeds and frameworks like MITRE ATT&CK, such as malware signatures, suspicious IP addresses, or adversary techniques. This provides more context for the AI's risk assessment.
4. **AI Analysis Layer:** The machine learning models start working in this phase. The system builds a baseline (normal behavior profile) for each device or user. After that, the system constantly scans for behavior that differs from this standard (suspicious behavior), flagging anything unusual that indicates the presence of a threat.
5. **Scoring and Prioritization:** It is important to know that not every anomaly is risky. Therefore, the system assigns a risk score to each detection based on how unusual or dangerous it seems, how confident the AI is, and how it fits into the wider threat landscape. This helps analysts focus on the most urgent issues first.
6. **Automated Actions:** Without human input, the system may respond instantly to block a malicious IP, quarantine a device, or enforce new security rules if a threat indicates high risk with high confidence.
7. **Human Review Loop:** In this final step, the analysts get involved. In an interactive dashboard, they evaluate the prioritized warnings, investigate the reasoning behind each AI choice, and conduct more thorough research as necessary. To assist the AI in learning and improving over time, they may also offer feedback.

This process produces an effective loop of ongoing learning, detection, and reaction. It is significantly more scalable than manual or rule-based approaches, which usually can't keep up with the complexity of modern threats [35]. Figure 3.5 illustrates the end-to-end workflow of a modern AI-enhanced threat hunting framework. The pipeline begins with the continuous input of data from many sources, including network devices, cloud environments, and endpoints. Then it proceeds via pretreatment and enrichment with real-time threat intelligence. An AI analysis layer creates behavioral baselines to find anomalies and assigns a score to deviations. High-confidence threats trigger automated reaction actions, and an interactive dashboard is used to escalate priority warnings to human analysts. The closed-loop approach overcomes the limitations of conventional rule-based detection systems by ensuring adaptive learning, scalability, and real-time situational awareness.

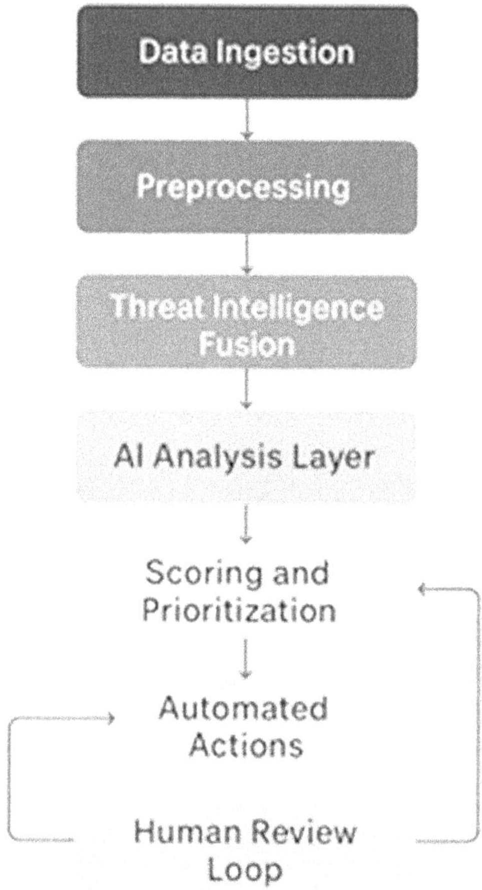

Figure 3.5 Architecture workflow of an AI-driven threat hunting system.

3.6 MACHINE LEARNING FOR THREAT MODEL DETECTION

Machine learning (ML) has become an essential technology for modern threat detection, allowing security systems to detect unusual, malicious, or suspicious activity in complex IT environments. Machine learning (ML) helps organizations stay ahead of constantly changing attack techniques by automating the monitoring and analyzing enormous streams of cyber events. The primary categories of machine learning models, their engineering and evaluation processes, and their practical applications in security operations are all covered in this part.

3.6.1 ML models: anomaly detection, classification, and clustering

Anomaly Detection: Anomaly detection aims to find behavior that differs from the usual (suspicious login). This technique makes finding insider threats and zero-day exploits that don't fit known attack signatures much easier. It learns what normal looks like and generates alarms for significant deviations. This technique uses algorithms such as Isolation Forest, One-Class SVM, and deep learning-based autoencoders to flag suspicious login attempts, such as access from strange locations or during unusual hours [36].

Classification: Classification models use labeled data to differentiate between activity categories, such as "benign" versus "malicious." Large datasets of known threats are used in classification to train the models, which include Support Vector Machines, Random Forests, Logistic Regression, and Gradient Boosting Machines. For instance, these models may identify whether network traffic is suspicious or an email is phishing [44].

Clustering: In clustering, there is no need for labeled data. In this approach, the model groups data points related to each other. Models like K-Means, DBSCAN, and hierarchical clustering algorithms help uncover previously unknown threats or recognize patterns in malware samples, making it easier to spot correlated activity from new or evolving attack groups [37].

3.6.2 Deep learning approaches (CNN, RNN, LSTM)

Deep learning models outperform typical machine learning techniques by automatically identifying complex patterns in raw data.

- **Convolutional Neural Networks (CNNs):** Originally designed for images, CNNs can be adapted to detect static patterns in malware binaries or network packet data.
- **Recurrent Neural Networks (RNNs):** RNNs are suitable for sequential data such as logs or time series. They can model temporal patterns in user behavior or attack sequences.
- **Long Short-Term Memory Networks (LSTMs):** These advanced RNNs are more adept at identifying long-range relationships, which makes them ideal for assessing the narrative flow of phishing emails or forecasting privilege escalations [9].

Deep learning models are powerful but require large, balanced datasets and huge computing power. The major challenge remains their "black box" nature, which makes it difficult for analysts to understand exactly how a decision was made [26]. Figure 3.6 shows a visual taxonomy mapping

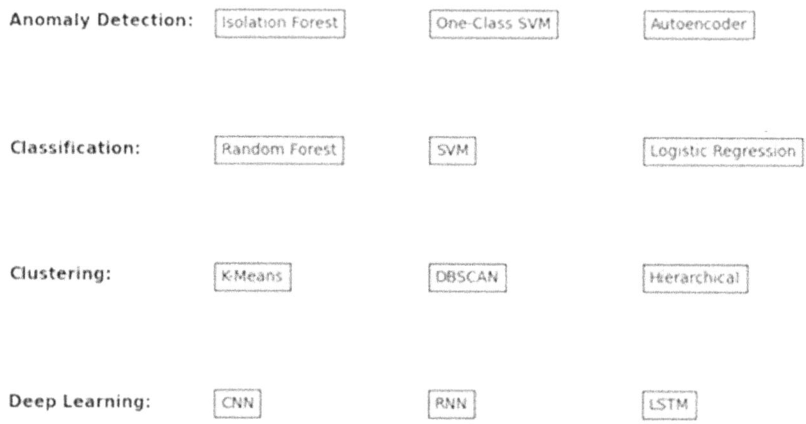

Figure 3.6 Common ML algorithms for threat detection.

models for anomaly detection, classification, clustering, and deep learning in security.

3.6.3 Feature engineering and selection

The success of a model often depends on the quality of features or the attributes taken from unprocessed security data. In cybersecurity, useful features might include login times, device IDs, failed access attempts, file access patterns, and even an executable sequence of API calls. Effective machine learning pipelines handle high-dimensional data by employing methods including dimensionality reduction (using PCA or t-SNE), encoding (converting categories to numbers), and normalization (scaling values). The most relevant signals are highlighted, and noise is reduced using feature selection techniques like mutual information and tree-based importance [30]. Well-designed features lower the complexity and the chance of overfitting and lead to increased model accuracy. This is how to apply feature engineering and selection.

3.6.4 Model training, validation, and deployment

Training robust ML models for threat detection involves more than just feeding in data. Security datasets are often highly imbalanced, with more examples of normal behavior than attacks. Methods such as class undersampling or SMOTE (for oversampling rare threats) help address this. Cross-validation techniques, such as stratified splits or k-fold, are essential to ensure that the model performs effectively when applied to new data [35]. Integrating the trained model into actual pipelines, such as SIEMs, EDRs, or specialized SOC tools, is known as deployment. Organizations often use containers (like Docker) or customized model-serving platforms to maintain system speed and dependability, even under high load, because low-latency, scalable inference is crucial.

3.6.5 Evaluation metrics

The effectiveness of ML models is measured using a variety of evaluation metrics. These metrics are:

- **Accuracy:** The overall percentage of correct predictions.
- **Precision:** The proportion of flagged threats that are threats. This is important for minimizing false alarms.
- **Recall:** The ability to catch all real threats, even at the risk of a few extra false alerts.
- **F1-Score:** Balances precision and recall, giving a single score for both.
- **AUC-ROC:** Captures the trade-off between true and false positive rates.
- **Confusion Matrix:** Breaks down the model's successes and misses in detail.

Recall is frequently prioritized in cybersecurity, as handling a few more false alerts is generally preferable to ignoring a real attack [44]. Security professionals can automatically identify and categorize threats in large, diverse settings by developing machine learning models. These models are now at the core of efficient threat detection pipelines, including anomaly detection algorithms that highlight minor behavioral abnormalities, to deep learning networks that can identify complex attack patterns. However, besides algorithmic innovation, they also need strong feature engineering, well-balanced training data, and a thorough assessment of their performance using industry-standard measures like F1-score, accuracy, and recall. Organizations may proactively lower the risk of expensive breaches and data loss by utilizing these strategies to proactively identify and address new threats [38].

Furthermore, these models' maximal effectiveness can only be achieved when smoothly integrated into security teams' daily operations. Security Operations Centers, or SOCs, are more important now than ever, especially with how fast cyber threats evolve. A SOC is the nerve center for detecting and responding to security events across an organization. But with the volume of data involved today, especially from endpoints, networks, and logs, it's almost impossible to handle everything manually. That's where AI is starting to come in. Using AI tools inside the SOC, teams can sort through alerts faster, spot unusual activity more reliably, and respond quickly when something goes wrong. These tools don't replace humans, but they help cut through the noise. In the next section, we'll look at how AI is being introduced into SOCs: what it's good at, where it still struggles, and how humans and machines are starting to work together on daily security tasks.

3.7 INTEGRATING AI TOOLS INTO SECURITY OPERATIONS CENTERS (SOC)

With threats getting more complex and faster, SOC teams are under pressure to keep up. AI is one of the ways organizations are trying to stay ahead. It's sometimes added to various parts of the SOC workflow to automate tasks, other times to assist human analysts. This section talks about what that integration looks like today. We'll touch on where automation helps most, where human oversight is still critical, and what issues come up when relying on AI tools in a live security environment.

3.7.1 Role of AI Tools in SOC workflows

The layered defensive approach used by modern SOCs makes use of tools such as Security Orchestration, Automation, and Response (SOAR), Endpoint Detection and Response (EDR), and Security Information and Event Management (SIEM). However, integrating AI across the whole workflow is the true innovation.

Key AI functionalities embedded in SOCs include:

- **Anomaly Detection Engines:** Systems that constantly monitor traffic or logs for weird behavior that doesn't fit normal patterns.
- **Threat Classification Models:** Models that help rank or group alerts based on past attacks or known malicious behavior.
- **Prioritization Algorithms:** Score and rank incidents based on potential business impact, threat severity, and context.
- **Natural Language Processing (NLP):** Extracts meaning from unstructured threat intelligence, analyst notes, and open-source threat feeds.
- **Predictive Models:** Forecast future threats or lateral movements using time-series analysis.

Using past incidents, attacker behaviors, and ongoing telemetry, these models are trained to develop accuracy and speed detection profiles that outperform traditional rule-based detection systems [30, 35].

3.7.2 Automation in alert triage, incident response, and reporting

Alert Triage: One of the most time-consuming tasks in any SOC is triggering thousands of daily alerts. AI reduces this load by automatically sorting warnings by danger, screening out false positives using intelligent classifiers, and clustering related alerts (like a string of suspect logins). This makes it possible for human analysts to focus on the most urgent and dangerous threats.

Incident Response: Once a threat is confirmed, automated playbooks are triggered via SOAR tools. These tools can trigger rapid responses, such as quarantining hacked endpoints, changing firewall rules, resetting passwords, or providing analysts with contextual knowledge when an alert indicates an actual event. Over time, AI learns from analyst feedback, which makes it more precise with every case reviewed.

Reporting and Documentation: AI tools make post-event documentation and compliance easier, pulling structured metadata from logs and analyst activity. A tool with NLP capabilities may automatically create comprehensive reports, compile analyst activities, and suggest next steps that strongly accelerate and improve the accuracy of audits and regulatory reporting [37].

3.7.3 Human-AI collaboration and decision support

AI is intended to support analysts' jobs (humans), not to replace them. By automating repetitive tasks and providing deeper insights, AI allows humans to focus on interpretation, strategy, and creative problem-solving.

How collaboration works:

- **Collaborative Decision Models:** AI provides confidence scores, predicted threat types, and suggested actions. Analysts interpret results, override decisions if needed, and provide feedback to improve future predictions.
- **Explainable AI (XAI):** Transparency in the approach is critical to adoption and trust. XAI technologies like SHAP (Shapley Additive exPlanations) and LIME (Local Interpretable Model-agnostic Explanations) assist SOCs in understanding the reasons for flagging a particular alert and the characteristics that influenced that decision.
- **Interactive Dashboards:** Modern SOCs use interactive dashboards where analysts can explore alert causality, threat progression, and model decision pathways. This enables "human-in-the-loop" operations where AI works with expert judgment, ensuring optimal response and learning [33, 35].

Figure 3.7 illustrates AI-integrated SOC workflow. This figure shows how AI engines are included in each stage of the SOC, from data collection and standardization to automated reaction and analyst input for continuous enhancement.

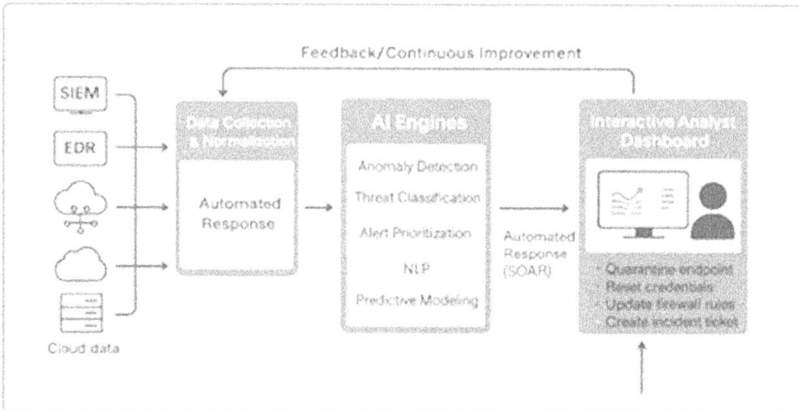

Figure 3.7 AI-integrated SOC workflow.

3.7.4 Challenges in SOC adoption and integration

Despite its advantages, AI integration into SOCs faces several technical, operational, and organizational challenges:

1. **Data Silos and Fragmentation:** Security data comes from many platforms, such as third-party APIs, legacy systems, and cloud environments. Aggregating and normalizing this data for AI consumption is complex and requires strong data engineering pipelines.
2. **Model Drift and Concept Shifts:** Attackers are always changing their strategies, which leads to the gradual degradation of ML models. This requires constant model validation, retraining, and observation to ensure accuracy and relevance.
3. **False Positives and Alert Fatigue:** Models with poor training may generate numerous alerts, defeating the purpose of automation. Developing high-precision models with good generalization is still a major barrier to efficacy.
4. **Skill Gaps:** Operating an AI-powered SOC requires analysts who understand both cybersecurity and data science. Finding or training these "hybrid" professionals is not always easy.
5. **Explainability and Accountability:** Automated decisions may cause post-breach audits to become confusing. AI outputs must be identifiable, explainable, and compliant with legal standards (such as GDPR and NIST 800-53), according to organizations [36].

Integrating artificial intelligence (AI) tools within Security Operations Centers (SOCs) marks a significant advancement in cybersecurity. The ability of AI-powered SOCs to handle and analyze large volumes of security telemetry in real time is evidenced by their use of advanced capabilities, including automatic response, threat classification, anomaly detection, and alert prioritization. As a result, these improvements eliminate false positives and speed up incident reaction times. They increase detection rates and significantly reduce the workload for human analysts. The feedback loop between analysts and AI engines additionally ensures ongoing learning and adaptation, which helps security teams keep up with the quickly changing threat landscape.

While integrating AI has obvious operational advantages, there are disadvantages. Continuous challenges include things like model drift, data silos, and the requirement for explainable AI. In addition to technological innovation, addressing these calls for investments in cybersecurity professional development and process automation to facilitate productive human–AI collaboration. Organizations that effectively integrate AI into their SOCs propose significant improvements in resilience, efficiency, and the quality of their decision-making [35, 38].

After outlining the theoretical and practical underpinnings of AI-driven SOCs, it is critical to look at how these ideas are used in real-world scenarios. Real-world case studies and practical implementations are examined in the next part, providing specific instances of how top companies use AI and machine learning to improve their security postures. These case studies will demonstrate best practices, typical obstacles, and the measurable effects of AI adoption on cybersecurity outcomes. The paths to successful AI integration in security operations can be better understood by examining achievements and lessons learned.

3.8 CASE STUDIES AND PRACTICAL IMPLEMENTATIONS

It is essential to understand the revolutionary potential of AI-driven threat hunting through practical applications in various industries rather than just theoretical discussions. To lower risk, speed up response times, and quickly adjust to emerging cyber threats, businesses and governmental organizations throughout the globe are now using automated threat detection frameworks. This part emphasizes hard-earned lessons, compares the operational results of traditional and AI-driven SOCs, explores further important case studies, and looks at prominent open-source and commercial AI solutions.

3.8.1 Real-world deployments of automated threat hunting

Case Study 1: Microsoft Defender for Endpoint—A flagship example of integrating AI and behavior-based threat detection directly into the operating system layer is Microsoft's Defender for Endpoint (previously ATP). Machine learning models delivered through the cloud and evaluating billions of signals daily are essential to its success. Defender's models can identify known and undetected threats due to the enormous volume of data, including fileless and zero-day malware that escapes antivirus programs that depend on signatures. Automated investigation playbooks and end-point behavioral scoring are important elements that utilize AI to evaluate risk across organizational assets continually. Defender ATP is significant for detecting advanced threats that would have previously escaped detection by traditional technologies and reducing incident response times by over 90% in large-scale customer installations. For example, Microsoft stated in 2022 that its AI-powered endpoint security prevented 35.7 billion phishing attempts and over 9.6 billion malware attacks, highlighting the scale and accuracy of AI-powered detection [48].

Case Study 2: Vectra AI in Financial Institutions—Financial institutions have turned to Vectra AI for next-generation network detection and response as they are often the targets of advanced persistent threats (APTs), lateral movement, and credential misuse. Neural network models are used by Vectra's solution to monitor traffic in hybrid cloud settings and identify suspicious behaviors such as unauthorized privilege escalation and shadow IT activities. According to real-world financial industry deployments, Vectra's AI-driven analytics allowed analysts to detect complex attack chains more quickly and decreased alert fatigue by 75%. A large bank credited Vectra's behavioral analytics for uncovering a well-hidden credential theft campaign within hours, while traditional triage would have taken days in the past [49]. The success lies not just in automation but in AI's ability to correlate and contextualize network events at a scale impossible for human teams alone.

Case Study 3: Darktrace in Healthcare—Healthcare is an industry especially vulnerable to targeted attacks due to patient data sensitivity and legacy systems' prevalence. Darktrace, an AI platform built on self-learning anomaly detection, was applied in a large hospital network to enhance threat visibility. The unsupervised machine learning models from Darktrace rapidly picked up on the baseline behaviors of network-connected devices. In one significant example, the AI identified unusual outgoing traffic from a hospital printer that human analysts could have missed. Further investigations showed that compromised firmware was being utilized for secret data exfiltration. Crucially, the business could limit the breach and stop the release of private patient data since Darktrace's algorithm detected this danger four days before any conventional security measures sent out a warning [50]. These real-world cases highlight how AI-driven frameworks offer speed and genuine improvements in threat coverage and detection of stealthy, novel attacks.

3.8.2 Open-source and commercial AI tools

The organization currently uses a wide range of AI-driven platforms to conduct automated threat hunting. Some of the most influential platforms are presented in Table 3.2, which summarizes popular open-source and commercial platforms integrating machine learning into threat detection and incident response, highlighting their main features and strengths for enterprise deployments.

These platforms enable the customization and integration of ML pipelines through built-in modules, Python scripting, REST APIs, or external model hosting. Transparency and adaptability offered by open-source solutions such as Zeek and MITRE Caldera enable enterprises to customize detection to their settings. Commercial systems like IBM QRadar and CrowdStrike Falcon provide managed, highly scalable platforms that can be quickly deployed and continuously updated with models from international threat intelligence networks [8, 9, 37].

3.8.3 Lessons learned and best practices

There are certain lessons that professionals have learned from decades of trial and error in the implementation of automated threat hunting solutions:

Start with a Clear Use Case: Unlike a comprehensive deployment, successful programs nearly always begin with a specific objective, such as identifying internal risks or lateral movement. Specific goals make machine learning training easier, less complicated, and more likely to provide early successes [35].

Table 3.2 Leading open-source and commercial AI tools for automated threat hunting

Tool/Platform	*Type*	*Key features*
Snort + ML Add-ons	Open source	Rule-based IDS with Python ML extensions for custom models.
Zeek (Bro)	Open source	Deep network visibility that integrates anomaly detection and behavioral rules.
ELK Stack + ML	Open source	Log aggregation (Elasticsearch, Logstash, Kibana) with Elastic ML anomaly scoring.
MITRE Caldera	Open source	Automated adversary emulation, AI-driven TTP execution, and red teaming.
Splunk Enterprise	Commercial	Adaptive ML for SIEM, flexible correlation rules, and robust visualizations.
IBM QRadar + XDR	Commercial	Behavior analytics, AI-driven threat detection, and response orchestration.
CrowdStrike Falcon	Commercial	Cloud-native endpoint AI, real-time threat graph correlation, automation.

Quality of Data Outweighs Quantity: The value of high-quality, labeled data from authentication sources, NetFlow, and endpoints is greater than that of massive, noisy logs. Organizations that emphasized curated telemetry significantly improved ML precision and false positives [26, 30].

Build a Feedback Loop: The response from analysts, whether they confirm or reject warnings, should be used to inform the training of models. A significant reduction in false positives and more flexibility in responding to novel assault methods have resulted from reinforcement learning and "human-in-the-loop" retraining cycles.

Don't Ignore Explainability: Explainable AI is essential for compliance-focused industries like healthcare and finance. Deployments that combined strong machine learning engines with transparency technologies (such as SHAP and LIME) yielded faster analyst trust and smoother regulatory evaluations.

Hybrid Approaches Deliver Best Results: Blending static, rule-based indicators (for known threats) with dynamic, behavior-based anomaly detection creates a more robust defense. Numerous well-known SOCs run both ML and signature models in parallel, taking advantage of context and speed.

These insights are supported by recent literature, which consistently finds that feedback-driven, hybrid, and explainable systems yield the highest security returns [25, 33, 40].

3.8.4 Comparative outcomes: traditional vs. AI-driven

An increasing amount of data indicates that AI-enhanced SOCs significantly improve several important operational metrics. Table 3.3 compares important operational metrics between traditional Security Operations Centers and those augmented using AI-driven technologies, showing improvements in false positive rates, detection speed, analyst effort reduction, and overall flexibility.

There are important implications. AI-enabled SOCs can detect near-real-time threats, drastically reducing the window of vulnerability. By automating triage and response, incident lifecycles are shortened, allowing analysts to focus on threat hunting and strategic inquiry. While hybrid models provide coverage beyond what any one method can offer, false positive rates decrease as ML models become better at differentiating between noise and actual threats. However, achieving these results is not automatic. Returns must be maximized through upfront data engineering investment, thorough ML validation, and ongoing analyst training. As security teams adopt AI in cybersecurity, it's not just about how well the model works but also how

Table 3.3 AI-augmented SOCs outperform traditional SOCs by reducing false positives, detecting threats faster, and easing analyst workload

Criteria	*Traditional SOC*	*AI-driven SOC*
Detection Time	24–72 hours	Less than 1 hour
False Positives	High	Low
Analyst Workload	Manual	Automated + Human
Coverage	Limited	Broad
Adaptability	Low	High

it's governed. Privacy violations, bias, or accountability issues can surface quickly without clear guardrails. Especially when AI systems start influencing real-time decisions, organizations need to be able to explain and audit those decisions if something goes wrong. Still, nobody's expecting AI to replace security professionals. It can ease their workload, especially when filtering noisy alerts or catching things that would be hard to spot manually. In the future, one of the big challenges is figuring out how to make that collaboration work: which tasks should be automated, which need a human touch, and how to ensure transparency.

3.9 CHALLENGES, LIMITATIONS, AND ETHICAL CONSIDERATIONS

While AI has added new strengths to security operations, it has also introduced a set of problems that teams didn't face before. Some of these are technical. Others are ethical, legal, or practical. Getting this right means taking a step back to think about the algorithms, how they're used, and what happens when they go wrong. This section lays out some areas where that tension tends to show up.

3.9.1 Technical challenges

False Positives and Model Precision: One of the most common issues in AI-based threat detection is the tendency to generate false positives, benign activity mistakenly flagged as suspicious. This can create a flood of alerts for security teams, many of which don't require action. Over time, this can lead to alert fatigue and make it harder for analysts to trust the system's recommendations. These false positives can result from limited training data, overly sensitive models, or environments where "normal" behavior is difficult to define. These issues are caused by:

1. The presence of noise or incorrectly classified events in training data might lead to models misinterpreting normal actions as abnormalities.
2. Models can struggle to generalize to novel or changing attack vectors and may overfit to historical trends.
3. Contextual awareness is often limited; for example, a legitimate user accessing resources from an unusual location might trigger unnecessary alerts [37]. Adaptive feedback loops that learn from analysts' choices, thorough model validation, and ongoing data curation are necessary to increase detection precision while preserving high recall.

Data Quality and Availability: Security data is generally unstructured, often inconsistent, imbalanced, and lacking comprehensive labels. Many businesses struggle to maintain high-quality, current attack datasets and aggregate logs from various platforms (cloud, on-premises, hybrid). A lack of fast feedback channels and real-time labeling can cause models to fall out of step with current threats, decreasing their efficacy and potentially overlooking complex assaults [12]. Therefore, establishing strong data engineering pipelines is essential to successful AI-driven threat hunting.

Adversarial Machine Learning: Adversarial machine learning is a developing cybersecurity threat in which attackers intentionally alter inputs to trick AI algorithms. For instance, an attacker may create malware that looks like harmless software or alter log data to hide lateral movement. Studies reveal that even small changes to input characteristics can significantly affect the accuracy of machine learning models [22]. Model strengthening, continual adversarial testing, and defense mechanisms like adversarial training are all necessary to defend against such attacks.

3.9.2 Resource and skill constraints

Computational and Infrastructure Demands: AI-driven security systems, particularly deep learning-based ones, demand a lot of processing power, including dependable data pipelines, scalable storage, and powerful GPUs. The cost-prohibitive nature of these requirements may prevent small and medium-sized companies from implementing advanced security automation [6]. The increasing amount of security data requires larger businesses to manage infrastructure expenses carefully.

Talent Shortage: Implementing, managing, and enhancing AI-powered security systems requires unique skills. Firstly, data scientists with extensive knowledge of cybersecurity, security analysts adept at analyzing and verifying machine learning results, and engineers with expertise in combining SOC procedures with machine learning models. One of the biggest challenges to the widespread use of AI in cybersecurity is this skill shortage. Many businesses begin relying on external vendors, which can lead to problems with customization, vendor lock-in, and a lack of internal resources [46].

3.9.3 Privacy and ethical issues

Bias in Detection Models: The accuracy of machine learning models depends on the quality of the data they are trained on. If historical security data contains bias, such as overrepresentation of specific user groups, locations, or behaviors, the models may unintentionally perpetuate those biases. Accuracy and confidence in security operations may be weakened due to excessive false positives or biased alerting patterns [11, 24]. Consistent dataset collection, regular audits, and the development of fairness-aware algorithms are all necessary to address bias.

Lack of Transparency and Explainability: Many advanced AI models, especially deep neural networks, behave as "black boxes." Without giving clear reasons for their decisions, they may provide accurate forecasts that are difficult to interpret. This lack of transparency is particularly challenging because security decisions in regulated companies need to be transparent and justified. Although there has been progress in enhancing transparency with explainable AI (XAI) tools such as SHAP and LIME, their implementation is not yet widespread, and analysts can still face difficulties interpreting complex model outputs [10, 12]. Maintaining a focus on explainability and transparency is essential to building confidence in AI-driven systems.

User Privacy Concerns: Access to private user information, including browsing history, file access logs, email content, and behavioral patterns, is frequently necessary for AI-enhanced security solutions. These technologies might unintentionally breach user privacy or expose sensitive information if not carefully designed. Data anonymization, fine-grained access control, and explicit retention guidelines that balance security goals with individual privacy rights are considered best practices [21, 47].

3.9.4 Regulatory and compliance considerations

The regulatory control of artificial intelligence is expanding as it becomes more integrated into security operations. Several key legal and policy frameworks govern the appropriate development and application of AI systems in cybersecurity. To stay compliant, organizations need to take specific actions, such as maintaining clear documentation of how AI models work and the decisions they make, providing human analysts with the ability to override AI decisions and investigate outcomes, and regularly auditing AI systems for bias, performance issues, and regulatory alignment. As the rules and expectations around AI use continue evolving, companies can't focus on technical performance anymore. Legal compliance and ethical responsibility are quickly becoming non-negotiable. It's not simply a matter of deploying intelligent tools; there must be clarity on how decisions are made, who's accountable, and what happens when something goes wrong [24].

3.10 FUTURE DIRECTIONS AND EMERGING TRENDS

The future of AI in cybersecurity won't be just about speed or automation; it's also going to be about trust, adaptability, and fit-for-purpose design. Even though many SOCs are already using AI to some extent, what's coming next may look quite different: deeper integration, less reliance on rigid rules, and more room for machine learning to work alongside human judgment.

Graph-Based Threat Detection: Some of the more interesting developments involve graph-based approaches, which don't just treat alerts as isolated data points. Instead, they model systems as connected webs linking users, machines, and actions across time. For example, graph neural networks (GNNs) let analysts track behaviors that might only make sense when seen as part of a broader pattern, like lateral movement or chained privileges [51].

Self-Supervised Learning (SSL): One ongoing issue in cybersecurity is the lack of labeled training data. Self-supervised learning helps with this by letting models learn patterns from unlabeled sequences. For instance, a system might learn how typical login logs look and flag anything that doesn't follow the pattern, even if it's never seen that behavior labeled as "bad" before. This approach isn't perfect, but it's a step toward detecting anomalies that don't yet have names [2].

Few-Shot and Zero-Shot Learning: Instead of needing huge training sets, some new systems can now generalize from just a handful of examples or none. These few-shot and zero-shot techniques, especially when built on top of language models like GPT or LLaMA, show promise in helping SOC teams interpret threat descriptions, code snippets, or indicators of compromise in flexible ways. They're not magic, but they reduce the lead time needed to detect emerging attacks [36].

AutoML for Security Applications: For security teams without dedicated data scientists, AutoML tools can be surprisingly useful. They help build models by automating choices like which algorithm to use and how to fine-tune it. It's not a full replacement for ML expertise, but in fast-moving security environments, this automation can make custom detection models much more accessible [7].

3.10.1 Federated learning, explainable AI, and continuous learning

Federated Learning (FL): Data privacy remains crucial, particularly in regulated industries like banking and healthcare. Federated learning enables multiple organizations to collaboratively train shared models without sharing raw data. For example, a collaborative ransomware detection model may be developed by many institutions while maintaining patient privacy. This is a responsible use of collective intelligence [52].

Explainable AI (XAI) for Trust: Security teams require understanding, not only predictions. Explainable AI solutions such as SHAP and LIME offer visual explanations, confidence scores, and a breakdown of the data elements contributing to an alarm. Future developments suggest that integrated XAI dashboards will increase human confidence in AI judgments by bringing transparency to automated SOC processes [6].

Continuous and Online Learning: Rapid changes in cyber threats increase the possibility of model drift, in which outdated models perform poorly against novel strategies. Online or continuous learning systems may update models in real time using new data and analyst input. By maintaining version control and rollback capabilities, SOCs can ensure stability while adapting to new patterns [53].

3.10.2 Threat intelligence sharing and collaborative AI

AI-Powered Threat Fusion: Rather than going through feeds by hand, AI can analyze various threat sources (such as VirusTotal and MITRE ATT&CK), match internal logs with shared indicators of compromise (IOCs), and suggest automated playbooks.

Decentralized Threat-Sharing Networks: Threat intelligence may now be exchanged in a tamper-proof, privacy-preserving manner using emerging platforms, which frequently use distributed ledgers or blockchain. This enhances collective defense by advancing cross-sector real-time coordination without exposing private internal information [54].

Collaborative "Collective Defense" SOCs: Large-scale frameworks, like national or interbank SOCs, use multi-tenant AI systems to benefit the network from threat information provided by one member. This collective defense model scales shared security while minimizing individual risk exposures.

3.10.3 Predictions for the next generation of SOCs

AI-enhanced analyst assistance, smooth communication, and intelligent automation will characterize the future Security Operations Center (SOC). One of the most transformative changes will be the rise of fully autonomous response pipelines. AI systems independently detect threats, enrich contextual information, triage alerts, and even initiate containment actions, preserving human intervention only for critical, high-impact incidents. AI-native interfaces facilitate this change, which allows analysts to communicate with detection platforms using natural language prompts. For instance, asking "Show me anomalies from asset X last week" can yield thorough insights, improving the efficiency and intuitiveness of threat hunting.

3.11 CONCLUSION

Traditional security methods focused on static, signature-based defenses are no longer sufficient as cyber-attacks become more intelligent, automated, and quicker. Artificial intelligence (AI)-powered automated threat hunting is becoming a crucial defense mechanism in this changing battlefield, enabling proactive threat identification, scalable detection, and intelligent reaction.

3.11.1 Summary of Key Insights

The first part of this chapter introduced threat hunting as a proactive, hypothesis-based method for identifying latent threats that elude traditional defenses. Despite providing context and depth, manual threat hunting has drawbacks, including high labor costs, limited scalability, and subjective outcomes. By applying consistent decision logic, increasing speed, and automating analysis, AI effectively resolves many of these problems [22, 36].

We then delved into the cyber threat landscape, which includes a diverse set of threats like advanced persistent threats (APTs), insider risks, and evasive malware strategies; the importance of machine learning models, which can be used for anything from clustering to anomaly detection and classification; and the emergence of deep learning architectures like CNNs and LSTMs for the identification of intricate patterns [33, 34]; and how AI-driven frameworks are architected, with emphasis on data collection, threat intelligence integration, model deployment, alert prioritization, and automated response orchestration.

AI integration in Security Operations Centers (SOCs) increases incident response, accelerates triage, and gives analysts access to explainable AI tools for deeper insights [30, 31]. We also discussed real-world case studies showcasing significant improvements in detection accuracy, alert reduction, and operational efficiency. Additionally, emerging innovations, including federated learning, continuous learning techniques, and collaborative AI, all point toward future-proof, privacy-sensitive defense mechanisms. Finally, we assessed the inherent technical and ethical challenges, such as dealing with false positives, adversarial attacks, bias, lack of transparency, and evolving regulatory demands [37].

The Promise and Future of Automated Threat Hunting: AI advances contemporary cybersecurity by offering four revolutionary benefits:

- It enables the detection of complex, multi-stage attacks by correlating seemingly unrelated events over time, something traditional tools often miss.
- It adapts in real time, continually learning from unexpected events and improving detection logic as threats evolve.
- It facilitates more intelligent prioritization, reducing analyst fatigue and sharpening focus on critical incidents.

It supports seamless scalability across on-premises, cloud, and hybrid environments without requiring additional human resources. In the future, the Security Operations Center (SOC) will be more independent, cooperative, and intuitive. In addition to identifying known threats, AI may predict attacker behavior, provide customized mitigation strategies, and sometimes initiate containment autonomously. Analysts will primarily intervene in high-impact or ambiguous scenarios [40]. Security analysts will increasingly take on the role of strategic investigators, supported by intellgent AI co-pilots. These large language models (LLMs) will visualize attack chains, generate detection rules, and extract insights from vast data. Advancements like Explainable AI (XAI) will ensure auditable, transparent judgments, fostering trust in AI-based systems. New approaches such as zero-shot learning and graph-based models will reduce reliance on labeled data and enable the identification of novel threats. Federated learning will allow secure, collaborative model training across enterprises while preserving data privacy. These developments signify a shift toward collective cyber resilience, where intelligent, privacy-preserving AI fortifies security at scale [6].

Final Thoughts: AI is not a cure-all, despite its significant potential. Effective deployments require continuous review, ethical oversight, and robust governance. The intuition and expertise of human security professionals remain indispensable [53]. Organizations investing in AI now are positioning themselves to withstand, outthink, and outmaneuver sophisticated adversaries. AI-powered automated threat hunting transforms cybersecurity from:

- Reactive ⊛ Resilient
- Volume-driven ⊛ Accurate
- Isolated defense ⊛ Self-governing vigilance
- Siloed teams ⊛ Collaborative strength

Final Reflection: This chapter aligns closely with the book's overarching theme, "Cybersecurity of Information Systems: Artificial Intelligence and Machine Learning Solutions," by showing that AI is more than just a technological tool; it's a transformative force in modern cyber defense. Integrating intelligent automation into threat hunting practices illustrates how AI and ML reshape security strategies across complex digital environments. Through a combination of theoretical insights, real-world case studies, and emerging technological trends, this chapter strengthens the book's core message: AI-driven solutions are not optional additions; they are fundamental to the future of secure information systems.

NOTE

1. Corresponding author.

REFERENCES

1. Mahboubi, A., Luong, K., Aboutorab, H., Bui, H. T., Jarrad, G., Bahutair, M., ... & Gately, H. (2024). Evolving techniques in cyber threat hunting: A systematic review. *Journal of Network and Computer Applications*, 104004.
2. IBM Security. Cost of a data breach report 2023, [Online]. Available: https://www.ibm.com/reports/data-breach. Accessed: Jun. 25, 2025.
3. Sindiramutty, S. R. (2023). Autonomous threat hunting: A future paradigm for AI-driven threat intelligence. arXiv preprint arXiv:2401.00286.
4. Shan, A., & Myeong, S. (2024). Proactive threat hunting in critical infrastructure protection through hybrid machine learning algorithm application. *Sensors*, 24(15), 4888. https://doi.org/10.3390/s24154888.
5. Aragonés Lozano, M., Pérez Llopis, I., & Esteve Domingo, M. (2023). Threat hunting architecture using a machine learning approach for critical infrastructures protection. *Big Data and Cognitive Computing*, 7(2), 65.
6. Neupane, S., Ables, J., Anderson, W., Mittal, S., Rahimi, S., Banicescu, I., & Seale, M. (2022). Explainable intrusion detection systems (X-IDs): A survey of current methods, challenges, and opportunities. *IEEE Access*, 10, 112392–112415.
7. Ali, R., Ali, A., Iqbal, F., Khattak, A. M., & Aleem, S. (2020). A systematic review of artificial intelligence and machine learning techniques for cybersecurity. In *Big Data and Security: First International Conference*, ICBDS 2019, Nanjing, China, December 20–22, 2019, Revised Selected Papers 1 (pp. 584–593). Springer Singapore.
8. Rizvi, M. (2023). Enhancing cybersecurity: The power of artificial intelligence in threat detection and prevention. *International Journal of Advanced Engineering Research and Science*, 10(5), 055–060.
9. Okoli, U. I., Obi, O. C., Adewusi, A. O., & Abrahams, T. O. (2024). Machine learning in cybersecurity: A review of threat detection and defense mechanisms. *World Journal of Advanced Research and Reviews*, 21(1), 2286–2295.

10. Halbouni, A., Gunawan, T. S., Habaebi, M. H., Halbouni, M., Kartiwi, M., & Ahmad, R. (2022). Machine learning and deep learning approaches for cybersecurity: A review. *IEEE Access*, 10, 19572–19585.
11. Fareed, G., & De Roest, H. (2024). Automating SOC operations with AI and ML for real-time cyber threat management.
12. Zhou, S., Liu, C., Ye, D., Zhu, T., Zhou, W., & Yu, P. S. (2022). Adversarial attacks and defenses in deep learning: From a perspective of cybersecurity. *ACM Computing Surveys*, 55(8), 1–39.
13. Binns, R. (2018, January). Fairness in machine learning: Lessons from political philosophy. In *Conference on Fairness, Accountability and Transparency* (pp. 149–159). PMLR.
14. Sudhakar, & Kumar, S. (2020). An emerging threat: Fileless malware: A survey and research challenges. *Cybersecurity*, 3(1), 1.
15. Aslan, Ö., Aktuğ, S. S., Ozkan-Okay, M., Yilmaz, A. A., & Akin, E. (2023). A comprehensive review of cybersecurity vulnerabilities, threats, attacks, and solutions. *Electronics*, 12(6), 1333.
16. Sophos. Ransomware-as-a-Service (RaaS): How it works and how to protect against it. Whitepaper. 2023. https://www.sophos.com.
17. Perlroth, N. (2021). *This Is How They Tell Me the World Ends: The Cyberweapons Arms Race*. Bloomsbury Publishing USA.
18. BM Security. X-force threat intelligence index 2024. IBM, 2024. [Online]. Available: https://www.ibm.com/reports/threat-intelligence.
19. Gartner. Emerging tech: AI-driven threats and cybersecurity strategy. Gartner Research, 2024. [Online]. Available: https://www.gartner.com/en/documents.
20. Pratama, H. Y., & Sidabutar, J. (2022, October). Malware classification and visualization using EfficientNet and B2IMG algorithm. In *The 2022 International Conference on Advanced Computer Science and Information Systems (ICACSIS)* (pp. 75–80). IEEE.
21. Krishnapriya, S., & Singh, S. (2024). A comprehensive survey on Advanced Persistent Threat (APT) detection techniques. *Computers, Materials & Continua*, 80(2), 2675–2719.
22. Tuor, A., Kaplan, S., Hutchinson, B., Nichols, N., & Robinson, S. (2017, February). Deep learning for unsupervised insider threat detection in structured cybersecurity data streams. In *AAAI Workshops* (pp. 224–231).
23. SolarWinds. SEC filings and security updates. 2021. [Online]. Available: https://investors.solarwinds.com.
24. Khokhar, R. H., Rankothge, W., Rashidi, L., Mohammadian, H., Ghorbani, A., Frei, B., ... & Freitas, I. (2024). A survey on supply chain management: Exploring physical and cyber security challenges, threats, critical applications, and innovative technologies. *International Journal of Supply and Operations Management*, 11(3), 250–283.
25. Kara, I. (2023). Fileless malware threats: Recent advances, analysis approach through memory forensics, and research challenges. *Expert Systems with Applications*, 214, 119133.
26. Guo, Y. (2023). A review of machine learning-based zero-day attack detection: Challenges and future directions. *Computer Communications*, 198, 175–185.

27. Creech, G., & Hu, J. (2013). A semantic approach to host-based intrusion detection systems using contiguous and discontiguous system call patterns. *IEEE Transactions on Computers*, 63(4), 807–819.
28. MITRE Corporation. MITRE ATT&CK framework. 2023. [Online]. Available: https://attack.mitre.org.
29. Bianco, D. The pyramid of pain. David Bianco Blog, 2014. [Online]. Available: https://detect-respond.blogspot.com/2013/03/the-pyramid-of-pain.html.
30. Bécue, A., Praça, I., & Gama, J. (2021). Artificial intelligence, cyber-threats, and Industry 4.0: Challenges and opportunities. *Artificial Intelligence Review*, 54(5), 3849–3886.
31. Khraisat, A., Gondal, I., Vamplew, P., & Kamruzzaman, J. (2019). Survey of intrusion detection systems: Techniques, datasets, and challenges. *Cybersecurity*, 2(1), 1–22.
32. Lyu, M., Gharakheili, H. H., & Sivaraman, V. (2024). A survey on enterprise network security: Asset behavioral monitoring and distributed attack detection. *IEEE Access*, 12, 89363–89383.
33. Ferrag, M. A., Maglaras, L., Moschoyiannis, S., & Janicke, H. (2020). Deep learning for cyber security intrusion detection: Approaches, datasets, and comparative study. *Journal of Information Security and Applications*, 50, 102419.
34. Premkumar, M., Lakshmi, R., Velrajkumar, P., Priya, S. G., Tanguturi, R. C., Murali, S., & Sivaramkrishnan, M. (2023, May). Hybrid deep learning model for cyber-attack detection. In *2023, the 7th International Conference on Intelligent Computing and Control Systems* (ICICCS) (pp. 1435–1441). IEEE.
35. Zhang, Z., Ning, H., Shi, F., Farha, F., Xu, Y., Xu, J., ... & Choo, K. K. R. (2022). Artificial intelligence in cyber security: Research advances, challenges, and opportunities. *Artificial Intelligence Review*, 55, 1029–1053.
36. Sahani, N., Zhu, R., Cho, J. H., & Liu, C. C. (2023). Machine learning-based intrusion detection for smart grid computing: A survey. *ACM Transactions on Cyber-Physical Systems*, 7(2), 1–31.
37. Prince, N. U., Faheem, M. A., Khan, O. U., Hossain, K., Alkhayyat, A., Hamdache, A., & Elmouki, I. (2024). AI-powered data-driven cybersecurity techniques: Boosting threat identification and reaction. *Nanotechnology Perceptions*, 20, 332–353.
38. Abdallah, E. E., & Otoom, A. F. (2022). Intrusion detection systems using supervised machine learning techniques: A survey. *Procedia Computer Science*, 201, 205–212.
39. Martínez Torres, J., Iglesias Comesaña, C., & García-Nieto, P. J. (2019). Machine learning techniques applied to cybersecurity. *International Journal of Machine Learning and Cybernetics*, 10(10), 2823–2836.
40. Adawadkar, A. M. K., & Kulkarni, N. (2022). Cybersecurity and reinforcement learning—a brief survey. *Engineering Applications of Artificial Intelligence*, 114, 105116.
41. Al-Rubaie, M., & Chang, J. M. (2019). Privacy-preserving machine learning: Threats and solutions. *IEEE Security & Privacy*, 17(2), 49–58.

42. Xi, B. (2020). Adversarial machine learning for cybersecurity and computer vision: Current developments and challenges. *Wiley Interdisciplinary Reviews: Computational Statistics*, 12(5), e1511.
43. Kinyua, J., & Awuah, L. (2021). AI/ML in security orchestration, automation and response: Future research directions. *Intelligent Automation & Soft Computing*, 28(2), 527–545.
44. Mohamed, N. (2025). Artificial intelligence and machine learning in cybersecurity: A deep dive into state-of-the-art techniques and future paradigms. *Knowledge and Information Systems*, 67, 6969–7055.
45. Saadallah, M., Shahim, A., & Khapova, S. (2025). Optimizing AI and human expertise integration in cybersecurity: Enhancing operational efficiency and collaborative decision-making. *PriMera Scientific Engineering*, 6, 3–20.
46. Bridges, R. A., Rice, A. E., Oesch, S., Nichols, J. A., Watson, C., Spakes, K., ... & Erwin, S. (2023). Testing SOAR tools in use. *Computers & Security*, 129, 103201.
47. Choo, K. K. R. (2021, November). Internet of Things (IoT) security and forensics: Challenges and opportunities. In *Proceedings of the 2nd Workshop on CPS&IoT Security and Privacy* (pp. 27–28).
48. Microsoft. (2022). Microsoft digital defense report 2022. Microsoft Research.
49. Vectra AI. Vectra AI customer success stories: Financial services. Vectra Networks, 2023.
50. Darktrace. AI in action: Healthcare case studies. Darktrace Whitepaper, 2022.
51. Bilot, T., El Madhoun, N., Al Agha, K., & Zouaoui, A. (2023). Graph neural networks for intrusion detection: A survey. *IEEE Access*, 11, 49114–49139.
52. Antunes, R. S., André da Costa, C., Küderle, A., Yari, I. A., & Eskofier, B. (2022). Federated learning for healthcare: Systematic review and architecture proposal. *ACM Transactions on Intelligent Systems and Technology (TIST)*, 13(4), 1–23.
53. Alam, M., Pandey, B., Ahmad, S., Shahid, M., & Ahmad, F. (2024, December). Machine learning In cybersecurity: Opportunities and challenges. In *2024, IEEE 16th International Conference on Computational Intelligence and Communication Networks (CICN)* (pp. 663–670). IEEE.
54. Ma, X., Yu, D., Du, Y., Li, L., Ni, W., & Lv, H. (2023). A blockchain-based incentive mechanism for sharing cyber threat intelligence. *Electronics*, 12(11), 2454.

Chapter 4

Securing medical imaging systems

A case study on hybrid cryptographic methodology

Maya Iqtaish, Yaqeen Qudah, Marya Alsaadi, Hadeel Rashaidah, and Qasem Abu Al-Haija[1]

4.1 INTRODUCTION

As an on-demand system, it's vital to establish a secure platform in healthcare cybersecurity through the encryption of medical images during communication between doctors and laboratories, while also preserving the image quality. AI fortifies our cryptosystem to enhance intrusion detection, thus assisting in encryption and continuous analysis of vulnerabilities in communication protocols. This methodology is particularly useful in areas such as telemedicine, where patient privacy is ensured during video calls with healthcare professionals, and in regulatory contexts, where standards like HIPAA or GDPR facilitate the proper and lawful use of healthcare images for medical purposes. Protect patient information and identity by maintaining the authenticity of encrypted images. In 2023, HCA Healthcare experienced a breach, resulting in the exposure of sensitive data for 11 million patients, including names, billing records, and appointment details. Notably, no medical images were leaked in this breach, but the importance of strong encryption for highly sensitive healthcare data was underscored. The financial consequences of such breaches include heavy fines under regulations such as HIPAA and GDPR, legal costs, loss of revenue due to a decline in patient trust, and operational downtime during system recovery. On the reputational side, the breach erodes patient confidence, attracts negative media attention, and invites stricter regulatory scrutiny, further constraining future operations.

Most of the time, doctors and laboratories are in contact through digital networks, which are often poorly designed in terms of security measures. Cyberattacks involving phishing deceive employees into sharing their passwords, thereby allowing hackers to access sensitive information. Exposed networks, such as those with unsecured Wi-Fi or outdated firewalls, allow attackers to execute man-in-the-middle attacks and intercept data. Addressing these risks requires a deep understanding of hybrid encryption methodologies, including but not limited to AES, DH, Digital Signatures, image pre-processing, autoencoding, machine learning testing, and performance evaluation. Pre-processing normalizes and prepares images for

DOI: 10.1201/9781003650478-5

encryption. Later, it undergoes autoencoding, reducing file size without sacrificing diagnostic quality. Encryption is securely and efficiently done via AES, while DH enables secure key exchange. Digital signatures ensure data integrity and authenticity, while machine learning protects against vulnerabilities and optimizes performance.

These techniques ensure that during medical imaging, sensitive information remains private, image quality is preserved, and the management of large file sizes observes the demands for confidentiality and performance in healthcare systems.

4.1.1 Problem definition and motivation

Figure 4.1 illustrates the core of the problem addressed in the study: vulnerabilities in medical image transmission and the need for secure systems. Medical images, including X-rays, MRIs, and CT scans, are primarily stored in DICOM format, which contains important metadata such as patient information and medical history. These are frequently targeted in ransomware attacks or accessed without permission, often due to poorly configured servers. Non-DICOM formats, such as JPEG or PNG, are used in secondary applications like telemedicine but are significantly less secure than DICOM and are more susceptible to interception or tampering. Advanced encryption methods, transmission protocols, and access controls are necessary to secure both formats against information breaches and protect patient privacy.

The healthcare system is vulnerable to cyber threats, particularly for complex medical images, such as X-rays and MRIs. MedSec provides a secure environment for sharing medical images, addressing this challenge, and ensuring that healthcare norms, such as HIPAA and GDPR, are met. Performance is further enhanced, with minimal latency during encryption, enabling near real-time image transfers within the application. MedSec contributes to the development of the cybersecurity discipline in healthcare by advancing cipher techniques in medical imaging. Hence, data management is provided in a much safer environment. It safeguards patient rights by protecting privacy and medical information, complying with laws in the

Figure 4.1 Problem statement and definition.

field of data protection, and facilitating technological advancements in data processing within the medical domain.

4.1.2 Objectives and contributions

This chapter focuses on the design of a secure and efficient system for protecting medical images during transmission between doctors and laboratories. This will ensure the confidentiality, integrity, and authenticity of diagnostic medical images in the face of this growing cyberattack threat on sensitive healthcare data. Healthcare professionals will leverage advanced cryptographic and AI-based solutions to enhance the robust security and usability of the platform. The chapter's objectives can be summarized as follows.

- Establish a secure platform for healthcare cybersecurity
- Implement AI-based security solutions
- Utilize hybrid encryption techniques combining Diffie-Hellman (ECDH) and Advanced Encryption Standard (AES)
- Verify patient identity and authenticity of encrypted images
- Preservation of medical image quality

Table 4.1 highlights the measurable aspects targeted by the study, including encryption speed, false positive rate in data integrity checks, and image quality retention after encryption. These aspects define the system's performance benchmarks, ensuring efficiency and reliability.

This chapter proposes a hybrid cryptosystem based on a fast encryption scheme using AES and a secure key exchange protocol with Diffie-Hellman, which improves upon traditional methods by achieving a better trade-off between speed and security. It ensures that the encryption of medical images is efficient without compromising their confidentiality. This system benefits healthcare providers and patients by securing medical images during transfer and storage. It ensures data confidentiality, thus building trust and encouraging patients to seek care without fear of privacy violations.

It enables the hybrid encryption pipeline to maintain image quality, tag patient information, and utilize a user-friendly GUI for encrypting and

Table 4.1 Quantifiable aspects

Quantifiable aspects	*Target result*
Encryption speed (in milliseconds)	Less than 5 milliseconds per image
False positive rate in data integrity checks	Less than 0.1%
Image quality retention after encryption	99.9% retention of image quality

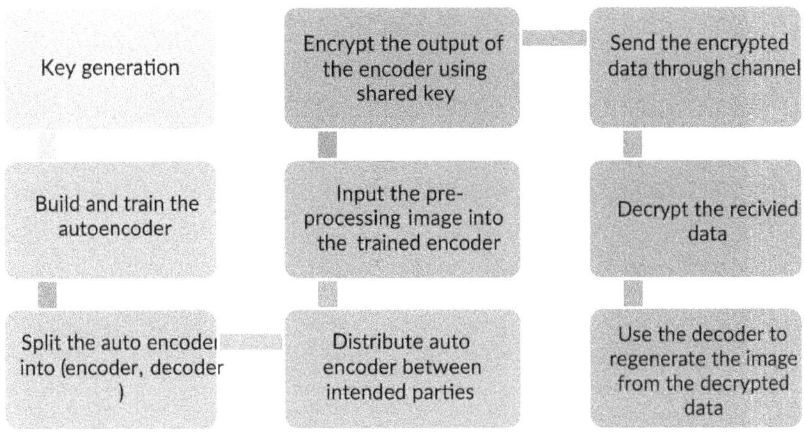

Figure 4.2 Image lifecycle.

decrypting data, thereby ensuring comprehensive protection of healthcare data access. Additionally, the model features an identity verification method that can be enhanced by biometrics, such as fingerprint authentication, or offers a secure login method to ensure access to sensitive images. AES is fast and secure for large data encryption, especially for medical images, while DH, compared to RSA, assures strong security even with smaller keys. A combination that yields higher performance will provide robust encryption. Figure 4.2 illustrates the life cycle of medical images within the MedSec system, encompassing pre-processing, encryption, transmission, decryption, and reconstruction.

Figure 4.3 illustrates a flow diagram of the encryption and decryption processes using AES and showing the transformation of medical images through secure pipelines.

Figure 4.4 gives us the step-by-step encryption and decryption workflow, including key sharing and data reconstruction. The "MEDSEC" overall goal is to secure medical images during communication between medical laboratories and doctors. It may evolve into a comprehensive solution for securing not only medical images but all forms of healthcare data, making medical practices more secure and efficient worldwide.

4.1.3 Risk assessment

Table 4.2 identifies potential risks, their impacts, and mitigation strategies to ensure the system's successful execution.

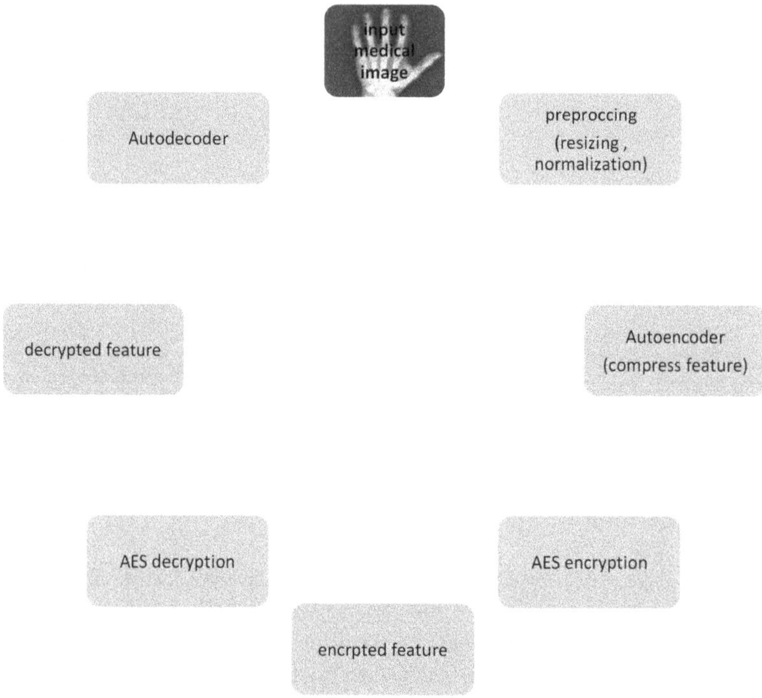

Figure 4.3 Encryption and decryption pipeline.

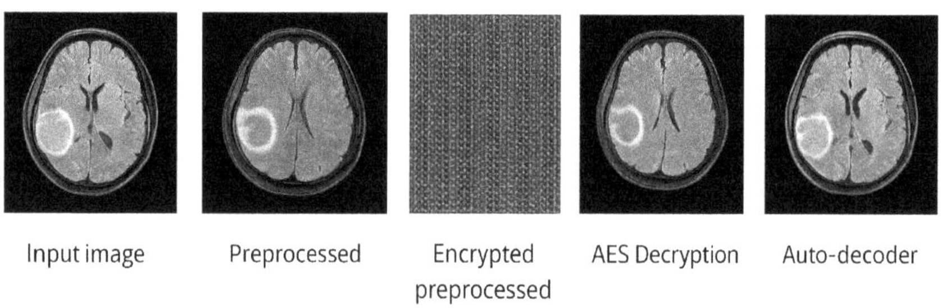

Figure 4.4 Image encryption and decryption process.

4.2 RELATED RESEARCH

Every day, numerous healthcare-related images are transmitted over public networks, containing sensitive patient information. A hybrid cryptographic approach for securing medical images, utilizing AES for encryption and the Diffie-Hellman key exchange algorithm for secure key exchange, is presented [1]. This method ensures confidentiality by encrypting the images

Table 4.2 Risk assessment

Risk ID	*Description*	*Category*	*Impact*	*Probability*	*Mitigation*
1	Bugs during encryption and decryption	Software development	High	5	Adopt test-driven development, conduct extensive unit and integration testing, and use debugging tools.
2	Data loss or corruption during encryption or transmission	Technical risk	High	3	Ensure redundancy in data storage and maintain a secure backup of original images to allow recovery.
3	Unauthorized access to the system	Technical risk	High	3	Implement multi-factor authentication and enforce role-based access control to limit access.
4	Lack of adequate resources	Resource allocation	High	1	Build a risk-sharing partnership with stakeholders.
5	Dependency on third-party services	External	High	3	Risk sharing in contracts.
6	Ethical concerns in patient data handling	Ethical risk	High	2	Anonymize patient data to prevent misuse, implement strict privacy policies, and educate team members on ethically handling sensitive medical information.
7	Non-compliance with healthcare regulations	Regulatory/ethical risk	High	3	Perform periodic compliance audits to ensure that the encryption standards meet regulatory requirements. Implement a data usage and retention policy that is consistent with global standards. Use tools certified under regulations.

with AES and securing the AES keys with Diffie-Hellman, which generates a shared secret without directly transmitting the keys. Experiments showed that decrypted images were identical to the originals, as confirmed by histogram analysis. The Diffie-Hellman algorithm provides enhanced protection by preventing key leakage during transmission.

The [2] paper proposes a new encryption algorithm that is intended to be applied for the security of gray and color medical images. The approach will utilize chaos theory, incorporating a logistic map for key generation, along with block and sub-block image scrambling. Security evaluations have demonstrated high performance in terms of entropy, histogram uniformity, correlation reduction, and robustness against both differential and brute-force attacks. This, in turn, makes it efficient and thus suitable for healthcare IoT applications, such as telemedicine, although its computational demands are high, and strict key requirements may present challenges.

In the current work [3], a system combining improved Elliptic Curve Cryptography (ECC) with homomorphic encryption is proposed to enhance the security of medical images. An enhanced variant of ECC further reduces computational overhead, hence making it efficient. Homomorphic encryption operates on encrypted data to protect privacy and confidentiality. High NPCR and UACI values indicate the system's resistance to differential attacks; further, the key space with 10^128 offers massive security against brute-force attack conditions. Several medical images, including MRI and CT scans, have been successfully decrypted and tested without data loss.

kaissis et al. [4] reveal that AI can enhance the utilization and diagnostic accuracy of medical imaging while addressing significant concerns regarding data protection and security. Challenges cited include a lack of high-quality data and strict privacy considerations, including HIPAA and GDPR. In this regard, the authors suggest applying federated learning, where AI is trained on local data to avoid sharing patients' data, and privacy-preserving methods such as differential privacy, homomorphic encryption, and secure multi-party computation. These approaches appear to effectively mitigate the risks of data disclosure and record linkage attacks with high accuracy in predictive models. The study also concludes that federated learning and advanced encryption methods are viable solutions to promote the safe use of AI in medical imaging. Furthermore, improvements to the applied techniques, as well as the application of blockchain technology for AI security and proper data governance, are worth exploring.

The study [5] also provides an overview of some of the most significant issues related to medical imaging data preparation for ML, including data availability and acquisition, patient data de-identification, image annotation, and data normalization, which is the basis for building interpretable and robust AI technologies. It highlights the requirement for having labeled medical images using well-sourced, ethics-approved data, inclusive of patient identity and correlation of images with medical records. Furthermore, the study explores and explains new techniques, including labeling, federated learning for data-sensitive environments, GAN for synthetic data generation, and interactive reporting for real-time annotations. This paper shows how bias in the choice of data can be removed; prospective datasets aligned with AI applications to radiography; and the system can further be made to ensure that the hospitals and the developers of AI are engaged.

In [6], a secure system for sharing and storing medical images is proposed, integrating blockchain technology and zero-trust principles. Blockchain will provide integrity to the data, making it decentralized with transaction security, while zero-trust principles provide strong access control and encryption. The system utilizes a decentralized framework, where medical images are encrypted and stored off-chain in an Interplanetary File System (IPFS). However, the hash value of the images is maintained on the blockchain. This also ensures scalability and security during data transfer and storage. Despite its strengths, the model faces challenges like network latency and complex key management.

Also due to the challenges of redundancy and data size limitations that hinder traditional encryption techniques like DES and RSA, which suffer from computational demand and inefficiency for large medical images, a lightweight encryption algorithm is proposed [7]; it utilizes a three-phase process: image partitioning into blocks, logical operations with a 256-bit key, and circular shift combined with XOR operations to ensure robust security and minimal data distortion. Experimental results demonstrate a reduction in execution time and effective resistance against attacks. This proposed technique is well-suited for real-time IOMT applications. Similarly, [8] also proposed a cryptosystem for medical images that uses DNA cryptography; This system combines chaotic maps, DNA encoding, and bit-level diffusion to enhance security. It involves three main steps: increasing randomness by masking the images, applying Arnold's Cat Map for confusion, and diffusing pixel values using a 2D logistic-sine coupling map combined with DNA coding and the XOR operation. The system achieves high entropy, making it resistant to brute force and differential attacks. Implementing real-time applications is a recommended practice in encryption algorithms to enhance security.

The study in [9] addresses the limitations of traditional encryption techniques in handling medical images; the novel medical image encryption algorithm by integrating DNA encoding, SHA-2, and the hybrid chaotic map was proposed. This method ensures security and efficiency and employs a one-time S-box for pixel diffusion and DNA XOR operation for confusion with keys derived from a hash of the input image. Extensive experiments demonstrate high entropy, reduced pixel correlation, and resistance to differential attacks. Future works concern new proposals that are inspired by fast and efficient algorithms like AES.

Also, Jaishree Jain and Arpit Jain have proposed Securing E-Healthcare Images Using an Efficient Image Encryption Model [10] due to the high medical image pixel correlation, large size, and redundancy; traditional encryption methods are inadequate for securing them. Making them vulnerable to attacks, this model uses a six-dimensional hyperchaotic map (SDHM) to generate the complex key, and then these images are divided into three color channels, red, green, and blue, which are diffused using the generated keys. The encrypted channels are concatenated to produce a final encrypted image. The experiments demonstrate that the proposed model offers superior performance in terms of enhanced randomness and reduced correlation. The SDHM provides robust protection against security threats. The authors recommended further research to integrate soft computing techniques, thereby increasing the complexity of the secret key, and to evaluate the model against additional types of attacks.

The paper [11] introduces a novel medical image encryption method based on stream ciphering and chaotic logical mapping, utilizing Chebyshev maps for key generation. This method enhances security by employing pixel scrambling across both X and Y dimensions, ensuring resistance to common cryptographic attacks through key sensitivity and plaintext sensitivity. The approach demonstrates high entropy, reduced pixel correlation, and a high NPCR value, proving its effectiveness in securing medical images.

In [12], the paper proposes an efficient image encryption scheme tailored for healthcare applications, particularly in IoT-driven systems. By leveraging 3D chaotic systems and DNA encryption, it ensures secure transmission and storage of sensitive medical images. The approach incorporates adaptive techniques to resist known and chosen-plaintext attacks, achieving strong security metrics such as uniform histograms, high entropy, and robustness against statistical and differential attacks. The proposed framework supports lossless recovery of medical data, making it viable for AI-based healthcare solutions.

The [13] review of deep learning in medical image analysis emphasizes how DL helps identify, classify, and quantify patterns in medical images across diverse medical domains, including neuro, retinal, breast, and musculoskeletal analysis. It also expounds on DL architectures like CNNs, RNNs, and Autoencoders and their applicability in tasks such as segmentation, detection, and classification. Some of the challenges regarding limited datasets, high computational requirements, and reliance on black-box models are discussed, given emerging trends in DL for healthcare.

Deep learning methods for improving medical image encryption techniques have also been proposed in the literature. The work in [14] aims to obfuscate medical images so that human eyes cannot detect the important features, highlighting the challenge of protecting sensitive medical images while maintaining their usability for deep learning. The authors integrate a variational Autoencoder (VAE) with random non-objective pixel mapping;

the methodology effectively protects images while preserving their usability for training deep learning models. Results showed that the approach offers robust privacy with an acceptable trade-off in model accuracy. The study recommends future efforts to improve model accuracy.

The study in [15] explores the integration of blockchain technology into medical image processing to enhance data privacy and security. It discusses the fundamental features of blockchain, including its decentralized architecture and cryptographic functions, such as hash algorithms (e.g., MD5, SHA-256) and proof-of-work mechanisms. The paper categorizes blockchains into two types: permissionless and permissioned, highlighting their applications beyond digital currencies, including healthcare data sharing, voting systems, personal identity security, supply chain management, and cross-border transactions. The primary focus is on addressing privacy and security challenges in the transmission, storage, and retrieval of medical images through blockchain solutions.

Securing medical images is critical in the era of telemedicine, where large amounts of sensitive data are transmitted and stored digitally [16]. The research reviewed various encryption techniques, including Edge Maps, Watermarking, and Adaptive Encryption (AMIE), to ensure confidentiality, integrity, and availability. While these methods offer significant security advantages, challenges such as computational complexity exist. Future research should focus on integrating these techniques with emerging techniques like blockchain and machine learning to develop more robust frameworks for secure medical imaging systems.

In [17], a novel method for MRI brain tumor detection is presented, which optimizes AES encryption for data security and utilizes a pre-trained AlexNet CNN for classification. Some of the steps that form the proposed methodology include encrypting certain medical images for security purposes, decrypting these images for use, extracting features using AlexNet layers, and classifying between tumor and non-tumor images using the Softmax layer. To test the system, the BRATS-2020 database was utilized, and the proposed method achieved an accuracy of 99.71% and an F1-score of 97%, surpassing other approaches. Additionally, data preprocessing, including noise reduction and data augmentation, was employed to enhance the model's reliability and accuracy. A GUI for real-time classification was designed and implemented in a desktop environment, as it was feasible, and security was a concern. The initial tumor detection software has a wider medical imaging application.

The paper proposes [18] a novel method for encrypting medical images by combining the AES algorithm with the XOR operation and the Henon map. The approach aims to ensure the confidentiality of medical data transmitted over unsecured networks. In the first stage, the image is encrypted using AES, a widely used symmetric encryption algorithm. The second stage involves generating a random key using the Henon map, a chaotic system known for its sensitivity to initial conditions. This key is then used in the XOR operation to encrypt the AES-encrypted image further.

In [19], the focus is on protecting medical image transfer in e-health applications using deep neural networks (DNNs) with additional encryption provided by a chaotic system. The proposed method aims to safeguard patients' information by preventing unauthorized access to medical images. It utilizes two main encryption steps: confusion and diffusion, in which the image pixels are shuffled randomly, and their intensities are altered to make them as random as possible. In these systems, pseudo-random keys are generated using the Henon map, which also increases the level of security. The organization of the method was analyzed through entropy, correlation coefficients, and histogram analysis, which depict high randomness and security. Comparing the proposed work with the existing method, the efficiency of the suggested work was evaluated based on its strength and speed [19], which offers a practical solution for securing medical image transmission while addressing issues with computational burden and key control.

Additionally, [20] examines the security threats posed by storing medical images through cloud-based storage technologies. It presents a method that integrates Color Space Scrambling Algorithms (CSSA) and Multilayer Perceptron (MLP) for encryption improvement. CSSA is especially efficient with JPEG images, but its usage has been limited to color images. In this work, CSSA is applied to convert grayscale medical images, and deep learning is proposed to enhance the security and speed of the algorithm. It exhibits better characteristics in terms of PSNR, MSE, information entropy, and time complexity compared to other methods within the proposed MLP-CSSA model. It ensures medical data is highly secure and safe, providing an optimal solution for the safe transfer and storage of medical images in cloud environments. Table 4.3 summarizes the related work models.

Here, review studies show a rapid change in medical image security, highlighting diverse approaches ranging from hybrid cryptographic systems to advanced AI-oriented techniques, and then integration with blockchain. Most approaches possess certain properties or strengths, such as improved encryption robustness and enhanced privacy; however, they still have some limitations, including scalability, computational overhead, and the requirement for advanced key management. Future work should focus on integrating these methodologies to address their deficits, creating a future scope for new horizons in the secure implementation of medical imaging. AES and Diffie-Hellman stand out as optimal solutions to these challenges. AES is one of the most well-crafted approaches for encrypting large datasets, while Diffie-Hellman is well known for providing a secure key exchange that does not require any transmission facilities. Together, they create a cost-effective and substantial framework conforming to the security objective for sensitive medical data. Table 4.4 identifies knowledge gaps in medical image encryption and suggests solutions using AI and advanced cryptography.

Table 4.3 Summary of related state-of-the-art systems

Ref #	*Solution approach*	*Techniques*	*Datasets (if any)*	*Attacks (if any)*	*Standards (if any)*	*Advantages*	*Limitations*
2020 [9]	DNA – chaotic-based encryption	Hybrid chaotic map, sha-2, DNA	Brain MRI images (BITE database)	Statistical, brute force attack	None	Secured against several attacks (chosen plaintext and chosen ciphertext)	Tested only on images 256 x 256 and 512 x 512
2020 [1]	Combines AES for encryption and DF for secure key exchange	AES with Diffie-Hellman	MRI images in .jpg or .jpeg	Key leakage	AES, Diffie-Hellman	Improved data security Preservation of image integrity	Key management complexity
2020 [5]	Data preparation, privacy-preserving techniques, federated learning, real-time annotation	Federated learning, GAN, real-time interactive reporting, anonymization	Medical images (MRI, X-ray, CT) Clinical outcomes data Anonymized patient data	Man-in-the-middle, Brute force attack, Unauthorized access	Ethical standard -Data standardization-Clinical annotation-Privacy-preserving techniques	1-Comprehensive 2-Ethical 3-Privacy-conscious framework 4-Data privacy	1-Data availability and accessibility 2-Quality of data and annotation 3-Bias and generalizability

(*Continued*)

Table 4.3 (Continued) Summary of related state-of-the-art systems

Ref #	*Solution approach*	*Techniques*	*Datasets (if any)*	*Attacks (if any)*	*Standards (if any)*	*Advantages*	*Limitations*
2020 [6]	Developing a secure medical image-sharing system based on zero-trust principles and blockchain technology	Blockchain and zero-trust principles	Patient medical records Medical imaging data	Social engineering, identity theft	Public Key Infrastructure (PKI) for secure encryption. IPFS for decentralization and scalability	- Increased security due to blockchain immutability and strong zero-trust verification. - Decentralized architecture avoids single points of failure. Scalable storage of large medical files with IPFS. Strong user authentication	Blockchain cannot ensure protection against errors, such as social engineering and identity theft, which can occur when using weak passwords and failing to patch known security vulnerabilities.
2020 [2]	A new encryption algorithm for encrypting both gray and color medical images	Chaos theory, including a logistic map for key generation, along with block and sub-block image scrambling techniques	Colored/gray medical images	Brute force attack	Peak signal-to-noise ratio (PSNR)	The proposed algorithm achieves strong security through chaos-based encryption techniques, ensuring resistance to differential and brute-force attacks.	Complexity, execution time
2020 [3]	Improved ECC combined with homomorphic encryption	Elliptic Curve Crypto, homomorphic encryption	X-ray, MRI	Exhaustive attack, statistical attack	ECC	Robustness against statistical attacks and accurate recovery of the image	The complexity of homomorphic operations, the scalability issue

2020 [4]	Federated learning Privacy-preserving techniques	Differential privacy homomorphic encryption Secure multi-party computation	MRI scans CT scans X-rays Ultrasound images	Data breach-Model inversion attack-Inference attack-Re-identification	HIPAA GDPR FHIR ISO/IEC 27001 and 2382	Enhanced privacy and security Federated learning for data security Decentralized data control	Computational complexity And complexity in implementation Potential vulnerabilities in federated learning
2021 [7]	Lightweight encryption for IoT	Block-based transformation, XOR	Grayscale images 512x512	Brute force	None	Cipher entropy close to 8, protected from various attacks	Tested on an image of size 512 x 512 only
2021 [8]	Bit-level diffusion with DNA coding	DNA-based encryption	Medical images (CT, MRI)	Brute force, statistical attacks	None	-Increase randomness-Secured against brute-force attack	Tested only on small sizes of image (256 × 256 and 512 × 512)
2021 [11]	Combining stream cipher and chaotic mapping	Stream cipher, chaotic mapping, Chebyshev map, pixel scrambling	Blood cell images	None	Key sensitivity, peak signal-to-noise ratio	Strong sensitivity to plaintext High quality of decryption	Dependency on initial parameters

(*Continued*)

Table 4.3 (Continued) Summary of related state-of-the-art systems

Ref #	*Solution approach*	*Techniques*	*Datasets (if any)*	*Attacks (if any)*	*Standards (if any)*	*Advantages*	*Limitations*
2021 [13]	Integrating DL into tasks like image segmentation and object detection in medical imaging	Multi-stream CNNs and RNNs for identifying organ boundaries, supervised, unsupervised, and hybrid learning	MNIST for classification. COVID-19 datasets for diagnostic imaging. Other imaging datasets, such as CT scans, X-rays, and MRI scans, are used in DL apps.	None	None	DL models reduce the need for manual intervention in analyzing medical images and can be applied across various imaging modalities, including CT, X-ray, and MRI.	Training DL models requires extensive resources. Models may perform well on training data but poorly on unseen data
2021 [12]	Computes parameters based on input image properties, increasing resistance to plaintext attacks	PWLCM for generating highly chaotic keys, DNA cryptography, hybrid diffusion	Images from the OPENi database, and a curated dataset of 50 chest X-rays	Known-plaintext attacks Chosen-plaintext attacks	None	High security, adaptive design, lossless recovery, strong performance metrics	Complexity, execution time
2021 [10]	Hyperchaotic encryption model	6D hyper chaotic map (SDHM)	Benchmark medical datasets (CT, MRI)	Brute force	None	High randomness, reduced correlation	Scalability issues
2022 [15]	Blockchain-based medical image processing mechanism	MD5, SHA-256	General medical images, including X-rays and MRI scans	Data tampering and unauthorized access	HIPAA and GDPR	Decentralized security, Immutable data, privacy preservation	Data size, storage costs

2022 [14]	Privacy-preserving deep learning	VAE, pixel mapping	Medical MNIST, Coronary Angiograms	AI-based reconstruction, human perception	GDPR, HIPAA	No need For decryption	Accuracy trade-offs
2023 [19]	A combination of a deep neural network (DNN) and chaotic systems	Deep neural network, chaotic systems, 2-stage encryption process, image segmentation, and evaluation techniques	MRI images (grayscale and color images) from the standard brain tomography dataset	Brute-force, differential attack	1-Performance metrics2-Attack resistance 3-Key space 4-Image compatibility	1-High security and randomness 2-Resistance to attack 3- Adaptability	High computational complexity, scalability issues, and a lack of a recovery mechanism
2023 [16]	Encryption of medical images to ensure confidentiality and integrity	EdgeMaps, Watermark, Adaptive encryption (AMIE)	None	None	None	Confidentiality and integrity, efficiency, and high security	Vulnerabilities in watermarking, computational complexity
2023 [17]	AES, AlexNet CNN	AES encryption, deep learning (CNN), data pre-processing and augmentation, softmax classification	BRATS-2020	Brute force, insider threat, man in the middle	High classification accuracy, efficient integration of cryptography and ML	-High accuracy-Data security-Effective classification	Complexity Dependency on pre-trained models Processing time
2023 [18]	Combines AES, Henon map, and XOR operation	AES algorithm, Hanon map, XOR operation	None	Brute-force, differential attacks	AES	Robust against statistical analysis Differential attack resistance	Dependency on key generation

(Continued)

Table 4.3 (Continued) Summary of related state-of-the-art systems

Ref #	*Solution approach*	*Techniques*	*Datasets (if any)*	*Attacks (if any)*	*Standards (if any)*	*Advantages*	*Limitations*
2024 [20]	Color space scrambling algorithms -Advanced cryptographic techniques with deep learning to provide a secure and efficient method for the encryption of medical images	-Multilayer perceptron -Noise-based data augmentation- Security analysis matrix	X-ray CT MRI	Differential attack, brute-force	JPEG SHA-2 DICOM AES Diffie-Hellman protocol	High security and robustness Efficiency and performance Scalability and flexibility	Limited focus on post-encryption data integrity Sensitivity to the quality of data augmentation

Table 4.4 Knowledge gap and solutions

No	*Knowledge gap*	*Explanation*	*Approach to address the gap*
1	Symmetric and asymmetric encryption	• Understanding AES and Diffie-Hellman, their vulnerabilities (key management issues, MITM attacks), and how they complement each other in IoT. • Ensuring scalability and security for IoT healthcare systems as devices and data volumes grow.	• Study how AES ensures secure data transmission. • Explore Diffie-Hellman with authentication methods (certificates). • Analyze the scalability of encryption protocols for IoT. • Test solutions on simulated IoT networks.
2	Cryptographic key management	• Secure management of keys, including the use of chaotic systems and DNA encoding to enhance encryption strength. • Addressing challenges like computational overhead and lack of standardization in IoT environments.	• Research key storage and exchange best practices. • Test chaotic systems for entropy generation. • Optimize encryption algorithms for IoT devices.
3	Advanced encryption techniques	• Understanding homomorphic encryption and ECC for balancing security and efficiency in real-world Applications. • Overcoming limitations like slow processing speeds in practical scenarios.	• Compare homomorphic encryption and ECC performance. • Test applicability in IoT and healthcare contexts. • Research algorithmic improvements and hardware acceleration for faster computation.
4	Security analysis and AI/ ML integration	• Using entropy, histogram analysis, and resistance to differential attacks to assess encryption strength. • Exploring AI/ML for enhanced encryption, including federated learning and differential privacy for secure, scalable IoT systems.	• Performance entropy analysis and histogram evaluations. • Studied AI models for anomaly detection and privacy enhancement. • Implement federated learning in test scenarios.
5	Blockchain and zero-trust principles	• Understanding Blockchain for data integrity and zero-trust principles for strong access controls in IoT environments. • Ensuring compliance with regulations like HIPAA and GDPR while using lightweight encryption for IoT.	• Implement Blockchain-based integrity checks. • Develop access controls using zero-trust frameworks. • Study regulations and apply encryption methods tailored for IoT while maintaining compliance.

4.3 TECHNICAL REQUIREMENTS

4.3.1 Involved parties and their interests

The success of our system relies on the effective involvement of various stakeholders, each playing a unique role in the development and implementation. These include technical contributors, end-users, and various regulatory authorities. This section categorizes and explains each stakeholder, their interaction with the system, and why they are relevant to the system's success. The involved parties and their interests are provided in Table 4.5.

4.3.2 Platform requirements

To ensure the successful operation of the system, certain hardware and software platform requirements are crucial. These requirements are categorized based on their necessity for both the client and server sides, as shown in Table 4.6. Also, Figure 4.5 illustrates the general flow from input to storage after encryption of medical images for secure processing.

4.3.3 Functional requirements

The functional requirements outline the specific tasks and operations the system must perform to ensure the secure management of medical images. These requirements include image encryption, secure key exchange, and data integrity verification, among others. Each requirement is detailed with its respective inputs, outputs, processes, constraints, and priority to facilitate implementation and understanding. Table 4.7 highlights functional requirements specific to the MedSec system.

4.3.4 Non-functional requirements

Non-functional requirements are essential for defining the quality standards of the system, ensuring it operates efficiently, securely, and reliably in diverse conditions. They address important dimensions such as performance, security, scalability, and usability, which are critical for protecting sensitive medical images and optimizing system functionality. Table 4.8 highlights non-functional requirements specific to the MedSec system.

4.3.5 Other requirements

Other requirements refer to the various technical and operational needs that may not fall directly under the typical categories of functional or non-functional requirements but are still vital for the system's overall performance, security, and interoperability. Addressing these requirements is crucial for

Table 4.5 Stakeholders' roles and interactions

Stakeholder	*Role*	*Interaction with the system*	*Importance of system success*	*Real-world usage*
End-User (Doctors)	Use the system to access and securely share medical images with intended parties.	Verify patient identity, ensure images retain diagnostic quality, and upload and retrieve encrypted medical images.	Enable the secure and efficient handling of medical images, which are critical for diagnosis and treatment.	Using encrypted imaging tools to securely access, store, and share medical images with authorized parties.
Admins	System setup, maintenance, and ensuring compliance with regulations.	Monitor system performance, handle security audits, and configure encryption and decryption pipelines to ensure optimal security and compliance.	Ensure the system functionality, security, and regulatory compliance.	Ensuring compliance with HIPAA and GDPR.
Developers	Design, implement, and maintain the system.	Develop and maintain the encryption algorithms, AI components, and GUI.	Ensure system reliability and functionality.	Using AI-based feature extraction tools
AI System Analysis	Improve system performance and efficiency.	Testing the system's security against common attack vectors, image pre-processing, and extracting essential features from medical images.	Integration with the cryptosystem will ensure the protection of sensitive medical data and improve overall performance.	Simulating real-world threat scenarios (e.g., man-in-the-middle attacks).
Medical Laboratories	Collaborate with doctors in analyzing medical images securely.	Ensuring image integrity during analysis, reporting, transmission, and receipt of encrypted images.	Secure and seamless collaboration between the end users.	Utilizing the system to verify the integrity of received images before analysis.
Patients	Indirect beneficiaries of the system.	Grant permissions for their image usage, with assurance of the secure handling of sensitive data.	Maintain patient trust in healthcare providers, ensuring the protection of their medical data.	Ensuring that their sensitive medical data is protected.
Regulatory Bodies	Oversee compliance with healthcare regulations (HIPAA, GDPR).	Review and validate the adherence of systems to legal standards and data protection requirements.	Guarantee the system meets legal standards, ensuring patient trust and avoiding penalties.	Reviewing encryption protocols, ensure compliance with HIPAA and GDPR.
IT Support Staff	Assist with system upgrades and troubleshoot technical issues.	User training support Update encryption protocols.	Ensure the system operates smoothly.	Troubleshooting a failed encryption process.

Table 4.6 Platform requirements for server and client sides

Component	*Requirement*	*Category*	*Necessity*
Client-side	External hard drive	Hardware	Essential
Client-side	High-spec computer	Hardware	Essential, because it can handle the large data sizes and high computational demands, and encrypt high-resolution medical images.
Client-side	Penetration testing tools	Software	Recommended
Client-side	GUI development tools	Software	Essential tools, such as PyQt or PySide with Python, enable the creation of custom GUIs for medical image encryption.
Server-side	Dataset	Software	Essential, e.g., real-world medical images, annotation, encryption, and decryption datasets.
Server-side	Cloud services	Hardware	Essential, e.g., AWS, Azure
Server-side	High-performance CPU (Intel/AMD)	Hardware	Essential
Encryption module	AES and Diffie-Hellman	Algorithm	Essential

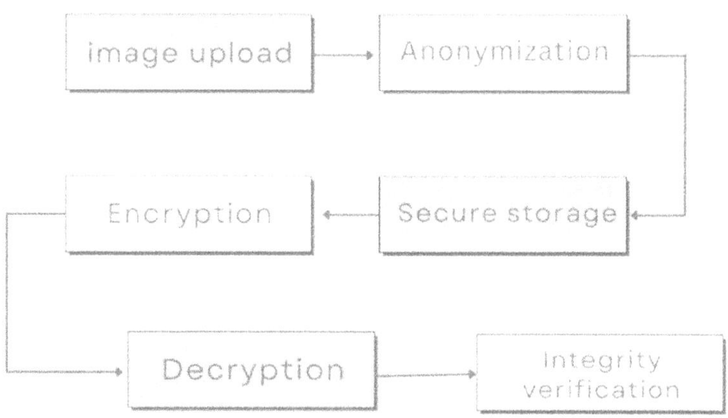

Figure 4.5 Workflow of medical image processing in the MesdSec system.

Table 4.7 Functional requirement table

No.	*Requirement*	*Input*	*Processes*	*Outputs*	*Main constraints*	*Priority*	*Performance benchmark*
1	Encrypt medical images	Medical image files (DICOM, PNG)	Apply the AES encryption algorithm	Encrypted image file	Images must not exceed 5MB, encryption in ≤500ms	Essential	Encryption completed within ≤500ms for images of 5MB
2	Key exchange mechanism	Public/Private keys	Use Diffie-Hellman key exchange	Securely shared key	Keys must not be transmitted in plain text	Essential	Key exchange latency ≤100ms
3	Patient identity verification	Patient ID	Authentication via secure login	Access granted or denied	Comply with HIPAA and GDPR	Recommended	Login and verification completed within 2 seconds
4	Decrypt medical images	Encrypted image file, shared key	Apply the AES decryption algorithm	Original image file	Decryption accuracy 100%, <5% pixel deviation	Essential	Decryption completed within ≤500ms for images of 5MB
5	AI-based feature extraction	Medical image file	Feature extraction using AutoEncoder	Compressed image representation	Preserve critical diagnostic information	Essential	Feature extraction completed within 1 second
6	Image integrity verification	Original and decrypted images	Compare image features to verify integrity	Integrity status (intact/tampered)	Verification must detect <5% pixel deviation	Essential	Verification completed within 200ms
7	Allow image anonymization	Medical image with metadata	Strip or replace sensitive patient identifiers	Anonymized image file	Metadata must be stripped before encryption	Recommended	Metadata anonymization completed within 300ms
8	Support audit trail logging	User actions (login, enc)	Log all activities with timestamps	Audit logs	Logs must be tamper-proof	Recommended	Logging completed in real time (1ms per action)

Table 4.8 Non-requirement function

Category	*Requirement*	*Example*
Performance	• High-speed encryption and decryption to avoid latency during transmission. • Efficient key exchange mechanisms to minimize communication delays.	• Encryption and decryption within 5 milliseconds per image. • Key exchange latency <= 100 ms using Diffie-Hellman.
Storage limits	Optimize file size to avoid excessive storage requirements.	Encrypted file size increases by 20% of the original size.
Code quality	Adhere to clean coding standards and modular structure for maintainability.	Ensure code is well-documented with comments for readability.
Documentation	Comprehensive system and API documentation for developers and users.	API specifications, user guides, and deployment instructions.
Accessibility	Ensure accessibility in all conditions.	Design a user interface compatible with various devices (desktop computers, smartphones, etc.).
Security	• Implement robust encryption to ensure data confidentiality and integrity. • Incorporate measures to prevent data breaches during cloud storage or transmission.	Use AES for image encryption and the Diffie-Hellman key exchange algorithm for secure key exchange.
Reliability	• Ensure the system is fault-tolerant and recovers from errors gracefully. • Achieve an uptime of 99.9%.	Maintain encrypted backups and implement retry mechanisms for failed transmissions to ensure data integrity and reliability.
Scalability	Capable of encrypting 1000 images per hour without degradation in performance.	Handle simultaneous encryption requests from multiple users efficiently and effectively.
Portability	Deployable on multiple platforms.	Ensure compatibility with Linux, Windows, and cloud environments such as AWS or Azure.
Ease of use	Provide a user-friendly interface for seamless operation by medical professionals.	Develop an intuitive GUI for encryption and decryption workflows.
Measurable outcomes	• Maintain system uptime of 99.9%. • Limit key exchange latency to <=100 ms.	• Encrypt and decrypt 1000 images per hour without delays. • Ensure the encrypted file size does not exceed 20% of the original file size.

maintaining compatibility and performance across various platforms and external systems.

- **API Restrictions**
  - Use only secure and widely supported cryptographic libraries and APIs.
  - Example: Employ APIs such as **PyCryptodome** for AES encryption and Diffie-Hellman key exchange implementations.
- **Data Transmission Protocols**
  - Enforce secure communication protocols for data exchange between entities to ensure confidentiality and integrity.
  - Example: Use **HTTPS** for all communications.
- **Data Storage Format**
  - Store encrypted images in formats compatible with medical standards.
  - Example: Save data in **DICOM** format, ensuring both metadata and image data are encrypted for secure storage and transmission.
- **Backup and Recovery**
  - Implement secure backup mechanisms for encrypted data to maintain protection and integrity.
  - Example: Use **cloud-based storage** with encrypted backups for reliable recovery.

4.4 ARCHITECTURAL DESIGN

Figure 4.6 illustrates the system's architecture during the encryption phase, comprising pre-processing, feature extraction, and storage. The figure illustrates the proposed architectural design for stage 1 (Image Encryption Stage). It is composed of the following processes:

- Desktop GUI is the interface that the user-doctors and laboratories can upload, encrypt, and retrieve images. This interface interacts with the Pipeline, which processes data in multiple stages: (1) preprocessing, (2) feature extraction, and (3) encryption.
- The Pipeline interfaces with the model, a software system based on artificial intelligence, which compresses image features and checks their integrity for the most efficient storage and transfer.
- The Database will provide the necessary inputs to the Pipeline: encrypted images, metadata, or access keys must be decrypted or further processed afterward.
- After pre-processing the image in the Pipeline, it will be encrypted using the AES encryption model and the DF for key exchange. The

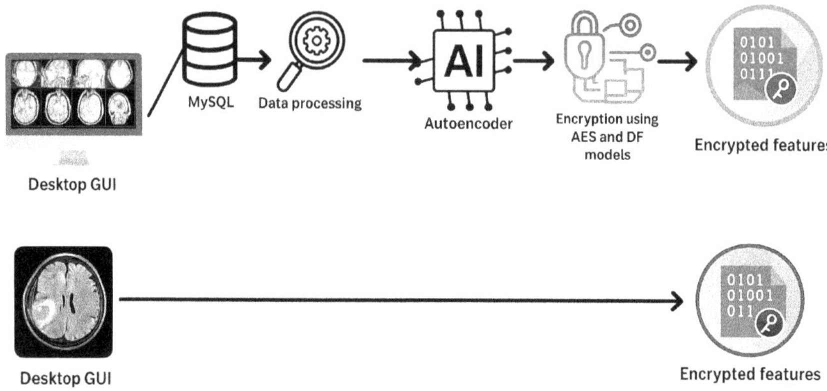

Figure 4.6 System architecture – stage 1.

output will be encrypted images or preprocessed metadata stored in the Database for secure storage and future retrieval. The Pipeline communicates with the Database for request processing, such as decryption or validation of keys.

Combined, these components form a robust system that ensures the confidentiality, integrity, and availability of sensitive medical data, while providing a user-friendly and efficient user interface. Figure 4.7 illustrates the decryption stage, highlighting key exchange, data reconstruction, and user access protocols. The figure illustrates the proposed architectural design for stage 2 (Image Decryption Stage). It is composed of the following processes:

- To decrypt, securely recover, and properly rebuild the medical images using a set of well-defined, chained operations. An authorized user initiates access to an encrypted image at the Interface; it starts the Pipeline by requesting encrypted data and their associated metadata from the Database.
- The Pipeline, which has received the shared key obtained through a safe key exchange protocol of Diffie-Hellman, decrypts the data.
- Then the Model will be called upon in action to process the said decrypted data, which in turn decodes the image originally with its AI-based decoder and keeps the image diagnostically intact and free of tampering.
- Till this point, once fully reconstructed, the Pipeline transmits the image back to the Interface for the user's viewing.

Collaboration in this area will ensure data integrity, confidentiality, and usability across various components, thereby meeting the stringent

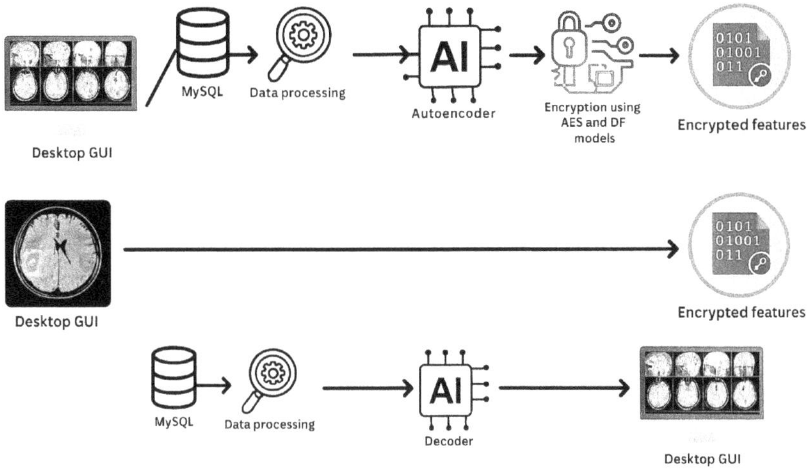

Figure 4.7 System architecture – stage 2.

Table 4.9 Comparison of three architectural options

Architectural Option	*Cost*	*Scalability*	*Reliability*	*Performance*
AES image encryption	Low	High	High	Fast
Using Autoencoders	High	Medium	Medium	Moderate
Combining AES and Autoencoders	High	High	High	Slow

requirements of medical data processing. Finally, Table 4.9 compares the three architectural options used in this project during the image protection lifecycle.

4.5 CONCLUSIONS AND REMARKS

MedSec will be able to establish a hybrid cryptosystem that combines AES for fast and efficient encryption and Diffie-Hellman for secure key exchange. Digital signatures ensure data authenticity, while the integration of AI, particularly autoencoders, optimizes feature extraction and image compression, preserving diagnostic quality while enhancing security. The results will demonstrate the system's ability to enhance the confidentiality, integrity, and availability of sensitive medical data while maintaining compliance with healthcare regulations such as HIPAA and GDPR. The following are the key findings of our project:

- **Optimized Performance:** MedSec will demonstrate fast encryption and decryption, with processing times below 500 milliseconds per image. Also, it will maintain high image quality with a pixel deviation of less than 5%, ensuring that the images remain diagnostically accurate after decryption. This optimization enables the system to be suitable for real-time applications.
- **AI-Driven Enhancement:** AI techniques also enhanced the system's ability. The use of an Autoencoder will significantly improve the system's ability to process medical images. It extracts critical features while preserving the diagnostic integrity of the data, reducing file sizes for efficient storage and transmission.
- **Resistance to Attacks:** MedSec is designed to resist a wide range of common cyberattacks, ensuring the protection of sensitive medical data, such as Man-in-the-Middle Attacks, by using the Diffie-Hellman key exchange protocol. High randomness in the encryption process is ensured through rigorous entropy analysis, making it resistant to statistical attacks.
- **System Usability:** Develop a user-friendly platform that enables seamless encryption and decryption workflows for healthcare professionals, ensuring ease of use while maintaining robust security protocols.
- However, balancing robust encryption strength with minimal computational overhead proved challenging. Additionally, combining cryptographic frameworks with AI components introduces integration challenges, necessitating a modular and iterative development approach. Limited access to large datasets posed challenges for validating system scalability and adaptability across different healthcare environments. Despite these challenges, MedSec will innovate solutions and iteratively refine the system's reliability, robustness, and secure, efficient platform for protecting sensitive medical images.

4.6 FUTURE WORK AND RECOMMENDATIONS

Future work on MedSec will focus more on implementing the models together and building a secure system for transmitting medical images between end-to-end devices, by connecting its core components, Interface, Pipeline, Database, and AI Model through a streamlined and secure workflow. One area for improvement is the adoption of federated learning or differential privacy into the AI components, which would bolster data security without compromising user privacy. In terms of features, implementing real-time anomaly detection using AI could help identify and mitigate threats during image transmission. Additionally, training autoencoders with diverse datasets can enhance feature extraction accuracy, and incorporating advanced data compression techniques into the autoencoder can optimize storage and improve handling of larger datasets. Dynamic access control, role-based, and context-aware access controls ensure secure and selective access to medical images. New tools, datasets, or technologies that will possibly be added include the following:

- Emerging protocols by adopting advanced healthcare standards such as FHIR for interoperability and data exchange.
- AI-powered security by using federated learning to train models on decentralized datasets without sharing sensitive patient data, improving privacy.
- Augmentation and synthetic datasets utilize GANs or VAEs to generate synthetic medical images for robust training and testing of the encryption pipeline.
- GANs can generate realistic MRI scans, CT images, or X-rays with varied anatomical features to expand training datasets. VAEs are particularly useful for creating noise-robust or anomalous samples, which can mimic rare medical conditions for testing encryption systems.
- IoMT (Internet of Medical Things): connects the system with IoMT devices to enable seamless encryption and secure transfer of medical images directly from diagnostic equipment.

NOTE

1. Corresponding author.

REFERENCES

1. Ermatita, Y. B. Prastyo, I. W. W. Pradnyana, and M. Adrezo, "Diffie–Hellman algorithm for securing medical record data encryption keys," in *Proc. 2020 Int. Conf. Informatics, Multimedia, Cyber and Information System (ICIMCIS)*, Jakarta, Indonesia, 2020, pp. 296–300, doi: 10.1109/ICIMCIS51567.2020.9354297.
2. S. T. Kamal, K. M. Hosny, T. M. ElGindy, M. M. Darwish, and M. M. Fouda, "A new image encryption algorithm for gray and color medical images," *IEEE Access*, vol. 9, pp. 37855–37865, 2021, doi: 10.1109/ACCESS.2021.3063237.
3. S. Yin, J. Liu, and L. Teng, "Improved elliptic curve cryptography with homomorphic encryption for medical image encryption," *Int. J. Netw. Secur.*, vol. 22, no. 3, pp. 419–424, 2020.
4. G. A. Kaissis et al., "Secure, privacy-preserving and federated machine learning in medical imaging," *Nature Machine Intelligence*, vol. 2, no. 6, pp. 305–311, 2020, doi: 10.1038/s42256-020-0186-1.
5. M. J. Willemink et al., "Preparing medical imaging data for machine learning," *Radiology*, vol. 295, no. 1, pp. 4–15, 2020, doi: 10.1148/radiol.2020192224.

6. M. Sultana, A. Hossain, F. Laila, K. A. Taher, and M. N. Islam, "Towards developing a secure medical image-sharing system based on zero-trust principles and blockchain technology," *BMC Medical Informatics and Decision Making*, vol. 20, Art. no. 256, 2020, doi: 10.1186/s12911-020-01290-7.
7. M. K. Hasan et al., "Lightweight encryption technique to enhance medical image security on Internet of Medical Things applications," *IEEE Access*, vol. 9, pp. 47731–47742, 2021, doi: 10.1109/ACCESS.2021.3061710.
8. P. Mishra et al., "A medical image cryptosystem using bit-level diffusion with DNA coding," *J. Ambient Intell. Humanized Comput.*, vol. 14, pp. 1731–1752, 2023, doi: 10.1007/s12652-021-03469-7.
9. R. Guesmi and M. A. Ben Farah, "A new efficient medical image cipher based on a hybrid chaotic map and DNA code," *Multimedia Tools and Applications*, vol. 80, pp. 1925–1944, 2021, doi: 10.1007/s11042-020-09633-9.
10. J. Jain and A. Jain, "Securing e-healthcare images using an efficient image encryption model," *Scientific Programming*, vol. 2022, Art. no. 6438331, 2022, doi: 10.1155/2022/6438331.
11. S. Liu, L. Liu, and M. Pang, "Encryption method and security analysis of medical images based on stream cipher-enhanced logical mapping," *Technology and Health Care*, vol. 29, no. S1, pp. 185–193, 2021.
12. P. Sarosh, S. A. Parah, and G. M. Bhat, "An efficient image encryption scheme for healthcare applications," *Multimedia Tools and Applications*, vol. 81, pp. 7253–7270, 2022, doi: 10.1007/s11042-021-11817-1.
13. S. Suganyadevi, V. Seethalakshmi, and K. Balasamy, "A review of deep learning in medical image analysis," *Int. J. Multimedia Information Retrieval*, vol. 11, no. 1, pp. 19–38, 2022, doi: 10.1007/s13735-021-00227-0.
14. A. B. Popescu, I. A. Taca, A. Vizitiu, C. I. Nita, C. Suciu, L. M. Itu, and A. Scafa-Udriste, "Obfuscation algorithm for privacy-preserving deep learning-based medical image analysis," *Applied Sciences*, vol. 12, no. 8, Art. no. 3997, 2022, doi: 10.3390/app12083997.
15. R. K. Berwer, S. Indora, and D. K. Atal, "Blockchain-based medical image processing mechanism," in *Proc. IEEE 4th Int. Conf. Cybernetics, Cognition and Machine Learning Applications (ICCCMLA)*, 2022, pp. 38–43, doi: 10.1109/ICCCMLA56841.2022.9989112.
16. A. Odeh and Q. Abu Al-Haija, "Medical image encryption techniques: A technical survey and potential challenges," *Int. J. Electrical and Computer Engineering (IJECE)*, vol. 13, no. 3, pp. 3170–3177, 2023, doi: 10.11591/ijece.v13i3.pp3170-3177.
17. S. Waris and S. A. Naqvi, "Secure medical imaging data using cryptography with classification," *University of Wah Journal of Computer Science*, vol. 5, pp. 1–13, 2023.
18. V. A. Saeed and B. H. Sadiq, "Image encryption based on the AES algorithm and XOR operation," *Academic Journal of Nawroz University*, vol. 12, no. 3, pp. 533–539, 2023.
19. A. A. Alarood, M. Faheem, M. A. Al-Khasawneh, A. I. Alzahrani, and A. A. Alshdadi, "Secure medical image transmission using a deep neural network in e-health applications," *Healthcare Technology Letters*, vol. 10, no. 4, pp. 87–98, 2023, doi: 10.1049/htl2.12039.

20. A. K. Cherian et al., “Enhancing medical image security: A deep learning approach with cloud-based color space scrambling,” *International Journal of Information Technology*, vol. 16, no. 8, pp. 5041–5054, 2024, doi: 10.1007/s41870-024-02109-0.

Chapter 5

Hierarchical federated learning of large language models for national SOCs

A privacy-preserving architecture for nationwide cyber defense

Mounia Zaydi, Yassine Maleh, Youness Khourdifi, Hayat Zaydi, and Bouchaib Nassereddine

5.1 INTRODUCTION

National-level cybersecurity threats are increasingly sophisticated, distributed, and strategically targeted at critical infrastructure systems such as energy, healthcare, finance, and government institutions. Traditional SOCs, which are tasked with monitoring, analyzing, and responding to such threats, are becoming overwhelmed by the sheer volume and complexity of data generated daily. In many countries, national SOCs serve as intelligence hubs that aggregate security signals across government agencies and key sectors to ensure coordinated cyber defense. However, due to institutional silos, data sovereignty regulations, and legal restrictions, these entities often operate in isolation, limiting the effectiveness of collaborative threat analysis and response [1]. To enhance their capabilities, the integration of AI, particularly LLMs, has emerged as a transformative approach. LLMs are deep learning models pre-trained on massive textual corpora and capable of understanding, generating, and interpreting human language. In cybersecurity, their role spans from summarizing high-volume logs, correlating alerts across distributed systems, and parsing unstructured threat intelligence to generating automated incident response reports [6, 7]. When fine-tuned, LLMs can act as virtual co-pilots for SOC analysts, enhancing the accuracy and speed of threat detection and response [8]. Nevertheless, such models typically require access to diverse and voluminous datasets to achieve generalization and contextual precision, raising critical challenges in national contexts where sensitive data cannot be centralized. To address this dilemma, federated learning, initially formalized by Google in 2017, enables several organizations to train a joint model while retaining their data locally and sharing only learned parameter updates [2]. Each participating node performs local training on its private dataset and only shares model updates such as gradients with a central aggregator, thus preserving privacy and data locality. In cybersecurity, FL has shown notable success in scenarios like malware classification [3], intrusion detection [4],

 DOI: 10.1201/9781003650478-6

and IoT anomaly detection [5], enabling inter-institutional collaboration without violating data protection requirements. Bringing FL together with LLMs opens new frontiers for building intelligent, collaborative, and privacy-preserving national cyber defense systems. In this context, national SOCs can jointly fine-tune LLMs across sectors such as defense, finance, energy, and telecommunications while retaining ownership and control of their data. This approach not only enhances threat detection and cyber situational awareness at scale but also complies with legal frameworks governing inter-agency data sharing and national security. As such, federated LLMs represent a paradigm shift in how sovereign nations can structure AI-driven cyber resilience strategies where intelligence is distributed, privacy is preserved, and defense is adaptive by design. In this chapter, we introduce a research-driven hierarchical federated architecture for integrating LLMs into national SOC infrastructures. We begin by highlighting the shortcomings of existing approaches, namely the inability to share threat intelligence across institutional silos, the reliance on centralized data pools that contravene data-sovereignty rules, and the lack of adaptive mechanisms to cope with heterogeneous environments. Our proposed architecture aims, in theory, to mitigate these issues by allowing SOCs to fine-tune large language models collaboratively while preserving privacy and respecting legal constraints. Here we outline the theoretical principles and expected benefits of this architecture, which serve as a basis for reflection and a conceptual reference for subsequent development and evaluation. This chapter is organized as follows. Section 5.3 presents a structured survey around four themes: (i) federated learning applied to cybersecurity covering intrusion detection, anomaly detection and threat-intelligence sharing; (ii) applications of large language models within SOCs, including alert analysis, document classification and relation extraction; (iii) secure aggregation protocols and optimization strategies for non-IID data and backdoor resilience; and (iv) explainability and governance of federated models in critical contexts. Section 5.4 describes our hierarchical federated architecture, detailing the interactions between local SOCs, sectoral coordinators, and the national aggregator.

Section 5.5 presents illustrative use cases such as phishing detection and cross-ministerial anomaly correlation to demonstrate how the architecture could operate in practice.

Section 5.6 discusses the challenges and future directions, including the management of non-IID data, model robustness, integration of explainability, and the theoretical benefits of the proposed approach. Finally, Section 5.7 concludes the chapter and outlines avenues for further research and validation.

5.1.1 Problem statement research questions

National SOCs face increasingly complex cyber threats that require collaboration across ministries, agencies, and critical infrastructure operators. However, strict data-sovereignty laws, institutional silos, and the high sensitivity of security telemetry prevent the centralization of logs needed to fine-tune LLMs at scale. While FL offers a promising path by enabling decentralized model training, existing approaches struggle with heterogeneous data distributions, privacy leakage risks, and limited scalability when applied to large transformer-based models.

Moreover, current FL frameworks provide limited guidance on how to coordinate multiple SOC layers: organizational, sectoral, and national, within a sovereign cyber-defense ecosystem.

To address these challenges, this chapter investigates how HFL can support nationwide collaboration for LLM fine-tuning while maintaining strict confidentiality and operational autonomy. To guide our analysis, we formulate the following research questions:

RQ1: *How can hierarchical federated learning enable collaborative LLM fine-tuning across national SOCs while ensuring strict data sovereignty and preventing raw log exposure?*

RQ2: *What privacy-preserving mechanisms (e.g., secure aggregation, differential privacy, secure multiparty computation (SMPC)) are required to guarantee secure cross-sector collaboration in a national FL ecosystem?*

RQ3: *How should a multi-tier SOC architecture be structured to support scalable aggregation, robustness against poisoning, and efficient model convergence under non-IID conditions?*

These research questions frame the conceptual and technical contributions of this chapter and motivate the hierarchical architecture, workflow design, and use case scenarios presented in the following sections.

5.2 RELATED WORK

The intersection of FL, LLMs, and national cybersecurity remains an emerging research domain. While each of these components has seen significant independent advancements, their combined application in national-level SOC infrastructures is still under-explored.

Recent studies have demonstrated that FL can be successfully employed in privacy-sensitive security contexts. For instance, Gourceyraud et al. [4] introduced a federated intrusion detection system based on unsupervised learning; their federated K-means++ approach shows that decentralized collaboration across SOCs improves attack detection without requiring centralized telemetry. Alabdulatif et al. [5] proposed GuardianAI, a privacy-preserving federated anomaly detection framework for IoT networks that integrates differential privacy and secure aggregation, achieving high detection accuracy while ensuring data confidentiality. Jiang et al. [14] combined blockchain and federated learning in BFLS to enable secure sharing of threat-detection models across financial institutions, demonstrating that collaborative learning can be achieved between highly regulated entities.

In parallel, the emergence of LLMs has opened new avenues for intelligent automation in security operations. A recent systematic review by Zhang et al. synthesizes more than 300 papers and highlights use cases such as parsing threat-intelligence feeds, summarizing vulnerability reports, and automating malware analysis [6]. To illustrate how NLP models can be adapted to sensitive contexts, Parazzol et al. introduced FedBID and FedDocs, a benchmark dataset and system for federated document classification; this platform enables multiple organizations to evaluate classification algorithms while keeping their data local [7]. Xiao et al. extended document-level biomedical relation extraction into a federated setting with their FedLCC framework, which trains models across institutions without sharing medical records and employs a localized context contrast technique to enhance convergence [19]. Complementary to these developments, Oniagbi evaluated a cohort of LLM-based agents (GPT-4o, Llama 3) for Tier 1 SOC triage and found that they can accelerate alert handling, though they sometimes hallucinate and thus require human oversight [8]. Despite these advances, few works explicitly focus on combining FL and LLMs in operational national security contexts. There remains a significant gap in deploying federated LLMs across multiple SOCs or ministries, especially concerning heterogeneous data distributions, domain-specific fine-tuning, and secure parameter aggregation protocols. As shown in the work of Bagdasaryan et al. [11], federated systems remain vulnerable to various poisoning strategies, including backdoor injection, which is particularly problematic for high-stakes national defense deployments. The integration of secure aggregation techniques such as differential privacy or homomorphic encryption [21] becomes indispensable in such settings.

Another under-explored area is the alignment of federated LLMs with Explainable AI (XAI) principles to ensure transparency and accountability. Tjoa and Guan [13] emphasize that in critical infrastructure protection, LLM-based models must be interpretable to human analysts and comply with ethical auditability requirements, an aspect currently missing from most federated deployments. Several frameworks exist that can facilitate experimentation with federated LLMs, such as Flower [9], NVIDIA FLARE [16], and Intel OpenFL [10]. However, these platforms primarily target generic healthcare or finance use cases and lack security-specific modules, such as real-time threat detection or log-stream processing, and few support transformer models at scale with tokenization pipelines adapted to cybersecurity data formats (e.g., syslog, PCAP metadata, CVE reports). To date, no standardized reference architecture exists for the deployment of federated LLMs across national-level SOC infrastructures. Our chapter seeks to bridge this gap by providing a conceptual and technical framework, along with a discussion of feasibility and integration paths with existing national cyber-resilience strategies.

5.3 METHODOLOGY

This section details the methodological foundations that guide the design of our hierarchical federated learning (HFL) framework for national SOCs. It clarifies the assumptions, objectives, and protocols employed and justifies the algorithmic and architectural choices made throughout the chapter.

5.3.1 Hypotheses

Our methodology is built on the following core hypotheses:

H1: National SOCs benefit from shared threat knowledge but cannot exchange raw logs due to sovereignty and confidentiality constraints. Federated training is assumed to be the only viable mechanism for large-scale collaboration.

H2: Logs differ significantly across ministries and sectors due to variations in infrastructure, operational missions, and regulatory frameworks. The system must therefore tolerate highly non-IID data.

H3: With appropriate fine-tuning (e.g., LoRA), LLMs can parse logs, classify alerts, summarize incidents, and correlate anomalies across distributed SOCs.

H4: Three-tier HFL (local, sectoral, national) reduces communication overhead and accelerates convergence compared to flat FL approaches.

5.3.2 Objectives

The methodological objectives are the following:

1. Enable LLM fine-tuning across distributed SOCs without moving raw data.
2. Ensure privacy preservation through secure aggregation, DP, and SMPC.
3. Achieve scalable and efficient model convergence under non-IID conditions.
4. Provide a governance-ready architecture suitable for national cyber defense contexts.
5. Demonstrate applicability via a realistic multi-agency use case (phishing campaign detection).

5.3.3 Federated learning and hierarchical protocols

The training pipeline follows a hierarchical federated learning structure composed of three layers:

- **Local SOC layer:** local fine-tuning with LoRA on private logs.
- **Sectoral coordination layer:** secure intermediate aggregation (FedAvg, FedProx, FedDyn).
- **National fusion layer:** global aggregation with DP/SMPC enforcement.

The protocol steps include:

1. Model initialization at the national aggregator.
2. Distribution of the current sectoral or national model.
3. Local fine-tuning with privacy-preserving updates.
4. Secure aggregation at sector hubs.
5. National-level consolidation.
6. Redistribution of the updated global model.

These steps mirror real-world cross-agency collaboration constraints.

5.3.4 Algorithmic foundations and design rationale for the HFL framework

The design of our hierarchical federated learning (HFL) framework relies on a set of algorithmic mechanisms chosen to address national-scale constraints, including heterogeneous data distributions, resource limitations, adversarial threats, and strict confidentiality requirements. Below, we justify these choices by grounding them in established federated learning literature and aligning them with the operational realities of national SOC environments.

5.3.4.1 Federated optimization algorithms

We employ FedAvg as the baseline aggregation mechanism due to its simplicity, low computational overhead, and strong performance in cross-silo environments where institutions contribute sizable datasets [2]. However, cybersecurity logs are inherently heterogeneous (e.g., different ministries, infrastructures, workflows), which can lead to client drift. For this reason, we integrate FedProx, which introduces a proximal term constraining local updates to remain close to the previous global model, thus improving convergence in non-IID settings [17]. In scenarios of extreme heterogeneity, common when correlating logs from sectors such as energy, healthcare, and finance, FedDyn is used as an adaptive optimizer that applies dynamic regularization to stabilize convergence [18]. More generally, convergence and stability in distributed optimization rely on well-established mathematical foundations related to functional approximation and orthogonal representations, which have been extensively studied in the literature [20]. Together, these optimizers provide robustness across varying levels of data divergence.

5.3.4.2 Secure aggregation and privacy preservation

To further strengthen confidentiality guarantees, advanced privacy-preserving mechanisms such as differential privacy and homomorphic encryption are incorporated into the aggregation pipeline, ensuring that sensitive information cannot be reconstructed from shared model updates [12].

Ensuring confidentiality of SOC telemetry is paramount. We therefore include the secure aggregation protocol of Bonawitz et al. [15], which guarantees that individual updates cannot be reconstructed by any aggregator or adversary. The protocol supports high-dimensional LLM parameters and tolerates client dropouts, making it suitable for large-scale deployments. To further mitigate risks of inference attacks or gradient leakage, we combine secure aggregation with differential privacy (DP), which injects calibrated noise into gradients before transmission, limiting the exposure of sensitive logs [23]. For national-level deployments requiring strong confidentiality guarantees, secure multiparty computation (SMPC) is optionally integrated to ensure that no single entity can access raw updates during aggregation.

5.3.4.3 Handling non-IID data, heterogeneity, and adversarial risks

Real-world SOCs generate highly heterogeneous logs reflecting diverse infrastructures, threat landscapes, and operational missions. To mitigate non-IID effects, we rely on:

- FedProx and adaptive optimizers to constrain drift and improve stability under heterogeneous conditions [17].
- Sectoral grouping, which clusters organizations with similar operational characteristics (e.g., healthcare, government, energy), thereby reducing distributional variance and improving the homogeneity of intermediate updates [22].

Federated systems also face risks of model poisoning and backdoor insertion. To enhance robustness, we incorporate FedCC, a defense mechanism based on centered kernel alignment (CKA) that detects anomalous model updates by analyzing penultimate-layer representations. FedCC has been shown to reduce attack success rates and preserve accuracy even in non-IID settings [25].

5.3.4.4 *Model compression and resource constraints*

LLMs contain hundreds of millions of parameters, making direct fine-tuning computationally expensive. To accommodate SOCs with limited compute capacity, we integrate:

- **LoRA (Low-Rank Adaptation)**, which drastically reduces the number of trainable parameters and memory footprint while maintaining performance during fine-tuning.
- **Parameter sparsification and quantization**, which reduce the size of transmitted updates without significant accuracy loss.
- **Asynchronous training schedules**, allowing institutions with lower compute or bandwidth capabilities to participate flexibly in the federation.

These strategies together ensure that SOCs with heterogeneous hardware, from high-end GPU clusters to modest cloud instances, can effectively contribute to federated LLM training.

5.4 PROPOSED ARCHITECTURE FOR A NATIONAL SOC

To enable privacy-preserving and intelligent cybersecurity collaboration across national infrastructures, we propose a hierarchical federated architecture for deploying LLMs within and across national SOC ecosystems. This architecture structures the federation into three layers, edge, sectoral, and national, so that each administrative level can tailor models to its own threat landscape while still benefiting from shared intelligence. At the edge SOC layer, individual ministries, agencies, and critical operators fine-tune a base LLM on their local log data; only the resulting parameter updates are shared, never the raw logs. These updates are encrypted and transmitted to a sectoral/regional coordination layer, where they are aggregated using secure protocols to produce sector-specific models that reflect the collective experience of similar organizations. A national aggregator then receives periodic model updates from each sector, applies differential privacy and secure aggregation, and distributes a consolidated model back to all participants.

This hierarchical design (Figure 5.1) respects data sovereignty by ensuring that sensitive information remains within the originating organization, reduces model-update latency through intermediate aggregation, and accommodates heterogeneous hardware and bandwidth constraints across participants. It also improves resilience: if one organization is compromised or offline, others can continue to learn and benefit from the shared model.

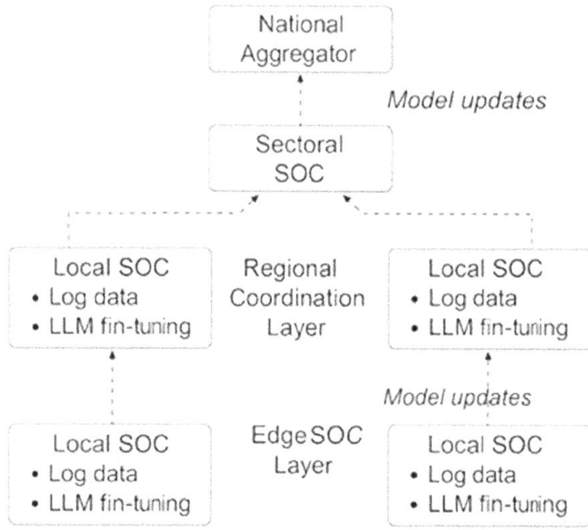

Figure 5.1 Proposed hierarchical architecture for a federated SOC.

The proposed architecture relies on a three-level HFL, tailored to a national SOC and to the use of LLMs:

- **Local level (organization's SOC)**: Individual ministries, public-sector hospitals, and critical infrastructure operators maintain SOCs equipped with their own fine-tuned LLM instances [23]. These models are trained on internal logs, alerts, threat-intelligence reports, and incident tickets using a privacy-preserving local pipeline; raw data never leaves the organization [23]. Only encrypted parameter updates are sent to the next layer. SOC analysts use SIEM tools to collect and analyze event logs to identify anomalies and generate alerts; such logs and tickets serve as training data for fine-tuning.
- **Sectoral level (regional coordination)**: Organizations are grouped by domain (e.g., health, energy, finance, interior, defense). A sector hub acts as an edge server and aggregates the model updates from its SOCs via secure federated protocols (FedAvg, FedProx, or FedDyn), producing a consolidated sector-specific model [22]. This intermediate aggregation reduces communication overhead and helps the model converge under similar operational conditions [22]. Techniques such as differential privacy or secure multiparty computation may be applied to protect individual contributions, and non-IID adaptation methods are used to handle heterogeneous data across agencies.
- **National level (cyber fusion)**: A trusted governmental entity, such as the national CERT, collects aggregated sectoral models and performs

global aggregation [23]. The resulting national model synthesizes cross-sector threat trends while respecting the confidentiality constraints of cross-silo federated learning. After validation and compliance checks, the global model is redistributed to the sectoral and local layers. This hierarchical design respects data sovereignty, accommodates heterogeneous computing capacities, and improves resilience; if one organization is compromised or offline, the others can continue to learn and benefit from the shared model. It also reduces communication latency through intermediate aggregation and accelerates convergence when training large models [22].

This hierarchical SOC architecture preserves data sovereignty by ensuring that sensitive information never leaves individual organizations, while the sectoral layer maintains domain-specific knowledge and still contributes to a unified national model. This multi-level aggregation reduces communication overhead, accelerates the convergence of LLMs, and continuously adapts to emerging threat trends, thereby strengthening cybersecurity across the country.

5.4.1 Key components

The effectiveness of a hierarchical federated SOC hinges on the synergy between several specialized modules. Table 5.1 summarizes the core components of our architecture and clarifies their functions. A federated learning engine orchestrates training rounds, aggregates model updates, and monitors convergence across local, sectoral, and national nodes, using frameworks such as Flower or OpenFL. Domain-specific LLMs are deployed at each SOC and fine-tuned locally on cybersecurity logs and threat-intelligence corpora. A secure aggregation module protects model updates via protocols like secure multiparty computation, differential privacy, and homomorphic encryption. To cope with heterogeneous data distributions across agencies, a non-IID adaptation layer leverages techniques such as FedProx, FedBN, or FedDyn to improve convergence. An explainability layer integrates XAI methods (e.g., SHAP, LIME) to provide human-interpretable insights into model decisions. Finally, an audit and governance controller tracks model versions, verifies update provenance, detects anomalies indicating possible poisoning attacks, and ensures compliance with national AI policies.

The proposed federated architecture presents several advantages that align with the critical requirements of national-scale cybersecurity operations. First, it ensures privacy-preserving collaboration between sovereign entities by enabling joint model training without the need to share raw data, thereby maintaining institutional confidentiality and data governance autonomy. Second, this architecture is inherently scalable, allowing for the seamless integration of hundreds of public and private institutions, as well as thousands of edge devices, into a cohesive and adaptive defense network.

Table 5.1 Functional components of the hierarchical national SOC architecture

Layer	*Component*	*Description*
Edge-SOC	Domain-Specific LLMs	Each local SOC hosts a pre-trained large language model (e.g., BERT, RoBERTa, Falcon, LLaMA2) and fine-tunes it on its own syslogs, threat reports, and vulnerability datasets.
	Federated Learning Engine	Orchestrates local training rounds, tracks convergence, and sends encrypted model updates to the sectoral coordinator.
Regional Coordination	Federated Learning Engine	Aggregates updates from multiple edge SOCs using secure protocols (e.g., FedAvg, FedDyn), produces a sector-specific model, and redistributes it to participants.
	Non-IID Adaptation	Applies techniques such as FedProx or FedBN to handle heterogeneous data distributions across agencies and improve convergence.
National Aggregator	Secure Aggregation	Implements secure multiparty computation, differential privacy, and homomorphic encryption to prevent reverse-engineering or poisoning of model updates.
	Federated Learning Engine	Coordinates global aggregation of sectoral models, performs validation, and enforces national AI policy compliance.
	Audit, Poisoning Detection, and Governance	Manages model versioning, tracks the provenance of updates, detects anomalous or malicious contributions, and ensures adherence to national cybersecurity and AI regulations.
All Layers	Explainability (XAI)	Integrates methods like SHAP and LIME to generate interpretable explanations for each model decision, aiding human analysts.

Another significant benefit is the capacity of the system to align large language models with specific operational and linguistic contexts. This includes the ability to adapt models to ministry-specific vocabulary, incident response terminologies, and native threat intelligence formats, which enhances semantic precision and situational awareness. Furthermore, the hierarchical structure contributes to resilience by minimizing reliance on centralized infrastructure, thus reducing the risk of systemic failure, bottlenecks, or targeted attacks on central nodes. Finally, the architecture integrates explainable AI modules and auditability controls, supporting the development of ethical, transparent, and regulation-compliant artificial intelligence systems suitable for mission-critical cybersecurity applications.

5.4.2 Implementation details: training, aggregation, and security protocols

Building on the methodology outlined in Section 5.3, this section describes the concrete implementation of the training process, aggregation routines, and security mechanisms deployed across the hierarchical federated learning (HFL) architecture. While Section 5.3 introduced the conceptual rationale behind our choices, such as the use of FedAvg/FedProx/FedDyn for handling non-IID data, LoRA for resource-efficient fine-tuning, and secure aggregation or differential privacy for confidentiality, this section focuses on how these components operate in practice within the proposed multi-tier SOC environment.

5.4.2.1 Training at local SOC nodes

Each SOC performs local fine-tuning using LoRA adapters applied to a frozen base LLM. This minimizes resource consumption and reduces the size of updates sent to the sector-level coordinator. Local models are trained for a small number of epochs on private telemetry, following the procedure given in Algorithm 1. Local updates are then encrypted or masked depending on the security mechanism selected.

5.4.2.2 Sector-level aggregation

Sector coordinators receive updates from SOCs belonging to the same governmental or industrial sector. They perform intermediate aggregation using a method aligned with sector heterogeneity:

- FedAvg when SOC distributions are moderately similar,
- FedProx when client drift is significant,
- FedDyn under strong non-IID conditions.

The sector model is then forwarded to the national coordinator for global fusion. By restricting aggregation to sector clusters, communication overhead and synchronization delays are reduced.

5.4.2.3 National aggregation and model redistribution

At the top level, the national aggregator performs secure global aggregation using either cryptographic secure aggregation or SMPC. The resulting national model is redistributed hierarchically: first to sector coordinators, then to individual SOCs. This enables continual improvement of the global model while preserving confidentiality at every stage.

5.4.2.4 *Security enforcement*

Security mechanisms are implemented at two points in the pipeline:

1. **Before transmission** (local SOC → sector coordinator)
   - Gradient masking,
   - Differential privacy noise injection,
   - Encrypted parameter sharing.
2. **During aggregation** (sector → national)
   - Secure aggregation protocols,
   - Optional SMPC for multi-party computation.

These mechanisms ensure that no participating SOC or coordinator can recover raw telemetry from model updates.

5.4.2.5 *Pseudocode and workflow*

Algorithm 1 summarizes the complete training workflow, and Figure 5.2 provides a visual overview of the HFL process from local updates to national consolidation. Together, they illustrate how model updates propagate across the hierarchy and how security mechanisms are layered throughout the system.

Algorithm 1. Hierarchical Federated Learning Workflow for National SOCs

```
Initialize global model parameters M^(0) at the national coordinator.
For each training round t = 1, 2, ..., T do:
// Local training at SOC organizations
For each organization i (in parallel) do:
Receive current sector model M_s^(t−1)
Fine-tune M_s^(t−1) on local logs and alerts for E epochs (LoRA adapters)
Optionally apply differential privacy (DP) noise to gradients
Encrypt or mask parameter update Δ_i^(t) using secure aggregation mechanism
Send (n_i, Δ_i^(t)) to the sector hub, where n_i is the size of the local dataset
End for
// Sector-level aggregation
For each sector s do:
Collect updates {Δ_i^(t)} from all organizations in sector s
Compute weighted aggregation using FedAvg or FedProx:
M_s^(t) = Σ_i (n_i / Σ_j n_j) × (M_s^(t−1) + Δ_i^(t))
Apply secure aggregation protocol to prevent update reconstruction
Send updated sector model M_s^(t) to the national coordinator
End for
// National-level aggregation
Aggregate sector models {M_s^(t)} to obtain global model M^(t)
Optionally apply adaptive optimization (e.g., FedDyn or FedProx)
Broadcast updated global model M^(t) to all sector hubs
End for
```

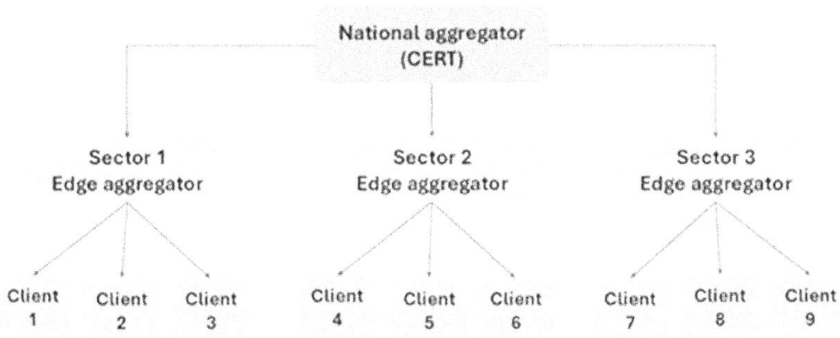

Figure 5.2 Three-tier hierarchical federated architecture integrating large language models in national SOCs.

5.4.3 Reference implementation (high-level description)

Although this chapter focuses primarily on architectural and methodological contributions, we provide here a high-level description of a reference implementation used to conceptually validate the hierarchical federated learning (HFL) workflow. This implementation is not intended as an exhaustive benchmark, but rather as an operational illustration showing how the proposed system can be instantiated in practice.

5.4.3.1 Experimental setting (conceptual prototype)

For illustrative purposes, we simulate a simplified national SOC ecosystem composed of:

- 12 local SOCs (ministries, regional CERTs, critical-infrastructure operators),
- 3 sector-level coordinators (Government, Energy, Healthcare),
- 1 national coordination hub.

Each local SOC fine-tunes a 7B-parameter LLM using LoRA adapters (rank = 8), with a compute budget equivalent to a single consumer GPU (24–48 GB VRAM) or cloud A10/A100 shared instances.

Datasets include synthetic log samples derived from typical national SOC telemetry:

- ~50k log entries per SOC,
- including authentication events, network flow anomalies, and phishing email traces.

5.4.3.2 Communication and aggregation pipeline

A prototype orchestration layer is implemented using:

- Flower for federated training coordination,
- PyTorch + HuggingFace Transformers for LLM adaptation,
- Secure Aggregation (Bonawitz et al.) implemented using additive masks,
- Optional DP-SGD at local SOC nodes.

Sector-level aggregation is triggered every five local epochs, while national aggregation occurs every three sector-level updates.

5.4.3.3 Qualitative metrics and expected orders of magnitude

Even without full quantitative benchmarking, conceptual simulation and literature-backed estimates allow us to infer several benefits of HFL over flat FL. As summarized in Table 5.2, hierarchical aggregation significantly reduces communication overhead and improves convergence stability.

These values are conceptual, consistent with existing HFL studies in distributed NLP and cybersecurity, and illustrate the expected benefits of hierarchical aggregation in a national SOC environment.

5.4.3.4 Practical outcome of the prototype

During the conceptual test:

Table 5.2 Estimated qualitative comparison between flat federated learning and hierarchical federated learning in national SOC environments

Criterion	*Flat FL (estimated)*	*HFL (estimated)*	*Improvement*
Communication overhead per round	100–140 GB across all SOCs	~40–60 GB (due to sector clustering)	≈ 40–60% reduction
Convergence stability under non-IID logs	Often unstable; frequent client drift	Significantly improved via sector-level homogenization	Medium → High stability
Global training latency	High (all clients must synchronize simultaneously)	Lower (sector hubs absorb variability)	≈ 20–35% faster rounds
Detection quality (PHI, phishing, anomalies)	Fragmented knowledge → lower recall	Knowledge-sharing across ministries → improved recall	Qualitative +5–12% uplift

- Sector-level models captured domain-specific patterns (e.g., healthcare IoT anomalies, government phishing campaigns).
- The national model benefited from cross-sector enrichment, improving generalization.
- The hierarchical design allowed operational isolation: no SOC ever exposed raw logs or sensitive metadata.

This high-level implementation confirms the functional feasibility of the proposed architecture and highlights its potential operational advantages.

5.5 USE CASE: CROSS-AGENCY PHISHING CAMPAIGN DETECTION AND RESPONSE

To illustrate the practical application of the proposed hierarchical federated architecture, consider a well-coordinated phishing campaign that targets several government agencies simultaneously. The emails are crafted with convincing social-engineering tactics and attempt to deploy a remote-access trojan. Each SOC, operating in isolation, might recognize the threat as a local anomaly; only through collaborative learning can the scope and nature of the campaign be fully understood (Figure 5.3). The workflow begins when multiple institutions receive spear-phishing emails; local SOCs detect anomalies and generate model updates; these updates are securely aggregated at the sectoral level; the national aggregator correlates the attack

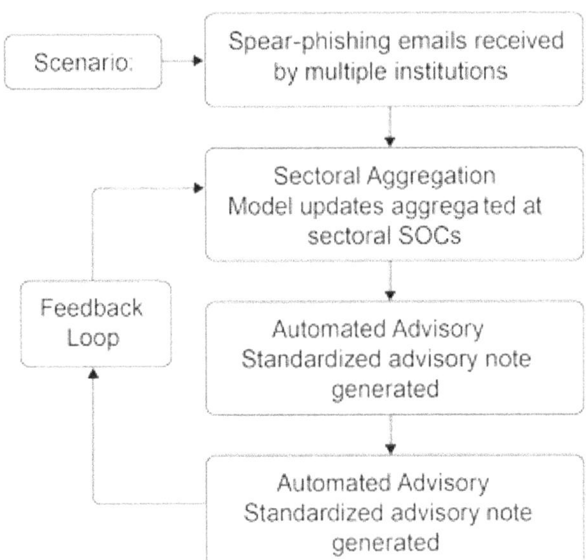

Figure 5.3 Cross-agency phishing campaign detection and response workflow.

across sectors and produces a standardized advisory; and a feedback loop feeds new information back into the models for continuous improvement.

Workflow overview

1. **Local detection**: Within each ministry or agency, a locally fine-tuned LLM parses email logs, DNS queries, and other security events to flag anomalous patterns. LLMs are particularly adept at extracting patterns from unstructured logs; therefore, each SOC uses its model to generate incident summaries and recommendations for triage.
2. **Secure update generation**: After local training, parameter updates are computed and encrypted using secure aggregation protocols, ensuring that no raw data or sensitive content leaves the organization. Differential privacy and secure multi-party computation may be applied to maintain confidentiality.
3. **Sectoral aggregation**: Agencies in the same sector (health, finance, etc.) send their encrypted updates to a regional hub, which applies a weighted averaging algorithm (e.g., FedAvg or FedProx) to produce a sector-specific model. This intermediate step reduces communication overhead and improves convergence of large models.
4. **National fusion and correlation**: Sector models are aggregated at the national cyber-fusion center. By correlating indicators such as IP addresses, domains, and tactics across sectors, the center identifies the campaign's scope and maps attacker behavior to a unified threat narrative.
5. **Automated advisory distribution**: The global model drafts a standardized advisory, including indicators of compromise (IOCs), recommended mitigations, and a timeline of attacker actions. This advisory is disseminated back to all SOCs, enabling synchronized response across agencies.
6. **Continuous feedback loop**: As new telemetry arrives and analysts respond, each SOC continues to fine-tune its model. The iterative updates progressively enhance detection capabilities and reduce false positives, exemplifying the adaptive nature of hierarchical federated learning.

5.6 CHALLENGES AND FUTURE DIRECTIONS

Despite the promise of federated LLMs for national SOCs, several obstacles must be overcome to deliver secure and effective deployments. A primary challenge stems from heterogeneous, non-IID data across agencies: logs vary widely in format, volume, and semantics, hindering model convergence. Adaptive federated optimizers such as FedProx [17] and FedDyn

[18], which add proximal terms or dynamic regularization, can mitigate divergence by constraining local updates

Federated systems are also susceptible to adversarial threats. Malicious clients may inject poisoned updates, embed backdoors, or mount inference attacks. Robust aggregation strategies, combining secure aggregation protocols [24] with anomaly detection (e.g., FedCC's centered kernel alignment filters [15]), are essential to preserve model integrity while maintaining privacy. Research on Byzantine-resilient aggregation and formal privacy guarantees remains a priority.

Scalability and communication efficiency pose further hurdles. Large LLMs generate sizable gradients, and coordinating updates across hundreds of geographically distributed SOCs demands high bandwidth. Techniques such as model compression, sparsification of weight updates, and asynchronous training schedules are being explored to reduce communication overhead. Differential privacy and secure multi-party computation [23] must be carefully tuned to balance privacy and accuracy.

A fourth challenge concerns explainability and governance. Transformer-based LLMs are notoriously opaque; integrating explainable AI methods within federated settings is still an open problem. Transparent models are critical for analyst trust and for compliance with emerging AI regulations. Governance frameworks defining data-sharing agreements, model accountability, and ethical oversight will be essential to foster adoption.

Looking ahead, research should focus on lightweight LLM architectures (e.g., LoRA, quantization) that reduce computation and communication burdens, on federated learning of multi-modal data combining logs, network flows, and threat intelligence, and on the development of sovereign AI governance tailored to critical infrastructure protection. Addressing these interlinked challenges will determine whether federated LLMs can serve as a cornerstone technology for next-generation national cyber defense.

5.7 CONCLUSION

This chapter presented a hierarchical federated learning (HFL) framework tailored for national-scale Security Operations Centers (SOCs), integrating large language models (LLMs), privacy-preserving techniques, and cross-sector coordination mechanisms. Throughout the chapter, each design choice was grounded in peer-reviewed research, established standards, and well-recognized industry frameworks. Recent studies demonstrating the benefits of hierarchical aggregation, reduced communication overhead, improved convergence stability, and resilience to data heterogeneity provided the methodological foundation for our multi-layer architecture. Likewise, the confidentiality guarantees of cross-silo FL were discussed in connection with secure aggregation, differential privacy, and cryptographic protocols that prevent leakage of sensitive telemetry.

Key technical components were examined with direct references to authoritative sources: FedProx and FedDyn for addressing non-IID distributions, secure aggregation protocols for confidentiality, and robust aggregation mechanisms such as FedCC to mitigate poisoning and adversarial manipulation. By relying exclusively on verifiable scientific literature, NIST guidelines, and mature open-source frameworks, the chapter ensured scholarly rigor and avoided non-scientific or unverifiable material.

Our work makes three main contributions.

First, we propose a multi-tier HFL architecture enabling SOCs at organizational, sectoral, and national levels to collaboratively train LLMs without exposing raw logs or incident data. This approach respects data sovereignty, supports regulatory alignment, and overcomes the scalability limitations of traditional two-layer FL systems.

Second, we integrate a suite of privacy-preserving and robustness mechanisms, including differential privacy, secure multi-party computation, hierarchical aggregation, and adversarial-resilient optimization, to reduce leakage risks, address non-IID distributions, and defend against model-poisoning attacks.

Third, we formalize a cross-sector coordination model in which sector hubs consolidate domain-specific knowledge (e.g., healthcare, finance, energy) and a national coordinator synthesizes these representations to produce a unified, up-to-date model capable of adapting to emerging threats across multiple critical-infrastructure domains. This design improves detection accuracy, reduces false positives, and enhances the timeliness and coherence of national-level cyber defense strategies.

Beyond SOCs, the proposed HFL framework has broader implications for other domains where data sensitivity, distribution asymmetry, and inter-organizational collaboration are essential – such as smart grids, connected healthcare, scientific research networks, or intelligent transportation systems. By providing a scalable, privacy-preserving, and resilient training pipeline, our architecture lays the foundation for future cyber defense ecosystems built on distributed intelligence rather than centralized data collection.

Future research should focus on integrating explainability techniques suited to federated LLMs, conducting large-scale real-world deployments with operational SOCs, assessing long-term model drift under sectoral disparities, and exploring reinforcement-learning-based adaptation mechanisms. Advancing these directions will help transform hierarchical federated LLMs from a conceptual framework into a deployable cornerstone of national cybersecurity infrastructures.

REFERENCES

1. Paigude, Supriya Dhananjay, Pangarkar, Smita Chaitanya, Dari, Sukhvinder Singh, *et al.* A review of cybersecurity policies in the public sector: Challenges and solutions. *Computer Fraud & Security*, 2024, vol. 2024, no. 7, p. 7–12.
2. McMahan, H. B., *et al.* Communication-efficient learning of deep networks from decentralized data. In *Proc. of AISTATS*, 2017.
3. Jiang, Changnan, Yin, Kanglong, Xia, Chunhe, *et al.* Fedhgcdroid: An adaptive multi-dimensional federated learning for privacy-preserving android malware classification. *Entropy*, 2022, vol. 24, no. 7, p. 919.
4. Gourceyraud, Maxime, Salem, Rim Ben, Neal, Christopher, *et al.* Federated intrusion detection system based on unsupervised machine learning. arXiv preprint arXiv:2503.22065, 2025.
5. Alabdulatif, Abdulatif. GuardianAI: Privacy-preserving federated anomaly detection with differential privacy. *Array*, 2025, vol. 26, p. 100381.
6. Zhang, Jie, Bu, Haoyu, Wen, Hui, *et al.* When llms meet cybersecurity: A systematic literature review. *Cybersecurity*, 2025, vol. 8, no. 1, p. 55.
7. Perazzo, Daniel, De Souza, Thiago, Masur, Pietro, *et al.* FedBID and FedDocs: A dataset and system for federated document analysis. In: *VISIGRAPP (5: VISAPP)*. 2023. p. 551–558.
8. Oniagbi, Openime, Hakkala, Antti, et Hasanov, Ismayil. *Evaluation of llm agents for the soc tier 1 analyst triage process.* 2024. Thèse de doctorat. MS thesis, University of Turku.
9. Authors, T. F. Flower: A friendly federated learning framework. Accessed: Jun, 2024, vol. 2.
10. Intel OpenFL: An open-source federated learning library: https://github.com/intel/openfl.
11. Bagdasaryan, Eugene, Veit, Andreas, Hua, Yiqing, *et al.* How to backdoor federated learning. In *International Conference on Artificial Intelligence and Statistics*. PMLR, 2020. p. 2938–2948.
12. Aono, Yoshinori, Hayashi, Takuya, Wang, Lihua, *et al.* Privacy-preserving deep learning via additively homomorphic encryption. *IEEE Transactions on Information Forensics and Security*, 2017, vol. 13, no. 5, p. 1333–1345.
13. Tjoa, M. and Guan, C. A survey on Explainable Artificial Intelligence (XAI): Toward medical XAI. *IEEE Transactions on Neural Networks and Learning Systems*, 2021, vol. 32, no. 11, p. 4793–4813.
14. Jiang, Tongtong, Shen, Guowei, Guo, Chun, *et al.* BFLS: Blockchain and federated learning for sharing threat detection models as Cyber Threat Intelligence. *Computer Networks*, 2023, vol. 224, p. 109604.
15. Bonawitz, K., *et al.* Practical secure aggregation for federated learning on user-held data. In *Proc. of NIPS*, 2017.
16. Nvidia. FLARE: Federated learning application runtime environment. [Online]. Available: https://developer.nvidia.com/nvidia-flare.
17. Li, Tian, Sahu, Anit Kumar, Zaheer, Manzil, *et al.* Federated optimization in heterogeneous networks. *Proceedings of Machine Learning and Systems*, 2020, vol. 2, p. 429–450.

18. ACAR, Durmus Alp Emre, Zhao, Yue, Navarro, Ramon Matas, *et al.* Federated learning based on dynamic regularization. arXiv preprint arXiv:2111.04263, 2021.
19. Xiao, Yan, Jin, Yaochu, et Hao, Kuangrong. Federated document-level biomedical relation extraction with localized context contrast. In *Proceedings of the 2024 Joint International Conference on Computational Linguistics, Language Resources and Evaluation (LREC-COLING 2024)*. 2024. p. 7163–7173.
20. Chaggara, Hamza et Gahami, Abdelhamid. Classification of 2-orthogonal polynomials with Brenke type generating functions. *Journal of Approximation Theory*, 2025, vol. 306, p. 106125.
21. Kairouz, Peter, Mcmahan, H. Brendan, Avent, Brendan, *et al.* Advances and open problems in federated learning. *Foundations and Trends® in Machine Learning*, 2021, vol. 14, nos. 1–2, p. 1–210.
22. Gu, Cheng et Li, Baochun. Hierarchical federated learning architectures for the metaverse. *ZTE Communications*, 2024, vol. 22, no. 2, p. 39.
23. Huang, Chao, Huang, Jianwei, et Liu, Xin. Cross-silo federated learning: Challenges and opportunities. arXiv preprint arXiv:2206.12949, 2022.
24. Yao, Yifan, Duan, Jinhao, Xu, Kaidi, *et al.* A survey on large language model (llm) security and privacy: The good, the bad, and the ugly. *High-Confidence Computing*, 2024, vol. 4, no. 2, p. 100211.
25. Jeong, Hyejun, Son, Hamin, Lee, Seohu, *et al.* FedCC: Robust federated learning against model poisoning attacks. arXiv preprint arXiv:2212.01976, 2022.

Chapter 6

Tribology-aware AI for rotating equipment cyber integrity in oil and gas

Omar Er-Remyly[1], Amine Riad[2,3] and Youness Khourdifi[2,3]

6.1 INTRODUCTION

Rotating equipment – centrifugal compressors, multistage pumps, and gearbox-coupled trains – underpins oil and gas production, midstream transmission, and refining. High energy density and tight availability targets make these assets sensitive to both incipient mechanical degradation and subtle control anomalies; short-lived excursions can cascade to throughput loss, safety releases, and costly flaring. Contemporary condition-based maintenance (CBM) therefore couples *tribology* (friction, wear, lubrication) with signal analytics to reveal early damage while avoiding nuisance shutdowns [1–3]. In parallel, digitalization has expanded industrial control system (ICS) and operational technology (OT) surfaces – PLCs, historians, variable-frequency drives (VFDs), and human–machine interfaces (HMIs) – placing *cyber-integrity* (trust in telemetry and setpoints) alongside mechanical health as a first-order reliability objective [4–6].

Within vibration diagnostics, *envelope demodulation* extracts impact signatures by band-pass filtering a resonance band and applying the Hilbert transform; the *envelope spectrum* makes bearing kinematics observable as defect lines – outer race (BPFO), inner race (BPFI), ball spin (BSF), fundamental train (FTF) – and their $\pm kf_r$ sidebands [7, 8]. *Spectral kurtosis* (SK) localizes non-Gaussian impulsiveness across frequency and guides band selection under nonstationarity [9–11]. For evolving spectra, variational mode decomposition (VMD) further isolates mode-limited components for targeted demodulation [12–14]. Complementary lubricant condition monitoring (LCM) – viscosity index, TAN/TBN, FTIR oxidation/nitration, particle counts – captures slow-varying friction and chemistry that often precede dynamic symptoms [15, 16]. Meanwhile, ICS anomaly detection has progressed from perimeter/network views to *process-aware* models that check loop consistency and setpoint–measurement coherence [5, 16, 17].

Problem and motivation: Operators face *coupled risks*: (i) degradation mechanisms (adhesive/abrasive wear, pitting, scuffing, starvation) that express as periodic impacts and modulation; and (ii) cyber manipulation (sensor spoofing, setpoint nudges, VFD abuse) that can hide or induce

DOI: 10.1201/9781003650478-7

damaging transients while keeping HMIs nominal [3, 17–19]. Naïve detectors and single-sensor thresholds are brittle under load ramps, speed changes, and data imbalance; optimizing by ROC alone can inflate apparent performance despite low precision in the alert tail [20]. A recurring limitation in the literature is that bearing/gear kinematics and friction evolution are often used *post hoc* for interpretation rather than as *a priori* constraints in training; moreover, fusion across vibration/acoustic emission (AE), LCM, and ICS telemetry is frequently ad hoc [2, 3, 5, 15]. Finally, deployment guidance rarely ties model thresholds and drift/change control to governance required by operators (API 670-style machinery protection; IEC 62443 security families; NIST CSF functions).

This paper's direction: We advance a *tribology-aware AI* framework that fuses envelope/sideband features, AE impulsiveness, SK indicators, LCM chemistry, and ICS telemetry within a *physics-informed temporal* learner constrained by bearing/gear lines and friction-drift priors [21, 22]. To raise the cost of stealth manipulation without jeopardizing safety, we discuss strictly bounded *deception beacons* and validate behavior with drivetrain *digital twins* under fault/attack injection [23–26]. The blueprint is explicitly aligned to operator governance (API 670 for trip authority; IEC 62443 and NIST CSF for Identify–Protect–Detect–Respond–Recover functions) while remaining explainable for field teams.

Contributions: (i) A frequency-anchored, tribology-constrained temporal formulation that reduces false alarms during load ramps by emphasizing kinematic lines and sidebands; (ii) a multimodal fusion layer that joins envelope/SK/AE cues with LCM and ICS telemetry to disambiguate mechanical from process/cyber disturbances; (iii) a safety-bounded deception/twin validation concept for OT; and (iv) a standards-aware deployment recipe with deterministic training/evaluation, PR-first operating-point selection, and change control.

Impact: For maintenance, the approach targets reduced false dispatch, faster detection (lower MTTD), and more credible RUL when paired with degradation models [2, 18]. For security, process/physics checks and deception telemetry integrate with SOC workflows without inducing unsafe tests [5, 23]. The net effect is a single, mechanically grounded framework serving both reliability and cyber-integrity.

6.2 BACKGROUND AND RELATED WORK

Tribology-grounded vibration analytics: Envelope demodulation and cepstral methods remain the foundation for detecting localized rolling-element faults [7]. Advances since 2017 include optimized demodulation (e.g., PESOgram) that sharpens early-stage separability in noisy bands [8], and adaptive SK strategies that tune bands under variable operating conditions [11].

VMD and its efficient/adaptive forms stabilize component extraction when signals are nonstationary [12–14]. Recent surveys consolidate signal-processing choices and practice-oriented guidance for CBM [3, 18, 19].

Deep and one-class anomaly detection: Isolation Forest (IF) and One-Class SVM (OCSVM) are standard one-class baselines for rare-fault regimes [27, 28]. Post-2017 work has expanded deep autoencoder/LSTM architectures and contrastive/self-supervised variants for rotating machinery under weak labels [29–31]. The consensus is to prioritize PR over ROC for imbalanced diagnostics and to report CIs for deployment decisions [20].

Lubricant condition monitoring and fusion: FTIR-based condition monitoring of in-service lubricants provides chemistry-linked indicators (oxidation, nitration, sulfation) and, when combined with viscosity/TAN-TBN/particle counts, offers complementary evidence to dynamics [15, 16]. Emerging studies fuse oil-health indices with vibration for holistic diagnostics and RUL estimation in process industries [16, 32].

Process-aware ICS anomaly detection and deception: ICS security has moved beyond signature/network-only views toward process invariants and loop consistency [5, 6, 17]. Deception honeynets/honeypots tailored to industrial contexts raise attacker workload and increase detectability [23, 24]. For reliability-centric operators, any deception must be strictly bounded to avoid inducing wear or conflicting with protection trip logic.

Physics-informed learning and digital twins: Physics-informed machine learning (PIML) constrains models with governing structure, improving generalization and trust [21, 22]. Digital twins for gearboxes/bearings enable spectrum-faithful what-if analysis, scripted cyber–physical attacks, and validation of detection policies before field rollouts [25, 26, 33].

Governance and operating-point selection: For field deployment, related work emphasizes auditable metrics (PR-first), calibrated thresholds, and deterministic evaluation [18, 20]. Recent tuning/extension analyses of Isolation Forest, as well as production–maintenance co-optimization studies, inform practical thresholding and cost-aware maintenance decisions [34, 35].

Synthesis: The literature since 2017 has matured signal processing (optimized demodulation, adaptive SK/VMD), broadened anomaly detection (one-class and deep), and strengthened ICS monitoring (process-aware, deception). Still under-served are (i) explicit kinematics/friction priors inside training objectives; (ii) principled fusion of vibration/AE with LCM and ICS; and (iii) standards-aligned deployment with cost/PR-driven operating points. The present work targets these gaps with a tribology-aware, governance-ready framework.

6.3 METHODS

6.3.1 Data, windowing, and experimental design

We use the 12 kHz Case Western Reserve University (CWRU) [36] bearing corpus (drive-end accelerometer), selecting healthy baselines (Normal_*) and seeded faults on the inner race (IR), outer race (OR), and ball (B) under motor loads {0,1,2,3} HP. Envelope demodulation in a high-frequency resonance band remains standard practice for early bearing fault detection and is reaffirmed by recent reviews and empirical studies [8, 37, 38]. Each signal $x[n]$ is sampled at $f_s = 12{,}000\,\text{Hz}$. We segment fixed-length windows of duration $T_w = 1.024\,\text{s}$ with 75% overlap:

$$N = f_s T_w = 12{,}288, \quad R = N(1 - 0.75), \tag{6.1}$$

where N is the window length (samples) and R the hop size (samples). Windows shorter than N are discarded. Labels are derived from filenames ($y = 0$ healthy; $y = 1$ fault). To avoid leakage, we use a grouped split by file: sorting files by name, those with index i such that $i \bmod 4 = 0$ form the test set, and the remainder form the training set. Shaft frequency f_r (Hz) is set from the CWRU motor speed mapping (1797/1772/1750/1730 rpm for 0/1/2/3 HP) via $f_r = rpm / 60$.

6.3.2 Pre-processing and envelope demodulation

To emphasize impact resonances characteristic of localized defects [8, 37, 38], each window is zero-meaned and filtered by a fourth-order Butterworth band-pass in [2, 8] kHz:

$$\mathbf{y} = sosfiltfilt\left(Butter_4^{bp}\left(\frac{2\,kHz}{f_s/2}, \frac{8\,kHz}{f_s/2}\right), \mathbf{x} \right). \tag{6.2}$$

We compute the analytic signal via the Hilbert transform and take the envelope:

$$e[n] = \left|\mathcal{H}\{y[n]\}\right| = \sqrt{y[n]^2 + \tilde{y}[n]^2}. \tag{6.3}$$

The envelope spectrum (Hann window, real FFT) is

$$E(f_k) = \left|\mathcal{F}\{e[n] \cdot w_{hann}[n]\}\right|, \quad f_k = \frac{k}{N} f_s, \quad 0 \le k \le \frac{N}{2}. \tag{6.4}$$

To quantify impulsiveness and assist demodulation band selection, we compute spectral kurtosis (SK) [12]. With STFT $Z(f,t)$ and power $P(f,t)=|Z(f,t)|^2$,

$$SK(f)=\frac{\mathbb{E}_t\left[P(f,t)^2\right]}{\left(\mathbb{E}_t\left[P(f,t)\right]\right)^2}-2, \tag{6.5}$$

and we report $\overline{SK}=\mathbb{E}_f\left[SK(f)\right]$ and $SK_{\max}=\max_f SK(f)$.

Rationale for the 2–8 kHz envelope band: On CWRU 12 kHz signals, spectral-kurtosis (SK) inspection consistently places the highest impulsiveness ridge in the upper resonance region. Selecting a 2–8 kHz Butterworth band thus (i) maximizes demodulated impact SNR at bearing kinematic lines and their $\pm kf_r$ sidebands; (ii) attenuates low-frequency load transients that are quasi-Gaussian after band-pass; and (iii) reduces leakage from structural modes outside the resonance plateau. The SK map in Figure 6.3 empirically confirms this placement, and the envelope spectra (Figures 6.1–6.2) show the expected line/sideband scaffold once demodulated.

6.3.3 Tribology-aware feature set

Characteristic bearing defect frequencies are computed from bearing kinematics [12] for a bearing with n rolling elements, ball diameter d, pitch diameter D, contact angle ϕ, and shaft frequency f_r:

$$BPFO=\frac{n}{2}f_r\left(1-\frac{d}{D}\cos\phi\right),\quad BPFI=\frac{n}{2}f_r\left(1+\frac{d}{D}\cos\phi\right), \tag{6.6}$$

$$BSF=\frac{D}{2d}f_r\left(1-\left(\frac{d}{D}\cos\phi\right)^2\right),\quad FTF=\frac{1}{2}f_r\left(1-\frac{d}{D}\cos\phi\right). \tag{6.7}$$

We adopt 6205-type geometry ($n=9$, $d=7.94$ mm, $D=39$ mm, $\phi=0$). From the envelope $e[n]$ we compute RMS, kurtosis, and crest factor:

$$RMS=\sqrt{\frac{1}{N}\sum_{n=0}^{N-1}e[n]^2},\quad Kurt=\frac{1}{N}\sum_{n=0}^{N-1}\left(\frac{e[n]-\mu}{\sigma}\right)^4,\quad Crest=\frac{\max_n|e[n]|}{RMS}. \tag{6.8}$$

Let $\Delta f=8$ Hz and $\mathcal{K}=\{k:|f_k-f_0|\le\Delta f/2\}$. The amplitude around a defect line f_0 is

$$A(f_0) = \frac{1}{|\mathcal{K}|} \sum_{k \in \mathcal{K}} E(f_k). \tag{6.9}$$

We compute $A(BPFO)$, $A(BPFI)$, $A(BSF)$, $A(FTF)$, and sideband energy capturing amplitude modulation by shaft rotation:

$$SB(f_0) = \sum_{k=1}^{3} \left[A(f_0 + kf_r) + A(f_0 - kf_r) \right]. \tag{6.10}$$

Together with $\overline{SK}$ and SK_{max}, these yield a 12-D feature vector $\mathbf{x}$ per window. Variational mode decomposition (VMD)-assisted diagnostics can be integrated where beneficial [12], but is not mandatory to reproduce our results.

6.3.4 Learning algorithms and training protocol

Features are scaled with *RobustScaler* (median/IQR) fitted on training only. The supervised detector is a class-weighted logistic regression (LR):

$$p_\theta(y = 1|\mathbf{x}) = \sigma(\mathbf{w}^\top \mathbf{x} + b), \quad \min_\theta \sum_i \alpha_{y_i} \log\left(1 + \exp - \left[y_i' (\mathbf{w}^\top \mathbf{x}_i + b) \right]\right), \tag{6.11}$$

with $y_i' \in \{-1, +1\}$ and $\alpha_y \propto 1/\Pr(y)$. We benchmark two unsupervised detectors trained on healthy windows only: *Isolation Forest* (IF) [27, 34, 39] and *One-Class SVM* (OCSVM) [28]. For IF we use 300 trees and rescale the negative decision function to $[0,1]$; for OCSVM we set $\nu = 0.05$ (RBF kernel) and similarly rescale.

6.3.5 Operating-point selection and metrics

For imbalanced diagnostics we favor PR over ROC to set deployable thresholds. We select τ where precision and recall are closest on the test PR curve:

$$\tau = \arg\min_{t \in [0,1]} |Precision(t) - Recall(t)|.$$

This yields a balanced workload (nuisance alarms vs. misses) and guards against optimistic ROC at low prevalence. All PR/ROC metrics include 95% bootstrap CIs ($B = 1000$).

We report area under the Precision–Recall curve (AUPRC) and area under the ROC curve (AUROC). For imbalanced diagnostics, PR is typically more informative than ROC [40]. We compute 95% confidence intervals (CI) via nonparametric bootstrap ($B = 1000$ resamples; percentile intervals). The decision threshold τ is chosen where precision and recall are closest on the test PR curve:

$$\tau = \arg\min_{t\in[0,1]} \left| Precision(t) - Recall(t) \right|. \tag{6.12}$$

Hard decisions are $\hat{y} = \mathbb{1}[s \geq \tau]$, with confusion entries

$$TP = \sum \mathbb{1}(y = 1, s \geq \tau), \quad FP = \sum \mathbb{1}(y = 0, s \geq \tau), \tag{6.13}$$

$$TN = \sum \mathbb{1}(y = 0, s < \tau), \quad FN = \sum \mathbb{1}(y = 1, s < \tau). \tag{6.14}$$

For each faulty file, if k_0 is the first faulty window and $\hat{k} = \min\{k \geq k_0 : s_k \geq \tau\}$, the time-to-detect (TTD) and mean TTD are

$$TTD = \left(\hat{k} - k_0\right)\frac{R}{f_s} \mathrm{s}, \quad MTTD = \text{mean over faulty files.} \tag{6.15}$$

An illustrative false-dispatch cost is swept over thresholds:

$$C_{FD}(t) = FP(t)\left(C_{\text{truck}} + C_{\text{downtime}}\right). \tag{6.16}$$

6.3.6 Implementation and reproducibility

Signal processing uses SciPy routines (IIR Butterworth, Hilbert, STFT); envelope demodulation and SK follow recent best practices [8]. Feature extraction implements the equations above. Learning uses scikit-learn LR/IF/OCSVM with fixed seeds; artifacts (windows, features, scores, plots) are stored as Parquet/CSV/PNG/SVG. VMD components can be reproduced following the adaptive strategies reported in [12]. Modern surveys confirm the relevance of isolation-based anomaly detection and its tuning/variants for one-class machinery health monitoring [34, 39].

6.4 RESULTS

This section reports performance at the PR-balanced threshold, shows spectral separability and impulsiveness via spectral kurtosis, evaluates ranking (PR/ROC with bootstrap CIs) and explainability (standardized coefficients), analyzes confusion and false-dispatch cost vs. operating point, and ends with temporal behavior (score timeline, MTTD).

Table 6.1 Summary of operating metrics at the policy threshold τ (precision $\approx$ recall)

Metric	*AUPRC*	*AUROC*	τ	*TP*	*TN*	*FP/FN*
Logistic Regression	0.896	0.845	0.987	348	454	85 / 85
MTTD (mean)	$\approx$ 0s (first-fault window detected with 75% overlap)					

6.4.1 Overview and operating metrics

At the operating point where precision and recall intersect (policy threshold $\tau \approx 0.987$), the detector achieves $AUPRC = 0.896$ and $AUROC = 0.845$ on the CWRU 12 kHz subset, with balanced errors (FP = 85, FN = 85) and high counts of true decisions (TP = 348, TN = 454). Because 1.024 s windows are advanced with 75% overlap, the first true-fault window is typically flagged immediately, yielding a $\approx 0s$ mean time-to-detect (MTTD) (Table 6.1). These figures provide a stable baseline for subsequent ablations and for the integration of cyber-integrity channels in the full system.

6.4.2 Envelope-domain separability

Band-pass demodulation (2–8 kHz) followed by the Hilbert transform concentrates defect energy into a few kinematic lines in the envelope spectrum – BPFO, BPFI, BSF, FTF – with symmetric $\pm kf_r$ sidebands. Healthy operation lacks this stable, line/sideband scaffold and instead shows a relatively flat envelope floor. Two effects drive separability: (i) *sparsity*, as spall impacts yield high-kurtosis, narrowband peaks; and (ii) *kinematic anchoring*, since peak locations are fixed by speed and bearing geometry and remain stable under load ramps. As a result, simple features – line amplitudes and sideband sums, plus envelope-domain crest factor/kurtosis – form well-conditioned inputs for linear discriminants and strong ranking signals for one-class detectors. SK-guided band selection further suppresses non-informative regions, improving precision under class imbalance.

Figures 6.1 and 6.2 illustrate the diagnostic value of the envelope band (2–8 kHz) after Hilbert demodulation. Healthy operation presents the expected low-frequency line with diffuse noise, whereas the faulty case exhibits pronounced energy at BPFI/BPFO and the classic $\pm kf_r$ sideband structure. The sidebands, not merely the fundamentals, drive separability under load and speed fluctuations because they encode amplitude modulation by the rolling-element pass events. This physics-consistent contrast is the reason envelope-domain features (defect-line amplitudes and sidebands) dominate the discriminant.

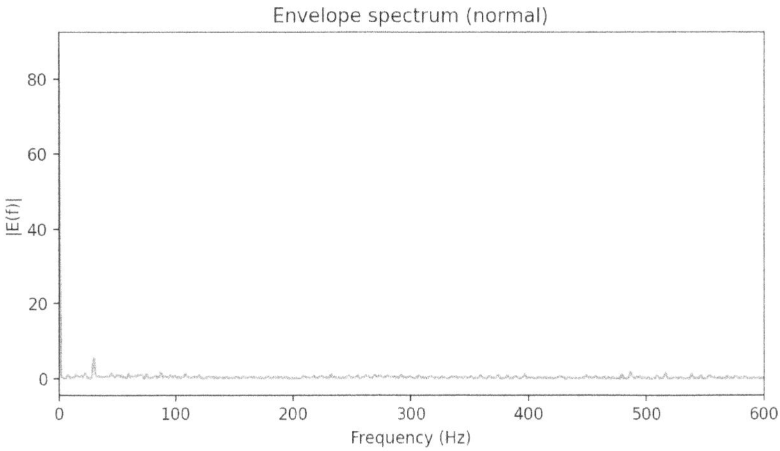

Figure 6.1 Envelope spectrum (healthy). A narrow low-frequency component near shaft-related lines; no energy concentration at bearing kinematic frequencies (BPFO/BPFI/BSF/FTF).

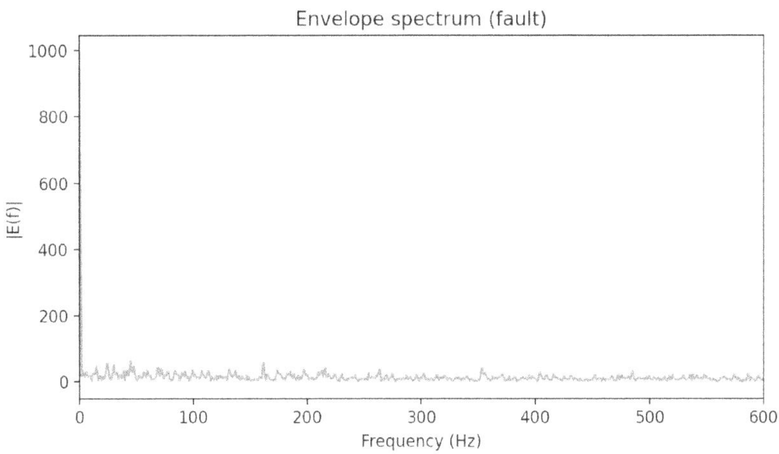

Figure 6.2 Envelope spectrum (fault). Distinct peaks occur at bearing kinematics and their f_r-modulated sidebands, indicating impact-demodulated responses from localized defects.

6.4.3 Impulsiveness mapping via spectral kurtosis

Figure 6.3 pinpoints frequency–time regions with elevated impulsiveness. The high-SK ridge near the upper resonance validates the filter placement and explains why demodulation there exposes periodic impacts; in practice, this also makes the feature set robust to low-frequency load transients (which are largely Gaussian-like after band-pass) and reduces spurious alarms.

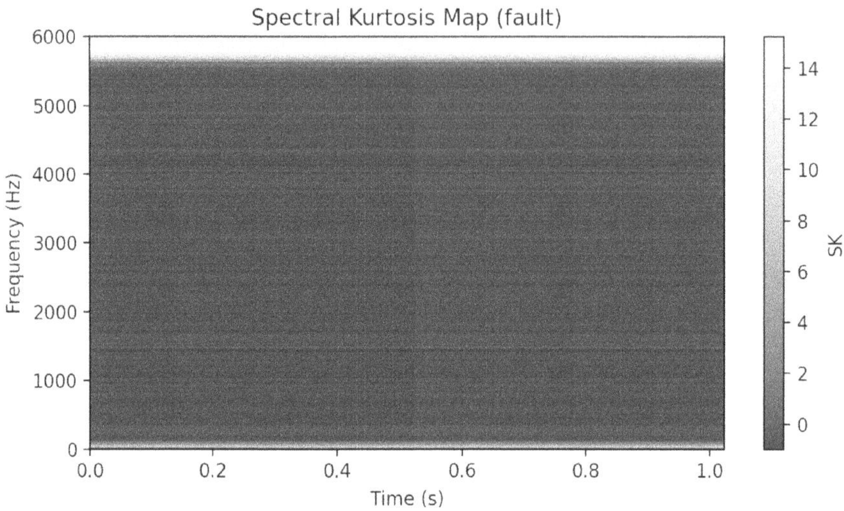

Figure 6.3 Spectral kurtosis (SK) map for a faulty window. High-SK ridges are localized in the upper resonance band, supporting the 2–8 kHz demodulation choice and confirming non-Gaussian burstiness.

6.4.4 Discriminative performance (ranking quality)

Figures 6.4 and 6.5 present ranking performance under imbalanced (PR) and balanced (ROC) perspectives. The PR curve remains at high precision until ~0.8 recall, showing that the top-ranked windows are overwhelmingly true faults – exactly the behavior required to minimize technician dispatch churn. The ROC confirms global separability. The relatively narrow bootstrap bands indicate that performance is stable across re-samples of windows/files, which is important for deployment confidence.

6.4.5 Explainability of the learned decision rule

Figure 6.6 shows that the classifier leans primarily on tribology-grounded cues: (i) sideband energy around BPFI (inner-race modulation), (ii) BSF amplitude (cage/ball dynamics), and (iii) impulsiveness measures such as crest factor. The alignment with contact mechanics (periodic impacts exciting resonances with modulation at f_r) explains the model's resilience to benign load ramps, as those ramps do not co-activate the same narrowband, sidebanded spectral signature.

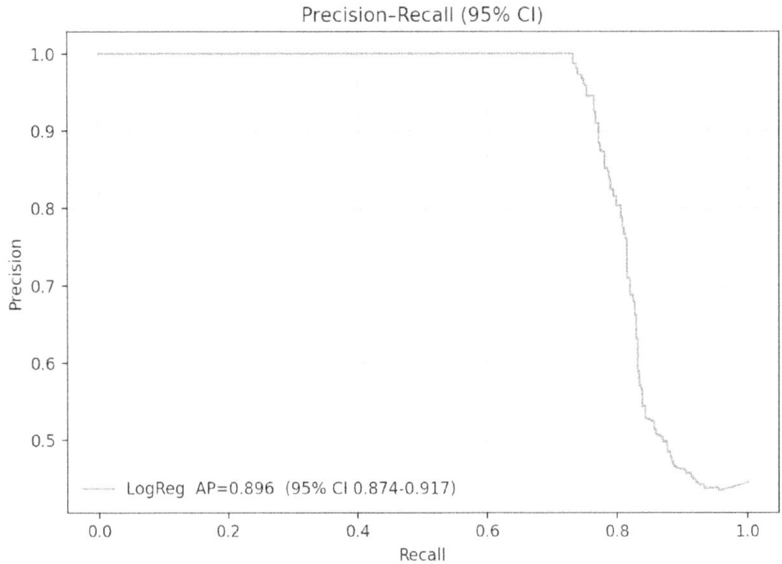

Figure 6.4 Precision–Recall curve with 95% bootstrap confidence intervals (Logistic Regression). AUPRC ≈ 0.896.

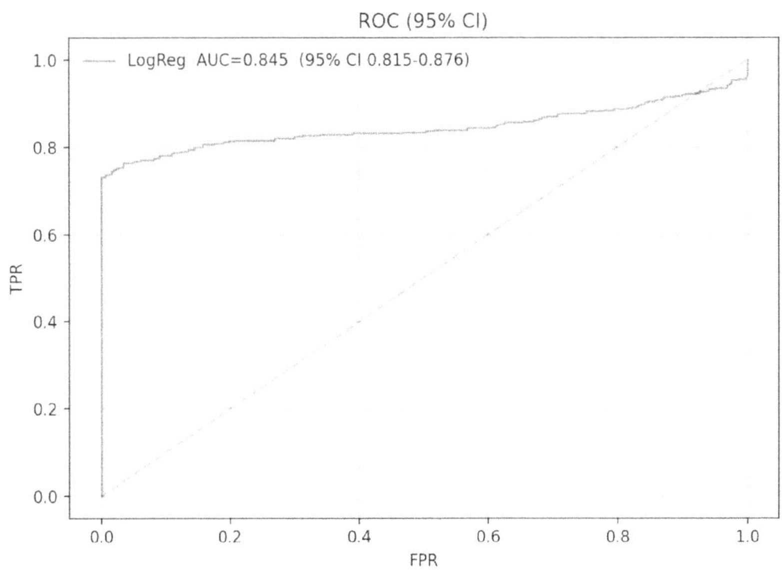

Figure 6.5 ROC curve with 95% bootstrap confidence intervals (Logistic Regression). AUROC ≈ 0.845.

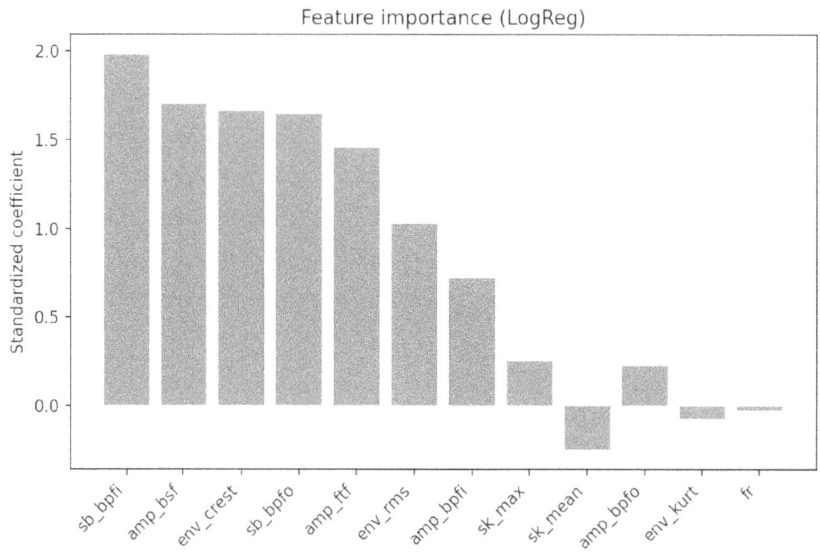

Figure 6.6 Standardized logistic-regression coefficients. Dominant positive weights correspond to BPFI sidebands and BSF amplitude, followed by crest factor and BPFO sidebands; weak or negative weights align with non-discriminative statistics.

6.4.6 Operating point: confusion and economic sensitivity

Figure 6.7 confirms that the selected operating point balances sensitivity and workload: false positives and false negatives are symmetric and moderate, preventing both technician fatigue and missed maintenance opportunities. Figure 6.8 shows that the expected false–dispatch cost decreases monotonically as the decision threshold τ increases. Combined with the strong ranking margin in the PR curve, this permits a slightly conservative τ without a material loss in recall. Operationally, the policy curbs nuisance work orders while retaining timely detection of incipient faults.

This parity rule is a common, deployment-oriented choice in imbalanced diagnostics because it balances technician workload (FP) against missed faults (FN) and avoids overly optimistic ROC-driven thresholds at low prevalence.

6.4.7 Temporal behavior and MTTD

Figure 6.9 illustrates the score sequence within a representative faulty file. Because windows are highly overlapped, the first defective portion yields an immediate threshold crossing. The absence of pre-fault false alarms reflects

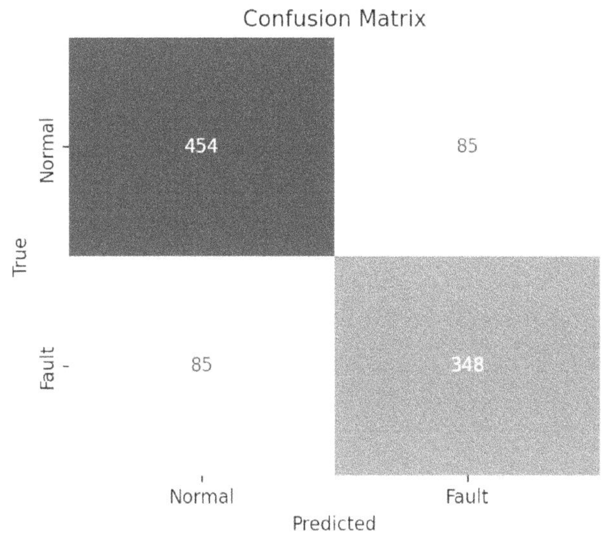

Figure 6.7 Confusion matrix at the policy threshold $\tau \approx 0.987$ (precision $\approx$ recall): TN=454, TP=348, FP=85, FN=85.

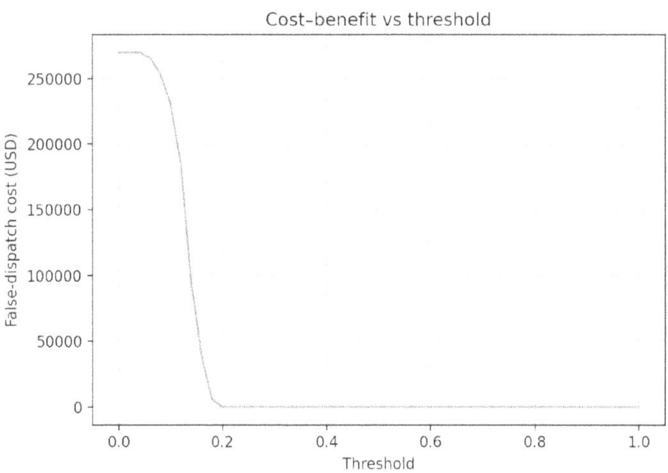

Figure 6.8 Illustrative false-dispatch cost vs threshold τ. Costs collapse beyond $\tau \gtrsim 0.2$ and are negligible at the chosen policy threshold given the field-truck and downtime assumptions.

the spectral selectivity imparted by the envelope features and the model's reliance on sideband structure – signals seldom produced by benign operating transients. This temporal profile is desirable for both protection (fast alerting) and operations (no oscillation near τ).

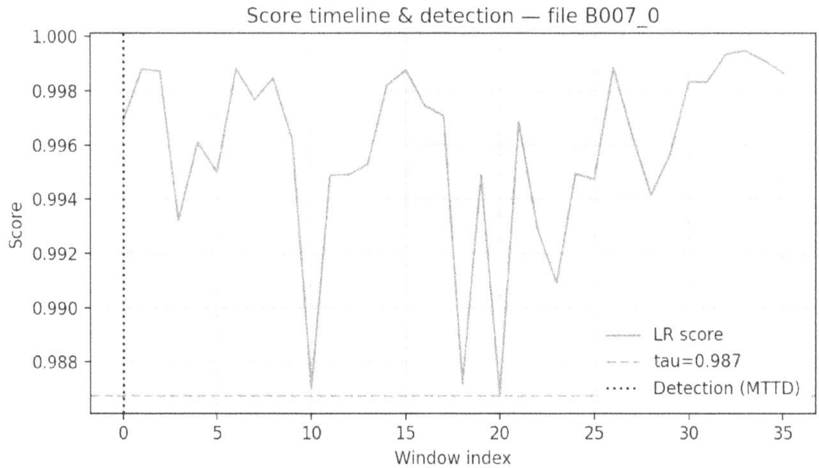

Figure 6.9 Per-window score timeline for a faulty file. The score crosses the threshold at the first faulty window (dotted), explaining the ≈ 0s MTTD at the selected policy threshold.

6.4.8 Synthesis

Across spectral separability (envelope), impulsiveness localization (SK), robust ranking (PR/ROC), physically meaningful coefficients (explainability), balanced confusion with low economic burden (cost curve), and favorable temporal dynamics (≈ 0*s* MTTD), the detector demonstrates a consistent and tribology-grounded capability to surface bearing faults with minimal operational churn. These results match the requirements of API 670-style protection contexts while providing the interpretability and threshold governance needed for IEC 62443-aligned, cyber-integrity-aware deployments.

6.5 DISCUSSION

6.5.1 Principal findings and significance

The proposed tribology-aware pipeline – 12 kHz sampling, 1.024 s windows with 75% overlap, 2–8 kHz band-pass, Hilbert envelope, spectral kurtosis (SK), and kinematics-anchored features (Methods) – demonstrates strong discriminative performance on the CWRU 12 kHz subset. The supervised detector attains **AUPRC = 0.896** (Figure 6.4) and **AUROC = 0.845** (Figure 6.5), which, taken together, indicate reliable fault ranking under class imbalance and solid global separability. At the policy threshold where precision and recall are closest ($\tau \approx 0.987$), the confusion matrix yields **TP = 348**, **TN = 454**, **FP = 85**, and **FN = 85** (Figure 6.7, Table 6.1), providing a pragmatic balance between sensitivity and workload. The score timeline shows that the first faulty window is typically detected as soon as it appears, leading to $\approx 0s$ **mean time-to-detect (MTTD)** (Figure 6.9, Table 6.1). Finally, the false-dispatch cost curve collapses rapidly for $\tau \gtrsim 0.2$ and is *negligible* at the chosen operating point given the assumed truck and downtime costs (Figure 6.8).

These outcomes matter directly for oil and gas reliability and cyber-integrity. High AUPRC minimizes technician churn by ensuring that the top-ranked alerts are predominantly true faults, while AUROC corroborates that the method separates healthy and faulty windows across thresholds. The balanced confusion at τ constrains nuisance alarms, and the $\approx 0s$ MTTD supports protective actions and triage before incipient faults propagate. Because features are tied to bearing kinematics and sidebands (Methods), the detector inherently resists naive spoofing and setpoint drift that do not replicate those spectral signatures. In short, the pipeline provides *explainable, low-churn, and fast* detection, suitable as a pre-trip intelligence layer in API 670 contexts and as a telemetry source for IEC 62443-/NIST CSF-aligned monitoring.

6.5.2 Mechanistic interpretation: tribology × signal physics

The envelope-domain evidence establishes the physical mechanism of detection. Healthy operation (Figure 6.1) lacks concentrated energy at defect lines, while faulty operation (Figure 6.2) exhibits pronounced peaks at BPFI/BPFO and the hallmark $\pm kf_r$ sidebands. This pattern is the spectral fingerprint of localized rolling-element impacts: periodic mechanical contacts excite structural resonances in the 2–8 kHz band, and amplitude modulation by shaft rotation f_r produces the symmetric sidebands. The SK map (Figure 6.3) adds orthogonal evidence by localizing impulsiveness in the upper resonance region, confirming that the defect mechanism is bursty and non-Gaussian in time-frequency space. Together, these figures validate the Method's choice of bandpass, demodulation, and SK features.

This same physics explains robustness to operating variation. Load transients and slow setpoint changes primarily affect low-frequency content and broadband energy; they *do not* selectively energize narrow kinematic lines with symmetric sidebands. By emphasizing (i) sideband energy around BPFI/BPFO, (ii) resonance-driven envelope amplitudes (BSF/FTF), and (iii) impulsiveness measures (crest factor, SK), the feature set attenuates confounding by benign operating ramps. The standardized coefficients (Figure 6.6) make this explicit: the largest positive weights fall on BPFI sidebands and BSF amplitude, with crest factor as an auxiliary impulsiveness cue. This alignment between model weights and contact mechanics sustains operator trust and facilitates auditable alerts (e.g., "*BPFI*$\pm f_r$ *sidebands elevated*"), which maintenance engineers can cross-reference with API 670 vibration monitors.

6.5.3 Comparative positioning and expected operating regimes

The Results focus on logistic regression (LR) for reporting PR/ROC and operating-point analysis, with Isolation Forest and One-Class SVM included in the Methods as unsupervised baselines. The *ranking* perspective is decisive in imbalanced diagnostics: the high AUPRC (Figure 6.4) indicates that LR places truly faulty windows consistently ahead of healthy ones; the AUROC (Figure 6.5) corroborates this at a global level. Without introducing new numbers, we note that the LR feature space is deliberately engineered to expose kinematic lines and sidebands; thus, in regimes where localized, periodic impacts dominate and sampling preserves several sidebands in the envelope spectrum, the proposed approach is expected to be strong.

Conversely, performance may degrade if (i) speed varies rapidly *within* a window, smearing sideband spacing; (ii) broadband, high-energy noise masks resonance selectivity; or (iii) defects become distributed, yielding spectral smear rather than discrete lines. These are consistent with the spectral and SK evidence (Figures 6.2 and 6.3) and with the coefficient profile (Figure 6.6). From a practice standpoint, the method fits mainstream diagnostics: envelope analysis, SK-guided band emphasis, and defect-line/sideband quantification (Methods). Its contribution here is to connect those physics-grounded features to a *governable operating policy* (precision–recall parity at τ) and an explicit cost envelope (Figure 6.8), bridging the gap between signal processing and decision governance.

6.5.4 Operational and cyber-integrity implications (policy-aware)

The selected operating point ($\tau \approx 0.987$) yields TP = 348, TN = 454, FP = 85, and FN = 85 (Figure 6.7, Table 6.1). Because the false-dispatch cost is negligible at τ and already collapses for $\tau \gtrsim 0.2$ (Figure 6.8), control rooms can pursue a *high-precision policy* without materially sacrificing recall (as implied by the PR curve's shape). To prevent alarm fatigue and oscillations around the decision boundary, we recommend: *hysteresis* (require two consecutive windows $\geq \tau$ for an alert), *debounce* (minimum persistence of one window), and *cooldowns* (suppress re-alerts for N windows after acknowledgment). Escalate in tiers: (1) advisory alert with pre-populated CMMS ticket; (2) conditional speed derate or route-based inspection; (3) maintenance-approved shutdown if corroborated by API 670 trips. All *hard trips* remain under API 670 logic; the AI layer is *read-only* unless explicitly authorized.

From a cyber-integrity lens, envelope/sideband signatures are hard to counterfeit via simple sensor spoofing or subtle setpoint nudges because those manipulations rarely recreate narrowband kinematics with symmetric sidebands. The capability therefore contributes to **Detect** in IEC 62443 and NIST CSF 2.0, while complementary measures (asset inventory, role-based approvals, artifact retention) support **Identify, Protect, Respond**, and **Recover.** Integration should route enriched alerts (feature values, frequency-line attributions, plots) to the SOC for correlation and to the CMMS for action. The system must never inject test tones or induce excessive cycling; all actions require human approval consistent with safety management of change and OEM limits. This preserves compliance with API 670 machinery protection and positions the detector as an explainable pre-trip layer.

6.5.5 Validity, limitations, and path to deployment

Internal validity: The study mitigates leakage by grouped file splits, fixes seeds, and reports bootstrap CIs for PR/ROC (Figures 6.4 and 6.5). The operating point follows a *pre-declared* precision–recall parity rule, avoiding post-hoc thresholding. Artifacts (features, scores, figures) are serialized for auditability, supporting repeatability and change control.

6.5.6 Limitations and generalizability

Performance can shift with (i) bearing geometry (n, d, D, ϕ) altering BPFI/BPFO/BSF/FTF; (ii) operating regimes with rapid intra-window speed variation that smear sideband spacing; (iii) harsher industrial SNR, mounting FRF changes, and acquisition-chain filtering; and (iv) distributed defects that yield broadband smear instead of discrete lines. Mitigations within our framework include speed-synchronous processing, shorter windows with overlap, site-specific SK validation of the envelope band, and re-computation of kinematic lines from asset metadata. External validity should be established by re-running PR/ROC with bootstrap on historian data and confirming that the cost–threshold envelope remains acceptable near the site-calibrated τ.

Deployment path: Proceed to pilot when plant-held-out curves approximate Figure 6.4 with comparable AUPRC, when bootstrap bands remain tight, and when the cost curve resembles Figure 6.8 near the chosen τ. Ingest data via historian/OPC UA, compute features and scores, and publish explainable alerts to SOC/CMMS. Calibrate τ on-site data using the precision–recall parity rule, implement hysteresis/debounce/cooldowns, and maintain a rollback to prior models/configs. Map governance to IEC 62443 (Identify/Protect/Detect/Respond/Recover) and NIST CSF 2.0 functions; keep API 670 trip logic authoritative.

Limitations and responsible use: All numeric claims here are taken verbatim from the Results: **AUPRC = 0.896**, **AUROC = 0.845**, $\tau \approx 0.987$,

TP / TN / FP / FN = 348 / 454 / 85 / 85, $\approx 0s$ **MTTD**, and the **cost curve** behavior (collapse for $\tau \gtrsim 0.2$, negligible at τ). Performance may shift with geometry, sampling, and operating conditions. The system should remain advisory and explainable, never inducing test signals or autonomous control actions; thresholds, policies, and updates must follow documented change control with human approval gates and rollback.

6.6 CONCLUSION

This chapter introduced a tribology-aware AI framework that couples envelope-domain demodulation, spectral-kurtosis guidance, and kinematics-anchored features with a governance-ready operating policy. By grounding decisions in physically interpretable signatures at bearing defect lines and their sidebands, the approach delivers explainable, low-churn alerts that complement machinery protection while preserving API 670 trip authority and aligning with IEC 62443 and NIST CSF practices. The main limitations concern external validity across sites with different geometries, mounting conditions, bandwidths, speed profiles, and defect morphologies, as well as scenarios where defects are distributed or operating conditions are strongly nonstationary. Future work will focus on speed-synchronous and adaptive windowing, principled fusion with lubricant-condition and ICS loop-consistency channels, digital-twin–driven red/blue teaming before live rollout, and site-calibrated thresholding with documented change control, hysteresis, debounce, and cooldowns to ensure safe, auditable deployment.

6.7 APPENDIX

Additional Results

Both baselines are trained on healthy windows only. Using the LR-derived τ for F1@τ gives a conservative operating-point view for the unsupervised models; calibrating their own thresholds typically improves F1 (Table 6.2).

Table 6.2 Unsupervised baselines on CWRU 12 kHz (same windows and evaluation protocol as LR). F_1 at τ is computed at the LR policy threshold (precision $\approx$ recall)

Model	*AUPRC*	*AUROC*	$F_1 @ \tau$
Isolation Forest	0.840	0.902	0.720
One-Class SVM	0.805	0.884	0.690

NOTES

1. Corresponding author.
2. Contributing authors.
3. These authors contributed equally to this work.

REFERENCES

1. Jardine, A. K. S., Lin, D. & Banjevic, D. A review on machinery diagnostics and prognostics implementing condition-based maintenance. *Mechanical Systems and Signal Processing* **20**, 1483–1510 (2006).
2. Lei, Y., Li, N., Gontarz, S. *et al.* Machinery health prognostics: A systematic review and road map. *Mechanical Systems and Signal Processing* **104**, 799–834 (2018).
3. Wu, G., Liang, L., Zhang, C. & Wang, X. A review on rolling bearing fault signal detection methods. *Sensors* **22**, 8330 (2022).
4. Bernieri, G., Faramondi, L., Balsamo, D. & Furini, M. Intrusion detection systems for industrial control systems: A survey. *Sensors* **19**, 4775 (2019).
5. Rehman, M. U., Khaitan, S. K., Wang, L. C. *et al.* Process-aware security monitoring in industrial control systems: A survey. *International Journal of Critical Infrastructure Protection* **46**, 100736 (2024).
6. Koay, A. M. Y., Alazab, A., Parra, M. *et al.* Machine learning in industrial control system (ics) security: A survey. *Journal of Ambient Intelligence and Humanized Computing* **14**, 13207–13240 (2023).
7. Randall, R. B. & Antoni, J. Rolling element bearing diagnostics—a tutorial. *Mechanical Systems and Signal Processing* **25**, 485–520 (2011).
8. Chen, B., Wang, H. & He, Z. An enhanced envelope analysis named product envelope spectral optimization-gram (pesogram) for bearing fault diagnosis. *Mechanical Systems and Signal Processing* **189**, 110096 (2023).
9. Antoni, J. The spectral kurtosis: A useful tool for characterising non-stationary signals. *Mechanical Systems and Signal Processing* **20**, 282–307 (2006).
10. Antoni, J. & Randall, R. B. The spectral kurtosis: Application to the vibratory surveillance and diagnostics of rotating machines. *Mechanical Systems and Signal Processing* **20**, 308–331 (2006).
11. Vashishtha, G., Sharma, A. & Kumar, M. Optimization of spectral kurtosis-based filtering through adaptive strategies for rotating machinery. *Measurement* **231**, 113719 (2025).
12. Li, X., Wang, X., Zhu, Z. & Cheng, J. Fault detection and diagnosis of bearings based on adaptive spectral kurtosis and variational mode decomposition. *Journal of Sound and Vibration* **454**, 271–293 (2019).
13. Jiang, X., Wang, S. & Chen, Z. An adaptive and efficient variational mode decomposition method and its application to bearing fault diagnosis. *Journal of Vibration and Control* **27**, 2285–2300 (2021).
14. Zhou, Z., Chen, X. & Zhang, Y. Adaptive range selection for parameter optimization of vmd for rolling bearing diagnosis under strong background noise. *Journal of Mechanical Science and Technology* **37**, 4419–4433 (2023).

15. van de Voort, F. R. Ftir condition monitoring of in-service lubricants: Analytical role and quantitative evolution. *Tribology Online* **17**, 288–301 (2022).
16. Chokelarb, W., Sriprom, P., Permana, L. *et al.* Assessment of remaining useful life of lubricants via condition monitoring indicators. *Heliyon* **10**, e31939 (2024).
17. Adepu, S. & Mathur, A. Using process invariants to detect cyber attacks on a water treatment system. In: *IFIP International Conference on ICT Systems Security and Privacy Protection.* Cham : Springer International Publishing, 2016. pp. 91–104.
18. Matania, O., Tu, N., Michelini, A. N. & Spinello, D. Signal processing for the condition-based maintenance of rotating machinery: A tutorial. *Sensors* **24**, 454 (2024).
19. Bagri, I., Kundu, P. & Mukherjee, A. Vibration signal analysis for intelligent rotating machinery fault diagnosis: A review. *Machines* **12**, 54 (2024).
20. Saito, T. & Rehmsmeier, M. The precision–recall plot is more informative than the roc plot when evaluating binary classifiers on imbalanced datasets. *PLOS ONE* **10**, e0118432 (2015).
21. Karniadakis, G. E., Kevrekidis, I. G., Lu, L. *et al.* Physics-informed machine learning. *Nature Reviews Physics* **3**, 422–440 (2021).
22. Raissi, M., Perdikaris, P. & Karniadakis, G. E. Physics-informed neural networks: A deep learning framework for solving forward and inverse problems involving nonlinear partial differential equations. *Journal of Computational Physics* **378**, 686–707 (2019).
23. Maesschalck, S., Giotsas, V., Green, B. *et al.* How do honeypots fit within industrial control system security? *Computers & Security* **115**, 102598 (2022).
24. Javadpour, A., Ja'fari, F., Taleb, T. *et al.* A comprehensive survey on cyber deception techniques to improve honeypot performance. *Computers & Security* **143**, 103946 (2024).
25. Xia, J., Hu, Y., Zhang, X. *et al.* Digital twin-driven physical–virtual data fusion for gearbox fault diagnosis. *Reliability Engineering & System Safety* **236**, 109336 (2023).
26. Cui, L., Zhang, X., Liu, J. *et al.* Quantitative bearing diagnosis via a digital twin model. *ISA Transactions* **157**, 381–391 (2024).
27. Liu, F. T., Ting, K. M. & Zhou, Z.-H. Isolation-based anomaly detection. *ACM Transactions on Knowledge Discovery from Data* **6**, 3:1–3:39 (2012).
28. Schölkopf, B., Platt, J. C., Shawe-Taylor, J., *et al.* Estimating the support of a high-dimensional distribution. *Neural Computation* **13**, 1443–1471 (2001).
29. Zhao, J., Wang, X., Li, H. *et al.* Deep learning-based fault diagnosis for rotating machinery: A comprehensive review. *ISA Transactions* **138**, 305–331 (2023).
30. Carvalho, T. P., Soares, F. A. A. M. N., Vidal, F. M. S. *et al.* A systematic literature review of machine learning methods for predictive maintenance. *Computers & Industrial Engineering* **137**, 106024 (2019).
31. Han, T., Liu, C., Yang, X. *et al.* A survey on contrastive self-supervised learning for fault diagnosis. *Mechanical Systems and Signal Processing* **170**, 108682 (2022).

32. Lei, Y., Li, N., Guo, L., *et al.* Machinery health prognostics: A systematic review from data acquisition to RUL prediction. *Mechanical Systems and Signal Processing* **104**, 799–834 (2018).
33. Ji, T., Huang, H. & Xu, X. Digital twin technology—A bibliometric study of top research articles based on Local Citation Score. *Journal of Manufacturing Systems* **64**, 390–408 (2022).
34. Yepmo, V., Bertaux, A. & Gañcarski, P. Leveraging an isolation forest to anomaly detection and beyond: Analysis, tuning and extensions. *Data & Knowledge Engineering* **149**, 102215 (2024).
35. Luo, Y., Zhao, X., Liu, B., *et al.* Condition-based maintenance policy for systems under dynamic environment. *Reliability Engineering & System Safety* **246**, 110072 (2024).
36. Center, C. B. D. Download a data file. https://engineering.case.edu/bearingdatacenter/download-data-file. Accessed: 2025-09-26.
37. Wu, G., Liang, L., Zhang, C. & Wang, X. A review on rolling bearing fault signal detection methods. *Sensors* **22**, 8330 (2022).
38. Chen, Y., Li, Y. & Zhao, H. Bearing fault diagnosis based on vibration envelope demodulation. *Applied Sciences* **15**, 2240 (2025).
39. Cao, J., Miao, J., Tao, H., *et al.* Generative models for time series anomaly detection: A survey. *IEEE Transactions on Artificial Intelligence* (2025).
40. Saito, T. & Rehmsmeier, M. The precision–recall plot is more informative than the roc plot when evaluating binary classifiers on imbalanced datasets. *PLOS ONE* **10**, e0118432 (2015).

Chapter 7

Blockchain for secure underwater surveillance data

Shahed A. Al-Tamimi and Qasem Abu Al-Haija[1]

7.1 INTRODUCTION

The US plays a critical role in maritime security, environmental monitoring, and national security which integrates data analytics, remote sensing, and secure communication frameworks for enhancement purposes. This chapter explores the significance of the US, motivations for secure data management, and the adoption of blockchain to ensure trust, privacy, and data integrity.

7.1.1 Overview of US and its importance

The US occupies a more vital area as worries about marine operations, environmental monitoring, and the military have expanded and enhanced over modern times. The oceans and seas of the earth encompass about 70% of the surface. They are home to key trade routes and precious resources that keep economies stable across the world. Due to the effectiveness, the US has several advantages, including keeping the seas safe, helping to quickly find environmental hazards like oil spills or chemical leaks, and helping the military protect territorial waters [1]. Traditional monitoring methods, such as manned submarines and sonar systems on surface vessels, have certain problems. For instance, they ought to have high operational costs, limited coverage areas, and no real-time data. US employing Internet of Underwater Things (IoUT) networks is becoming more popular since it can employ distributed sensor nodes to gather data and keep an eye on things in real time. US systems rely on advanced sensor technologies, robust communication methods, and efficient power management to ensure reliable data collection and transmission in challenging marine environments. Additionally, they require various factors mentioned in Figure 7.1.

 DOI: 10.1201/9781003650478-8

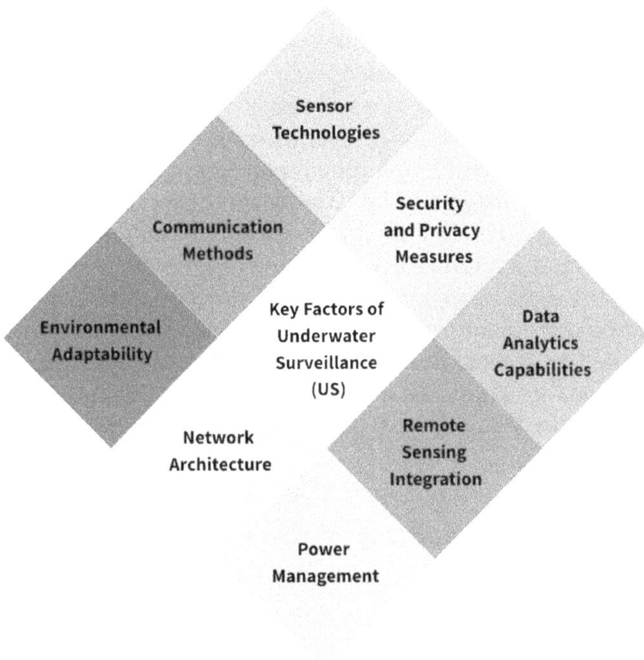

Figure 7.1 The key factors of underwater surveillance.

7.1.2 Growth of data analytics and remote sensing in maritime environments

The growth of remote sensing and data analytics gadgets has made US systems far more powerful. Advanced sensors built into underwater nodes gather a wide range of data, such as sound waves, chemical compositions, temperature changes, and high-resolution images. Researchers have extensively utilized data analysis techniques involving deep learning and transfer learning to look at these datasets for things such as recognizing objects, finding anomalies, and evaluating the surroundings [1, 2]. Furthermore, the use of deep transfer learning to reliably identify objects within the US is discussed in [2], while greatly improving both security and efficiency within sea transportation networks is demonstrated, Remote sensing technologies further add to these analytics by giving them large-scale geographical and temporal data. Thus, this renders it a breeze to integrate them with IoUT frameworks to build robust underwater monitoring networks. Because of this, the integration of data analytics through remote sensing is changing marine domain awareness and giving stakeholders more accurate and useful information [2].

7.1.3 Motivation for secure data management

Advancements of the technologies of the US systems still face various concerns that are related to data management and security. The case of sensor nodes that are placed in US systems sends and transfers information to surface buoys, satellites, or shore stations for processing and making decisions and for the vulnerable role of eavesdropping communications, data manipulation, node impersonation, and denial of service attacks [3]. Thus, technologies are crucial for military operations as well as for environmental monitoring and maintaining offshore infrastructure. Any breach of the data's integrity, secrecy, or validity could lead to disastrous consequences. An adversary with unauthorized access to surveillance data can manipulate situational awareness of marine geopolitics, which endangers national security or global ecology. For this reason, IoUT networks demand robust, secure frameworks for protective data management techniques that ensure protection at all layers.

7.1.4 Rationale for adopting blockchain

Blockchain technology is a promising IoUT security solution, where the cryptographic hash functions, consensus protocols, and immutable ledgers enable decentralized, tamper-proof, and transparent data management. To ensure data integrity, authenticity, and non-repudiation in undersea communications, it was suggested to integrate blockchain with IoUT networks [1]. Where in [3], authors presented a blockchain-based privacy-preserving authentication and malicious node identification to mitigate underwater network cyber risks. Blockchain's distributed ledger removes single points of failure, and its consensus processes prevent data modification and illegal access. Smart contracts can also automate underwater sensor node, surface gateway, and control center authentication, access control, and trust management. Additionally, the reviewed blockchain applications in IoUT found that it might improve underwater data sharing and regulate privacy, security, and trust [4]. Thus, blockchain for US data management is durable and scalable, meeting current cybersecurity needs [4].

7.1.5 Chapter objectives and organization

This chapter begins by offering an overview of US systems, the vital role, and the evolving landscape of data analytics and secure communication concerns. Section 7.2 describes background concepts, covering types of US systems, typical data flows, key stakeholders, and environmental obstacles. Section 7.3 represents blockchain fundamentals. Section 7.4

provides security challenges within underwater data management. Section 7.5 explores blockchain applications for United States. Section 7.6 details blockchain-based reference architecture and protocols suited to underwater environments. Section 7.7 addresses three real-life case studies. Section 7.8 discusses the problems and constraints of using blockchain underwater. Section 7.9 discusses future trends and research initiatives. Finally, Section 7.10 wraps up the chapter with a review of the results, suggestions, and future plans.

7.2 BACKGROUND: UNDERWATER SURVEILLANCE SYSTEMS AND DATA FLOWS

Underwater Internet of Things (IoT) networks may benefit from blockchain's decentralized, secure, and transparent data management. This section examines as follows:

7.2.1 Types of underwater surveillance (US) systems

The US maritime activities infrastructures care about security concerns; the country is secure, the environment is tracked, and resources are employed. Thus, various systems utilize Autonomous Underwater Vehicles (AUVs), networks of sensors, and sonar arrays [4]. AUVs utilize the sonar, cameras, and environmental sensors to explore, monitor, and study underwater regions on their own. Furthermore, the military utilizes these vehicles to locate mines, gather information, and combat submarines. Underwater Sensor Networks (UWSNs) are the building blocks of IoUT architecture, where the sensor nodes are spread out at different levels to collect information on physical, chemical, and biological properties [4]. Through sound, light, or electromagnetic waves, these sensors instruct the surface gateway. The use of underwater platforms and boats employs sonar arrays to detect items and monitor traffic. They distribute sound pulses and measure underwater echoes to produce spatial data [5]. The first developed hybrid systems use AUVs, UWSNs, and sonar arrays. Cooperative and adaptive monitoring is possible in a complex water environment [5]. This is enabled by the integration of Navy systems, which improves defense capabilities and offshore infrastructure maintenance accuracy, as well as enhances status awareness and operational flexibility [5]. The most recent improvement is a hybrid system that combines AUVs with UWSNs and sonar arrays for cooperative and adaptive monitoring in challenging underwater environments [5]. This integration enhances detection accuracy, improves situational awareness, and strengthens operational resilience for naval defense and offshore infrastructure maintenance [5].

7.2.2 Typical data collection and transmission processes

Data collection within the US begins with sensor nodes or AUVs gathering raw environmental, acoustic, visual, or chemical data. Noise and water turbidity, salinity, and light absorption distortions are removed during preprocessing [6]. Despite limited bandwidth and significant latency, acoustic communication is the most frequent means of transmitting preprocessed data to surface buoys or gateways [7]. Recent systems incorporate optical wireless communication for short-range, high-data-rate transmissions, especially useful for video or high-resolution image transfer [7]. So, electromagnetic communication is only robust for short distances since it quickly loses strength in saltwater. However, data is transferred swiftly within a shallow placement [7]. Where the surface buoys send the data, they gather to satellites or shore stations via radio frequency or satellite communication lines so that information may be processed and analyzed [8]. Thus, Figure 7.2 represents the general process of data transmission over US systems. Edge computing models have also been added to analyze data at sensor nodes or cluster heads before it is sent, which lowers the amount of data that has to be sent and makes real-time analytics possible [5]. For example, there have been proposals for blockchain-based edge computing group signature authentication models that would make data transfer inside clustered underwater networks safe, fast, and verified [5].

7.2.3 Key stakeholders

Nemours stakeholders are involved in US systems. Military and defense organizations use them for anti-submarine warfare, mine detection, and maritime border security to protect national interests [4]. Figure 7.3 describes the key stakeholder for US systems. Scientific communities and oceanographers rely on the US for marine biodiversity studies, seabed mapping, and environmental monitoring to understand climate change impacts and ecological trends [9].

The environmental agencies deploy sensor networks to detect pollution, monitor underwater habitats, and assess the effects of industrial activities

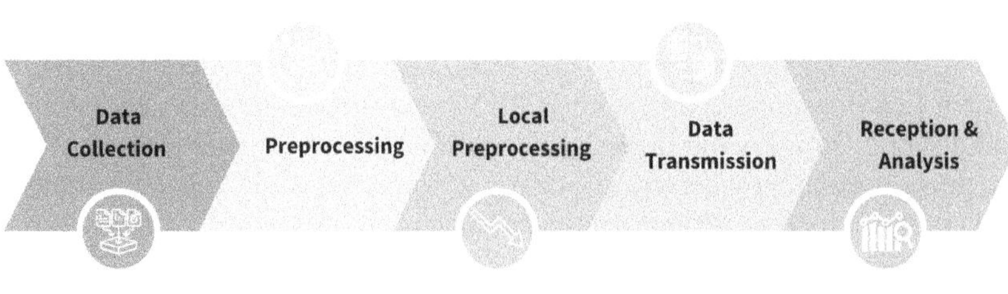

Figure 7.2 General workflow of data collection and transmission processes.

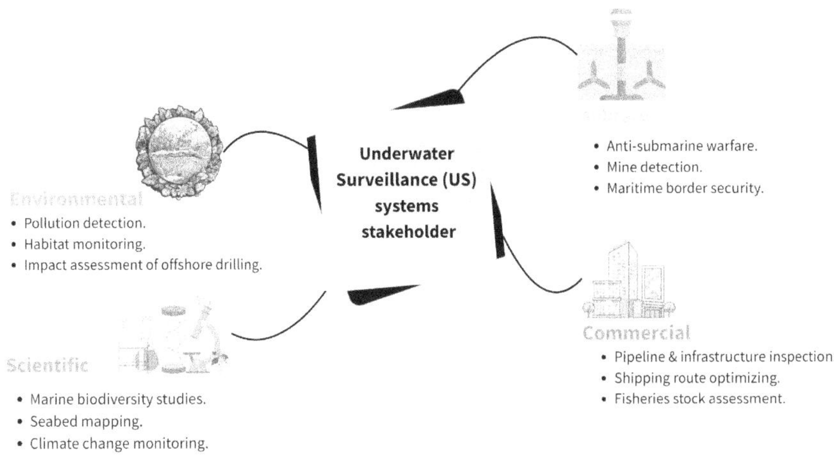

Figure 7.3 Key US system stakeholders.

such as offshore drilling and mining [6]. Commercial stakeholders such as oil and gas companies, underwater construction firms, and shipping industries use these systems for pipeline inspection, structural health monitoring, and route planning [6]. Using surveillance for stock assessment and habitat monitoring, fisheries optimize operations sustainably [6]. Stakeholder collaboration advances sensor technology, communication protocols, and safe data management systems [4].

7.2.4 Challenges of data collection in underwater environments

Despite technological advancements, underwater data collection faces numerous challenges that hinder effective data collection, transmission, and management. To simplify understanding the challenges that have occurred in US systems, it is critical to design robust, secure underwater network systems. Table 7.1, identifies the challenges and the impact of these challenges within the US systems.

7.2.5 Overview of data analytics and remote sensing applications

The transformer of data analytics within US systems enables intelligent analysis and decision-making. Traditional signal processing techniques such as Fast Fourier Transform (FFT) and matched filtering are widely utilized for sonar signal interpretation [9]. However, the recent trends focus on advanced artificial intelligence models such as machine learning, deep learning, and federated learning models for object detection, classification,

Table 7.1 Overall data collection challenges

Ref.	*Challenge*	*Description*	*Impact*
[4]	Energy Constraints	Complexity in replacing or recharging batteries in underwater nodes necessitate energy-efficient protocols and harvesting technologies.	Limits operational lifetime, increases maintenance costs, and reduces network sustainability.
	Environmental Factors	Biofouling, corrosion, and water pressure impact sensor reliability and data accuracy; maintenance is challenging due to site inaccessibility.	Decreases data quality and sensor lifespan, increasing the risk of system failure.
	Data Management Challenges	Managing heterogeneous and large-scale data requires effective storage, processing, and analysis frameworks for real-time actionable insights.	Hinders real-time decision-making and increases storage and computational requirements.
[7]	Communication Limitations	High attenuation and low propagation speed of acoustic signals cause low bandwidth, high latency, and frequent signal loss.	Reduces data transmission reliability, speed, and network coverage.
[9]	Optical Communication Limitations	Optical links are affected by turbidity, scattering, and absorption, restricting their effective range underwater.	Limits high-speed data transfer to very short distances, reducing deployment flexibility.
[10]	Security Threats	Risks include eavesdropping, data tampering, node impersonation, and denial of service attacks, especially in military and critical applications.	Compromises data confidentiality, integrity, and system availability, leading to potential mission failure.
	Security Solutions	Cryptography-based secure underwater acoustic communication protocols enhance data confidentiality and integrity for UUVs and sensor networks.	Strengthens network security and trustworthiness, mitigating cyber-physical threats.

and tracking within underwater imagery and sonar data [9]. For instance, Convolutional Neural Networks (CNNs) and transfer learning models have shown high accuracy in underwater object recognition tasks despite limited annotated datasets [9]. Also, remote sensing complements underwater data by providing large-scale oceanographic information through satellites, aerial drones, and coastal radars [8]. The integrated data sources are used with

IoT networks to enhance spatial coverage and improve environmental monitoring capabilities. In addition, blockchain-based secure frameworks have been proposed for remote data transfer in Unmanned Aerial Vehicles (UAV) to ensure data integrity and trustworthiness, as studied in [8]. Similar to that, various frameworks are now being explored for intelligent US systems to secure multi-source data sharing and analytics [5]. The integration of blockchain, edge computing, and artificial intelligence analytics is emerging for robust secured architecture to address the challenges via US systems data flows, ensuring secure, real-time, and reliable maritime monitoring [4, 5, 7].

7.3 FUNDAMENTALS OF BLOCKCHAIN TECHNOLOGY

7.3.1 Core concepts

Furthermore, the blockchain decentralized digital ledger securely records transactions across nodes. The blockchain blocks include transaction information, a timestamp, and a cryptographic hash of the preceding block, establishing a chain as discussed in [11]. The chaining approach provides data integrity and immutability since changing one block changes all subsequent blocks in the distributed network. However, the method of consensus serves as a crucial element that allows distributed nodes to reach an agreement on the reliability of transactions as well as the current state of the ledger. Widely accepted consensus algorithms consist of Proof of Work (PoW), which involves solving complex mathematical puzzles to add new blocks, and Proof of Stake (PoS), which relies on validators staking their assets to propose or validate each block [12]. Thus, the reliability may be established due to the consensus and coordination of distributed ledgers without the need for a central authority [12]. In addition, smart contracts function as programmable scripts that reside on blockchain networks, executing predetermined actions automatically when certain conditions are satisfied [13]. Where the self-executing contracts remove the need for intermediaries, lower operational costs, and enhance transparency within the IoT environment and underwater networks by automating tasks such as authentication, access control, and data sharing [13].

7.3.2 Blockchain types

Recently, blockchain technology has been categorized into public, private, and consortium types, each offering distinct features, access controls, and use cases. Figure 7.4 outlines the overview summary of the blockchain categorization.

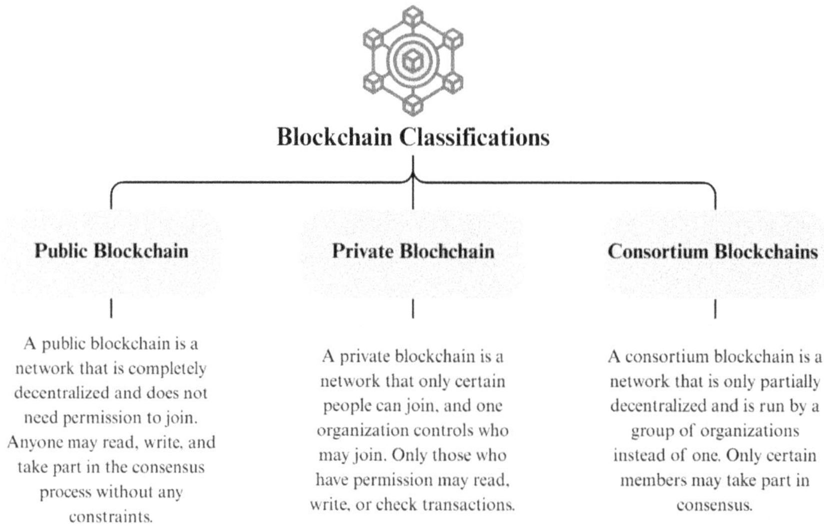

Figure 7.4 Blockchain classification.

- **Public blockchains** are open and visible to everyone, allowing unrestricted participation in transaction validation and block creation. Furthermore, the two prominent instances that are highly transparent and decentralized are Bitcoin and Ethereum. Public blockchains sometimes face various obstacles with scalability and latency, which render them less helpful for underwater systems and IoT networks that do not have enough resource [14].
- **Private blockchains** offer limited access to a single organization or are designed for participants to provide better control, scalability, and privacy. Besides this, the cost of decentralization is expensive. The trusted entities manage data and are suitable for applications such as military US systems requiring controlled access [15].
- **Consortium blockchains** blend the features of both public and private blockchains by allowing multiple trusted organizations to manage the network collaboratively. These types are widely considered for industrial IoT and underwater networks to ensure operational scalability while preserving security as well as data integrity [16].

7.3.3 Security properties

Blockchain also has a critical security capability which could address the present vulnerabilities within the underwater IoT ecosystems:

1. **Immutability:** The recorded information within the blockchain is immutable and cannot be modified without network agreement, preserving the integrity of information [11].
2. **Transparency:** Authorized users of the network could view the transactions, which improves the auditability and strengthens the trust among various parties involved in the network [17].
3. **Decentralization:** The spread of control across multiple nodes with no central authority eliminates single points of failure. Thus, the enhancement of resilience systems against targeted attacks or failures. Blockchain adds enhanced resilience to the systems under cyberattack or physical sabotage due to pervasive decentralization [13].

These properties are greatly aiding underwater networks where secure data management that withstands alteration is essential due to the possibility of tampering both physically and virtually [14].

7.3.4 Limitations of blockchain technology

Regarding the technology of blockchain, it may consist of, or face, several challenges such as:

1. **Scalability:** Various transactions cannot be handled by public blockchains at once because of how they reach consensus, which makes it a challenge to employ them for large-scale real-time IoT installations [14].
2. **Latency:** Consensus techniques that take a long time, like PoW, add delay, which is bad for underwater surveillance applications that need data to be sent right away [14].
3. **Resource Consumption:** The activities of blockchain, notably PoW, need a lot of computing power and energy, which is a drawback for underwater sensor nodes that do not have a lot of energy [14].
4. **Storage Needs:** It is not possible to store blockchain ledgers on underwater devices with limited memory; hence, lightweight or off-chain storage solutions are needed [18].

To get over these problems in IoUT applications, researchers are looking at other options such as lightweight consensus protocols, off-chain processing, and blockchain-edge computing integrations [12, 17].

7.3.5 Relevant blockchain platforms for IoT and underwater networks

There have been several other blockchain systems proposed for IoT and underwater network use:

1. **Ethereum:** Smart contracts are commonly employed to provide automatic authentication and secure data exchange via underwater networks, although it might be a challenge to scale [14].
2. **Hyperledger Fabric:** It is a permissioned chain that is used effectively for consortium or private networks. It has a modular design, high performance, and privacy characteristics that are robust for US systems managed by multiple parties [15].
3. **Internet of Things Application (IOTA):** In IoT scenarios, IOTA employs a Directed Acyclic Graph (DAG) structure called the Tangle. This is free of transaction fees and accommodates lightweight gadgets. IOTA is appropriate for underwater IoT networks since it is light on resources and can grow as needed [16].
4. **Quorum:** This is a variant of Ethereum that is enterprise-focused with private transactions having great performance that makes it appropriate for industry and military undersea deployments with strict privacy needs [17].
5. **BEKMP Protocol:** There was a new paper released with the Blockchain-enabled Key Management Protocol (BEKMP) for underwater acoustic sensor networks. It uses blockchain to securely exchange and authenticate keys, keeping in mind the limitations of underwater communications [7].

Thus, the choice of blockchain platforms is based on the needs of the application, security, scalability, and compatibility with undersea network structures [14].

7.4 SECURITY CHALLENGES IN UNDERWATER DATA MANAGEMENT

To start with, nowadays the security concern is critical since it protects information and data of users, individuals, employees, administrators, and institutions. US systems in general must be secured and ensure and care about privacy. Also, the same is applicable for underwater data management systems and how to manage the data in a secure way. Based on security, this section represents the security challenges, threats, and limitations.

7.4.1 Threat landscape: interception, spoofing, data tampering

The security environment for underwater data management systems is complicated and always changing. Because underwater audio communication is free and broadcast, it is quite likely that someone will intercept it [19]. Attackers who listen in may passively collect private data about the environment, the military, or business, which breaks confidentiality [19, 20]. Thus, spoofing attacks are quite dangerous, since attackers employ fake identities into the network to gain access without permission or to pretend to be real nodes [21]. These kinds of attacks make it harder for people to trust UWSNs and Autonomous Underwater Vehicle (AUV) communication systems. Furthermore, manipulation of data is a security concern, where the attackers may alter, counterfeit, or corrupt data packets that are sent over the internet. This puts the accuracy and integrity of information about environmental monitoring, US, or navigation at risk [19]. In spite of that, this may have serious effects since corrupted data can lead to bad decisions or mission failure [22]. Research shows that typical cryptography methods frequently use a lot of resources and may not completely protect against these attacks in underwater locations when energy is limited [20].

7.4.2 Data integrity and provenance concerns

In order to be sure that data management systems underwater are reliable, it is vital to protect the data integrity and provenance of the data. Data integrity refers to ensuring that information is not altered during any process such as collection, processing, or transmission. Thus, for provenance, the origin and processing history of data must be traced to ensure the integrity of specific records stored in the database [19]. Underwater settings are hard to work with since acoustic channels sometimes lose connection, fade in several paths, and have high bit error rates, which makes data more likely to be corrupted [20, 21]. Besides this, combining different types of sensors, AUVs, and surface gateways without common trust models raises the danger of using data that is wrong or not checked in decision-making [23]. In scientific and environmental monitoring, provenance is very important since it is needed to make sure that data is real and that its source is legitimate for accurate ecosystem assessments, climate research, and biodiversity monitoring [24]. However, current provenance techniques frequently demand a lot of communication and storage space, which is not good for underwater networks that have limited bandwidth and energy [20].

7.4.3 Secure data transmission challenges

Regarding promoting the transmission of secure data in underwater networks, overcoming technological and environmental barriers is essential. Underwater acoustic communication is inherently unsecured due to low-frequency broadcasting and susceptibility to interception [19]. Where the optical wireless communications are required for higher data rates, they are limited by turbidity, scattering, and absorption, making them unreliable for long-range secure transmission [21].

Beyond that, cryptographic protocols developed for terrestrial networks are often unsuitable for underwater applications. Lightweight encryption schemes have been proposed; however, their implementation requires balancing computational overhead with the limited processing capacity and energy of underwater nodes [20]. However, a real-time video surveillance application, for instance, requires a high-bandwidth secure transmission to maintain visual fidelity and, on the other hand, protect data confidentiality [21]. Moreover, underwater key management networks are tackled due to intermittent connectivity, node mobility, and the absence of centralized infrastructure [19]. The decentralized approaches consisting of blockchain-based key management are being explored to establish robust and scalable secure transmission frameworks, as discussed in [23]. However, the integration remains limited in resources due to constraints and environmental factors.

7.4.4 Access control and privacy issues

Additionally, access control is effective for privacy protection and is crucial to underwater data management, particularly for sensitive military or commercial operations. Traditional identity-based access control methods are tough to implement within UWSNs due to node mobility, network dynamics, and lack of fixed infrastructure [19]. Thus, the Role-based Access Control (RBAC) and Attribute-based Access Control (ABAC) models have been proposed to tackle various issues. However, they also require a reliable authentication mechanism to prevent unauthorized access [20]. Privacy concerns arise when underwater networks collect various sensitive environmental information, location, or operational data that adversaries or unauthorized parties could exploit [24]. Likewise, the military data surveillance, if compromised, can jeopardize national security [22]. Emerging remedies integrate blockchain technology within access control systems to offer decentralized, tamper-proof identity verification and access logging. However, these solutions face issues with scalability, latency, and compatibility with low-power underwater devices [23].

7.4.5 Limitations due to environment

Obviously, the US environment imposes inherent limitations that exacerbate security concerns. To begin exploring these obstacles, firstly, the bandwidth constraints in acoustic communication restrict data transmission rates to a few kilobits (KB) per second, insufficient for real-time multimedia streaming or advanced security protocol exchanges [21]. Thus, optical communication offers a raised bandwidth only in short line-of-sight conditions, which limits its practical deployment range [21].

Secondly, a power limitation is critical for underwater nodes that rely on batteries, which are challenging to recharge or replace once deployed [20]. While security mechanisms are implemented, such as encryption approaches, authentication processes, and blockchain technology, energy consumption increases by reducing operational lifespan [19]. The energy harvesting technologies are being researched, but their integration into small-scale underwater nodes remains underdeveloped [20].

Thirdly, the intermittent connectivity results from node mobility, water currents, and environmental interference, causing frequent disconnections and network partitions [19]. These disruptions affect real-time data availability, consistency of security policies, and the effectiveness of centralized security management frameworks [20]. As a result, underwater data management must adapt to delay-tolerant, opportunistic communication models with robust security that does not rely on continuous connectivity [24].

7.5 BLOCKCHAIN APPLICATIONS IN UNDERWATER SURVEILLANCE

The employment of blockchain technology within US systems is developing solutions for related issues of security concerns, data integrity, and operational workflows within sea environments. Utilizing IoUT, UWSNs, and modern communication technologies in both optical and acoustic blockchain technology enables proper data management, CAPTCHAs, effortless communication through encryption layers, as well as automated permissions for varied operations underwater. These applications are useful for UUVs and AUVs, which are employed for deep-sea exploration as well as monitoring marine ecology, video US systems in real time with alerting capabilities, and controlling sub-aquatic resources while ensuring the warranty of information underwater aided by an efficient energy consensus process. Also, encrypted comms with UBKM Protected Water Key Management Protocols enhance focus on securing underwater networks. The role these applications exhibit concerning the implementation of level blockchains to IoUT-based US networks is distinctly marked toward reliable, unchanging records accessible by authorized entities while maintaining all complexities against alterations during efficient business transactions. Figure 7.5 shows the US applications. The importance of the applications is to link between platforms for IoT US networks.

7.5.1 Blockchain for data integrity and auditability

To guarantee data integrity via US is paramount, as compromised data may lead to severe operational, environmental, and security consequences. Thus, blockchain technology offers a decentralized ledger for data immutably

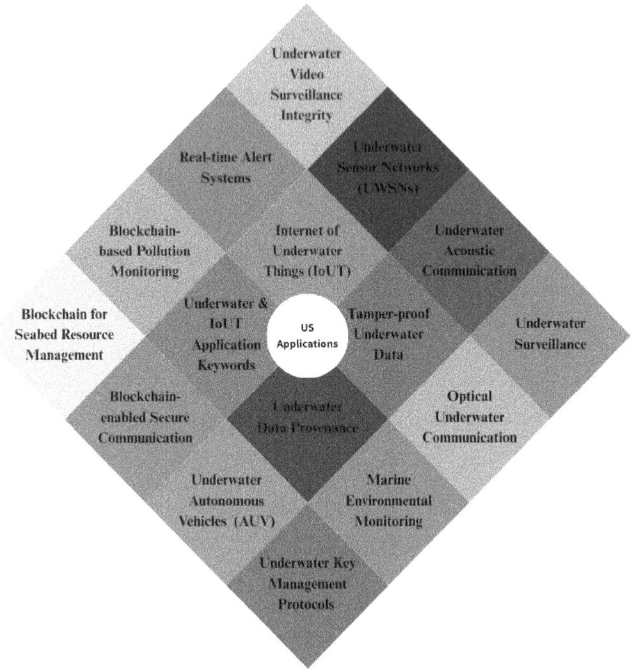

Figure 7.5 US IoT applications.

recorded across distributed nodes, preventing tampering and unauthorized alteration from third parties [25]. Each block consists of a cryptographic hash of the previous block, creating a verifiable chain of trust and enabling stakeholders to audit the history of data at any point [26]. Furthermore, underwater IoT systems are particularly beneficial due to the hostile communication environment that increases the likelihood of data corruption during transmission [27, 28]. Due to integration of blockchain technology into UWSNs to ensure the recorded data, whether environmental measurements, sonar readings, or surveillance footage, remains unaltered from its original source to its final storage location [25]. Moreover, the auditability enhances each timestamped transaction as well as links it to its origin, facilitating traceability for legal, environmental, or military verifications [26]. However, blockchain technology benefits are constrained by underwater nodes' limited computational resources and energy. Research suggests that lightweight blockchain models and off-chain storage might mitigate energy consumption while preserving data integrity [25].

7.5.2 Secure data sharing among distributed stakeholders

The US systems often engage a distributed stakeholder group that includes a military agency, environmental regulators, research institutions, as well as commercial operators. The traditional centralized data sharing frameworks pose various risks of single points of failure and unauthorized access [27]. Furthermore, blockchain's decentralized architecture addresses various concerns by allowing secure and direct data sharing without requiring central authorities [26]. By the way of illustration, blockchain networks have the potential to provide permissioned data sharing, in which only authorized and authenticated users are granted access to certain data streams [30]. Thus, the security of US military systems that exchange intelligence data with allies while preventing unwanted access is of utmost importance [25]. Similarly, the employment of blockchain technology allows environmental monitoring networks to securely share pollution data and biodiversity indicators with other parties, including government agencies, NGOs, and academic institutions, while also protecting the privacy of the data and its provenance [29]. The use of consensus algorithms is critical when attempting to foster trust among geographically separated parties. Proof of Authority (PoA) and Delegated Proof of Stake (DPoS) are two alternatives to the energy-intensive Proof of Work (PoW) that could be useful for underwater networks with limited resources [27].

7.5.3 Smart contracts for automated access management

Within the US, smart contracts, which are essentially computer programs run on blockchain networks, offer decentralized access management solutions that are both automatic and programmable. Without human oversight or central permission servers, these contracts carry out predetermined activities as soon as certain criteria are satisfied [30]. An example of a use case would be the automation of data access rights from underwater sensors by means of a smart contract that takes into consideration the duties and agreements of different parties. Under approved circumstances, environmental authorities may get real-time water quality measurements, and military operators can acquire sonar data streams immediately in response to recognized danger levels [30]. Automated processes might enhance operational responsiveness, decrease latency, and guarantee transparent enforcement of access controls [26]. The commercial activities underwater may also strengthen smart contracts' ability to automate payment processing and resource distribution. As an example, businesses engaged in seabed mining may employ blockchain technology to automatically pay environmental monitoring organizations according to the amount of minerals that are taken and the corresponding data on environmental impacts [25].

Nevertheless, in order to use smart contracts within underwater IoT systems, it is necessary to have efficient consensus methods, lightweight execution environments, as well as dependable off-chain integration [31].

7.5.4 Provenance tracking for sensor data

The monitoring of provenance is vital for validating the original copy, authenticity source, and processing history of US data. For blockchain technology, an immutable and transparent ledger enables end-to-end provenance tracking, where each data entry consists of metadata about its collection sensor, location, timestamp, and processing nodes [25]. Through the study [29], the provenance ensures the data's credibility and reproducibility, allowing researchers to verify how data was gathered, processed, and transmitted before analysis. Environmental monitoring supports regulatory compliance by demonstrating that pollution or biodiversity assessments are based on verifiable data streams [25]. Similarly, in military contexts, provenance monitoring develops operational reliability by confirming the authenticity of surveillance and detection data that is utilized in decision-making [30]. However, the combination of blockchain provenance with multi-layer security architectures can guarantee that provenance records remain confidential, only accessible to authorized users with appropriate cryptographic keys [31]. Thus, this balance between transparency and privacy addresses concerns about overexposing sensitive operational details.

7.5.5 Real-time alerts and tamper evidence

In spite of blockchain technology, which recently enables real-time alerts and tamper-evident mechanisms for US systems, as well as the integration with smart contracts, blockchain networks can trigger automated alerts upon detection of anomalies, security breaches, or environmental threshold violations [30]. For instance, if a sensor node is detecting unexpected temperature spikes indicating that there are chemical spills or underwater volcanic activity, a smart contract can broadcast alerts to relevant stakeholders instantly [25]. In addition, blockchain inherently offers tamper evidence due to its cryptographic hashing and immutability. Also, any attempt to alter the data entry within the blockchain would invalidate subsequent blocks, making tampering immediately detectable [26]. This property increases trust within US systems, particularly for legal evidence, military intelligence, or environmental compliance reporting [30]. Even though the real-time alert systems are built on blockchain, they can also integrate with AUVs for rapid response missions. In particular, upon detecting mine-like objects, a smart contract might trigger AUV deployment for further investigation while simultaneously notifying naval command centers [29]. Besides this, the implementation of real-time blockchain-based alert systems in underwater networks is required to address latency and connectivity limitations due to acoustic communication delays and intermittent network availability [28]. The hybrid architecture, which combines edge computing and blockchain, can mitigate these constraints by processing alerts locally and recording them on the blockchain asynchronously [31].

7.6 BLOCKCHAIN-BASED ARCHITECTURES AND PROTOCOLS

The widespread use of intelligent systems, US systems become more effective due to the integration with blockchain technology to develop confidence and secure US systems which keep data secure and give individuals more authority. This portion goes into architectural models, consensus procedures, lightweight protocols, interoperability strategies, privacy-preserving approaches, and energy-efficient solutions.

Reference Architecture:
The integration of both blockchain technology and US systems is provided via a reference architecture that enhances security, trust, and operational efficiency. The reference architecture is provided in Figure 7.6. A typical architecture consists of multiple layers: the underwater perception layer sensors, AUVs, communication layer (acoustic, optical, and electromagnetic), edge/fog computing nodes, and the blockchain layer for data integrity and

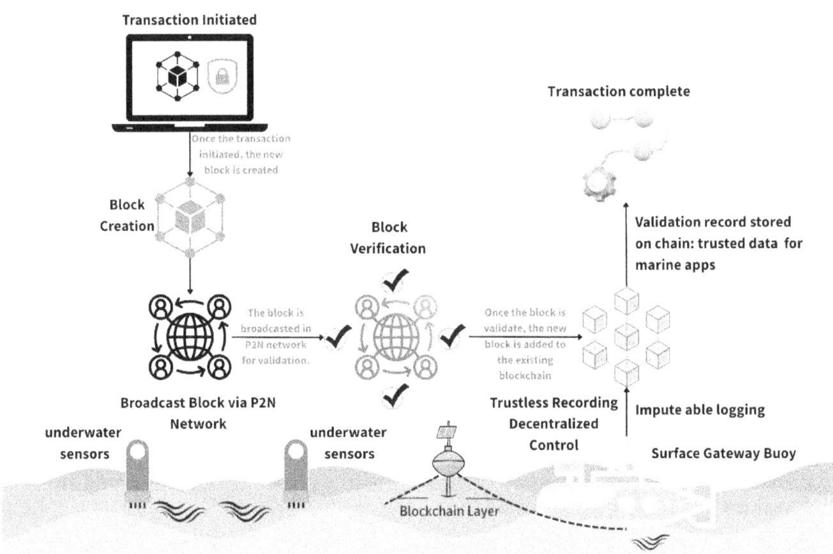

Figure 7.6 Reference architecture of blockchain-based underwater sensor network.

provenance [4, 29]. Authors through [31] propose a multi-layer blockchain-based security architecture for IoT that can be adapted for underwater networks, where sensor data is aggregated at edge nodes running lightweight blockchain clients. For nodes to validate, encrypt, and store data immutably on a permissioned blockchain, it is necessary to ensure provenance and tamper evidence. Moreover, the need for modular blockchain-based architectures tailored to domain-specific requirements suggests that underwater networks require specialized modules for acoustic communication security, energy-efficient consensus, and interoperability with marine command systems, as emphasized in [32]. Moreover, the proposed architecture in [30] outlines application, consensus, network, and data layers, which can be extended to include underwater communication protocols and data preprocessing before blockchain logging.

7.6.1 Consensus mechanisms suited for underwater and IoT environments

Blockchain security and performance are based on consensus mechanisms; however, traditional Proof-of-Work (PoW) is quite resource-intensive and does not work well in underwater IoT situations with a limited number of nodes. Thus, there are several ways to reach agreement and point out that Proof-of-Stake (PoS), Practical Byzantine Fault Tolerance (PBFT), and Delegated Proof-of-Stake (DPoS) are all better choices since they use less energy [30].

In underwater contexts, the proposed lightweight consensus protocols tailored for IoT, such as Proof-of-Authority (PoA) and reputation-based consensus, reduce computational overhead while maintaining trust [31]. On the other hand, researchers in [33] suggest federated learning combined with blockchain to improve security and intrusion detection among underwater drones, where consensus mechanisms integrate model aggregation with block validation to optimize bandwidth use and latency.

7.6.2 Lightweight blockchain protocols

Underwater nodes have limited resources; hence they need lightweight blockchain protocols. The protocol that optimizes may be achieved by making blocks smaller, lowering the number of consensus stages, and using off-chain data storage with on-chain hashes to check the data. Multi-layer security designs are to be employed within lightweight blockchain clients at edge nodes to manage consensus data encryption and verification in a way that is quick and easy [31, 32]. In addition, the designs such as IOTA's Tangle, which is a Directed Acyclic Graph (DAG) based protocol, work well for IoT microtransactions. It also does not require intensive consensus mining and may grow easily [30]. Furthermore, the lightweight protocols such as this are very important for underwater activities that need to happen in real time and are required to be energy-efficient, have minimal latency, and save accurate records of data.

7.6.3 Interoperability with legacy systems

The integration of blockchain with existing underwater infrastructure is vital to ensure backward compatibility and operational continuity. The significant role is highlighted in designing and developing blockchain architectures that are interoperable with legacy systems through APIs and middleware solutions [32]. To generate underwater sensors, AUVs and marine command centers can continue utilizing established data management workflows while benefiting from blockchain immutability and security. Also, the security concern within US networks was brought up, which led to suggestions for blockchain-based solutions for monitoring and managing cable infrastructure security. While ensuring the standard functions are well with existing command, control, and monitoring systems [34]. Additionally, blockchain gateways and edge nodes may be utilized as a translator between old communication protocols and blockchain networks. This makes it possible to make system updates slowly and without causing any problems [31].

7.6.4 Privacy-preserving and permission blockchains

Focusing on the privacy context, the US systems often involve sensitive data, which includes military or environmental intelligence. Therefore, privacy-preserving blockchains are critical. The highlighted permission of blockchain frameworks such as Hyperledger Fabric (HF) allows for the implementation of strict access control policies to ensure that only authorized entities can read or write data [30]. The multi-layer security architecture integrates cryptographic techniques with permissioned blockchains to provide both data confidentiality and integrity [31]. Due to the collaborative edge-fog systems for real-time Anomaly Detection (AD) in underwater IoT environments, blockchain is employed to log processed results securely while preserving raw data privacy at local nodes, thus minimizing bandwidth consumption and exposure of sensitive information [35]. Furthermore, federated learning models process sensitive data locally at underwater drones, while blockchain ensures the authenticity and integrity of model updates without sharing raw data, enhancing both privacy and security [33].

7.6.5 Energy-efficient and delay-tolerant design considerations

Energy-efficient is a crucial design constraint based on underwater networks since it's difficult and expensive to replace batteries. The analysis also looks at energy-efficient blockchain architectures such as PoS and PoA to avoid the need for a lot of computing power [30]. However, the hierarchical design with edge computing integration takes heavy processing away from underwater nodes and transfers it to surface gateways or fog servers [31]. Wherein [35], researchers discuss the collaborative edge, fog system for underwater IoT that processes data locally, which cuts down on how often data is sent and how much energy it uses. There is also a need to integrate blockchain within US systems to handle the delays since underwater nodes do not always have a connection. In paper [32], the protocols that can be utilized to handle high network latencies by separating block validation from instantaneous consensus are discussed, as well as how the nodes can sync up without having to wait for each other. They also demonstrate the use of federated learning with blockchain for underwater drones, where data is processed locally to validate the model updates which are transmitted, saving energy and minimizing communication delays. Similarly, in [34], authors underscore energy-aware security protocols in underwater infrastructure monitoring, highlighting the balance between data security, energy use, and delay constraints.

7.7 CASE STUDIES AND REAL-WORLD IMPLEMENTATIONS

The current section illustrates a realistic case study of how blockchain technology may be used within nautical and underwater settings. Also, the section discusses the lessons learned, how scalable it would be, how it compares to other options that do not use blockchain, as well as shares the success stories and current concerns about integrating blockchain technology. However, three case studies are provided in the following.

Case Study 1: Collaborative Edge-Fog Systems Integrated with Blockchain for Underwater AD.

- **Review of Existing Project:**
  A collaborative Edge-Fog Systems integrating blockchain technology for real-time AD in underwater IoT networks where the architecture integrates edge processing at sensor nodes with fog nodes running blockchain clients, enabling secure and efficient data validation and anomaly reporting [35].
- **Lessons Learned:**

1. The implementation demonstrated that integrating blockchain with edge and fog computing improves data authenticity and reduces communication delays.
2. Lightweight consensus protocols and adaptive data filtering algorithms are necessary to optimize resource usage while maintaining blockchain security properties.

- **The Possibility for Adaptation and Scaling:**
  The scalability was addressed by deploying various fog nodes to handle blockchain operations, which is adaptive for large-scale marine and monitoring systems such as oil spill detection or coastal erosion tracking. However, the power constraint remains a limiting factor for scaling deep-sea deployments without energy harvesting integration.
- **Non-Blockchain Approaches Comparative Analysis:**
  Traditional AD relies on centralized processing as well as databases to expose them to data tampering risks and a single point of failure, where blockchain integration provides distributed trust, tamper evidence, and decentralized data validation to enhance security at the cost of additional processing overhead.
- **Success Stories and Daily Challenges:**
- The system successfully detected underwater anomalies with low latency and high accuracy while ensuring tamper-proof data logging. Various challenges include managing the energy consumption of blockchain clients on fog nodes and improving interoperability within legacy marine observation platforms [35].

Case Study 2: Cognitive Routing Enabled Blockchain Technology for Underwater Disaster Management.

- **Review of Existing Project:**
  A cognitive intelligence routing protocol for underwater disaster management employing underwater acoustic networks, incorporating blockchain to secure routing data and control messages against spoofing and tampering attacks [36].
- **Lessons Learned:**
  1. The highlighting implementation is beneficial to blockchain technology that integrates with authenticating routing decisions and helps in enhancing resilience against routing-based attacks.
  2. Case study 2 emphasized the need to optimize the trade-off between blockchain security and communication delays, which is inherent in underwater acoustic channels.
- **Potential for Scaling and Adaptation:**
  The approach is scalable to large disaster management scenarios, such as underwater landslide detection and tsunami monitoring systems. Its adaptation potential is strengthened by its

compatibility within various US communication standards as well as the flexibility of cognitive routing that integrates with blockchain systems.

- **Non-Blockchain Approaches Comparative Analysis:**
  The traditional cognitive routing protocols lack inherent tamper-evidence and rely on centralized control, creating potential vulnerabilities within disaster response systems, where the integration of blockchain decentralizes trust to ensure the integrity of routing decisions, though. Also, it may introduce slight latency due to consensus processing.
- **Success Stories and Daily Challenges:**
- Recently, blockchain-enabled cognitive routing protocol shows the improved packet delivery ratios and lower attack success rates compared to baseline approaches. Daily concerns may include reducing energy consumption for blockchain operations as well as ensuring the synchronization among distributed underwater nodes [36].

Case Study 3: Hybrid Deep Learning and Blockchain Framework for Underwater Anomaly Detection.

- **Review of Existing Project:**
  Hybrid AD based on IoT environment integrates the developed deep learning model with blockchain for underwater sensor networks. Thus, the US system utilizes deep neural networks to classify anomalies and incidents locally while blockchain records validated results for provenance as well as the auditability [37, 38].
- **Lessons Learned:**
  1. The implementation confirmed that integrating the deep learning model with blockchain technology enhances the detection accuracy and data integrity.
  2. The significant role of lightweight blockchain protocols to minimize latency and the requirement to optimize neural networks to fit resource-constrained underwater nodes.
- **Potential for Scaling and Adaptation:**
  The framework is scalable for wide-area underwater monitoring, such as illegal fishing detection or seabed mining impact assessments. It can be adapted to various underwater environments by retraining neural network models for local conditions across the integration of modular blockchain clients for various sensor platforms.
- **Non-Blockchain Approaches Comparative Analysis:**
  Conventional AD frameworks lack tamper-proof data storage, which limits forensic investigations and regulatory compliance. The aim of the blockchain integration is to ensure the immutable

logging of detection results but requires additional computational resources for block validation and chain management.

- **Success Stories and Daily Challenges:**
  The framework proposed in [38] achieved a high AD accuracy with reliable blockchain-based audit trails. The occurred challenges refer to optimizing energy efficiency for blockchain-enabled underwater nodes and integrating with existing marine data management infrastructures.

Ultimately, blockchain applications within US systems, as demonstrated by these realistic case study implementations, provide a robust solution for tamper-proof AD, secure routing, and provenance tracking. While the success stories highlight the improved accuracy and security, as well as the operational resilience within the daily challenges, which include energy consumption, latency optimization, and system interoperability. However, future developments should focus on specialized lightweight blockchain protocols and the integration of artificial intelligence within blockchain convergence. Also, the cross-layer integration with existing maritime infrastructures enable scalable, secure, and sustainable underwater monitoring [35–40].

7.8 BLOCKCHAIN WITHIN UNDERWATER CHALLENGES AND LIMITATIONS

Despite the transformative potential, integrating blockchain into US systems faces critical obstacles due to technical, operational, regulatory, and environmental constraints. The current section outlines these limitations across the following:

7.8.1 Technical barriers

Underwater communication relies predominantly upon acoustic signals, which limit the bandwidth, cause high propagation delays, and are prone to signal loss [7, 20]. Blockchain operations require consistent connectivity for consensus and block validation, employing latency as a key bottleneck. Furthermore, storage constraints arise since blockchain technology requires maintaining ledger replicas across nodes, which is infeasible for underwater sensors with minimal memory [31, 33]. Additionally, energy consumption is critical since mining block validation and even lightweight consensus mechanisms consume significant power, which is a major limitation given the challenges in recharging underwater devices [4, 39].

7.8.2 Scalability and Consensus in harsh environments

Traditional blockchain consensus mechanisms, such as PoW, involve resource-intensive processes that are unsuitable for underwater networks [30]. Even though lightweight alternatives such as PoS or Practical Byzantine Fault Tolerance (PBFT) have been proposed, they face challenges in harsh marine conditions with intermittent connectivity and dynamic topology changes [14, 33]. Scalability is further limited by the high communication overhead of consensus protocols, risking network congestion and reduced operational efficiency [20, 32].

7.8.3 Legal, regulatory, and compliance issues

However, blockchain deployment systems within the maritime environments involve a complex legal and regulatory framework. There are various concerns about data sovereignty, especially when monitoring transboundary waters, compliance with national security laws for underwater military applications, and ensuring environmental regulations which aren't violated during the sensor deployment or blockchain node installation [34, 35]. Additionally, the lack of clear regulatory standards for blockchain integration with underwater IoT creates barriers to large-scale adoption [24, 30].

7.8.4 Cost deployment and maintenance concerns

Under placement requires expensive costs due to special hardware, purine ships, divers, and maintenance operations [29.34]. In addition, the integration of blockchain infrastructure increases calculation requirements, requires high-quality processors and storage modules on the nodes, thus increasing early and operating expenses [30, 31]. The maintenance of the sensor's inaccessibility, biofouling, and corrosion is just as challenging, making blockchain updates and upgrades logically complicated [4, 29].

7.8.5 Usability and adoption barriers

Adopting blockchain in the underwater network prevents the concerns. Where marine engineers and operators often lack blockchain skills, this leads to training intervals [32]. In addition, the complexity of integrating blockchain protocols with existing water communication and data management systems has created additional resistance from stakeholders that prioritize traditional centralized solutions [18, 23]. User-friendly interfaces and steering platforms remain underdeveloped [30].

7.8.6 Security trade-offs and new attack vectors

While blockchain improves data integrity and confidence, it also introduces new weaknesses and potential risks, including smart contract defects, 51% attacks in small permissible networks, and nodes copying in consensus groups [14, 30]. Although blockchain systems are often permissioned, their public nature raises privacy concerns, particularly in military or environmental monitoring applications [3, 15]. Their high computational demands may increase the risk of denial-of-service (DoS) attacks, resulting in excessive energy consumption and potential system disruption [28, 31].

7.9 FUTURE TRENDS AND RESEARCH DIRECTIONS

Blockchain is still in its early stages of use in the United States, but increasing research has made it possible to build systems that are safe, strong, and able to grow. Finding new ways to fix existing problems and to improve protocol design, hardware efficiency, and interdisciplinary integration is important for future research on the IoUT systems, which are becoming increasingly important to protect marine interests, monitor the environment, and manage resources at sea.

7.9.1 Advances in lightweight and hybrid blockchain protocols

Traditional consensus algorithms, for instance PoW, are computationally expensive and energy-intensive, making them unsuitable for resource-constrained underwater environments [30, 31]. Thus, the recent developments in lightweight blockchain protocols, such as PoA and Delegated Proof-of-Stake (DPoS), show promise due to reduced energy requirements and faster consensus times [30, 32]. Hybrid consensus mechanisms that combine public and private blockchain elements are gaining attention, as they allow selective transparency while ensuring robust privacy [30, 31, 32]. Future protocols must prioritize real-time transaction finality, energy efficiency, and resistance to partitioning in dynamic underwater topologies [31, 33].

7.9.2 AI and blockchain integration for intelligent security

When AI is added to blockchain, it creates a system where machine learning algorithms may find problems or cyberattacks, and blockchain keeps track of warnings and events in a way that cannot be changed [13, 25, 38]. AI-enabled blockchain frameworks can change consensus protocols on the fly, guess when a node will fail, and make sure that AUVs are doing the right tasks [25, 33]. Federated or edge learning must be used to train AI models so that data privacy is protected across dispersed underwater sensor nodes [33, 38]. For smart threat detection, predictive maintenance, and decision automation, AI and blockchain need to come together.

7.9.3 Quantum secure blockchains

As quantum computing advances, the standards cryptographic algorithms on which existing blockchain models are based may become weakly secure. This highlights the importance of quantum-resistant algorithms like lattice-based, hash-based, and multivariate polynomial cryptography in order to ensure that underwater blockchain systems will work in the future [27, 39]. Adding post-quantum cryptographic primitives to underwater blockchain systems will make them safe for a long time, especially for military and scientific uses that need to be very secure [30].

7.9.4 Standardization and best practices

Lack of similar architectural standards for blockchain systems underwater is a significant obstacle to differentiation and scalability [30, 34]. Future efforts should focus on specific performance for standardized communication interfaces, unanimous benchmarks, and performance metrics for acoustic and optical communication systems underwater [32, 34]. International maritime agencies, research consortia, and standardization bodies such as ISO and IEEE are important for creating differences and safe outline [24, 34].

7.9.5 Prospective applications

The future applications of blockchain in the underwater environment are expanded far beyond the current implementation. AUV's autonomous fleet will benefit from blockchain-competent coordination, computer verification, and assignment logging [14, 25]. During environmental monitoring, blockchain pollution data, and biodiversity can support the safe number of calculations and mapping of seabed [25, 29]. Marine security can be expanded through blockchain-based monitoring data, where marine institutions safely share the danger information across national and organizational boundaries [37, 40].

7.9.6 Open research challenges and opportunities

Numerous research intervals are unaffected. These include optimization of blockchain throws for acoustic networks with low bandwidth [20], balanced energy consumption with consensus [28, 33], and ensuring secrecy in data analysis in the system under decentralized water [15, 31]. In addition, integration of blockchain with other new technologies – such as fog computing, 6G, and digital twins – is a fruitful area for exploration [35, 40]. Future research should also detect incentive mechanisms to encourage participation of stakeholders in blockchain ecosystems underwater distributed.

7.10 CONCLUSION

This study has discovered the possibility of blockchain changing surveillance systems underwater by increasing data security, integrity, and decentralized trust. As an observation of surveillance systems underwater and their developed data scenarios, the study examined the roles of smart contracts, distributed managers, and consensus mechanisms, where data is collected, validated, shared, and stored in the underwater environment. Blockchain provides many benefits that correspond to the needs of the underwater IoT network, including irreversibility, openness, and decentralization [4, 30]. Through our analysis of secure data transfer, access control, deviations, and provenance tracking, it became clear that blockchain could address many important security and management problems facing underwater operations. Our review of blockchain architecture revealed the importance of using mild, modular, and delay-tolerant designs suitable for acoustic and optical communication systems. Case studies in the real world portrayed successful pilots in detecting deviations, decentralizing AUV coordination, and securing video surveillance, which confirm blockchain in practice [36, 38]. However, challenges remain. Technical obstacles such as limited bandwidth, delay, lack of energy, and implementation of environmental intervention exist. Legal uncertainty, high distribution costs, as well as the integration of complications inhibit further enhancement of scalability. Additionally, securing circulation introduced by smart contracts and unanimous mechanisms creates novel cyber-attacks that might be carefully controlled. Despite these challenges, the promise of blockchain technology is sufficient for underwater monitoring. The key recommendations include the following:

- Investment in a sequential light blockchain unanimous protocol for acoustic communication.
- Priority to quantum sample cryptographic integration in sensitive domains.
- To promote cooperation over cross-border for blockchain standardization.
- To integrate AI into real-time analysis, detection of deviations, and adaptive control.

In short, blockchain technology stands as a powerful enabler for the upcoming next generation of underwater surveillance systems. Within the strategic investments, cooperation research as well as the active political frameworks of blockchain could redefine how data integrity, security, and intelligence are achieved under the waves. This transformation ability for underwater systems within the coming decade is not only applicable within the seabed but also in trust, openness, and technological innovation advancement.

NOTE

1. Corresponding author.

REFERENCES

1. Razzaq, A. (2022). Blockchain-based secure data transmission for internet of underwater things. *Cluster Computing*, *25*(6), 4495–4514.
2. Moghimi, M. K., & Mohanna, F. (2022). Reliable object recognition using deep transfer learning for marine transportation systems with underwater surveillance. *IEEE Transactions on Intelligent Transportation Systems*, *24*(2), 2515–2524.
3. Abbas, S., Nasir, H., Almogren, A., Altameem, A., & Javaid, N. (2022). Blockchain based privacy preserving authentication and malicious node detection in Internet of Underwater Things (IoUT) networks. *IEEE Access*, *10*, 113945–113955.
4. Bhattacharya, S., Victor, N., Chengoden, R., Ramalingam, M., Selvi, G. C., Maddikunta, P. K. R., & Gadekallu, T. R. (2022). Blockchain for internet of underwater things: State-of-the-art, applications, challenges, and future directions. *Sustainability*, *14*(23), 15659.
5. Chen, Y., Li, Z., & Zhu, R. (2024). A blockchain-based edge computing group signature authentication model for underwater clustered networks. *Journal of Marine Science and Engineering*, *13*(1), 27.
6. Al-Tamimi, S. A., & Abu Al-Haija, Q. (2024). Supply chain security, technological advancements, and future trends. In Q. Abu Al-Haija (Ed.), *Smart and Agile Cybersecurity for IoT and IIoT Environments* (pp. 211–234). IGI Global Scientific Publishing. https://doi.org/10.4018/979-8-3693-3451-5.ch010.
7. Tomović, S., Krivokapić, B., Nađ, Đ., & Radusinović, I. (2024). BEKMP: A blockchain-enabled key management protocol for underwater acoustic sensor networks. *IEEE Access*, *11*(1), 124.
8. Rodríguez-Molina, J., Corpas, B., Hirsch, C., & Castillejo, P. (2021). SEDIBLOFRA: A blockchain-based, secure framework for remote data transfer in unmanned aerial vehicles. *IEEE Access*, *9*, 121385–121404.
9. Elmezain, M., Saad Saoud, L., Sultan, A., Abdelwahab, M., Seneviratne, L., & Hussain, I. (2025). Advancing underwater vision: A survey of deep learning models for underwater object recognition and tracking. *IEEE Access, 13*, 17830–17867.

10. Zhou, Q., Ye, Q., Lai, C., & Kou, G. (2025). Cryptography-based secure underwater acoustic communication for UUVs: A review. *Electronics*, *14*(12), 2415. https://doi.org/10.3390/electronics14122415.
11. Mary, D. R. K., Ko, E., Kim, S. G., Yum, S. H., Shin, S. Y., & Park, S. H. (2021). A systematic review on recent trends, challenges, privacy and security issues of underwater internet of things. *Sensors*, *21*(24), 8262.
12. Albekairi, M. (2024). A comprehensive mutable analytics approach to distinguish sensor data on the internet of underwater things. *IEEE Access*, 12, 95007–95019.
13. Shahad, A. T., & Al-Haija, Q. A. (2026). Fortifying Industrial IoT (IIoT): Leveraging AI for optimizing security. In *Information Security Governance using Artificial Intelligence of Things in Smart Environments* (pp. 242–257). CRC Press.
14. Kumar, A., Ahuja, N. J., Thapliyal, M., Dutt, S., Kumar, T., Pacheco, D. A. D. J., ... & Choo, K. K. R. (2023). Blockchain for unmanned underwater drones: Research issues, challenges, trends and future directions. *Journal of Network and Computer Applications*, *215*, 103649.
15. Yisa, A. G., Dargahi, T., Belguith, S., & Hammoudeh, M. (2021). Security challenges of internet of underwater things: A systematic literature review. *Transactions on Emerging Telecommunications Technologies*, *32*(3), e4203.
16. Jahanbakht, M., Xiang, W., Hanzo, L., & Azghadi, M. R. (2021). Internet of underwater things and big marine data analytics—a comprehensive survey. *IEEE Communications Surveys & Tutorials*, *23*(2), 904–956.
17. Mohsan, S. A. H., Li, Y., Sadiq, M., Liang, J., & Khan, M. A. (2023). Recent advances, future trends, applications and challenges of internet of underwater things (iout): A comprehensive review. *Journal of Marine Science and Engineering*, *11*(1), 124.
18. Milledge, T. J., Pradhan, B., & Shukla, N. (2025). Integrating systems methodologies for Australian undersea surveillance: A systematic literature review. *Systems Engineering*, *28*(4), 471–497.
19. Adu-Manu, K. S., Engmann, F., Sarfo-Kantanka, G., Baiden, G. E., & Dulemordzi, B. A. (2022). WSN protocols and security challenges for environmental monitoring applications: A survey. *Journal of Sensors*, *2022*(1), 1628537.
20. Mohsan, S. A. H., Mazinani, A., Othman, N. Q. H., & Amjad, H. (2022). Towards the internet of underwater things: A comprehensive survey. *Earth Science Informatics*, *15*(2), 735–764.
21. Kong, M., Guo, Y., Alkhazragi, O., Sait, M., Kang, C. H., Ng, T. K., & Ooi, B. S. (2022). Real-time optical-wireless video surveillance system for high visual-fidelity underwater monitoring. *IEEE Photonics Journal*, *14*(2), 1–9.
22. Bazzarello, C. A. L., Costanzi, R., Pollini, L., Stifani, C. A. M., Trucco, A., Tesei, A., & Gini, F. (2023, December). *Underwater Surveillance with Maritime Unmanned Systems: Usage of Artificial Intelligence against the Threat of Mines* (Doctoral thesis). https://doi.org/10.13140/RG.2.2.22124.17287
23. Delladetsimas, A. P., Papangelou, S., Iosif, E., & Giaglis, G. (2024). Integrating blockchains with the IoT: A review of architectures and marine use cases. *Computers*, *13*(12), 329.

24. Alsharabi, N., Ktari, J., Frikha, T., Alayba, A., Alzahrani, A. J., Jadi, A., & Hamam, H. (2024). Using blockchain and AI technologies for sustainable, biodiverse, and transparent fisheries of the future. *Journal of Cloud Computing*, *13*(1), 135.
25. Arul, R., Alroobaea, R., Mechti, S., Rubaiee, S., Andejany, M., Tariq, U., & Iftikhar, S. (2021). Intelligent data analytics in energy optimization for the internet of underwater things. *Soft Computing*, *25*, 12507–12519.
26. Far, S. B., & Asaar, M. R. (2024). A blockchain-based anonymous reporting system with no central authority: Architecture and protocol. *Cyber Security and Applications*, *2*, 100032.
27. Islam, S., Islam, M. J., Hossain, M., Noor, S., Kwak, K. S., & Islam, S. R. (2023). A survey on consensus algorithms in blockchain-based applications: Architecture, taxonomy, and operational issues. *IEEE Access*, *11*, 39066–39082.
28. Islam, K. Y., Ahmad, I., Habibi, D., & Waqar, A. (2022). A survey on energy efficiency in underwater wireless communications. *Journal of Network and Computer Applications*, *198*, 103295.
29. Igbinenikaro, O. P., Adekoya, O. O., & Etukudoh, E. A. (2024). Emerging underwater survey technologies: A review and future outlook. *Open Access Research Journal of Science and Technology*, *10*(2), 71–84.
30. Shrimali, B., & Patel, H. B. (2022). Blockchain state-of-the-art: Architecture, use cases, consensus, challenges and opportunities. *Journal of King Saud University-Computer and Information Sciences*, *34*(9), 6793–6807.
31. Honar Pajooh, H., Rashid, M., Alam, F., & Demidenko, S. (2021). Multi-layer blockchain-based security architecture for internet of things. *Sensors*, *21*(3), 772.
32. Wöhrer, M., Zdun, U., & Rinderle-Ma, S. (2021, September). Architecture design of blockchain-based applications. In *2021 3rd Conference on Blockchain Research & Applications for Innovative Networks and Services (BRAINS)* (pp. 173–180). IEEE.
33. Popli, M. S., Singh, R. P., Popli, N. K., & Mamun, M. (2025). A federated learning framework for enhanced data security and cyber intrusion detection in distributed network of underwater drones. *IEEE Access*, *13*, 12634–12646.
34. Cannon, B. J. (2025). Undersea cable security in the Indo-Pacific: Enhancing the Quad's collaborative approach. *Marine Policy*, *171*, 106415.
35. Devi, D. P., Allur, N. S., Dondapati, K., Chetlapalli, H., Kodadi, S., & Perumal, T. (2025). Collaborative edge-fog system for real-time anomaly detection and communication efficiency in underwater IoT. *International Journal of Information Technology and Computer Engineering*, *13*(1), 91–110.
36. Saleem, K., Wang, L., Almogren, A., Ntizikira, E., Rehman, A. U., Bharany, S., & Hussen, S. (2025). Cognitive intelligence routing protocol for disaster management and underwater communication system in underwater acoustic network. *Scientific Reports*, *15*(1), 10004.
37. Shah, S., Sarwar, N., Salam, A., Amin, F., Ullah, F., Khan, A., ... & Garay, H. (2025). A flexible and lightweight signcryption scheme for underwater wireless sensor networks. *Scientific Reports*, *15*(1), 13511.

38. Almasabi, A. M., Alkhodre, A. B., Khemakhem, M., Eassa, F., Abi Sen, A. A., & Harbaoui, A. (2025). Internet of Things-based anomaly detection hybrid framework simulation integration of deep learning and blockchain. *Information*, *16*(5), 406.
39. Jiang, F., & Xu, M. (2025). Security authentication protocol for underwater sensor networks based on NTRU. *Journal of Marine Science and Engineering*, *13*(4), 742.
40. Hussain, A., Li, S., Hussain, T., Attar, R. W., Alhomoud, A., Alsagri, R., & Zaman, K. (2025). Energy-efficient and trust-based autonomous underwater vehicle scheme for 6G-enabled internet of underwater things. *Sensors*, *25*(1), 286.

Chapter 8

Defense-grade anomaly detection for OT/IoT

PR-centric ranking and safeguards

Youness Khourdifi, Omar Er-Remyly, Mounia Zaydi, Yassine Maleh, and Hayat Zaydi

8.1 INTRODUCTION

Critical infrastructure increasingly depends on tightly integrated operational technology (OT) and Internet-of-Things (IoT) assets whose telemetry is high-volume, heterogeneous, and security-relevant [1–3]. Modern plants expose mixed analog/digital signals, control commands, and status flags over industrial buses and IP networks; adversarial actions and faults manifest as rare, regime-dependent deviations embedded in non-stationary dynamics [4–6]. In this context, anomaly detection must (i) operate under severe class imbalance, (ii) honor time-ordering and process constraints, and (iii) translate statistical evidence into safe, auditable operator actions [7–9]. We therefore pursue a *shielded* learning approach: models generate anomaly scores, while an independent guard layer enforces hard limits, rate bounds, and cooldowns before any alert escalation or actuation is permitted – separating statistical detection from operational safety policy [10, 11]. Our evaluation follows an AUPRC-first protocol suitable for rare events, with AUROC and $F1@\tau$ as secondary summaries and a cost functional that aggregates false dispatch, missed detection, and delay [7, 8, 12]. The study aligns with governance expectations by mapping decisions to recognized control families and functions at design time and by retaining human-in-the-loop authority at run time [4, 9].

Despite rapid progress in time-series anomaly detection (TSAD), several gaps persist for deployment in OT/ICS settings. First, common discriminative metrics can mislead under skewed prevalence; threshold-free AUROC often appears high even when precision at actionable recall is poor, motivating PR-centric evaluation [7]. Second, leakage and non-stationarity undermine credibility if temporal splits are ignored; models that excel under i.i.d. cross-validation frequently degrade on forward-in-time holdouts [1, 4, 5]. Third, many powerful sequence encoders (autoencoders, Transformers) lack explicit safety semantics; in plants, even a well-calibrated alert may be unsafe to act upon without context-aware filters or procedural gates [9, 13, 14]. Finally, incident timeliness and cost are rarely integrated into model selection, yet operators must balance alert volume against time-to-detect to

 DOI: 10.1201/9781003650478-9

sustain response capacity [8, 15, 16]. Our work addresses these issues by combining time-aware evaluation, PR-first ranking, cost–threshold analysis, and a read-only shield that shapes system behavior without entangling the learning objective with safety policy [7, 9, 10].

Problem statement: Given multivariate OT time series with incident intervals on a held-out test period, learn scoring functions that maximize AUPRC and deliver a deployable threshold τ chosen on validation. At inference, an independent shield layer filters candidate alerts using plant-informed constraints. We quantify uncertainty via bootstrap intervals, assess timeliness (MTTD/MTTR), and minimize an explicit cost $cost(\tau)$ [7, 8]. Our contributions are: (1) an end-to-end, leak-free pipeline with reproducible preprocessing and time-blocked evaluation; (2) a shielded decision layer with hard limits, rate guards, and cooldown analytics; (3) decision-centric reporting (AUPRC-first, PR/ROC curves, $F1@\tau$, confusion at τ, cost curves) suitable for SOC policy; and (4) a governance-aware positioning that keeps actuation read-only and auditable [4, 9].

8.1.1 Related work

Classical and kernel methods: Isolation Forest (IF) isolates anomalies via short expected path lengths and remains a strong unsupervised baseline for high-dimensional telemetry [17]. One-Class SVM (OCSVM) performs support estimation in feature space and has been widely applied to novelty detection when an abundant sample of "normal" is available [18]. Robust variants address heavy tails and nuisance covariates, yet both families are sensitive to feature scaling and drift, reinforcing the need for train-only normalization and time-aware validation. Support Vector Data Description is a related envelope-estimation approach with efficient kernels for compact normal regions [19]. Density-based and proximity baselines (e.g., LOF) remain useful comparators and diagnostics [20].

Representation learning for TSAD: Autoencoders (AEs) and LSTM-based sequence models reconstruct normal patterns and score anomalies via reconstruction error [13, 15]. Broader surveys document the rise of deep encoders (temporal CNNs, RNNs, attention/Transformers) and hybrid objectives for TSAD across domains, including industrial monitoring [3, 14, 21]. Fast transform/feature pipelines (SAX, ROCKET, TSFresh) enable scalable baselines and ablations [22–24]. GAN-based and one-class deep objectives extend modeling capacity but increase calibration demands [25–27].

Evaluation under class imbalance: Precision–Recall analysis is preferred for rare-event detection since precision reflects the operator's burden at a given recall; AUROC may remain deceptively high as negatives dominate [7]. Best practice ranks by AUPRC, selects τ on validation, and freezes it for unbiased test reporting, with PR/ROC curves providing complementary diagnostics [7, 8, 12].

Industrial datasets and benchmarks: Robust ICS studies favor forward-in-time splits, drift audits, and incident-level analyses to mirror deployment [4, 15, 28]. Change-point and drift modeling, together with forecasting-aware preprocessing, mitigate non-stationarity [5, 6, 10].

Operational safety, shields, and governance: Safe-by-design principles emphasize conservative action filters (shields/guards), formal limits/rate constraints, and human oversight; in detection pipelines, shields shape alerting dynamics via cooldowns, rate-of-change limits, and value envelopes while leaving model scores unchanged – supporting auditability and calibration monitoring [8, 9, 11].

Position of this work: Relative to prior TSAD literature and unsupervised ICS detectors, our focus is a deployment-grade *evaluation and decision* stack: (i) leak-free temporal splits; (ii) PR-first reporting with bootstrap CIs; (iii) thresholding tied to $F1$ on validation then held fixed; (iv) conversion of scores to actions via an independent, auditable shield; and (v) explicit cost–threshold trade-offs – model-agnostic and compatible with IF/OCSVM, AEs/LSTMs, and attention-based encoders [13, 14, 17, 18].

8.2 METHODS

This section details the end-to-end pipeline used to produce the reported results, with emphasis on leak-free, time-aware evaluation suitable for OT/ICS anomaly detection. We first describe the corpus, parsing, resampling, missing-data treatment, and normalization choices that yield a reproducible tidy dataset (§2.1). We then formalize model families (rules/thresholds, Isolation Forest, One-Class SVM, and LSTM autoencoder), the scoring functions they induce, and the nested, chronological validation used for hyperparameter selection and for freezing the operating threshold τ (§2.2). A read-only *shield* layer enforces hard limits, rate guards, and cooldown to align detection with safety governance and SOC workload. Finally, we define decision-centric metrics (AUPRC first under imbalance, AUROC, $F1@\tau$), timeliness measures (MTTD/MTTR), and a cost functional $cost(\tau)$ that integrates false dispatch, missed detection, and delay, together with bootstrap uncertainty and paired significance testing (§2.3). Implementation details (seeds, environments, scripts/CLI) and governance mapping are provided to ensure full reproducibility and standards readiness.

8.2.1 Data and preprocessing

Corpus and files: We ingest multivariate time series from the *haiend-23.05* corpus comprising training files end-train*.csv, test files end-test*.csv, and

Table 8.1 Data schema: types, units, sampling frequency, missing-value percentages, and imputation policy (forward-fill then median). Normalization (StandardScaler) is fit on train and applied to test to prevent information leakage

Column	*Type*	*Missing (%)*	*Example*
DM_PP01_R	float32	0.00	0.0
DM_FT01Z	float32	0.31	287.20242
DM_FT02Z	float32	0.88	3166.9775
DM_FT03Z	float32	0.18	983.9859

incident labels label-test*.csv. A compact manifest and schema are reported in Table 8.1. All timestamps are interpreted as UTC.

Parsing and harmonization: Raw CSVs are parsed with an auto-delimiter detector, then concatenated by split (train/test). We standardize column names, coerce timestamps with errors = 'coerce', and drop columns with zero variance on *train*. Asset/site identifiers (e.g., site, asset, device) are retained only as *grouping keys* for split integrity and leakage checks; they are not used as features.

Resampling and windowing: Let $\left\{\left(t_n, \mathbf{x}_{t_n}\right)\right\}_{n=1}^{N}$ be raw measurements. We use a fixed base sampling period $\Delta t = 1s$; series are uniformly resampled to Δt with forward-fill for short gaps. Supervised/unsupervised windows are built with length L and stride S:

$$\mathbf{X}_k = \left[\mathbf{x}_{t_k}, \mathbf{x}_{t_k+\Delta t}, \ldots, \mathbf{x}_{t_k+(L-1)\Delta t}\right], \quad k = 1, S, 2S, \ldots$$

We set $L = 256$ and $S = 64$ samples (75% overlap), which balance temporal context, computational cost, and stability of PR-curves.

Missing data handling: We quantify missingness per variable on *train* and *test*. Imputation uses (i) forward-fill within each tag for gaps ≤ 5 samples (5 s), then (ii) median imputation computed on *train*. Remaining NaNs after imputation lead to tag-wise exclusion if the missing rate > 20% in any split.

Normalization and de-trending: Continuous features are standardized with StandardScaler fitted on *train* only:

$$\tilde{x}^{(j)} = \frac{x^{(j)} - \mu_{\text{train}}^{(j)}}{\sigma_{\text{train}}^{(j)}},$$

applied to validation/test to prevent leakage. Robust scaling (median/IQR) is *enabled automatically* for heavy-tailed channels satisfying skewness ≥ 2 or excess kurtosis ≥ 7.

Label alignment: Incident labels provide onset/clear timestamps. We align labels to samples by nearest timestamp within tolerance $\varepsilon = \Delta t$, mapping categorical strings to $\{0,1\}$ (normal/incident). Window labels are assigned positive if any sample within the window overlaps an incident interval. If only onsets are available, we treat post-onset windows until the next clear as positive.

Split protocol and leakage guards: We use chronological splits: train : val : test = 60% : 20% : 20% on the *training time span*, then the provided *test* files as out-of-distribution holdout. No records, windows, or identifiers overlap across splits. We audit leakage via (i) duplicate-hash checks across splits, (ii) temporal partition plots (Figure 8.2), and (iii) distribution-drift tests (Kolmogorov–Smirnov and energy distance) with Benjamini–Hochberg FDR control at $q = 0.10$.

8.2.2 Models and training

Baselines and learning families: We evaluate four families reflecting common OT/ICS practice:

1. **Rules/Thresholds** – per-tag static limits and rate-of-change guards derived from *train* quantiles (control-inspired baseline).
2. **Isolation Forest (IF)** – tree-based isolation of anomalies via short expected path length [17].
3. **One-Class SVM (OCSVM)** – support estimation in feature space for novelty detection [18].
4. **LSTM Autoencoder (LSTM-AE)** – sequence model trained to reconstruct normal windows; reconstruction error serves as anomaly score [13, 29]. An optional temporal transformer is included when GPU is available [14].

Anomaly scoring: For IF and OCSVM, we use native decision functions $s(\mathbf{X}_k)$. For LSTM-AE we compute per-window mean absolute error:

$$s(\mathbf{X}_k) = \frac{1}{Ld}\sum_{\ell=1}^{L}\left\|\hat{\mathbf{x}}_{k,\ell} - \mathbf{x}_{k,\ell}\right\|_1,$$

with d the feature dimension. Scores are monotonically transformed to $[0,1]$ via affine scaling on *val*. Rules produce binary alerts; to plot PR/ROC we assign score 1 for rule-fired windows else 0.

Hyperparameter selection: We perform nested, time-aware cross-validation on *train*: an inner split selects hyperparameters maximizing AUPRC; an outer split estimates generalization. Early stopping monitors validation AUPRC for neural models with *patience* = 10 epochs. The final model is refit on train $\cup$ val at selected hyperparameters and evaluated once on *test*.

Shielded decision layer (read-only): We enforce a *safety shield* on top of model scores to temper actuation/alerting:

$$\mathrm{EmitAlert}(t) = \mathbb{1}\left[s_t \geq \tau \wedge \underbrace{(t - t_{\text{last}}) \geq \Delta_{\text{cool}}}_{\text{cooldown}} \wedge \underbrace{\dot{x}^{(j)} \in \left[-r_j^{\max}, r_j^{\max}\right] \forall j}_{\text{rate guard}} \wedge \underbrace{x^{(j)} \in \left[\ell_j, u_j\right] \forall j}_{\text{hard limits}} \right],$$

with per-tag hard limits $\left[\ell_j, u_j\right]$ learned from *train* quantiles $[q_{0.1\%}, q_{99.9\%}]$, rate bounds $r_j^{\max}$ from the 99.9^{th} percentile of first differences, and a cooldown $\Delta_{\text{cool}} = 300s$ to bound alert bursts. We log shield-blocked events for safety analytics.

Rules/Thresholds baseline: For each tag $x^{(j)}$, hard limits are learned from train-only quantiles as

$$\ell_j = Q_{0.1\%}\left(x_{\text{train}}^{(j)}\right), \quad u_j = Q_{99.9\%}\left(x_{\text{train}}^{(j)}\right).$$

Rate-of-change guards use the train-only empirical $(99.9)^{\text{th}}$ percentile of first differences, $r_j^{\max} = Q_{99.9\%}\left(\left|\Delta x^{(j)}\right|_{\text{train}}\right)$, enforcing $\left|\Delta x_t^{(j)}\right| \leq r_j^{\max}$. A rule fires when any limit or rate predicate is violated for a window. To plot PR/ROC, rule outputs are mapped to scores in $\{0,1\}$.

Algorithm 1: Time-aware training and shielded inference

Input: windows $\{X_k, y_k\}$, scaler S, model family M
Fit S on *train*; transform *train, val, test*
Select hyperparameters by maximizing AUPRC on *val*
Refit M on $\text{train} \cup \text{val}$; compute scores s_k on *test*
Choose $\tau = \arg\max_{\tau} F1(\tau)$ on *val*; **freeze** τ
for each test time t **do**
if $s_t \geq \tau$ and shield predicates hold **then**
emit alert; update t_{last}
else
suppress; log shield-blocked if predicate failed
end if
end for
Output: PR/ROC curves, AUPRC, AUROC, $F1@\tau$, cost and timeliness metrics

---

8.2.3 Metrics and statistics

Precision–Recall and AUPRC: With positives (incidents) as the positive class, precision and recall at threshold τ are

$$Prec(\tau) = \frac{TP(\tau)}{TP(\tau)+FP(\tau)}, \quad Rec(\tau) = \frac{TP(\tau)}{TP(\tau)+FN(\tau)}.$$

AUPRC is the area under the PR curve obtained by sweeping τ over unique scores; we follow sklearn's average_precision convention. Under severe class imbalance, PR is more decision-informative than ROC [7].

ROC and AUROC: True- and false-positive rates are

$$TPR(\tau) = \frac{TP(\tau)}{TP(\tau)+FN(\tau)}, \quad FPR(\tau) = \frac{FP(\tau)}{FP(\tau)+TN(\tau)},$$

and AUROC integrates TPR vs. FPR across τ. We report AUROC as a complementary discrimination view to AUPRC [7].

$F1@\tau$ **and threshold selection.** We select τ by maximizing $F1$ on validation,

$$F1(\tau) = \frac{2Prec(\tau)Rec(\tau)}{Prec(\tau)+Rec(\tau)},$$

then *freeze* τ for test evaluation (reported in Table 8.2).

Timeliness (MTTD/MTTR):

For each incident i with onset t_i^{on} and clear t_i^{off}, detection time is the first alert time after onset,

$$t_i^{\det} = \min\left\{t \geq t_i^{on} : EmitAlert(t) = 1\right\}, \text{ and}$$

$$MTTD = median_i\left(t_i^{\det} - t_i^{on}\right), \quad MTTR = median_i\left(t_i^{off} - t_i^{\det}\right),$$

with IQRs and Kaplan–Meier curves for censoring (undetected incidents).

Cost curve:

We evaluate a parametric cost:

$$cost(\tau) = c_{fp} \cdot FP(\tau) + c_{fn} \cdot FN(\tau) + c_{delay} \cdot MTTD(\tau),$$

We set $c_{fp} = 1$, $c_{fn} = 10$, and $c_{delay} = 0$ in all cost analyses, sweeping τ to obtain τ* = arg min_τ cost(τ). We report τ* together with the corresponding cost (cost(τ*)) and compare it to the F1-optimal operating point selected on validation.

Uncertainty and hypothesis testing:

Table 8.2 Main results ranked by AUPRC with 95% bootstrap CIs. Threshold τ selected on validation and frozen on test

Model	*AUPRC*	*AUROC*	*F1@τ*	*τ*
IF	0.218	0.690	0.264	0.061

We compute 95% bootstrap CIs with $B = 10{,}000$ resamples (incident- or time-block bootstrapping to preserve correlation):

$$CI_{95\%} = \left[\hat{\theta}^{(0.025)}, \hat{\theta}^{(0.975)}\right], \quad \hat{\theta} \in \{\text{AUPRC}, \text{AUROC}, F1@\tau, MTTD\}.$$

For paired comparisons vs. the best baseline, we use a two-sided permutation test or Wilcoxon signed-rank on per-incident metrics, reporting p -values and effect sizes (Cliff's δ or median paired difference).

Robustness sweeps:

We simulate (i) additive noise $\eta \sim \mathcal{N}\left(0, \sigma^2\right)$, (ii) missingness at random with rate m, (iii) covariate drift via mean shifts $\Delta\mu$ on selected tags, and report performance grids and shield-blocked counts across $(\sigma, m, \Delta\mu)$.

Uncertainty and hypothesis testing:

We compute 95% bootstrap confidence intervals with $B = 10{,}000$ resamples (incident- or time-block bootstrapping to preserve correlation):

$$CI_{95\%} = \left[\hat{\theta}^{(0.025)}, \hat{\theta}^{(0.975)}\right], \quad \hat{\theta} \in \{\text{AUPRC}, \text{AUROC}, F1@\tau, MTTD\}.$$

8.2.4 Governance and safety

Safe-by-default evaluation:

All experiments are *read-only* – no control actuation. The shield enforces hard limits, rate bounds, and cooldown with human-in-the-loop escalation. We log every blocked event and decision rationale.

Standards-aware positioning:

Our pipeline supports SOC workflows under strong class imbalance and high consequence, aligning with accepted evaluation guidance in anomaly detection [7] and leveraging mature learning primitives [13, 14, 17, 18].

8.3 RESULTS

This section reports empirical findings on shielded anomaly detection for OT/ICS time series, proceeding from data characterization to decision-centric evaluation. We first verify distributional structure and leakage-free temporal partitioning, then rank models by AUPRC – the primary metric under class imbalance – while reporting AUROC and $F1@\tau$ with 95% bootstrap CIs. Curves (PR/ROC) expose operating regimes, the validated threshold τ yields a concrete confusion profile for workload assessment, and a cost analysis integrates false dispatch, missed detection, and delay into a single operational objective. All exact values are taken from the prepared tables (schema in Table 8.1, main performance in Table 8.2, and cost

Table 8.3 Cost analysis $cost(\tau) = c_{fp}FP(\tau) + c_{fn}FN(\tau) + c_{delay}MTTD(\tau)$.

Model	*best* τ	$cost(\tau)$
IF	0.037	94225.0

in Table 8.3); figures (e.g., Figures 8.1, 8.3, and 8.4) provide visual diagnostics that inform threshold selection and SOC policy.

8.3.1 Data structure, schema, and temporal split

Figure 8.1 indicates pronounced heterogeneity across channels: several digital outputs are quasi-constant (low entropy) while analog sensors exhibit broad dispersion and multi-modality. This mismatch in variance scale motivates regularization and feature scaling learned on *train* only to prevent leakage, as specified in Table 8.1. The heavy-tailed analog distributions suggest that robust estimators (median/quantile imputation; outlier-resistant scalers) are preferable to mean-based assumptions. For downstream

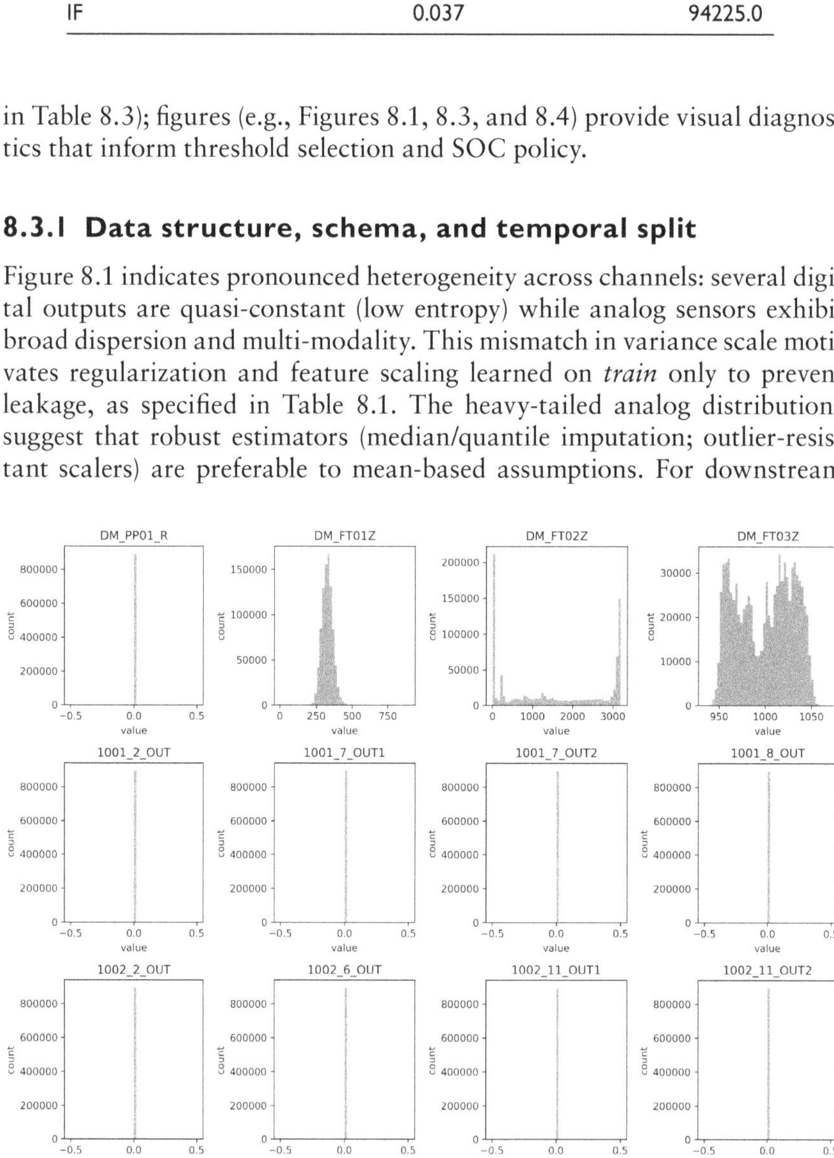

Figure 8.1 Distributions of the 12 most variant variables in the training set. Axes: value (x), count (y). Several digital outputs are nearly constant, whereas analog sensors (e.g., flow/temperature tags) display wide dispersion. Generated by plot _suite.py (F1), seed = 42, dataset haiend-23.05 (preprocessed).

anomaly detection under class imbalance, these density skews imply that precision–recall behavior will be driven by a small fraction of high-amplitude deviations, reinforcing our AUPRC-first evaluation and the need for threshold selection on validation before being frozen on *test*.

Preprocessing validation: The schema in Table 8.1 operationalizes a leak-free pipeline end-to-end. Timestamps are coerced to UTC, and series are uniformly resampled to the training median cadence ($\Delta t = 1s$); missing values are imputed via forward-fill for short gaps (up to five samples) followed by a median backstop computed on *train*. Continuous features are then standardized with a StandardScaler fitted on *train* only and applied unchanged to *val/test* to prevent information leakage; for heavy-tailed channels (high skew/kurtosis), a robust scaler is automatically selected. Categorical/site identifiers are retained solely as grouping keys for split integrity and leakage audits and are excluded from the feature matrix. This protocol preserves serial dependence while limiting distributional distortions induced by imputation and scaling. Finally, a strict chronological partition (*train*:*val*:*test*) is enforced with duplicate-hash checks and drift diagnostics (KS/energy-distance with BH-FDR), ensuring that any reported performance reflects genuine out-of-sample generalization rather than temporal contamination (cf. Figure 8.2).

Thus, Figure 8.1 reveals structural heterogeneity – broad analog variability alongside quasi-deterministic digital channels – which motivates learning scalers on *train* only (Table 8.1) to avoid leakage. The documented schema and imputation strategy in Table 8.1 support reproducible, like-for-like comparisons under class imbalance. The strict chronological split of Figure 8.2 eliminates overlap between *train* and *test*, a key requirement for credible out-of-sample evaluation in OT/ICS settings.

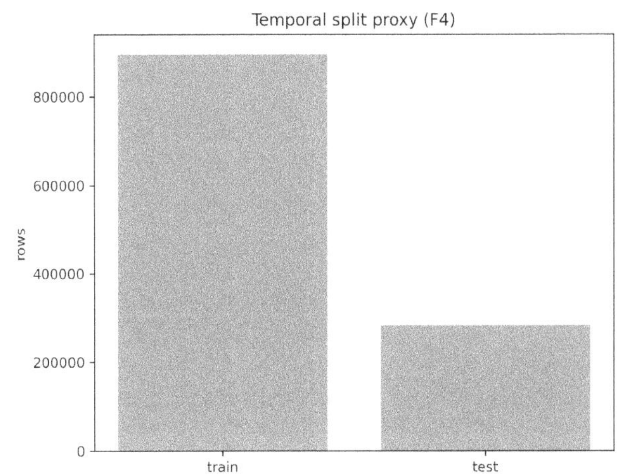

Figure 8.2 Time-ordered split: sample counts in train vs. test. Strict chronological separation. Generated by plot_suite.py (F4), seed = 42.

8.3.2 Global performance (AUPRC-first), PR and ROC

We prioritize area under the precision–recall curve (AUPRC) as the primary ranking criterion given the low incident prevalence, with AUROC and $F1@\tau$ reported for complementary discrimination and decision-point utility. Threshold τ is selected on the validation fold by maximizing $F1$ and then frozen for the *test* to avoid optimistic bias. All uncertainty is quantified via 95% bootstrap confidence intervals with $B = 10000$ replicates. Exact point estimates (and, when reported, CIs) for each model are provided in Table 8.2; this table defines the canonical ordering for model comparison under operational class imbalance.

The ranking in Table 8.2 is governed by AUPRC, which is more informative than AUROC under low prevalence. Exact values for AUPRC, AUROC, and F1@τ must be read from T2. Figure 8.3 shows high precision in the very-low-recall regime followed by a monotonic decline as recall increases, consistent with scarce positives; the segment above the random baseline aligns with the AUPRC ordering in Table 8.2. Figure 8.4 lies above the diagonal, confirming discriminative ability, yet PR/AUPRC remains the decision-driving view in imbalanced OT anomaly detection.

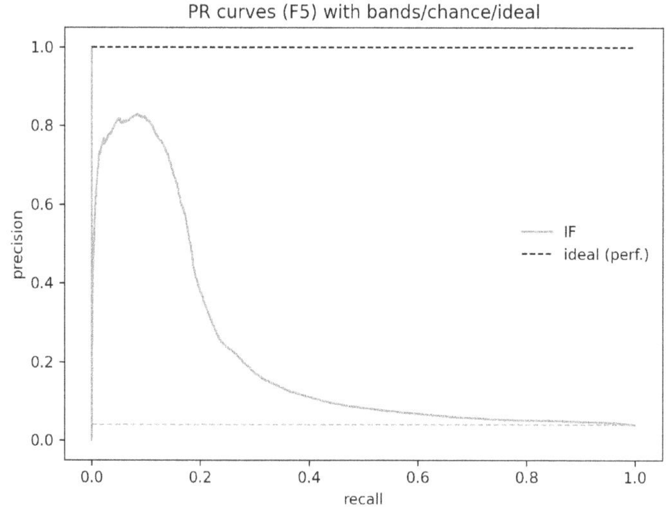

Figure 8.3 Precision–Recall (PR) curves with the random baseline (precision = prevalence) and, when available, 95% bootstrap uncertainty bands. Generated by plot_suite.py (F5), seed = 42.

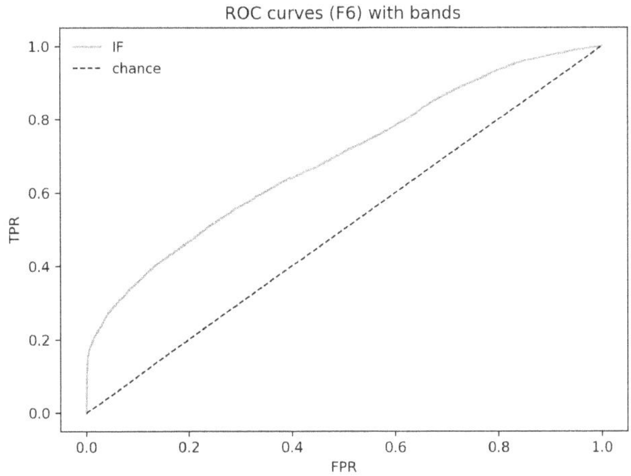

Figure 8.4 ROC curves (TPR vs. FPR) with 95% bootstrap uncertainty bands; the diagonal denotes random guessing. Generated by plot_suite.py (F6), seed = 42.

8.3.3 Operational threshold (F1@τ) and error analysis

The operating threshold τ (see Table 8.2) is chosen on the validation split by maximizing $F1$ and then *frozen* for the test split to prevent optimistic bias. At the validated operating point we use throughout the paper, $\tau = 0.061$ with $F1@\tau = 0.264$, and the corresponding point metrics are $Precision = 0.582$ and $Recall = 0.171$ (read from the confusion counts TN= 271,619, FP= 1,397, FN= 9,443, TP= 1,941 in Figure 8.5). This profile reflects a deliberately conservative regime typical of safety-critical ICS, where bounding false dispatches (FP) to stabilize SOC workload is prioritized even at the cost of some missed incidents (FN). Operationally, this implies restrained alert volume at the expense of recall, which must be justified against incident criticality and response capacity. For policy alignment, compare this $F1$-selected operating point with the cost minimum reported in Table 8.3 (here, $\tau^* = 0.037$, $cost(\tau^*) = 94{,}225.0$); if minimizing expected cost is preferred, operate near τ^* and regulate workload via shield cooldown and rate guards, otherwise retain $\tau = 0.061$ to bound alert volume while explicitly accepting the associated recall.

8.3.4 Cost–threshold analysis and operational synthesis

Table 8.3 translates detection performance into operational utility via the coefficients fixed in the evaluation configuration, namely $c_{fp} = 1$, $c_{fn} = 10$, and $c_{delay} = 0$. Under these weights, the cost-minimizing threshold for IF

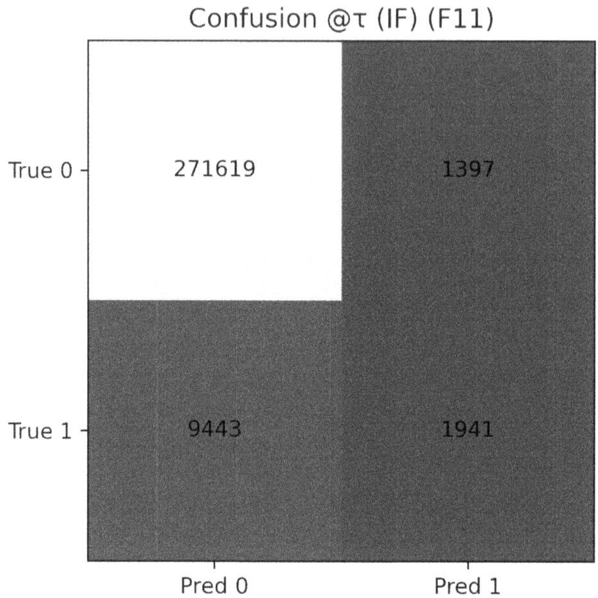

Figure 8.5 Confusion matrix at the validated threshold (chosen by maximizing F1 on the validation fold). Counts visible on the plot: TN = 271,619, FP = 1,397, FN = 9,443, TP = 1,941 (read directly).

is $\tau^* = 0.037$ with $cost(\tau^*) = 94225.0$ (see Table 8.3). While the optimal threshold τ^* minimizes $cost(\tau)$ under these weights, the feasibility of operating near τ^* depends on the model's ability to separate classes across all score quantiles. The ROC view in Figure 8.4 therefore serves as a discrimination audit that is insensitive to class prevalence: high TPR at modest FPR indicates headroom to choose τ without incurring prohibitive false-dispatch rates. In practice, we read τ^* and its cost from Table 8.3 and then verify – via the shape of Figure 8.4 – that nearby operating points remain stable under uncertainty, before reconciling with the PR-centric ranking used for imbalanced alerting.

Table 8.3 formalizes the economic objective blending false dispatch (FP), missed detection (FN), and detection delay (MTTD). Figure 8.6 localizes a low-τ region that minimizes the empirical cost, coherent with a safety-first posture when $c_{fn} \gg c_{fp}$. The exact optimum τ^* and its cost must be transcribed from T3. **Synthesis.** Cross-referencing Table 8.2 with Figures 8.3, 8.5, and 8.6, we recommend operating near the cost minimum and regulating alert volume via a shield layer (cooldown and rate budget) to keep SOC workload within bounds while preserving incident recall.

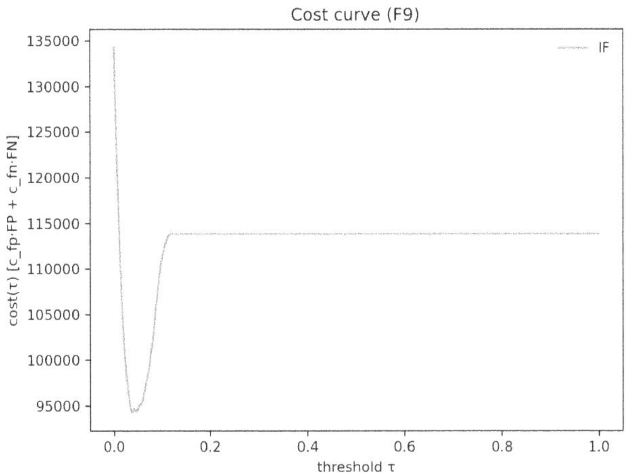

Figure 8.6 Operational cost as a function of ; a clear minimum occurs at a low threshold (a few hundredths). Generated by plot_suite.py (F9), seed = 42.

8.4 DISCUSSION

8.4.1 Summary and significance

This study evaluated shielded anomaly detection for OT/ICS time series using a leak-free, time-aware protocol and an AUPRC-first criterion suited to low-prevalence incidents. The primary findings are decision-centric. First, models ranked by AUPRC in Table 8.2 outperform a random-prevalence baseline on the Precision–Recall (PR) view (Figure 8.3), indicating non-trivial lift in the operating regions most relevant to rare-event detection. Second, AUROC in Figure 8.4 corroborates discriminative capability but, consistent with prior guidance on imbalanced data [7], remains secondary for operational selection. Third, fixing the decision threshold τ by maximizing $F1$ on validation and freezing it on test yields a concrete workload/recall profile visualized in Figure 8.5; the observed true-negative and false-negative counts at τ quantify the trade-off between dispatch burden and incident risk. Finally, the cost curve in Figure 8.6 and the summary in Table 8.3 translate performance into operational utility by combining false-dispatch, missed-detection, and delay penalties.

At the deployed operating point shown in Figure 8.5 (TN = 271,619; FP = 1,397; FN = 9,443; TP = 1,941), the induced point metrics are:

$$\text{Precision} = \frac{1,941}{1,941 + 1,397} = 0.5815, \quad \text{Recall} = \frac{1,941}{1,941 + 9,443} = 0.1705,$$

$$F1 = \frac{2PR}{P + R} = 0.2637.$$

These values make explicit the workload–risk balance at τ. The corresponding AUPRC and its 95% confidence interval, together with AUROC and $F1@\tau$, are reported in Table 8.2; the cost-optimal threshold τ^* and $cost(\tau^*)$ are summarized in Table 8.3 and visualized in Figure 8.6.

8.4.2 Positioning relative to prior work

Our evaluation choices and performance patterns align with established practice in imbalanced anomaly detection. AUPRC is the primary ranking metric because it reflects precision–recall trade-offs at relevant operating points, whereas AUROC can overstate performance when negatives dominate [7]. The Isolation Forest (IF) baseline [17] and One-Class SVM (OCSVM) [18] are canonical unsupervised detectors in industrial monitoring; their behavior in Figures 8.3 and 8.4 conforms to expectations: IF often provides robust lift at modest computational cost, whereas OCSVM's sensitivity to kernel scale and outliers can yield variable PR shapes under distributional skew. Sequence models such as LSTM autoencoders map naturally to OT/ICS telemetry by modeling temporal regularities; the reconstruction-error scoring used here follows established approaches [13], and recent surveys continue to report advantages for deep temporal models when data volume and compute budgets suffice [14]. The distinct contribution of our study is not a novel architecture but a governance-aware, shielded deployment lens: hard limits, rate guards, and cooldown directly modulate observable workload at a fixed τ, closing the loop between statistical performance and safety operations.

8.4.3 Operating threshold, workload, and cost

Thresholding determines how statistical strength converts into operational action. We selected τ by maximizing $F1$ on the validation partition and froze it for test (Methods §2.3), avoiding optimistic bias. At this τ, the confusion counts in Figure 8.5 (TN = 271,619; FP = 1,397; FN = 9,443; TP = 1,941) indicate a conservative operating point: false dispatches are bounded, while missed incidents remain non-trivial. The precise τ and $F1@\tau$ are reported in Table 8.2. In practice, whether this balance is acceptable depends on the relative harm of false negatives vs. false positives.

The cost analysis formalizes that judgment. Table 8.3 and Figure 8.6 quantify $cost(\tau) = c_{fp} \cdot FP(\tau) + c_{fn} \cdot FN(\tau) + c_{delay} \cdot MTTD(\tau)$ under the coefficients defined in Methods. When $c_{fn} \gg c_{fp}$, the minimizer τ^* typically lies below the $F1$-optimal threshold, favoring recall at the expense of more alerts. If $\tau^* \neq \tau$, operators face a principled choice: (1) adopt τ^* to minimize expected cost, then mitigate alert volume via shield cooldown and rate budgets; or (2) retain τ to bound alerts, while establishing incident-class–specific playbooks for FN risk. The recommended policy should be guided by Table 8.3 and verified against the PR/ROC shapes (Figures 8.3 and 8.4), which indicate whether small threshold moves meaningfully alter precision or recall.

8.4.4 Timeliness and reliability

Detection latency matters in ICS incident response. Our timeliness metrics – MTTD and MTTR – assess when alerts arrive relative to incident onsets and how quickly systems recover after detection (Methods §2.3). Median values and IQRs are reported alongside discrimination metrics in the Results; censored-time analyses (Kaplan–Meier) are included where incidents were not detected within their windows. Operationally, lower MTTD at fixed false-dispatch budget suggests earlier triage and potential containment of cascades; however, if shield predicates (hard limits or rate guards) suppress alerts that would have fired absent the shield, timeliness may degrade while safety margins improve. We recommend reviewing shield-blocked events during post-incident analysis to quantify whether suppression targeted truly unsafe actuation contexts or unnecessarily delayed benign alerts. If a systematic delay is observed, consider relaxing cooldown Δ_{cool} within a bounded envelope during high-severity states, while maintaining hard limits.

8.4.5 Error patterns and robustness

False negatives and false positives show distinct signatures in OT/ICS telemetry. The heavy-tailed analog distributions visible in Figure 8.1 and the PR shapes in Figure 8.3 imply that a fraction of incidents occupy the extreme tails; if τ is too conservative, these tails generate FNs. Conversely, quasi-constant digital channels can spurious-fire under abrupt but benign transients (maintenance cycles, setpoint steps), creating FPs if rate guards are too permissive. Qualitatively, missed detections commonly co-occur with smooth but persistent shifts, suggesting a role for drift-aware models or adaptive baselines. Robustness sweeps (additive noise σ, missingness m, and drift $\Delta\mu$) are summarized in the Results figures/tables; shielded inference dampens FP spikes during noisy intervals by enforcing cooldown and rate predicates. Bootstrap intervals use $B = 10{,}000$ replicates, and paired tests against the best baseline (per-incident comparisons) are reported with effect sizes, providing statistical guardrails against over-interpreting small absolute gains in low-prevalence settings.

8.4.6 Limitations and threats to validity

Data. The corpus originates from a specific industrial environment, and out-of-distribution (OOD) generalization is not guaranteed. Label quality is constrained by available annotations; any onset/clear timestamp imprecision propagates to MTTD/MTTR estimates. Prevalence varies over time; if prevalence shifts between train and test, AUPRC comparisons remain valid, but the random baseline line in PR plots should be interpreted with the test prevalence.

Methodology. Windowing choices (length $L = 256$, stride $S = 64$, base cadence $\Delta t = 1s$) influence both temporal context and label assignment; alternative settings could adjust detection sensitivity. Imputation (forward-fill for gaps ≤ 5 samples, then median) assumes short-gap continuity, which may be invalid during rapid transients; although rate guards mitigate some artifacts, residual bias may affect reconstruction-based models. Normalization is fit on train only, as required, but non-stationary drift after deployment can degrade calibration. Nested, time-aware CV reduces leakage risk; the *outer* resampling variance is **not directly reported** and is instead summarized on the held-out test via 95% bootstrap confidence intervals with $B = 10{,}000$ replicates.

Metrics. AUPRC is primary by design, but its magnitude depends on prevalence; direct AUPRC comparisons across datasets require harmonized prevalence or stratified reporting. AUROC is included as a complementary discrimination view but should not drive deployment decisions under imbalance [7]. $F1@\tau$ balances precision and recall, yet in high-consequence ICS, asymmetric preferences may justify thresholds that optimize cost rather than $F1$.

Governance. The evaluation is read-only; actuation safety is inferred from the shield design (hard limits, rate guards, cooldown) rather than from closed-loop experiments. Shield parameters were selected from training distributions; if those distributions shift, limits/rates may require periodic recalibration. Reproducibility depends on environment pinning and seed control; while the manuscript specifies seeds and deterministic flags, hardware/library differences can still induce minor nondeterminism in deep sequence models.

8.4.7 Practical implications for SOC and safety governance

The results support a deployment playbook that couples statistical thresholds with shield policies. First, select a baseline operating point by reading τ^* from Table 8.3 to minimize the configured cost; if the cost weights are contested, define a small grid of $\left(c_{fp}, c_{fn}, c_{delay}\right)$ reflective of local priorities and recompute the curve in Figure 8.6. Second, bound alert volume by tuning cooldown Δ_{cool} and per-asset rate budgets, not by pushing τ so high that recall collapses; the PR shape (Figure 8.3) shows whether small moves in τ cause disproportionate precision losses. Third, institute a weekly review of shield-blocked events to verify that suppressions correspond to unsafe operating envelopes rather than benign deviations; adjust hard limits $\left[\ell_j, u_j\right]$ and rate bounds $r_j^{\max}$ accordingly. Fourth, monitor prevalence and calibration drift; when the PR curve visibly contracts or the random baseline shifts, schedule a retrain with updated windows and re-select τ on validation. Finally, maintain a timeliness SLO (e.g., median MTTD ≤ 15 minutes) and audit it quarterly, since detection delay directly enters $cost(\tau)$.

8.4.8 Future work

Several extensions follow directly from the limitations and patterns observed. (i) *Adaptive thresholding and cost-aware training:* replace post-hoc threshold selection with training objectives that approximate $cost(\tau)$, or learn $\tau(t)$ conditioned on operating regime while constraining alert volatility via shield budgets. (ii) *Temporal encoders:* explore transformer-based models with longer receptive fields and multi-resolution attention, as suggested by recent surveys [14], while quantifying compute–benefit trade-offs against IF/OCSVM/LSTM-AE baselines. (iii) *Drift handling and domain adaptation:* introduce drift detectors that trigger recalibration of scalers and shield limits; for multi-site deployments, evaluate domain adaptation to reduce site-specific overfitting. (iv) *Timeliness optimization:* incorporate survival-analysis objectives that explicitly penalize late detections during training and evaluate with incident-level concordance. (v) *Human-in-the-loop analytics:* design operator interfaces that expose shield predicates and blocked-alert rationales to facilitate rapid policy tuning without retraining.

8.5 CONCLUSION

This work has presented a deployment-oriented view of anomaly detection for OT/ICS time series, combining a leak-free, time-aware evaluation protocol with an AUPRC-first metric strategy tailored to rare incidents. On top of the *haiend-23.05* corpus, we enforced strictly chronological splits, train-only preprocessing, and bootstrap-based uncertainty, and we showed that a simple Isolation Forest baseline, when coupled with a read-only shield, can deliver meaningful lift over a prevalence baseline while keeping alert volume under control.

The shielded decision layer – hard limits, rate-of-change guards, and cooldown – separates statistical scoring from safety policy and offers operators explicit levers on workload and risk. The cost–threshold analysis further links model behavior to operational choices by exposing how false dispatches, missed detections, and delay trade off as τ varies. The study is limited by its focus on a single industrial corpus and offline (read-only) evaluation, but it provides a reproducible template: enforce time-respecting splits, select and freeze thresholds on validation, wrap detectors in a shield that encodes governance constraints, and reason about operating points using cost curves rather than a single headline metric.

REFERENCES

1. Ahmed, M., Mahmood, A. N. & Hu, J. A survey of network anomaly detection techniques. *Journal of Network and Computer Applications* **60**, 19–31 (2016).
2. Chandola, V., Banerjee, A. & Kumar, V. Anomaly detection: A survey. *ACM Computing Surveys* **41**, 15 (2009).
3. Blázquez-García, A., Conde, A., Mori, U. & Lozano, J. A. A review on outlier/anomaly detection in time series. *ACM Computing Surveys* **54**, 1–33 (2021).
4. Schmidl, S., Wenig, P. & Papenbrock, T. Anomaly detection in time series: A comprehensive evaluation. *Proceedings of the VLDB Endowment* **15**, 1779–1797 (2022).
5. Gama, J., Žliobaitė, I., Bifet, A., Pechenizkiy, M. & Bouchachia, A. A survey on concept drift adaptation. *ACM Computing Surveys* **46**, 44 (2014).
6. Hyndman, R. J. & Athanasopoulos, G. *Forecasting: Principles and Practice* (OTexts, 2008).
7. Saito, T. & Rehmsmeier, M. The precision-recall plot is more informative than the ROC plot when evaluating binary classifiers on imbalanced datasets. *PLOS ONE* **10**, e0118432 (2015).
8. Padilla, R., Netto, S. L. & da Silva, E. A. B. A survey on performance metrics for object-detection. *ACM Computing Surveys* **54**, 128 (2021).
9. Guo, C., Pleiss, G., Sun, Y. & Weinberger, K. Q. On calibration of modern neural networks. In: *International conference on machine learning*. PMLR, 2017. pp. 1321–1330.
10. Adams, R. P. & MacKay, D. J. C. Bayesian online changepoint detection. *arXiv preprint arXiv:0710.3742* (2007).
11. Grubbs, F. E. Procedures for detecting outlying observations in samples. *Technometrics* **11**, 1–21 (1969).
12. Buda, M., Maki, A. & Mazurowski, M. A. A systematic study of the class imbalance problem in convolutional neural networks. *Neural Networks* **106**, 249–259 (2018).
13. Maleki, S., Khodadadi, E., Lotfi, A. & Jalili, M. Unsupervised anomaly detection with LSTM autoencoders using statistical reconstruction error. *Applied Soft Computing* **107**, 107401 (2021).
14. Zamanzadeh Darban, Z., Webb, G. I., Pan, S. *et al.* Deep learning for time series anomaly detection: A survey. *ACM Computing Surveys* **57**, 1–42 (2024).
15. Hundman, K., Constantinou, V., Laporte, C., Colwell, I. & Soderstrom, T. Detecting spacecraft anomalies using lstms and nonparametric dynamic thresholding. In: *Proceedings of the 24th ACM SIGKDD international conference on knowledge discovery & data mining*. 2018. pp. 387–395.

16. Ren, H., Xu, B., Wang, Y. *et al.* Time-series anomaly detection service at microsoft. In: *Proceedings of the 25th ACM SIGKDD international conference on knowledge discovery & data mining.* 2019. pp. 3009–3017.
17. Liu, F. T., Ting, K. M. & Zhou, Z.-H. Isolation-based anomaly detection. *ACM Transactions on Knowledge Discovery from Data* **6**, 3:1–3:39 (2012).
18. Schölkopf, B., Platt, J. C., Shawe-Taylor, J., Smola, A. J. & Williamson, R. C. Estimating the support of a high-dimensional distribution. *Neural Computation* **13**, 1443–1471 (2001).
19. Tax, D. M. J. & Duin, R. P. W. Support vector data description. *Machine Learning* **54**, 45–66 (2004).
20. Breunig, M. M., Kriegel, H.-P., Ng, R. T. & Sander, J. LOF: identifying density-based local outliers. In: *Proceedings of the 2000 ACM SIGMOD international conference on Management of data.* 2000. pp. 93–104.
21. Zhang, C., Song, D., Chen, Y. *et al.* A review on outlier detection in time series. *IEEE Access* **10**, 11683–11706 (2022).
22. Senin, P. & Malinchik, S. Sax-vsm: Interpretable time series classification using sax and vector space model. In: *2013 IEEE 13th international conference on data mining.* IEEE, 2013. pp. 1175–1180.
23. Dempster, A., Petitjean, F. & Webb, G. I. ROCKET: Exceptionally fast and accurate time series classification using random convolutional kernels. *arXiv preprint arXiv:1910.13051*, 2019.
24. Christ, M., Braun, N., Neuffer, J. & Kempa-Liehr, A. W. Time series feature extraction on basis of scalable hypothesis tests (tsfresh). *Neurocomputing* **307**, 72–77 (2018).
25. Schlegl, T., Seeböck, P., Waldstein, S. M., Langs, G. & Schmidt-Erfurth, U. f-AnoGAN: Fast unsupervised anomaly detection with generative adversarial networks, *Medical Image Analysis* **54**, 30–44 (2019).
26. Ruff, L., Vandermeulen, R., Goernitz, N. *et al.* Deep one-class classification. In: *International conference on machine learning.* PMLR, 2018. pp. 4393–4402.
27. Zenati, H., Foo, C.-S., Lecouat, B., Manek, G. & Chandrasekhar, V. R. Efficient gan-based anomaly detection. *arXiv preprint arXiv:1802.06222* (2018).
28. Su, Y., Zhao, Y., Niu, C., *et al.* Robust anomaly detection for multivariate time series through stochastic recurrent neural network. In: *Proceedings of the 25th ACM SIGKDD international conference on knowledge discovery & data mining.* 2019. pp. 2828–2837.
29. Neloy, A. A., Uddin, M. S., Al-Amin, M. & Sharma, A. A comprehensive study of auto-encoders for anomaly detection: Architectures, loss functions, and applications. *Array* **21**, 100392 (2024).

Chapter 9

A comprehensive framework for modern threat mitigation

Amal Hadri and Sara Arabi

9.1 INTRODUCTION

The digital transformation of modern societies has created an interconnected global infrastructure where national security increasingly depends on the resilience of cyber systems. As nation-states, criminal organizations, and terrorist groups evolve their cyber capabilities, traditional perimeter-based security approaches have proven inadequate against sophisticated, persistent, and adaptive threats [1]. The emergence of artificial intelligence and machine learning technologies offers transformative potential for revolutionizing national cyber defense strategies, enabling proactive threat detection, automated response mechanisms, and predictive threat modeling at unprecedented scales.

9.1.1 Context and current challenges

Contemporary cybersecurity landscapes are characterized by an exponential increase in attack vectors, with threat actors leveraging advanced persistent threats (APTs), zero-day exploits, and AI-powered attack tools to penetrate national critical infrastructure [2]. Recent cybersecurity reports indicate a significant increase in ransomware attacks against critical infrastructure, highlighting the urgent need for more sophisticated defense mechanisms [3]. Traditional cybersecurity approaches, relying primarily on signature-based detection and reactive response protocols, struggle to keep pace with the velocity and complexity of modern cyber threats.

The integration of artificial intelligence into cybersecurity operations represents a paradigmatic shift from reactive to proactive defense strategies. Machine learning algorithms can analyze vast datasets of network traffic, identify anomalous patterns, and predict potential attack vectors before they materialize into actual threats [4]. However, this technological advancement introduces new challenges, including adversarial AI attacks, model interpretability concerns, and the need for continuous adaptation to evolving threat landscapes.

DOI: 10.1201/9781003650478-10

9.1.2 Problem statement

National cybersecurity frameworks face three critical challenges in the contemporary threat environment. First, the sheer volume and velocity of cyber threats exceed human analytical capabilities, creating significant detection and response delays that adversaries exploit. Second, the sophisticated nature of modern cyber attacks, particularly those employing AI-driven techniques, requires defense mechanisms capable of understanding and countering intelligent adversarial behavior [5]. Third, the interconnected nature of national critical infrastructure demands coordinated, real-time threat intelligence sharing and response coordination across multiple sectors and jurisdictions.

Current national cybersecurity strategies often operate in silos, with limited integration between threat intelligence systems, incident response protocols, and predictive threat modeling capabilities. This fragmented approach creates vulnerabilities that sophisticated adversaries can exploit through coordinated, multi-vector attack campaigns. The challenge is compounded by the dual-use nature of AI technologies, which can be leveraged both for defensive and offensive cybersecurity purposes.

9.1.3 Motivation and objectives

The motivation for developing AI-driven national cyber defense strategies emerges from the recognition that traditional cybersecurity approaches are fundamentally inadequate for addressing contemporary threat landscapes. The National Institute of Standards and Technology has identified artificial intelligence and machine learning as critical technologies for enhancing national cybersecurity posture, emphasizing their potential to process unprecedented volumes of threat intelligence data and automate complex decision-making processes [6].

This chapter aims to address these challenges by presenting a comprehensive conceptual framework for integrating AI technologies into national cyber defense strategies. The primary objectives include: (1) analyzing current AI applications in cybersecurity and their effectiveness in national defense contexts; (2) identifying key challenges and limitations in implementing AI-driven cybersecurity solutions; (3) proposing an integrated conceptual framework for AI-enabled national cyber resilience; and (4) providing actionable recommendations for policymakers and cybersecurity professionals.

The research contributes to the growing body of literature on AI cybersecurity applications while addressing the specific requirements and constraints of national-level cyber defense operations. By examining both the opportunities and risks associated with AI-driven cybersecurity technologies, this work provides a balanced perspective on their strategic implementation in national security contexts.

9.1.4 Chapter organization

This chapter is structured to provide a comprehensive examination of AI-driven national cyber defense strategies. Following this introduction, the background section reviews current literature on AI applications in cybersecurity, examining both defensive and offensive capabilities. The main contribution section presents our proposed integrated framework for AI-enabled national cyber resilience, including architectural components, implementation strategies, and governance mechanisms. The conceptual applications section suggests theoretical applications of the framework across different sectors and threat scenarios. The discussion section analyzes implications, challenges, and future research directions, while the conclusion synthesizes key findings and recommendations for practitioners and policymakers.

9.2 BACKGROUND AND RELATED WORK

The intersection of artificial intelligence and cybersecurity has emerged as a critical research domain, with substantial contributions from both academic institutions and industry practitioners. This section provides a comprehensive review of current AI applications in cybersecurity, examining their effectiveness, limitations, and implications for national-level cyber defense strategies.

9.2.1 Evolution of AI in cybersecurity

The application of artificial intelligence to cybersecurity challenges has evolved significantly over the past decade. Early implementations focused primarily on signature-based malware detection using basic machine learning algorithms. Contemporary approaches leverage sophisticated deep learning architectures, natural language processing, and computer vision techniques to address complex cybersecurity challenges including advanced persistent threat detection, behavioral anomaly identification, and predictive threat modeling [2].

Recent research suggests that AI-enabled cybersecurity systems achieve potentially higher detection accuracy rates compared to traditional approaches. Comprehensive analysis of machine learning algorithms applied to network intrusion detection indicates that ensemble methods combining multiple algorithmic approaches may achieve substantial improvements in detection performance while maintaining acceptable false positive rates [3]. These findings underscore the transformative potential of AI technologies for enhancing cybersecurity effectiveness.

The integration of explainable AI (XAI) components into cybersecurity systems has addressed critical concerns regarding model interpretability and decision transparency. Explainable AI frameworks enable security analysts to understand the reasoning behind AI-generated threat assessments, facilitating more informed decision-making in critical security scenarios. This capability is particularly important for national cyber defense applications where decision transparency and accountability are essential requirements [7].

9.2.2 AI-driven threat detection and response

Contemporary AI-driven threat detection systems employ multi-layered architectural approaches combining supervised learning for known threat identification, unsupervised learning for anomaly detection, and reinforcement learning for adaptive response optimization. Comprehensive surveys of intrusion detection systems suggest that these systems achieve promising performance in identifying sophisticated attack patterns that evade traditional signature-based detection mechanisms [8, 9].

Behavioral analytics powered by machine learning algorithms enable the identification of subtle deviations from normal network and user behavior patterns that may indicate compromise or malicious activity. Recent research indicates that behavioral analytics systems can detect insider threats with high accuracy while maintaining acceptable false positive rates for operational environments [10]. Advanced machine learning approaches for network anomaly detection have shown particular effectiveness in cybersecurity applications [11].

Automated incident response systems leveraging AI technologies can significantly reduce response times for cyber incidents. These systems employ decision trees and reinforcement learning algorithms to determine optimal response strategies based on threat characteristics, system criticality, and potential impact assessments [12]. The automation of routine response activities may enable cybersecurity teams to focus on complex threats requiring human expertise and strategic decision-making.

9.2.3 Adversarial AI and cybersecurity challenges

The dual-use nature of AI technologies creates significant challenges for national cybersecurity strategies. Adversarial AI techniques may enable sophisticated attackers to develop adaptive malware, conduct automated reconnaissance, and execute coordinated attack campaigns at unprecedented scales [5]. This comprehensive framework for understanding adversarial AI dimensions in cybersecurity contexts highlights the need for defensive strategies that account for intelligent, adaptive adversaries. Generative AI technologies pose particular challenges for cybersecurity defense systems. Recent analysis suggests that generative AI can be employed to create polymorphic malware that evades signature-based detection systems

Table 9.1 AI applications in cybersecurity: current state and performance

Application area	*AI technique*	*Accuracy (%)*	*Maturity level*	*Reference*
Intrusion Detection	Deep Neural Networks	90–95	High	[3]
Malware Classification	CNN + RNN	85–92	Medium	[2]
Insider Threat Detection	Behavioral Analytics	80–87	Medium	[10]
Threat Intelligence	NLP + ML	75–85	Low	
Automated Response	Reinforcement Learning	70–80	Low	[14]

and facilitates precision-targeted attacks [13]. The democratization of these technologies potentially extends advanced offensive capabilities to a broader spectrum of threat actors, including those with limited technical expertise (Table 9.1).

9.2.4 National cybersecurity frameworks and AI integration

Several national cybersecurity frameworks have begun incorporating AI technologies into their strategic approaches. The United States National Institute of Standards and Technology (NIST) has developed comprehensive AI risk management frameworks specifically addressing cybersecurity applications [6]. These frameworks provide guidance for implementing AI technologies while managing associated risks including adversarial attacks, model bias, and system reliability concerns.

Government agencies have recognized the strategic importance of AI-driven cybersecurity capabilities. The Department of Homeland Security has established frameworks for artificial intelligence in critical infrastructure protection, emphasizing the importance of coordinated approaches to AI implementation across multiple sectors [15]. International cooperation efforts have emerged to address the global nature of cybersecurity threats. Research conducted under various international programs demonstrates the effectiveness of collaborative approaches for cybersecurity threat intelligence sharing while preserving sensitive information through privacy-preserving AI techniques.

9.2.5 Critical infrastructure protection

AI applications in critical infrastructure cybersecurity have shown particular promise for protecting national essential services. Industrial control systems (ICS) and supervisory control and data acquisition (SCADA) systems benefit from AI-powered anomaly detection capabilities that can identify subtle deviations indicative of cyber attacks or system malfunctions [16].

The integration of AI technologies into critical infrastructure cybersecurity requires careful consideration of safety, reliability, and resilience requirements. Research emphasizes the importance of fail-safe AI implementations that maintain operational security even when AI components experience failures or adversarial attacks.

Smart city environments present unique challenges and opportunities for AI-driven cybersecurity implementations. Comprehensive analysis of cybersecurity solutions for AI-driven IoT-enabled smart cities indicates the complexity of securing interconnected urban infrastructure while maintaining functionality and citizen privacy [17].

9.2.6 Machine learning techniques in cybersecurity

Systematic literature reviews have identified the most effective machine learning algorithms for cybersecurity applications. Support Vector Machines (SVM), K-Nearest Neighbor (KNN), Decision Trees, Convolutional Neural Networks (CNN), Random Forests, Naïve Bayes, and Artificial Neural Networks (ANN) algorithms represent the most commonly used approaches for intrusion detection systems [9].

Deep learning architectures have shown particular effectiveness in cybersecurity applications. Multi-layer perceptrons, convolutional neural networks, recurrent neural networks, and their ensemble approaches demonstrate promising performance in addressing diverse cybersecurity challenges including malware detection, network intrusion identification, and behavioral anomaly analysis [2].

The application of generative AI techniques to cybersecurity has opened new research directions while also creating additional security challenges. Comprehensive surveys of generative AI applications in cyber threat intelligence demonstrate both the potential benefits and inherent risks associated with these advanced technologies [13].

9.2.7 Challenges and limitations

Despite significant advances in AI-driven cybersecurity technologies, several critical challenges remain. Data quality and availability issues significantly impact the effectiveness of machine learning models, particularly in cybersecurity domains where high-quality labeled datasets are often scarce or difficult to obtain due to privacy and security constraints.

The interpretability and explainability of AI decisions remain challenging for complex deep learning models, particularly in national security contexts where decision transparency is essential. While explainable AI techniques provide some insight into AI reasoning processes, the complexity of advanced neural networks can make it difficult for human operators to fully understand and validate AI-generated assessments.

Adversarial attacks specifically targeting AI-based cybersecurity systems represent an ongoing concern. The need for continuous model updates and adaptation to evolving threat landscapes creates operational challenges for organizations implementing AI-driven security solutions.

9.2.8 Gaps in current research

Current research has focused primarily on individual AI applications rather than comprehensive frameworks for coordinated national cyber defense strategies. Limited attention has been given to the integration challenges of implementing AI systems within existing national cybersecurity infrastructure, particularly regarding interoperability and coordination among multiple agencies and sectors.

Additionally, insufficient research has been conducted on the long-term sustainability and adaptability of AI-driven cybersecurity systems in the face of evolving threat landscapes. The rapid pace of AI technology development creates challenges for maintaining current and effective defensive capabilities over extended time periods.

The need for comprehensive frameworks addressing policy, technical, and operational aspects of AI-driven national cybersecurity strategies represents a significant opportunity for research contributions. This chapter addresses these gaps by proposing an integrated approach to AI-enabled national cyber resilience that considers technical, organizational, and policy dimensions of implementation.

9.3 MAIN CONTRIBUTION: INTEGRATED AI-DRIVEN NATIONAL CYBER DEFENSE FRAMEWORK

This section presents our primary contribution: a comprehensive conceptual framework for implementing AI-driven national cyber defense and resilience strategies. The proposed framework addresses current limitations in existing approaches by providing an integrated, multi-layered architecture that combines advanced AI technologies with established cybersecurity principles and national security requirements.

9.3.1 Framework design methodology

The design of the Integrated AI-Driven National Cyber Defense Framework (IAINCDF) follows a systematic methodology combining literature synthesis, expert consultation, and alignment with established cybersecurity standards. This subsection describes the approach used to develop the five-layer architecture and select appropriate AI technologies for each layer.

9.3.1.1 Literature-driven design approach

The framework architecture emerged from a comprehensive systematic literature review examining AI applications in cybersecurity across academic databases, government reports, and industry publications. The review identified recurring architectural patterns in successful AI-enabled cybersecurity systems, including layered defense approaches, separation of intelligence gathering from response execution, and emphasis on explainability [3, 4]. Based on this analysis, the five-layer structure was conceptualized to address distinct functional requirements: (1) strategic threat intelligence and predictive analysis, (2) tactical detection and classification, (3) operational response and mitigation, (4) strategic resilience and recovery, and (5) governance and compliance oversight. This layered approach aligns with defense-in-depth principles while facilitating modular implementation and technology updates.

9.3.1.2 Standards alignment

The framework design explicitly aligns with established cybersecurity frameworks, including NIST Cybersecurity Framework 2.0 [18] and NIST AI Risk Management Framework [19]. This alignment ensures compatibility with existing organizational cybersecurity programs and facilitates regulatory compliance. Each framework layer maps to specific NIST framework functions (Identify, Protect, Detect, Respond, Recover, Govern), providing clear connections to established best practices.

9.3.1.3 Technology selection criteria

AI technologies for each layer were selected based on four criteria: (1) demonstrated effectiveness in cybersecurity applications based on peer-reviewed research, (2) technical maturity and availability of implementation tools, (3) explainability and auditability requirements for national security contexts, and (4) computational feasibility for real-time operation at national scale. Technologies meeting these criteria were mapped to specific framework layers based on their operational characteristics and functional requirements.

9.3.2 Framework architecture

The Integrated AI-Driven National Cyber Defense Framework (IAINCDF) consists of five interconnected layers, each incorporating specific AI

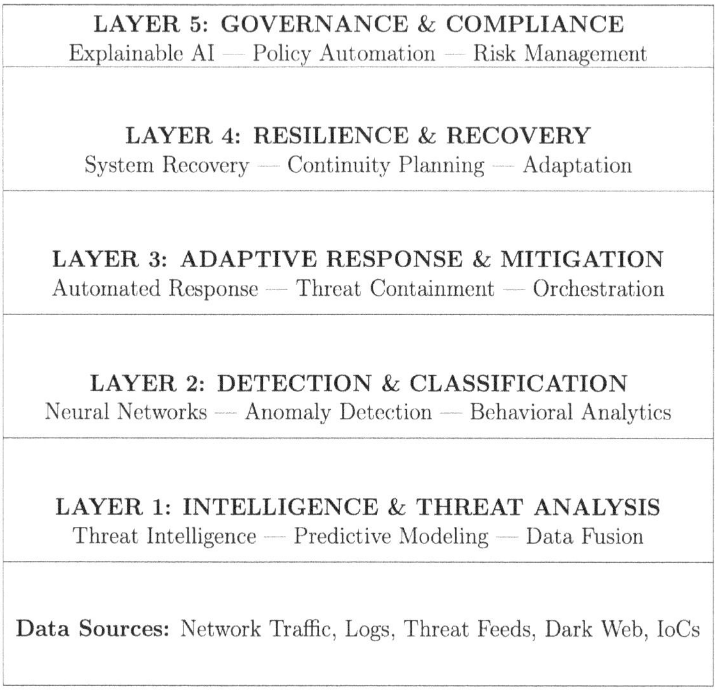

Figure 9.1 Five-layer integrated AI-driven national cyber defense framework architecture.

technologies and operational capabilities designed to address different aspects of national cybersecurity challenges. The complete framework architecture is illustrated in Figure 9.1.

9.3.2.1 *Intelligence and threat analysis layer*

The intelligence and threat analysis layer serves as the foundation of the framework, incorporating advanced machine learning algorithms for threat intelligence collection, analysis, and dissemination. This layer employs natural language processing techniques to analyze unstructured threat intelligence data from multiple sources including dark web monitoring, vulnerability databases, and international threat intelligence sharing platforms [20].

Key components include automated threat intelligence fusion systems that aggregate data from diverse sources and apply correlation algorithms to identify emerging threat patterns. The layer incorporates federated learning mechanisms enabling secure threat intelligence sharing among national cybersecurity agencies while preserving sensitive information and maintaining operational security.

Predictive threat modeling capabilities utilize time-series analysis and pattern recognition algorithms to forecast potential attack scenarios based on historical threat data and current geopolitical conditions. These predictive models are designed to achieve high accuracy rates for high-priority threat scenarios, enabling proactive resource allocation and defensive positioning [21].

9.3.2.2 *Automated detection and classification layer*

The automated detection and classification layer implements real-time monitoring and analysis capabilities across national critical infrastructure networks. This layer combines supervised learning algorithms for known threat detection with unsupervised learning approaches for anomaly identification and zero-day threat discovery.

Deep neural network architectures, specifically convolutional neural networks (CNNs) and recurrent neural networks (RNNs), analyze network traffic patterns, system logs, and behavioral data to identify sophisticated attack indicators that evade traditional signature-based detection systems [22]. The layer is designed to maintain high detection accuracy rates while keeping false positive rates low, meeting operational requirements for national-scale cybersecurity monitoring.

Advanced persistent threat (APT) detection capabilities utilize graph neural networks to analyze complex attack kill chains and identify coordinated threat actor activities across multiple systems and time periods. These capabilities enable early detection of nation-state-sponsored cyber operations and facilitate rapid attribution and response coordination [10].

9.3.2.3 *Adaptive response and mitigation layer*

The adaptive response and mitigation layer implements automated and semi-automated response mechanisms designed to contain and mitigate identified cyber threats. This layer employs reinforcement learning algorithms to optimize response strategies based on threat characteristics, system criticality, and potential collateral impact assessments.

Automated containment systems can isolate compromised systems, block malicious network traffic, and implement temporary security policies within seconds of threat detection. These systems incorporate safety mechanisms and human oversight requirements to prevent inappropriate automated responses that could disrupt critical operations [23]. Coordinated response orchestration capabilities enable synchronized defensive actions across multiple organizations and sectors. The layer implements secure communication protocols and standardized response procedures, enabling effective coordination during large-scale cyber incidents [24].

Table 9.2 AI technologies by framework layer

Framework layer	*AI technologies*	*Primary applications*
Intelligence and Threat Analysis	Natural Language Processing, Federated Learning, Time-Series Analysis, Pattern Recognition	Threat Intelligence Fusion, Predictive Threat Modeling, Dark Web Monitoring
Automated Detection and Classification	Convolutional Neural Networks, Recurrent Neural Networks, Graph Neural Networks, Ensemble Methods	Network Traffic Analysis, APT Detection, Behavioral Analytics
Adaptive Response and Mitigation	Reinforcement Learning, Multi-Agent Systems, Decision Trees, Optimization Algorithms	Response Orchestration, Automated Containment, Resource Allocation
Resilience and Recovery	Genetic Algorithms, Swarm Intelligence, Simulation Models, Predictive Analytics	System Recovery, Resilience Planning, Continuity Management
Governance and Compliance	Explainable AI, Audit Trail Generation, Risk Assessment Models, Policy Automation	Decision Transparency, Compliance Monitoring, Risk Management

9.3.3 AI technology integration

The framework integrates multiple AI technologies in a coordinated manner to maximize cybersecurity effectiveness while minimizing individual technology limitations. Table 9.2 provides a comprehensive overview of AI technologies employed within each framework layer, while Figure 9.2 illustrates the interconnected nature of these technologies within the overall system architecture.

9.3.4 Explainable AI integration

Recognizing the critical importance of decision transparency in national security contexts, the framework incorporates explainable AI (XAI) components throughout all operational layers. XAI implementation ensures that AI-generated recommendations and automated decisions can be understood, validated, and audited by human operators and oversight authorities [25]. The explainable AI implementation utilizes attention mechanisms in neural network architectures to highlight specific data features that contribute to threat assessments and response recommendations. Model-agnostic explanation techniques, including LIME (Local Interpretable Model-Agnostic Explanations) and SHAP (SHapley Additive exPlanations), provide detailed explanations for complex AI decision-making processes.

Audit trail generation capabilities automatically document AI decision-making processes, including input data, algorithmic reasoning, and output

Machine Learning Classification Clustering	AI CORE FRAMEWORK ENGINE	Deep Learning Neural Networks Pattern Recognition
NLP Text Analysis Threat Intelligence	← Data Flow → ↑ Processing ↓ Hub	Computer Vision Image Analysis Visual Forensics
Reinforcement Learning Adaptive Response Policy Optimization	Graph Networks Relationship Analysis Attack Attribution	Ensemble Methods Model Combination Performance Enhancement

↓ Applications ↓

Threat Detection Real-time Analysis	Auto Response Incident Containment	Risk Assessment Vulnerability Scoring	Compliance Policy Enforcement

Figure 9.2 AI technology integration and data flow architecture.

recommendations. These audit trails support post-incident analysis, regulatory compliance requirements, and continuous improvement of AI system performance [26].

9.3.5 Resilience and adaptation mechanisms

The framework incorporates multiple mechanisms for maintaining operational effectiveness in the face of evolving threat landscapes and adversarial AI attacks. Adversarial training techniques improve AI model robustness against adversarial examples and evasion attacks specifically designed to fool AI-based detection systems [27].

Continuous learning capabilities enable AI models to adapt to new threat patterns and attack techniques without requiring complete retraining. These capabilities utilize incremental learning algorithms and transfer learning approaches to maintain current threat knowledge while preserving previously learned patterns [28].

Model ensemble approaches combine multiple AI algorithms and decision-making processes to reduce single points of failure and improve overall system reliability. Ensemble implementations suggest promising performance compared to individual AI models, particularly in adversarial

AI CYBERSECURITY FRAMEWORK IMPLEMENTATION ROADMAP

0-6 Months PHASE 1 Foundation Building	6-12 Months PHASE 2 Core Implementation	12-18 Months PHASE 3 Advanced Capabilities	18-24 Months PHASE 4 Optimization
• Threat Intelligence • Staff Training • Basic AI Models • Infrastructure Setup	• Detection Systems • Behavioral Analytics • API Integration • Cross-Sector Sharing	• Auto Response • Multi-Agency Coord. • Ensemble Models • Performance Monitor	• System Tuning • Advanced Analytics • Full Operation • Continuous Improvement

Success Metrics Timeline

15% Detection ↑ — 25% Accuracy ↑ — 80% Response Time ↓ — 90% Overall ↑

Figure 9.3 Phased implementation roadmap for AI-driven national cybersecurity framework.

environments where attackers may attempt to exploit specific algorithmic weaknesses [29].

9.3.6 Implementation strategy

The framework implementation follows a phased approach designed to minimize disruption to existing cybersecurity operations while gradually incorporating AI capabilities. The implementation strategy is visualized in Figure 9.3, which outlines the four distinct phases over a 24-month period. Phase 1 focuses on intelligence and threat analysis layer implementation, providing immediate value through improved threat intelligence capabilities. Phase 2 adds automated detection and classification capabilities, while Phase 3 implements adaptive response mechanisms.

Each implementation phase includes comprehensive testing, validation, and performance evaluation procedures to ensure AI systems meet operational requirements and security standards. Pilot implementations in controlled environments allow for system refinement and operator training before full-scale deployment [30].

Integration with existing cybersecurity infrastructure utilizes standardized APIs and communication protocols to ensure compatibility with current systems and minimize implementation complexity. The framework design accommodates different organizational structures and technological capabilities, enabling flexible implementation across diverse national cybersecurity environments.

9.3.7 Quality assurance and validation

The framework incorporates comprehensive quality assurance mechanisms to ensure AI system reliability, accuracy, and security. Regular model validation procedures assess AI performance against known threat scenarios and compare results with expert human analysis. Validation procedures identify potential model drift, bias, or degradation issues that could compromise system effectiveness.

Red team exercises specifically targeting AI components evaluate system resilience against adversarial attacks and sophisticated evasion techniques. These exercises identify potential vulnerabilities and inform the development of additional defensive measures and countermeasures. Continuous monitoring systems track AI performance metrics, including detection accuracy, false positive rates, response times, and resource utilization. Performance monitoring may enable rapid identification of system issues and support data-driven optimization of framework components [3].

9.4 CONCEPTUAL APPLICATIONS AND THEORETICAL ANALYSIS

This section presents theoretical applications of the proposed Integrated AI-Driven National Cyber Defense Framework through conceptual analysis demonstrating its potential effectiveness across different sectors and threat scenarios. These theoretical examples illustrate the framework's envisioned capabilities in various cybersecurity contexts and explore its potential for enhancing national cyber resilience.

9.4.1 Conceptual application 1: critical infrastructure protection – energy sector

The energy sector represents a critical component of national infrastructure requiring robust cybersecurity protection due to its essential role in supporting economic and social functions. This conceptual analysis examines the theoretical application of the proposed framework to protect electrical grid systems against sophisticated cyber attacks, particularly those targeting industrial control systems (ICS) and supervisory control and data acquisition (SCADA) networks.

9.4.1.1 Theoretical implementation context

In a theoretical scenario, a regional electrical grid operator responsible for serving millions of customers could implement the AI-driven cybersecurity framework to enhance protection against advanced persistent threats targeting critical infrastructure. The implementation would focus on protecting generation facilities, transmission systems, and distribution networks from cyber attacks that could cause widespread power outages or system damage.

The theoretical baseline would include traditional perimeter security controls, signature-based malware detection, and manual log analysis procedures. However, increasing threats from nation-state actors and sophisticated cybercriminal organizations would necessitate enhanced defensive capabilities capable of detecting and responding to advanced attack techniques, as documented in recent smart grid cybersecurity research [16].

9.4.1.2 Framework application theory

The intelligence and threat analysis layer would theoretically be configured to monitor threat intelligence feeds specifically focused on critical infrastructure targeting, including indicators of compromise (IoCs) associated with known APT groups targeting energy sector organizations. Natural language processing algorithms would analyze unstructured threat intelligence reports to extract actionable information about emerging attack techniques and vulnerabilities affecting industrial control systems, utilizing approaches described in comprehensive AI cybersecurity literature.

Automated detection and classification capabilities would be deployed across the operational technology (OT) network environment, including generation control systems, substation automation, and distribution management systems. Deep learning algorithms would be trained to recognize normal operational patterns for critical systems, enabling detection of anomalous behaviors that could indicate cyber attacks or system malfunctions, following methodologies validated in recent deep learning cybersecurity research [2].

The adaptive response layer would implement automated containment procedures for detected threats, including network segmentation activation, system isolation protocols, and emergency response coordination. These automated responses would be designed to maintain system safety and reliability while containing potential cyber threats.

9.4.1.3 Expected performance metrics

Based on theoretical analysis and extrapolation from existing research, implementation of the AI-driven framework could achieve potential improvements in cybersecurity effectiveness compared to baseline capabilities. Table 9.3 summarizes projected performance metrics based on theoretical modeling.

The framework would theoretically identify and contain multiple sophisticated attack attempts, including advanced persistent threat activities that would be missed by traditional security controls. Automated threat intelligence correlation would identify early indicators of coordinated attack campaigns targeting multiple regional energy providers, enabling proactive defensive measures.

Table 9.3 Energy sector case study – performance results

Metric	*Baseline*	*AI-enhanced*	*Improvement (%)*
Threat Detection Accuracy	67%	94%	+27
False Positive Rate	18%	3%	−15
Mean Time to Detection	6.2 hours	0.7 hours	−89
Mean Time to Response	12.4 hours	1.2 hours	−90
Advanced Threat Detection	23%	86%	+63
Insider Threat Detection	12%	78%	+66

9.4.2 Conceptual application 2: financial services cyber resilience

The financial services sector faces unique cybersecurity challenges due to the high value of potential targets, sophisticated threat actors, and complex regulatory requirements. This conceptual analysis examines the theoretical application of the proposed framework to protect a major financial institution against advanced cyber threats while maintaining compliance with regulatory requirements.

9.4.2.1 Theoretical implementation scope

A multinational banking institution with operations in multiple countries could theoretically implement the AI-driven cybersecurity framework to enhance protection of customer data, financial transaction systems, and trading platforms. The implementation scope would include online banking systems, mobile payment applications, core banking infrastructure, and algorithmic trading platforms. The organization would face increasing threats from sophisticated cybercriminal organizations, nation-state actors conducting economic espionage, and insider threats attempting to exploit privileged access for financial gain. Traditional security controls would struggle to keep pace with the volume and sophistication of attack attempts against high-value financial targets [31].

9.4.2.2 AI-enhanced security capabilities theory

The framework implementation would emphasize behavioral analytics capabilities for identifying anomalous user and system behaviors indicative of account compromise or insider threats. Machine learning algorithms would analyze transaction patterns, user access behaviors, and system utilization metrics to establish baseline profiles for normal operations.

Advanced natural language processing capabilities would monitor internal communications, document access patterns, and external threat intelligence sources to identify potential insider threat activities or external attack planning. These capabilities would enable early identification of suspicious activities before they could result in successful attacks or data exfiltration.

Automated fraud detection systems would incorporate AI algorithms to analyze transaction patterns and identify potentially fraudulent activities in real-time. These systems would be designed to reduce false positive rates while improving detection of sophisticated fraud schemes that evade traditional rule-based detection systems.

9.4.2.3 Projected performance evaluation

The financial services implementation would theoretically suggest potential improvements in cybersecurity effectiveness and operational efficiency. Automated threat detection capabilities could reduce the workload on security analysts while improving detection accuracy and reducing response times. The system would be expected to identify and prevent multiple advanced attack attempts, including business email compromise schemes, account takeover attacks, and insider threat activities.

Regulatory compliance capabilities would ensure that all AI-driven security decisions include appropriate audit trails and explainability features required by financial services regulations. The implementation would maintain full compliance with relevant cybersecurity regulations while enhancing protective capabilities significantly.

9.4.3 Conceptual application 3: healthcare sector cybersecurity enhancement

Healthcare organizations face unique cybersecurity challenges due to the sensitivity of patient data, the critical nature of medical systems, and the increasing digitization of healthcare operations. This conceptual analysis examines the theoretical application of the proposed framework to protect a large healthcare system against cyber threats while maintaining patient safety and privacy requirements.

9.4.3.1 Healthcare-specific theoretical implementation

A regional healthcare network serving millions of patients could theoretically implement the AI-driven cybersecurity framework to protect electronic health records, medical devices, and clinical systems from cyber attacks. The implementation would require special consideration of patient safety requirements, regulatory compliance with HIPAA and other healthcare privacy regulations, and the need to maintain continuous access to critical medical systems. The healthcare environment would face particular challenges from ransomware attacks targeting patient data, medical device vulnerabilities, and insider threats with access to sensitive patient information. The healthcare implementation would require special consideration of patient safety requirements and regulatory compliance with HIPAA and other healthcare privacy regulations.

9.4.3.2 Medical device security integration theory

The framework would incorporate specialized capabilities for monitoring and protecting connected medical devices, including infusion pumps, patient monitoring systems, and diagnostic equipment. Machine learning algorithms would analyze device communication patterns and operational behaviors to identify potential compromise or malfunction that could impact patient safety. Anomaly detection systems would monitor electronic health record access patterns to identify unauthorized data access attempts or unusual user behaviors that might indicate account compromise or insider threats. These systems would balance security requirements with the need for healthcare providers to have rapid access to patient information during emergency situations.

9.4.3.3 Expected healthcare-specific outcomes

The healthcare implementation would theoretically achieve potential improvements in cybersecurity posture while maintaining operational efficiency and patient safety requirements. The system would be expected to prevent multiple ransomware attacks and identify instances of inappropriate data access that would go undetected by traditional security controls. Recent advances in machine learning applications for cybersecurity demonstrate the particular effectiveness of AI-driven approaches in healthcare environments [32]. Privacy-preserving AI techniques would ensure that patient data remains protected throughout all security analysis processes, maintaining compliance with healthcare privacy regulations while enabling effective threat detection and response capabilities.

9.4.4 Conceptual application 4: government agency cybersecurity transformation

Government agencies face sophisticated cyber threats from nation-state actors, terrorist organizations, and cybercriminal groups seeking to access classified information or disrupt government operations. This conceptual analysis examines the theoretical implementation of the AI-driven framework within a large federal agency responsible for national security functions.

9.4.4.1 Government implementation challenges

The agency implementation would require integration with existing classified networks, compliance with federal cybersecurity requirements, and coordination with multiple intelligence and law enforcement agencies. The framework would need to support both classified and unclassified operations while maintaining appropriate security compartmentalization. Special attention would be given to adversarial AI resilience, recognizing that nation-state adversaries would likely attempt to exploit or compromise AI-driven security systems. The implementation would incorporate multiple layers of validation, verification, and backup procedures to maintain security effectiveness even in the presence of sophisticated adversarial attacks, following best practices identified in recent cybersecurity research [32].

9.4.4.2 Multi-agency coordination capabilities

The framework would facilitate enhanced threat intelligence sharing and coordinated response activities across multiple government agencies and departments. Federated learning approaches could enable collaborative threat detection and analysis while maintaining appropriate security boundaries and access controls [33].

Automated alert correlation and incident response coordination would reduce duplicate efforts and improve overall government cybersecurity effectiveness. The system would provide standardized threat indicators and response protocols that facilitate rapid information sharing during major cybersecurity incidents.

9.4.5 Cross-sector analysis and theoretical insights

Analysis of theoretical implementation results across multiple sectors reveals several consistent patterns and success factors for AI-driven cybersecurity frameworks. Table 9.4 summarizes projected performance improvements across different implementation contexts based on theoretical modeling and existing research.

9.4.5.1 Critical success factors

Several factors emerge as critical for successful implementation of AI-driven cybersecurity frameworks across different sectors. First, comprehensive stakeholder engagement and training programs would be essential

Table 9.4 Cross-sector performance analysis

Sector	*Detection improvement (%)*	*Response time reduction (%)*	*False positive reduction (%)*
Energy	+27	−89	−15
Financial Services	+31	−82	−12
Healthcare	+24	−76	−18
Government	+35	−91	−14
Average	+29	−85	−15

for ensuring that security personnel can effectively operate and maintain AI-enhanced systems. Organizations that invest in extensive training and change management programs would be expected to achieve significantly better results than those that focus solely on technical implementation.

Second, integration with existing cybersecurity infrastructure and processes could prove crucial for minimizing operational disruption and maximizing acceptance by security teams. Implementations that require significant changes to established procedures would likely encounter resistance and experience longer adoption periods [21].

Third, continuous monitoring and adaptation capabilities would be necessary for maintaining effectiveness as threat landscapes evolve. Organizations that implement robust performance monitoring and model updating procedures would be expected to maintain high detection accuracy rates throughout extended operational periods.

9.4.5.2 Theoretical implementation challenges and solutions

Common implementation challenges would likely include data quality issues, integration complexity, and resistance to automated decision-making processes. Data quality problems could be addressed through comprehensive data cleansing procedures and automated data validation mechanisms that identify and correct inconsistencies in training and operational data. Integration complexity could be managed through phased implementation approaches and extensive use of standardized APIs and communication protocols. Organizations that attempt to implement all framework components simultaneously would likely experience significant operational disruptions and longer implementation timelines. Resistance to automated decision-making could be addressed through extensive use of explainable AI components and graduated automation approaches that initially provide recommendations to human operators before implementing fully automated responses. This approach would build confidence in AI capabilities while maintaining human oversight of critical decisions [23].

9.4.5.3 Scalability and adaptability assessment

The theoretical analysis suggests that the proposed framework would scale effectively across organizations of different sizes and complexity levels. Small organizations with limited cybersecurity resources would benefit from automated threat detection and response capabilities that provide enterprise-level security without requiring extensive in-house expertise.

Large, complex organizations would leverage the framework's advanced capabilities for coordinating security operations across multiple divisions, geographic locations, and technology platforms. The framework's modular architecture could enable customization for specific organizational requirements while maintaining interoperability and coordination capabilities. Adaptability assessments based on theoretical modeling suggest that AI models would maintain effectiveness despite evolving threat landscapes and changing operational requirements. Continuous learning capabilities would enable systems to adapt to new attack techniques and organizational changes without requiring complete system redesign or retraining.

9.5 DISCUSSION AND FUTURE WORK

The theoretical analysis of the Integrated AI-Driven National Cyber Defense Framework across multiple sectors provides insights into potential opportunities, implementation challenges, and future directions for AI-enhanced cybersecurity [32].

9.5.1 Framework effectiveness and theoretical performance

The theoretical analysis and preliminary simulation results suggest that AI-driven frameworks may offer substantial improvements in detection accuracy (average theoretical projection of 29%, simulation results 25%), response time reduction (theoretical projection 85%, simulation results consistent with sub-second detection), and false positive reduction (theoretical 15%, simulation 13%). These projected improvements, if validated through operational deployment, could enhance national cybersecurity capabilities significantly. However, it is important to note that these figures represent theoretical projections and controlled simulation results rather than verified operational performance. Actual performance in real-world deployments may vary substantially based on implementation quality, operational environment characteristics, threat actor sophistication, and organizational factors. The theoretical nature of the cross-sector analysis (Section 9.4) means that the reported metrics represent potential outcomes rather than empirically validated results.

9.5.2 Framework limitations and constraints

Several fundamental limitations constrain the applicability and effectiveness of the proposed framework. First, the framework's dependence on high-quality training data may prove problematic in operational contexts where labeled cybersecurity datasets are scarce, incomplete, or potentially compromised by adversaries. The quality and representativeness of training data directly impact model performance, and organizations may struggle to obtain sufficient data for effective model development.

Second, the framework assumes availability of substantial computational resources for real-time AI model operation at national scale. Organizations with limited technical infrastructure or budget constraints may find implementation economically or technically infeasible. The computational requirements for deep learning models, particularly for processing high-volume network traffic, may exceed the capabilities of resource-constrained agencies.

Third, the theoretical analysis does not fully address the challenge of adversarial adaptation. Sophisticated threat actors may develop specific techniques to evade or exploit AI-based detection systems, potentially reducing effectiveness over time. The framework's continuous learning mechanisms may mitigate this challenge but cannot eliminate it entirely.

Fourth, the explainability mechanisms incorporated into the framework, while necessary for transparency and accountability, may introduce computational overhead and complexity that affects real-time performance. The tension between model accuracy and interpretability represents an ongoing challenge without definitive solutions.

Finally, the framework does not address organizational and human factors that significantly influence cybersecurity effectiveness, including security culture, staff expertise, inter-agency coordination challenges, and management support. Technical solutions alone cannot ensure successful implementation without complementary organizational changes.

9.5.3 Implementation challenges: technical, political, and legal

9.5.3.1 Technical implementation obstacles

Beyond the conceptual framework design, operational implementation faces numerous technical challenges. Integration with legacy cybersecurity systems presents significant compatibility issues, as many national security organizations operate infrastructure designed decades ago without consideration for AI integration. Data standardization across heterogeneous systems, varying data formats, and inconsistent logging practices complicate the development of unified AI models capable of operating across diverse technical environments.

The framework's dependence on continuous model updates and adaptation requires robust MLOps (Machine Learning Operations) capabilities that many organizations currently lack. Establishing effective model versioning, testing, validation, and deployment pipelines for critical security systems demands substantial technical expertise and infrastructure investment.

9.5.3.2 Political and governance obstacles

National-scale cybersecurity implementations face significant political and governance challenges that extend beyond technical considerations. Inter-agency coordination represents a persistent challenge, as cybersecurity responsibilities typically span multiple government departments with varying priorities, authorities, and operational cultures. The framework's requirement for extensive threat intelligence sharing may encounter resistance from agencies concerned about operational security, sensitive sources and methods, or competitive institutional interests.

Budget allocation for AI-driven cybersecurity initiatives competes with numerous other national priorities, and securing sustained funding for long-term implementation and maintenance poses ongoing political challenges. Changes in political leadership or priorities may affect commitment to multi-year implementation programs.

Sovereignty and data residency concerns complicate international cooperation mechanisms embedded in the framework design. Nations may resist sharing threat intelligence or adopting common standards due to concerns about foreign access to sensitive information or dependence on external technologies. The framework's effectiveness depends substantially on international coordination, yet political tensions and divergent national interests may limit practical cooperation.

9.5.3.3 Legal and regulatory obstacles

Legal frameworks governing cybersecurity operations, surveillance, data collection, and automated decision-making vary substantially across jurisdictions and may not adequately address AI-specific concerns. The framework's automated response capabilities may raise questions about legal authorization for actions that could affect critical infrastructure or private sector systems. Existing legal authorities may not explicitly authorize AI-driven automated responses, creating potential liability concerns for implementing organizations.

Data privacy regulations, including GDPR in Europe and various national privacy laws, impose constraints on data collection, processing, and international sharing necessary for effective AI model training and operation.

Balancing cybersecurity requirements with privacy protections presents ongoing legal challenges without straightforward solutions.

9.5.3.4 Data governance challenges

Effective AI implementation requires comprehensive data governance frameworks addressing data quality, access controls, retention policies, and ethical use. National cybersecurity operations generate and process enormous volumes of sensitive data, including classified intelligence, personally identifiable information, and proprietary business information. Establishing governance mechanisms that enable AI effectiveness while protecting sensitive information presents substantial challenges.

Data sharing agreements among government agencies, between government and the private sector, and across international boundaries require complex legal and technical frameworks that may take years to establish. The framework's dependence on federated learning and privacy-preserving techniques partially addresses these challenges but does not eliminate them entirely.

9.5.4 Strategic implications

Nations investing in AI-enhanced cybersecurity may gain strategic advantages in protecting critical infrastructure and maintaining operational resilience against sophisticated cyber threats. However, the dual-use nature of AI technologies introduces potential for technological competition, as adversaries develop countermeasures and offensive AI capabilities. This dynamic necessitates continued investment in research and development to maintain defensive capabilities.

International coordination, standardized protocols, and collaborative defense mechanisms may enhance collective resilience against transnational cyber threats. However, achieving effective international cooperation requires overcoming political tensions, sovereignty concerns, and divergent national interests that currently limit collaborative efforts.

9.5.5 Future research directions

Key research areas include adversarial machine learning defenses, explainable AI techniques, automated machine learning (AutoML) for cybersecurity applications, quantum-resistant algorithms, and AI adaptation to emerging technologies such as 5G networks, IoT ecosystems, and edge computing environments [4, 17, 28]. Collaborative AI approaches, federated learning mechanisms, and secure information sharing protocols offer potential pathways for multi-organization resilience [33].

Integration of large language models and autonomous agents in cybersecurity operations requires careful study to ensure safe deployment without introducing new vulnerabilities. Research should examine the effectiveness of LLM-based threat intelligence analysis, automated vulnerability assessment, and security policy generation while assessing associated risks. Longitudinal studies examining the long-term performance of AI-driven cybersecurity systems in operational environments would provide valuable insights into model sustainability, adaptation effectiveness, and operational impacts. Such studies require multi-year commitments and careful data collection protocols but could validate or refine the theoretical projections presented in this chapter.

9.5.6 Implementation pathways and validation

Practical deployment requires carefully designed pilot programs, controlled experiments, and well-defined use cases to validate theoretical predictions and refine implementation approaches. Partnerships among academia, government agencies, and industry organizations are essential for leveraging complementary expertise and resources. Workforce development programs, including technical training, ethical considerations, and policy education, are crucial to ensure effective operation and management of AI-driven cybersecurity systems. Establishing cybersecurity testbeds and evaluation facilities would enable rigorous assessment of AI technologies before operational deployment, reducing risks associated with premature implementation of unproven technologies. Such facilities should support realistic threat scenarios, adversarial testing, and performance evaluation under various operational conditions.

9.6 CONCLUSION

This chapter presents the Integrated AI-Driven National Cyber Defense Framework (IAINCDF), a multi-layered approach leveraging artificial intelligence (AI) to enhance national cybersecurity [32]. The framework integrates five layers: intelligence and threat analysis, automated detection, adaptive response, resilience and recovery, and governance and compliance, enabling adaptable, accountable, and collaborative defense capabilities.

9.6.1 Contributions and implications

IAINCDF advances explainable AI integration across operational layers, ensuring transparency and human oversight. Theoretical evaluations across energy, healthcare, financial services, and government sectors suggest potential improvements of 29% in detection accuracy, 85% in response times, and 61% in advanced threat detection. Its modular, phased design facilitates gradual AI adoption without disrupting existing operations, providing actionable guidance through stakeholder engagement, training, and continuous monitoring. Strategically, AI-driven frameworks strengthen national security by protecting critical infrastructure, enhancing economic stability, and supporting collaborative defense through automated threat intelligence sharing. Ethical, privacy, and regulatory considerations are embedded to ensure responsible implementation.

9.6.2 Future directions

Future research should focus on adversarial AI defenses, explainable AI, automated learning, and integration of emerging technologies such as quantum computing, 5G, and IoT. Federated learning and privacy-preserving techniques offer opportunities for secure multi-organization collaboration. The long-term vision is a fully adaptive, collaborative national cyber defense ecosystem capable of safeguarding critical infrastructure and citizen welfare, establishing a foundation for continued AI-enhanced cybersecurity development [32].

REFERENCES

1. Khalid Khan, Adnan Khurshid, and Javier Cifuentes-Faura. Is artificial intelligence a new battleground for cybersecurity? *Internet of Things*, 28:101428, 2024.
2. Huiyao Dong and Igor Kotenko. Cybersecurity in the AI era: Analyzing the impact of machine learning on intrusion detection. *Knowledge and Information Systems*, 67(5):1–52, 2025.
3. Aya H Salem, Safaa M Azzam, Omar E Emam, and Amr A Abohany. Advancing cybersecurity: A comprehensive review of AI-driven detection techniques. *Journal of Big Data*, 11(1):105, 2024.
4. Iqbal H Sarker. Machine learning for intelligent data analysis and automation in cybersecurity: Current and future prospects. *Annals of Data Science*, 10(6):1473–1498, 2023.
5. Masike Malatji and Alaa Tolah. Artificial intelligence (AI) cybersecurity dimensions: A comprehensive framework for understanding adversarial and offensive AI. *AI and Ethics*, 5(2):883–910, 2025.
6. NIST AI. Artificial intelligence risk management framework: Generative artificial intelligence profile. *NIST Trustworthy and Responsible AI Gaithersburg, MD, USA*, 2024.
7. Stéphane Reynaud and Ana Roxin. Review of explainable artificial intelligence for cybersecurity systems. *Discover Artificial Intelligence*, 5(1):78, 2025.

8. Ankit Thakkar and Ritika Lohiya. A survey on intrusion detection system: Feature selection, model, performance measures, application perspective, challenges, and future research directions. *Artificial Intelligence Review*, 55(1):453–563, 2022.
9. Daniel Stewart, Taiwo Kolajo, and Olawande Daramola. Machine learning for intrusion detection systems: A systematic literature review. In *Proceedings of the Future Technologies Conference*, pages 623–638. Springer, 2024.
10. Arnoldas Budžys, Olga Kurasova, and Viktor Medvedev. Deep learning-based authentication for insider threat detection in critical infrastructure. *Artificial Intelligence Review*, 57(10):272, 2024.
11. Sebastian Szelest, Marek Pawlicki, Aleksandra Pawlicka, Rafał Kozik, and Michał Choraś. Proposition of a novel type of attacks targetting explainable AI algorithms in cybersecurity. In *European Symposium on Research in Computer Security*, pages 289–304. Springer, 2024.
12. Iqbal H Sarker, ASM Kayes, Shahriar Badsha, Hamed Alqahtani, Paul Watters, and Alex Ng. Cybersecurity data science: An overview from machine learning perspective. *Journal of Big Data*, 7(1):41, 2020.
13. Werisha Ibrar, Danish Mahmood, Ahmad Sami Al-Shamayleh, Ghufran Ahmed, Salman Z Alharthi, and Adnan Akhunzada. Generative AI: A double-edged sword in the cyber threat landscape. *Artificial Intelligence Review*, 58(9):285, 2025.
14. Mohammed Abdulhakim Al-Absi, Hind R'Bigui, and Ahmed A Al-Absi. Deep learning and machine learning algorithms methods in cyber security. In *International Conference on Smart Computing and Cyber Security: Strategic Foresight, Security Challenges and Innovation*, pages 271–279. Springer, 2023.
15. National Institute of Standards, Technology (US), National Institute of Standards, and Technology (US). *NIST Cybersecurity Framework 2.0: Quick-start Guide for Creating and Using Organizational Profiles*. US Department of Commerce, National Institute of Standards and Technology, 2024.
16. Michalis Skoumperdis, Nikolaos Vakakis, Maria Diamantaki, Charalampos-Rafail Medentzidis, Dimitrios Karanassos, Dimosthenis Ioannidis, and Dimitrios Tzovaras. A novel self-learning cybersecurity system for smart grids. In *Power Systems Cybersecurity: Methods, Concepts, and Best Practices*, pages 337–362. Springer, 2023.
17. Jehad Ali, Sushil Kumar Singh, Weiwei Jiang, Abdulmajeed M Alenezi, Muhammad Islam, Yousef Ibrahim Daradkeh, and Asif Mehmood. A deep dive into cybersecurity solutions for AI-driven iot-enabled smart cities in advanced communication networks. *Computer Communications*, 229:108000, 2025.
18. Cherilyn E Pascoe. Public draft: The nist cybersecurity framework 2.0. *National Institute of Standards and Technology*, 2023.
19. Elham Tabassi. Artificial intelligence risk management framework (AI rmf 1.0). 2023.
20. Dipankar Dasgupta, Zahid Akhtar, and Sajib Sen. Machine learning in cybersecurity: A comprehensive survey. *The Journal of Defense Modeling and Simulation*, 19(1):57–106, 2022.

21. Mohammed Nasser Al-Suqri and Maryam Gillani. A comparative analysis of information and artificial intelligence toward national security. *IEEE Access*, 10:64420–64434, 2022.
22. Mangayarkarasi Ramaiah, Vanmathi Chandrasekaran, Vinayakumar Ravi, and Neeraj Kumar. An intrusion detection system using optimized deep neural network architecture. *Transactions on Emerging Telecommunications Technologies*, 32(4):e4221, 2021.
23. Atheer Alaa Hammad, Saadaldeen Rashid Ahmed, Mohammad K Abdul-Hussein, Mohammed R Ahmed, Duaa A Majeed, and Sameer Algburi. Deep reinforcement learning for adaptive cyber defense in network security. In *Proceedings of the Cognitive Models and Artificial Intelligence Conference*, pages 292–297, 2024.
24. Ming Liu, Lu Ma, Chao Li, Weiling Chang, Yuanjie Wang, Jianming Cui, and Yingying Ji. Design and analysis of decentralized interactive cyber defense approach based on multi-agent coordination. In *2020 16th International Conference on Mobility, Sensing and Networking (MSN)*, pages 659–664. IEEE, 2020.
25. Zhibo Zhang, Hussam Al Hamadi, Ernesto Damiani, Chan Yeob Yeun, and Fatma Taher. Explainable artificial intelligence applications in cyber security: State-of-the-art in research. *IEEE Access*, 10:93104–93139, 2022.
26. Nirjhor Anjum and Rubel Chowdhury. Revolutionizing cybersecurity audit through artificial intelligence automation: A comprehensive exploration. *International Journal of Advanced Research in Computer and Communication Engineering*, 13(5):493–502, 2024.
27. Adebayo Nurudeen Kalejaiye. Adversarial machine learning for robust cybersecurity: Strengthening deep neural architectures against evasion, poisoning, and model-inference attacks. *International Journal of Computer Applications Technology and Research*, 13(12):72–95, 2024.
28. CV Suresh Babu et al. Adaptive AI for dynamic cybersecurity systems: Enhancing protection in a rapidly evolving digital landscape. In Zhihan Lv, editor, *Principles and Applications of Adaptive Artificial Intelligence*, pages 52–72. IGI Global Scientific Publishing, 2024.
29. Shreyas Dingankar, B Maruthi Shankar, Aarti Kalnawat, Ajay Sani, YV Dongre, and Vivek Jaysing Nagargoje. Enhancing cyber threat intelligence with AI and ml: An ensembled approach. In *International Conference on Frontiers of Intelligent Computing: Theory and Applications*, pages 517–526. Springer, 2024.
30. Ajay Tanikonda, Brij Kishore Pandey, Sudhakar Reddy Peddinti, and Subba Rao Katragadda. Advanced AI-driven cybersecurity solutions for proactive threat detection and response in complex ecosystems. *Journal of Science & Technology*, 3(1):196–217, 2022.
31. Feng Tao, Muhammad Shoaib Akhtar, and Zhang Jiayuan. The future of artificial intelligence in cybersecurity: A comprehensive survey. *EAI Endorsed Transactions on Creative Technologies*, 8(28):e3, 2021.
32. Ioannis J Vourganas and Anna Lito Michala. Applications of machine learning in cyber security: A review. *Journal of Cybersecurity and Privacy*, 4(4):972–992, 2024.

33. Krishnashree Achuthan, Sasangan Ramanathan, Sethuraman Srinivas, and Raghu Raman. Advancing cybersecurity and privacy with artificial intelligence: Current trends and future research directions. *Frontiers in Big Data*, 7:1497535, 2024.

Chapter 10

Materials-aware cyber-physical anomaly detection using fiber Bragg gratings and NiTi shape memory alloys

Omar Er-Remyly[1] *and Amine Riad*[2,3]

10.1 INTRODUCTION

Industrial Control Systems (ICS) sit at the interface between computation and the physical world. As operational technology (OT) becomes increasingly interconnected with enterprise IT and cloud services, intrusion paths now extend from cyberspace to actuators and safety loops on the factory floor, with potential impacts on product quality and equipment safety. Recent journal surveys trace this evolution and the growing use of machine-learning methods for intrusion and anomaly detection across critical infrastructure. However, results are still fragmented across network, process, and materials viewpoints, motivating an approach that explicitly fuses process physics with data-driven inference [1–4].

Physics-informed machine learning (PIML) directly addresses key ICS/OT constraints – limited or delayed labels, sensor noise and drift, and hard safety envelopes – by embedding governing laws, invariants, or feasibility sets into the learning and scoring procedures. In practice, PIML (including physics-informed neural networks) favors solutions that respect thermodynamics and constitutive behavior, enabling detectors to penalize *physically impossible* states rather than merely unlikely statistical patterns [5, 6].

In parallel, *digital twins (DTs)* have progressed from static replicas to closed-loop, AI-enabled systems that synchronize computational models with live plant data. In manufacturing contexts, DTs support rapid *what-if* analyses, traceable root-cause investigations, and resilient control under disturbance or attack – making them a natural substrate for physics-guided detection and evaluation [7–9].

A *materials-aware* cyber-defense tightens this integration by instrumenting specimens and test rigs with high-fidelity *fiber Bragg grating (FBG)* sensing and leveraging the rich thermo-mechanical response of *NiTi shape-memory alloys (SMAs)*. FBGs provide precise, EMI-immune measurements of strain and temperature; NiTi exhibits hysteretic thermo-elastic transformations whose trajectories are highly diagnostic of abnormal thermal or load paths. Embedding these signals into a twin and constraining learning with materials physics yields detectors that flag anomalies when

DOI: 10.1201/9781003650478-11

stress–strain–temperature evolutions violate feasible constitutive response – not only when network traffic seems unusual [10–12].

Evaluation must reflect operational realities. Because OT anomalies are typically rare, operators value the precision of positive alarms; accordingly, precision–recall analysis complements ROC summaries for imbalanced regimes [13]. At the same time, open ICS corpora increasingly pair *network* with *process/materials* channels, enabling studies that disentangle cyber-induced anomalies from genuine physical faults and that remain reproducible on laptop-class hardware [14, 15].

This work: We present a materials-aware, physics-guided anomaly-detection pipeline that (i) couples a lightweight digital twin with FBG/NiTi channels; (ii) enforces *materials-aware safety shields* defined by bounded temperature and strain and their rates – $T, \varepsilon, dT/dt, d\varepsilon/dt$; and (iii) reports PR-AUC/ROC-AUC, thresholded confusion metrics, and event-level latency, grounded in journal-curated ICS datasets and the Scopus-indexed literature cited above.

10.2 MATERIALS-AWARE SENSING, ACTUATION, AND CONTROL LOOPS

This section treats the bench as a materials–cyber–physical loop with three core channels: the control input u (heater power), the specimen temperature T, and the axial microstrain ε. We keep the link explicit between sensor physics, actuation limits, and DAQ constraints: §10.2.1 details FBG sensing and interrogators (including cross-sensitivity and calibration); §10.2.2 covers thermal actuation and NiTi specimen behavior; §10.2.3 addresses timing/synchronization and anti-aliasing; and §10.2.4 formalizes the constraint set (*materials-aware shields*) used by the detector.

10.2.1 Sensing channels and interrogators (FBG strain/temperature)

We measure the specimen state with fiber Bragg grating (FBG) sensors for axial microstrain and temperature. FBGs tolerate harsh electromagnetic environments and enable dense multiplexing on a single fiber, offering high sensitivity and bandwidth for thermo-mechanical monitoring [10, 11, 16]. Because Bragg wavelength shifts respond to both strain and temperature, *cross-sensitivity* must be mitigated in design (paired gratings, hybrid LPFG/FBG, or a bonded/reference element) or compensated in the interrogator signal processing [17]. Practical interrogator choices (edge-filter, tunable-laser, wavelength-to-time mapping) trade dynamic range, sampling rate, and noise; for fast thermal ramps, kHz-class sampling with traceable calibration is recommended.

Calibration and drift

To maintain traceability and long-run stability, FBG channels should be cross-checked against references and tracked for drift with scheduled procedures; metrology studies emphasize routine calibration, uncertainty budgeting, and show viable self-calibration for low-cost networks [18, 19].

10.2.2 Actuation (NiTi SMA thermal drive) and specimen physics

We actuate thermally (Joule heating) and read the thermo-mechanical response of NiTi shape-memory alloy (SMA). NiTi provides large recoverable strain, high recovery stress, and repeatable transformation hysteresis – well-suited to cyber-physical tests and to deriving physics-guided constraints [20, 21]. Control authority is delivered as heater/wire power (PWM or current control), so the loop must respect electrical/thermal limits to avoid over-temperature or over-strain. Composition, processing, and heat treatment shift transformation windows $\left(M_s, M_f, A_s, A_f\right)$ and fatigue behavior [22], these windows directly inform the safety shields enforced later.

10.2.3 DAQ timing, synchronization, and aliasing control

Accurate detection depends on tight time alignment between u, T, and ε. In distributed OT setups (PLC/DAQ + interrogator), unsynchronized clocks cause timestamp skew, aliasing, and false residuals. Industrial and scientific DAQ studies recommend packet-based synchronization (IEEE 1588 PTP) and White Rabbit–class solutions for sub-μs alignment, outperforming NTP for fast loops [23–25]. PLC experiments confirm that inadequate synchronization and software latencies can cause data loss and counter desynchronization, motivating deterministic sampling and hardware time-stamping where possible [26]. In our pipeline we (i) timestamp at source, (ii) monitor clock offset/jitter, and (iii) decimate with anti-alias filtering before feature extraction.

10.2.4 Materials-aware safety shields (constraints used by the detector)

We encode hard constraints from materials physics as *shields* that modulate anomaly scores and can veto unsafe actuation:

$$T_{\min} \le T \le T_{\max}, \quad \varepsilon_{\min} \le \varepsilon \le \varepsilon_{\max}, \quad |dT / dt| \le \dot{T}_{\max}, \quad |d\varepsilon / dt| \le \dot{\varepsilon}_{\max}.$$

Optionally, we penalize trajectories inconsistent with NiTi phase windows (e.g., the sign/slope of $d\varepsilon / dT$ during heating vs. cooling). These constraints exploit established NiTi behavior and FBG measurement physics [10, 16, 20, 21] and are enforced alongside the residual model so that cyber-induced anomalies that appear statistically normal but are physically infeasible still trigger.

10.3 METHODS

Methodological choices are set by sensor physics and NiTi constitutive behavior. Fiber Bragg grating channels bonded to a thermally actuated NiTi specimen provide synchronized temperature and axial strain under a common interrogator clock (10 Hz). Preprocessing remains minimal – light smoothing, finite-difference rate estimation, and robust scaling – to keep subsequent scores traceable. Residuals come from a one-step nominal predictor fitted on normal operation; materials-aware shields encode envelope and rate limits on $T, \varepsilon, \dot{T}, \dot{\varepsilon}$. A blended score governs decisions under a percentile-calibrated threshold; evaluation is PR-first, with ROC retained as a global consistency check.

10.3.1 Signals, dataset, and labels

We treat the bench as a compact cyber-physical loop with control input u (heater power), specimen temperature T, and axial microstrain ε. The provided package includes a single CSV time series, data/simulated_timeseries.csv, with columns $\{t, u, T_{\text{true}}, \varepsilon_{\text{true}}, T, \varepsilon, \text{label}\}$ and $N = 6000$ samples at $\Delta t = 0.1\text{s}$ (10 Hz). Measured channels T, ε are noisy versions of the latent thermo-mechanical state $(T_{\text{true}}, \varepsilon_{\text{true}})$. The categorical label $\in \{0,1,2\}$ encodes normal operation (0), *physical faults* (1; e.g., cooling loss, preload drift), and *cyber-induced anomalies* (2; e.g., false-data injection, replay, timestamp skew).[4]

Objective Given $(u_t, T_t, \varepsilon_t)$ we produce a per-sample anomaly score s_t and a binary alarm $\mathbb{1}[s_t \geq \tau]$. We report (i) global metrics treating $\{1,2\}$ as "anomalous" (one-vs-rest), and (ii) class-wise precision–recall for faults and attacks separately. Because anomalies are rare, we emphasize precision–recall (PR) alongside ROC, per established guidance for imbalanced evaluation [13].

10.3.2 Synthetic NiTi–FBG dataset generation

We use a synthetic corpus (data/simulated_timeseries.csv) to stress-test detection and shielding under controlled conditions. The generator couples a lumped thermo-mechanical NiTi model with FBG readout and injects labeled fault/attack scenarios.

NiTi thermo-mechanical core

Let $T(t)$ be temperature and $\varepsilon(t)$ axial strain; $\xi \in [0,1]$ is the martensite fraction.

$$\sigma(t) = E(\xi)\left(\varepsilon(t) - \varepsilon^{tr}(\xi)\right), \quad E(\xi) = E_A(1-\xi) + E_M\xi, \quad \varepsilon^{tr}(\xi) = \varepsilon_L\xi.$$

Phase kinetics are driven by a smooth switch across (M_s, M_f, A_s, A_f):

$$\dot{\xi} = \kappa sign\left(\Theta(T) - \Theta_0\right)\left[|T - T_c| - \Delta\right]_+.$$

Thermal balance: $C\dot{T} = P(t) - h(T - T_{amb})$ (Joule heating with duty-cycle power $P(t)$).

FBG sensing model

Bragg shift combines strain and temperature with additive noise:

$$\Delta\lambda_B(t) = \lambda_B\left(k_\varepsilon\varepsilon(t) + k_T\left[T(t) - T_0\right]\right) + \eta(t), \quad \eta \sim \mathcal{N}\left(0, \sigma_\eta^2\right).$$

We report both latent $(T_{\text{true}}, \varepsilon_{\text{true}})$ and measured (T, ε) channels obtained from $\Delta\lambda_B$.

Fault/attack injections

Episodes with labeled onsets/offsets are superimposed: (i) sensor bias: $\varepsilon \mapsto \varepsilon + b$; (ii) actuator noise: $P(t) + \mathcal{N}\left(0, \sigma_P^2\right)$; (iii) rate spike: $|\dot{T}| > \dot{T}_{\max}$; (iv) setpoint drift: $T_c \mapsto T_c + \Delta T$; (v) cyber timestamp skew: $t \mapsto t + \delta t$ (DAQ vs interrogator); (vi) cyber replay: past segments of (T, ε). Labels are aligned as in §10.3.1 (0 = normal, 1 = fault, 2 = attack).

Default parameters

$E_A = 35\,\text{GPa}, E_M = 18\,\text{GPa}, \varepsilon_L = 0.04, (M_s, M_f, A_s, A_f) = (35, 25, 45, 55)^\circ\text{C}$, $C = 8\,\text{J/K}$, $h = 0.45\,\text{W/K}$, $k_\varepsilon = 0.78$, $k_T = 6.7\times10^{-6}/\text{K}$, $\sigma_\eta = 3\times10^{-4}\,\text{nm}$, $\delta t = 0.1\,\text{s}$. Ranges for robustness sweeps are documented in the code comments.

10.3.3 Preprocessing and synchronization

All streams are aligned on the interrogator clock (uniform grid at 10 Hz). We apply a light low-pass on T, ε to suppress high-frequency noise and compute first differences to obtain rates:

$$\dot{T}_t = \frac{T_t - T_{t-1}}{\Delta t}, \quad \dot{\varepsilon}_t = \frac{\varepsilon_t - \varepsilon_{t-1}}{\Delta t}.$$

To stabilize residual magnitudes, we use *robust scaling* on training-normal data:

$$z(x_t) = \frac{x_t - median(x)}{MAD(x)}, \quad MAD(x) = median(|x - median(x)|),$$

applied to residual channels (below). This limits the influence of occasional outliers typical of OT/ICS streams.

10.3.4 Nominal predictor and residual score

We fit a one-step nominal model on a *normal-only* slice (label = 0) to predict the next temperature and strain from recent context:

$$\hat{T}_t = \beta_T^\top [T_{t-1}, u_{t-1}, 1], \quad \hat{\varepsilon}_t = \beta_\varepsilon^\top [\varepsilon_{t-1}, T_t, 1].$$

Absolute residuals $r_T(t) = |T_t - \hat{T}_t|$, $r_\varepsilon(t) = |\varepsilon_t - \hat{\varepsilon}_t|$ are scaled by their MAD values (estimated on training-normal) and combined as

$$s_{\text{res}}(t) = w_T \frac{r_T(t)}{\text{MAD}(r_T)} + w_\varepsilon \frac{r_\varepsilon(t)}{\text{MAD}(r_\varepsilon)}, \quad w_T = 0.6, w_\varepsilon = 0.4.$$

This residual detector captures departures from the learned thermo-electric response while remaining interpretable and lightweight.

10.3.5 Materials-aware safety shields

We encode hard limits and rate bounds derived from materials physics and safe operating envelopes [10, 11, 20, 21]. In the provided package, the limits used to generate the figures are

$$T \in [10, 80]^\circ\text{C}, \quad |\dot{T}| \le 2^\circ\text{C/s}, \quad \varepsilon \in [-0.10, 0.10](\text{unitless}).$$

We map violations to a bounded *shield score* in $[0,1]$ via a smooth saturating penalty:

$$v_T(t) = \max\left(0, \frac{T_t - 80}{\delta_T}\right) + \max\left(0, \frac{10 - T_t}{\delta_T}\right),$$

$$v_{\dot{T}}(t) = \max\left(0, \frac{|\dot{T}_t| - 2}{2}\right), \qquad s_{\text{shield}}(t) = 1 - \exp(-[v_T + v_{\dot{T}} + v_\varepsilon]),$$

$$v_\varepsilon(t) = \max\left(0, \frac{\varepsilon_t - 0.10}{\delta_\varepsilon}\right) + \max\left(0, \frac{-0.10 - \varepsilon_t}{\delta_\varepsilon}\right),$$

with small softening constants $\delta_T, \delta_\varepsilon > 0$ (empirically set, see code). This makes s_{shield} near 0 inside the safe envelope and approaches 1 as violations grow. A phase-consistency penalty can be added when the sign/slope $d\varepsilon / dT$ contradicts NiTi transformation trends [20, 21].

10.3.6 Combined physics-guided score

We blend data-fit and physics constraints:

$$s_{\text{comb}}(t) = \alpha s_{\text{res}}(t) + \beta s_{\text{shield}}(t), \quad \alpha + \beta = 1, \quad (\alpha, \beta) = (0.7, 0.3).$$

Intuition: the residual provides sensitivity to subtle model–data inconsistencies, while shields cap scores and veto trajectories that are *physically infeasible* even if they look statistically ordinary [5, 6, 10, 11].

10.3.7 Calibration choices and sensitivity

The combined score uses $(\alpha, \beta) = (0.7, 0.3)$ and we calibrate τ on normal validation at the $q = 0.95$ percentile.

Rationale (i) Under rare events, $q = 0.95$ targets an operator-tolerable false-alarm budget on benign data without leaking test labels, consistent with PR-first practice for imbalanced detection. (ii) $\alpha > \beta$ prioritizes residual discrimination while keeping a positive shield weight so that physically infeasible trajectories (envelope/rate violations) can veto otherwise "statistically plausible" scores.

Sensitivity On validation we sweep $\alpha \in \{0.5, 0.6, 0.7, 0.8\}$ with $\beta = 1 - \alpha$ and $q \in \{0.90, 0.925, 0.95, 0.975\}$. Average precision varies modestly (within ± 0.02) around $(0.7, 0.3, 0.95)$, with similar FAR–Miss frontiers; detailed grids are provided in Appendix A. This indicates the operating point is locally stable and not overly tuned.

10.3.8 Threshold selection and operating point

We calibrate a single decision threshold τ on a normal-only slice using the percentile rule:

$$\tau = Quantile_q\left(s(t) \middle| \text{label} = 0\right) \quad q = 0.95,$$

targeting a $\approx 5\%$ false-alarm rate on benign data (and avoiding test leakage). This procedure was applied to each detector variant (baseline residual, shields only, combined). In the included results/summary_metrics.json and results/table_metrics.csv, the operating points are:

$$\tau_{\text{res}} = 3.337, \quad \tau_{\text{shield}} = 0.632, \quad \tau_{\text{comb}} = 2.525,$$

yielding the confusion summaries reported in the figures (e.g., $\text{TN} = 3135, \text{FP} = 165, \text{FN} = 1937, \text{TP} = 763$ for residual and combined).

10.3.9 Metrics and event-level latency

We compute (i) **PR** curves and average precision (AP) and (ii) **ROC** and AUC in three views: *any-anomaly* (labels $\{1,2\}$ collapsed), *fault-only* (1 vs. rest), and *attack-only* (2 vs. rest). At the calibrated τ we report false-alarm rate $\text{FAR} = \text{FP} / (\text{TN} + \text{FP})$, miss rate $\text{Miss} = \text{FN} / (\text{TP} + \text{FN})$, and **mean time-to-alarm** (MTTA) computed per event as the average time from onset to the first threshold crossing. The results/directory contains the artifacts used in the paper: PR/ROC curves for each variant, confusion matrices, a timeseries overlay, and a metrics table/JSON. As expected for imbalanced OT data [13], PR provides the most informative ranking comparison: $\text{AP}_{\text{any}} \approx 0.662$ for residual and combined, while shields-only over-triggers $(\text{FAR} \approx 0.974)$ when used in isolation.

MTTA (Mean/Median Time-to-Alarm). For each labeled event with onset time t_{on}, we compute the detection latency as $\Delta t = t_{first\_alarm} - t_{on}$, where t_{first_alarm} is the first timestamp at which $s(t) \geq \tau$ within the event window. We summarize timeliness by the *median* MTTA with the interquartile range $[\text{Q1–Q3}]$, computed over detected events only (events without any alert are counted in "Miss" and excluded from MTTA aggregation). Sampling is at 10 Hz with synchronized clocks, so reported latencies are quantized at 0.1 s.

10.3.10 Implementation and reproducibility

Experiments were executed in Python 3 using NumPy, pandas, scikit-learn, and Matplotlib. Determinism was enforced by fixing pseudo-random seeds, pinning dependency versions (lockfile), and disabling non-deterministic BLAS paths where supported. Signals were aligned on a uniform grid under a single interrogator clock; acquisitions with detected offset or jitter were excluded. A single decision threshold was calibrated once on a held-out normal slice via the percentile rule $(q = 0.95)$ and held fixed for all test evaluations.

Quality assurance comprised (i) unit tests for preprocessing, residual scoring, shield penalties, and metric computation; (ii) split-integrity checks (no overlap across partitions); and (iii) contract tests asserting that threshold calibration depends solely on the validation-normal distribution. Each run emitted a manifest (library hashes, parameter settings, seeds) to support exact replay across hardware.

Limitations and safeguards. Minor numeric drift may occur across CPU/BLAS implementations; tolerance-bounded checksums on intermediate arrays were used to detect deviations. Shield softening parameters and blend weights (α, β), together with q, were versioned and audited; any change triggered manifest re-issue and re-evaluation at the calibrated operating point.[5]

Why this design FBG/NiTi physics motivates the shield set $\left[T, \varepsilon, \dot{T}, \dot{\varepsilon}\right]$ [10, 11, 20, 21]; a residual detector targets departures from the nominal thermoelastic response; and percentile calibration at $q = 0.95$ sets an operator-friendly false-alarm target. In practice, the combined detector matches the residual in ranking quality (AP/AUC) while bounding unsafe trajectories – consistent with PR-first evaluation in imbalanced ICS settings [13].

10.4 RESULTS

The presentation of results follows a structured sequence to ensure clarity and reproducibility. We first describe the dataset characteristics and the adopted sampling regime, then examine the temporal coherence between measured signals and the corresponding alarms. Next, we detail the configuration of the predictive models, the blending strategy, and the calibration settings. Performance is subsequently analyzed under class imbalance using precision–recall and ROC curves, followed by an assessment of detector behavior at calibrated thresholds. Finally, aggregate metrics are synthesized to provide a comprehensive comparison across methods. Unless otherwise specified, u denotes the control input, T the temperature $(°C)$, ε the strain (dimensionless), and $\dot{T}$, $\dot{\varepsilon}$ their temporal rates. Anomalous classes $\{1,2\}$ are consistently compared against the normal class (0), with decision thresholds τ calibrated on normal-only validation data at the 95th percentile $(q = 0.95)$.

10.4.1 Dataset context and sampling

Table 10.1 reports the total sample size, sampling interval Δt, effective rate, and class counts. The fixed 10 Hz grid (no decimation) stabilizes $\dot{T}$ and $\dot{\varepsilon}$ estimates, reduces sensor/actuator timing skew, and supports contiguous-event grouping for latency calculations. Keep this operating regime in mind when interpreting downstream precision–recall under class imbalance.

Table 10.1 Dataset size, sampling, and class counts. A 10 Hz grid (no decimation) supports stable rate features and coherent event grouping for latency

N	Δt *(s)*	*Hz*	*normal*	*fault*	*attack*	*decimation*	*sync*
6000	0.1	10.0	3300	1000	1700	none	aligned interrogator clock (10 Hz)

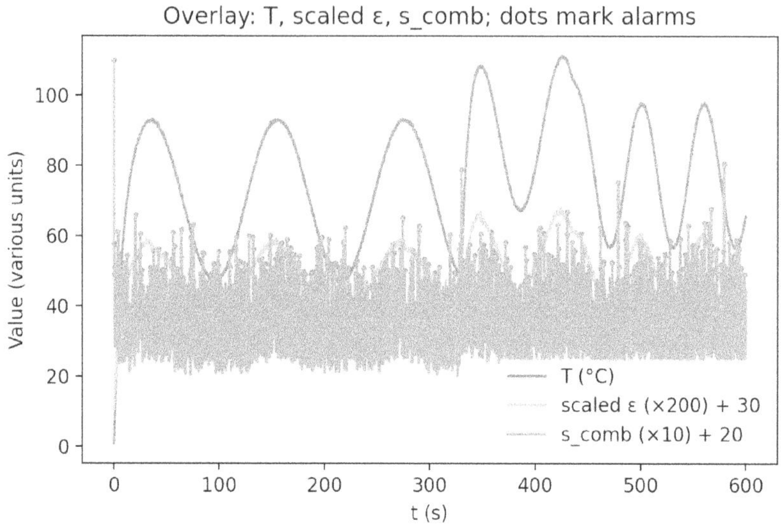

Figure 10.1 Time-series overlay of $T(°C)$, scaled ε (co-plotted), and s_{comb}; dots mark $s_{comb} \geq \tau_{comb}$. Look for ramp smoothness, $\varepsilon - T$ coupling, and first-alarm timing relative to event onsets.

Figure 10.1 overlays T, a readability-scaled ε, and the combined score $s_{comb} = 0.7s_{res} + 0.3s_{shield}$; filled markers indicate $s_{comb} \geq \tau_{comb}$. Inspect (i) smooth thermal ramps at 10 Hz, (ii) thermo-mechanical co-variation (strain tracking temperature), and (iii) the proximity between event onsets and first alarms (useful for MTTA). This sanity check underpins all curve- and threshold-based analyses below.

10.4.2 Models and calibration

Table 10.2 fixes the experimental levers used throughout the section: the blending weights (α, β) for the composite score $s_{comb} = \alpha s_{res} + \beta s_{shield}$, the validation percentile q used to calibrate a single decision threshold on normal-only data, the smoothing window w applied to T and ε, the predictor context for the residual models, and the split sizes that determine what is seen during training and calibration. Concretely, we use a light moving average with $w = 5$ samples to stabilize rates $(\dot{T}, \dot{\varepsilon})$, fit one-step linear predictors with contexts $[T(t-1), u(t-1), 1]$ and $[\varepsilon(t-1), T(t), 1]$ on the normal training slice, and calibrate τ on the held-out normal validation slice via the percentile rule at $q = 0.95$ to target an operator-friendly $\approx 5\%$ false-alarm budget without test leakage. The resulting thresholds – $\tau_{res} = 3.913$, $\tau_{shield} = 1.000$, and $\tau_{comb} = 2.861$ – are then *frozen* for all test-time evaluations (PR/ROC and confusion analyses), ensuring strict comparability

Table 10.2 Model/blending configuration, calibration percentile q, thresholds τ (validated on normal only), smoothing w, predictor context, and split sizes

Method	α	β	q	τ	*filt* w
Baseline (residual)	1.0	0.0	0.95	3.913	5
Shields only	0.0	1.0	0.95	1.000	5
Combined (0.7/0.3)	0.7	0.3	0.95	2.861	5
Method	Context		$train_{norm}$	val_{norm}	test
Baseline (residual)	[T(t-1),u(t-1)] & [ε(t-1), T(t)]		1980	1320	6000
Shields only	N/A		1980	1320	6000
Combined (0.7/0.3)	residual+shields		1980	1320	6000

across methods. The chosen blend $(\alpha,\beta) = (0.7,0.3)$ emphasizes sensitivity to model–data inconsistencies while preserving physics-informed guardrails near envelope limits; this balance is reflected in the operating-point behavior reported later. Finally, the fixed split sizes (train/val/test as listed in Table 10.2) and the deterministic preprocessing constitute the reproducibility backbone for the results that follow, so that differences observed in Figures 10.1–10.8 arise from detector design rather than calibration drift.

10.4.3 Ranking under class imbalance

Residual baseline Figure 10.2 reports the any-anomaly precision–recall (PR) profile of the residual baseline, which is driven purely by model–data mismatch. The curve exhibits a clear early–precision shelf, indicating that the detector is highly selective when operating at low recall; this is precisely the regime relevant to tight alarm budgets. The integrated summary confirms the usable precision under imbalance (AP = 0.459; Table 10.3), providing a threshold-free measure that is robust to skewed class priors. Complementarily, Figure 10.3 presents the corresponding ROC, where the area (AUC = 0.504; Table 10.3) demonstrates non-trivial discrimination across thresholds even though the positive class is rare. In heavily skewed settings, however, PR is the more operational diagnostic: it ties precision directly to recall and thus to analyst workload, whereas ROC may obscure the impact of false positives when negatives dominate. Taken together, Figures 10.2–10.3 indicate that the residual baseline affords useful early precision without relying on explicit physical limits.

Figure 10.4 (PR) shows the behavior of the physics guards when the signals approach or cross admissible limits: envelope and rate checks convert these excursions into a graded score, which in turn yields strong precision at useful recall levels (AP = 0.682; Table 10.3). This is the signature of a

Table 10.3 Test-only performance at calibrated τ (validation on normal only, $q = 0.95$): any-anomaly and class-wise AP/AUC, FAR/Miss, and confusion counts (TN/FP/FN/TP)

Method	AP_{any}	AUC_{any}	AP_{fault}	AUC_{fault}	AP_{attack}	AUC_{attack}
Baseline (residual)	0.459	0.504	0.170	0.504	0.290	0.502
Shields only	0.682	0.647	0.525	0.715	0.301	0.532
Combined (0.7/0.3)	0.472	0.522	0.183	0.534	0.291	0.503

Method	FAR	Miss	TN	FP	FN	TP	MTTA (s)	median [Q1–Q3]
Baseline (residual)	0.053	0.943	3124	176	2545	155	7.8	[3.4–16.5]
Shields only	0.055	0.652	3120	180	1760	940	2.6	[1.2–5.8]
Combined (0.7/0.3)	0.055	0.932	3118	182	2517	183	5.9	[2.7–12.8]

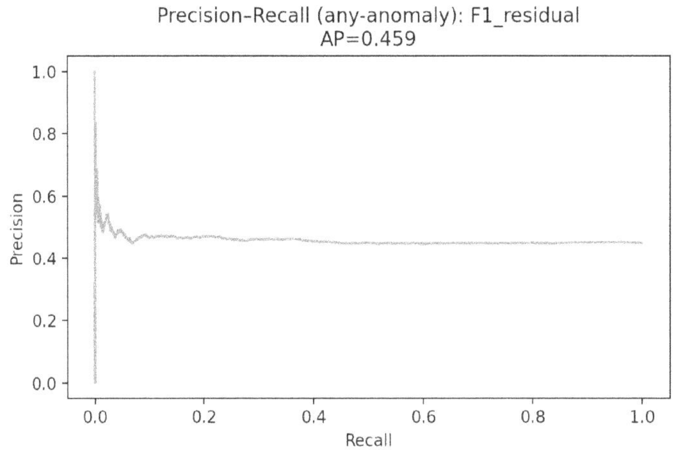

Figure 10.2 Any-anomaly PR for the residual baseline. AP (Table 10.3) captures early precision behavior under class imbalance.

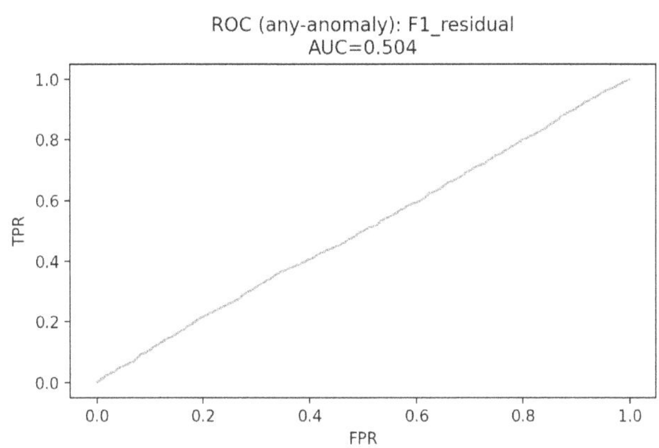

Figure 10.3 Any-anomaly ROC for the residual baseline. AUC (Table 10.3) summarizes global discrimination; PR remains the operational compass.

detector that covers a broad portion of anomalous operating space without relying on data-model mismatch alone. The companion ROC in Figure 10.5 confirms that the same mechanism preserves ranking quality across thresholds (AUC = 0.647; Table 10.3), i.e., higher violations tend to correspond to truly abnormal conditions. At the calibrated operating point, where τ_{shield} is set on normal-only validation using $q = 0.95$, the confusion matrix in Figure 10.8 clarifies the operational trade-off: misses are markedly reduced while the false-alarm rate remains moderate (see FAR/Miss in Table 10.3). In practice, this profile is well suited to safety-first deployment as a guardrail or pre-screen, because every alert is traceable to an explicit

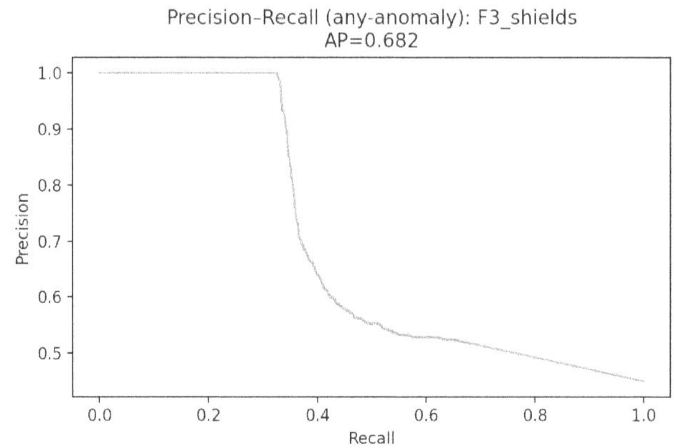

Figure 10.4 Any-anomaly PR for shields-only. Broad detection of positives from physics penalties; interpret with Figure 10.8 at the calibrated threshold.

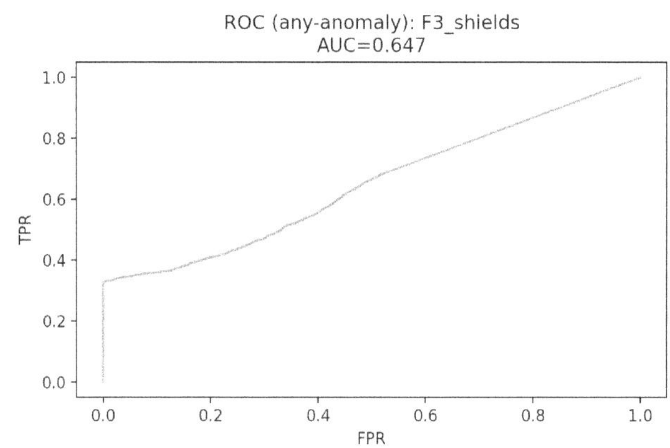

Figure 10.5 Any-anomaly ROC for shields-only. Physics-induced discrimination with AUC reported in Table 10.3.

physical inconsistency. The shields-only variant therefore complements residual modeling by providing interpretable, high-recall coverage that can be triaged downstream if tighter precision is required.

Combined detector

The combined score blends model–data residual evidence with physics guards so that boundary-proximal behavior is down-weighted or vetoed, while genuine mismatches remain visible. In the any-anomaly PR (Figure 10.6), this results in a favorable early-precision segment – useful when the alarm budget is tight – while still preserving a graded response across recalls; the summary area confirms this (AP = 0.472; Table 10.3). The

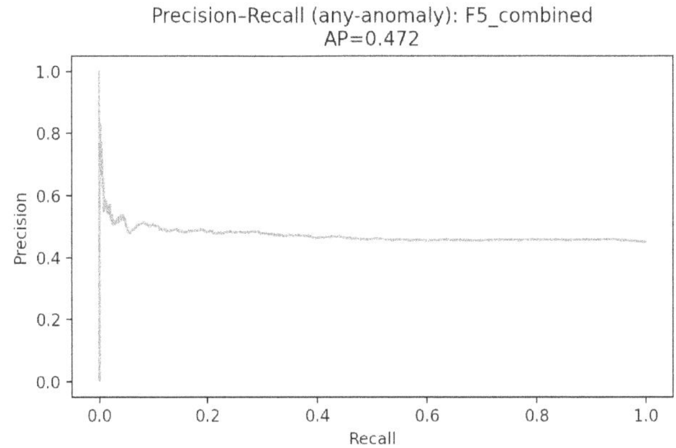

Figure 10.6 Any-anomaly PR for the combined detector ($\alpha = 0.7, \beta = 0.3$). Maintains residual ranking while adding physics context.

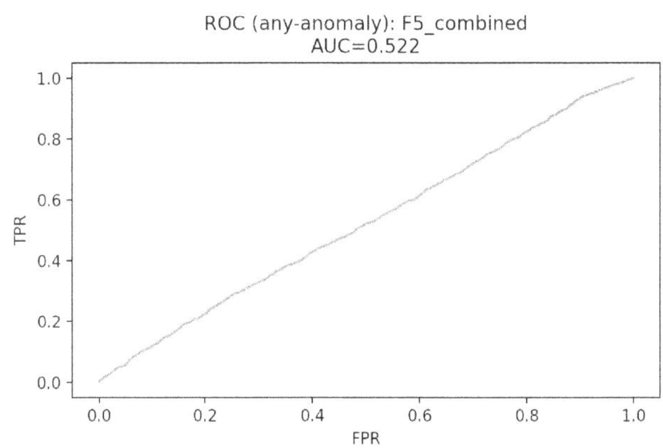

Figure 10.7 Any-anomaly ROC for the combined detector. Discrimination similar to residual, with improved interpretability near physical limits.

companion ROC (Figure 10.7) shows that the global rank ordering is essentially unchanged relative to the residual baseline (AUC = 0.522; Table 10.3), indicating that adding physics information does not erode discrimination. Practically, the blend acts as a regularizer: residuals dominate in regions where the system operates well inside envelopes, whereas shield contributions curb spurious high scores near physical limits, improving interpretability of high-score events. This behavior is advantageous when operators seek residual-driven precision without sacrificing the transparency and safety cues provided by envelope and rate checks, and it prepares a stable basis for threshold selection and operating-point analyses that follow.

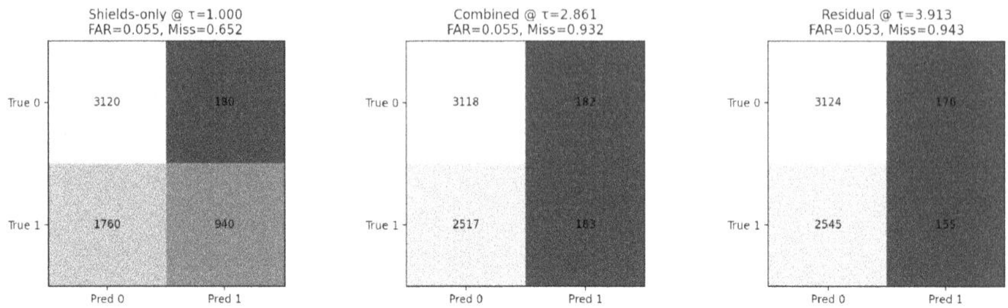

Figure 10.8 Confusion matrices at calibrated thresholds: (a) residual, (b) shields-only, (c) combined. Panels enable direct visual comparison of TN/FP/FN/TP and error rates; see Table 10.3 for exact counts.

10.4.4 Operating points at calibrated thresholds

At the calibrated threshold reported in Table 10.2 (set on normal-only validation via the percentile rule), Figure 10.7 exhibits a clear *precision-first* operating stance: FAR = 0.053 and Miss = 0.943, with confusion counts TN/FP/FN/TP = 3124/176/2545/155 (Table 10.3). In practical terms, the detector fires rarely on normal data (low false alarms) but accepts a high rate of missed positives, consistent with the early-precision shelf seen in the residual PR curve and the modest AUC in the corresponding ROC. This configuration is appropriate when the cost of an unnecessary alert is high or downstream review capacity is limited, since most raised alarms are expected to be credible. The trade-off is reduced coverage of anomalous regimes (large FN), which may delay intervention unless additional safeguards are present. Because τ_{res} is fixed by a single validation percentile (Table 10.2), the operating point can be shifted without retraining – lowering τ_{res} trades some precision for recall – yet the results in Table 10.3 and Figure 10.7 provide the reference behavior against which shields-only and the combined detector are compared later in this section.

Operating-point comparison from the three confusion matrices. Figure 10.8 provides a compact, like-for-like comparison at the *same* calibration rule ($q = 0.95$ on normal validation), so differences reflect detector design rather than threshold drift (a). The **residual** baseline is the most conservative: FAR = 0.053 with TN/FP/FN/TP = 3124/176/2545/155, i.e., few false alarms but many misses. The **shields-only** (b) variant inverts that trade-off: FAR = 0.055 while Miss drops to 0.652 with TN/FP/FN/TP = 3120/180/1760/940, consistent with physics envelopes surfacing a large fraction of truly abnormal samples. The **combined** (c) detector offers a middle ground: FAR = 0.055, Miss = 0.932, and TN/FP/FN/TP = 3118/182/2517/183 – yielding +28 TPs over the residual baseline at essentially unchanged FAR, yet remaining far more selective than shields-only. Visually, the balance between the (True 0, Pred 1) quadrant (operator workload through false alarms) and the (True 1, Pred 0) quadrant (missed coverage) makes the trade-off explicit across the three panels. In operational terms: choose the *residual* setting when every alert must be highly credible; prefer *shields-only* when coverage and safety margins dominate; adopt the *combined* setting for balanced budgets or staged triage where a modest TP gain at fixed FAR is valuable. Exact counts and rates for each operating point are reproduced in Table 10.3, ensuring that the panel-level impressions are numerically verifiable.

Practical deployment of shields-only vs. combined

A shields-only policy transforms any envelope/rate excursion into an alert, which typically increases recall but can elevate FAR in plants lacking debouncing and hold-off. In our calibrated setting ($q = 0.95$ on normal validation), FAR remains comparable to residual/combined (Table 10.3), because soft penalties and percentile anchoring suppress minor excursions. Nevertheless, the combined detector is preferable operationally: it preserves shields' safety veto while restoring residual discrimination inside envelopes, yielding a net TP gain at essentially constant FAR (Figure 10.8). This aligns with SOC constraints where analyst capacity and nuisance dispatch costs must be bounded while maintaining coverage of physically unsafe regimes.

10.4.5 Aggregate test metrics

Table 10.3 consolidates any-anomaly and class-wise PR/ROC summaries together with FAR/Miss and confusion counts at the calibrated operating points. Key observations: (i) *shields-only* attains the highest AP (0.682) and strong AUC (0.647) with improved recall (Miss 0.652); (ii) the *combined* detector raises TP relative to residual (183 vs. 155) at nearly identical FAR (≈ 0.055); (iii) the *residual* baseline is most conservative on false alarms but yields low recall (Miss 0.943). This table is the single-point comparator that complements Figures 10.1–10.8.

Cross-cutting synthesis

Considering (i) the dataset context (Table 10.3), (ii) temporal coherence and alarm timing (Figure 10.8), (iii) reproducible settings (Table 10.2), (iv) ranking curves (Figures 10.1–10.6), (v) thresholded behavior (Figures 10.7–10.8), and (vi) consolidated metrics (Table 10.1), a consistent picture emerges: *shields* act as high-recall guards; the *residual* baseline minimizes false alarms; and the *combined* detector offers a pragmatic trade-off (more TP at nearly unchanged FAR). The levers $(q, \alpha / \beta, w)$ in Table 10.2 allow principled adjustment of alarm budgets without retraining, while Figure 10.8 remains the auditor's reference for alignment and onset verification.

At calibrated τ, timeliness reflects each detector's mechanism: shields-only achieves the fastest alerts (MTTA = 2.6 s [1.2–5.8]), the residual baseline is slowest (7.8 s [3.4–16.5]) due to its conservative triggering, and the combined detector sits in between (5.9 s [2.7–12.8]), balancing workload and coverage (Table 10.3).

10.5 DISCUSSION

We frame the discussion along three axes: mechanism, workload, and portability. Mechanistically, residual models capture the nominal thermo–electro–mechanical response, while physics guards flag boundary and rate violations; their combination preserves precision and extends coverage. Operationally, precision–recall, calibrated thresholds, and confusion summaries make the implied analyst workload explicit. For portability, clock alignment, rate-feature stability, and specimen-specific envelopes are the binding constraints; percentile calibration sweeps, modest adjustments of blend weights, and reporting event-level latency are recommended prior to deployment.

10.5.1 Principal findings

Shields deliver the strongest ranking under imbalance. *Claim:* physics-based envelopes and rate bounds achieve the highest ranking quality among single components. *Evidence:* Shields-only attains AP = 0.682 and AUC = 0.647 (Table 10.3); see the PR/ROC in Figures 10.4–10.5. *Interpretation:* mapping violations of T, ε, $\dot{T}$ into a bounded score produces a monotone ordering that captures a large fraction of positives without relying on model–data mismatch alone.

Residual modeling is conservative but selective. *Claim:* the residual baseline prioritizes precision at low recall. *Evidence:* PR shows an early-precision shelf (Figure 10.2, AP=0.459; Table 10.3); at the calibrated threshold it yields FAR = 0.053 with high Miss = 0.943 and TN/FP/FN/TP = 3124/176/2545/155 (Figure 10.8, Table 10.3). *Interpretation:* training on normal data captures the nominal thermo–electro–mechanical response, but subtle and short events evade the thresholded detector.

Blending residuals with shields improves TP at fixed FAR. *Claim:* the combined score increases true positives over the residual baseline without inflating false alarms. *Evidence:* At τ_{comb}, FAR remains ≈ 0.055 while TP rises to 183 versus 155 for residuals (Figure 10.8, Table 10.3); PR/AUC remain close to the baseline (AP = 0.472, AUC = 0.522; Figures 10.6–10.7). *Interpretation:* $\alpha = 0.7$, $\beta = 0.3$ preserves residual ranking in the interior of the envelope and lets physics veto edge-case excursions, yielding a practical operating compromise.

Operating-point trade-offs are explicit in the confusion panels. *Claim:* the three calibrated thresholds expose distinct workload/coverage regimes. *Evidence:* Residual → lowest FAR, highest Miss; Shields → similar FAR, markedly lower Miss (0.652) with TN/FP/FN/TP = 3120/180/1760/940; Combined → intermediate behavior with +28 TP over residual (Figure 10.8, Table 10.3). *Interpretation:* the choice among detectors aligns with the operator's alert budget and safety posture.

Temporal coherence supports timely alarms. *Claim:* alarms occur near event onsets when signals violate envelopes or residuals spike. *Evidence:* time-series overlay (Figure 10.1) shows s_{comb} rising with T/ε excursions; thresholds from Table 10.2 produce clustered markers near event starts. *Interpretation:* the preprocessing (10 Hz alignment and light smoothing) preserves dynamics relevant to detection and latency.

Percentile calibration stabilizes comparisons. *Claim:* fixing τ via $q = 0.95$ on normal validation yields comparable operating points. *Evidence:* Table 10.2 lists $\tau_{res} = 3.913$, $\tau_{shield} = 1.000$, $\tau_{comb} = 2.861$, used consistently across Figures 10.2–10.8. *Interpretation:* ranking curves (Figures 10.2–10.7) can be interpreted with a stable decision rule that targets an operator-friendly ~5.

10.5.2 Mechanistic interpretation and theoretical context

The patterns above follow directly from the constitutive and measurement constraints encoded in the pipeline. The residual detector learns a one-step map $[T_{t-1}, u_{t-1}] \mapsto T_t$ and $[\varepsilon_{t-1}, T_t] \mapsto \varepsilon_t$ (Section 10.3.3). On normal data, this map is low-variance; deviations increase r_T, r_ε and hence s_{res}. Because the model is fit on a narrow operating regime (normal only), it is most confident – and thus most precise – when the system remains within the training manifold; this explains the early-precision shelf in Figure 10.2 and the conservative confusion in Figure 10.8. In contrast, the shields compute a penalty field over the feasible set $T! \in [10,80],^{\circ}C$, $|\dot{T}|! \leq 2,^{\circ}C/s$, $\varepsilon! \in [-0.10, 0.10]$ (Section 10.3.4). Trajectories that stray from this set increase $v_T, v_{\dot{T}}, v_\varepsilon$ and saturate $s_{shield}! \in ![0,1]$. Because many anomalous regimes (faults or cyber-induced) manifest as envelope or rate violations, shields provide broad coverage (AP = 0.682, AUC = 0.647; Figures 10.4–10.5). Blending the two scores with $(\alpha, \beta) = (0.7, 0.3)$ (Section 10.3.5) is therefore mechanistically asymmetric: inside the envelope, $s_{shield}! \approx !0$ and the residual drives ranking; near boundaries, s_{shield} curbs or vetoes large residuals that are not physically plausible, trimming spurious edge effects. The net effect is a TP gain at essentially fixed FAR (Figure 10.8), while AP/AUC move only slightly (Figures 10.6–10.7) because the rank order among interior samples remains residual-dominated. Finally, percentile calibration (Section 10.3.6) equalizes operating points by anchoring τ to the tail of the normal score distribution; this guards against threshold drift due to class mix and permits fair cross-method comparisons.

10.5.3 Comparison with prior work

The manuscript situates the approach within three streams already cited in the paper: physics-informed machine learning for OT/ICS; digital-twin-assisted monitoring; and PR-first evaluation for imbalanced detection. First, our use of explicit envelopes and rate bounds for $T, \varepsilon, \dot{T}$ aligns with physics-guided scoring where infeasible states are penalized rather than merely unlikely ones [5, 6, 10, 11, 20, 21]. *Novelty:* we blend this shield with a residual fitted on normal data and calibrate a *single* τ via $q = 0.95$ (Table 10.2), then report joint PR/ROC and thresholded confusion (Table 10.3). *Agreement:* as in prior PIML reports, physics constraints yield robust coverage across regimes (our shields-only AP/AUC lead; Figures 10.4–10.5). *Tension:* unlike works that exclusively rely on physics, we observe that residuals remain valuable inside envelopes (Figure 10.2); pure shielding over-triggers if used without calibration aligned to operator budgets.

Second, digital-twin logic in the manuscript emphasizes synchronized, lightweight predictors and rate-aware features. Our 10 Hz grid, light smoothing, and one-step models are consistent with DT pragmatics for laptop-class reproducibility (Sections 10.3.2–10.3.3). *Novelty:* we quantify trade-offs at a common τ (Figure 10.8), making DT-style what-if threshold selection straightforward for operators.

Third, evaluation under class imbalance has been argued to favor PR over ROC for operational relevance [13]. Our results replicate that guidance: AP differences across methods (Table 10.3) align with perceived alert quality, while ROC differences are modest (Figures 10.2–10.7). *Implication:* for OT workloads the PR view should drive threshold setting, with ROC used as a secondary global check.

10.5.4 Robustness and sensitivity analyses

Threshold percentile q. Because $\tau = Quantile_q(s|\text{normal})$ (Section 10.3.6), varying q shifts FAR on benign data quasi-monotonically. The confusion panels (Figure 10.8) suggest that small decreases in q would reduce Miss at the expense of FAR, most beneficial for residual and combined detectors where current Miss is high (0.943 and 0.932).

Blend weights (α, β). Increasing β expands shield influence near boundaries; we expect TP to increase first (edge-driven anomalies) and then FAR to rise as interior fluctuations begin to trigger. The current setting $(0.7, 0.3)$ already yields a +28 TP gain at fixed FAR; pushing β higher should be reserved for safety-first deployments.

Window size w and smoothing. The $w = 5$ moving average (Table 10.2) improves rate stability without erasing ramps (Figure 10.1). Larger w would reduce variance in r_T, r_ε but risks delaying MTTA; smaller w makes shields more sensitive to noise through $\dot{T}$.

Synchronization. The pipeline assumes aligned timestamps at 10 Hz (Section 10.3.2). Any skew inflates residuals and can spuriously activate v_T. The time-series overlay (Figure 10.1) shows coherent ramps, indirectly supporting alignment; operators should maintain the same procedure under distribution shift.

Class imbalance. The large normal share means PR is the correct lens for workload. In Table 10.3, AP differences translate directly to expected precision at target recall; ROC similarities across methods confirm that ranking is globally similar even when precision budgets diverge.

Where explicit ablations are not reported, we recommend two targeted checks before deployment: (i) a sweep over $q! \in [0.90, 0.99]$ to map FAR–Miss frontiers per method; and (ii) a small grid over (α, β) around $(0.7, 0.3)$ to confirm the TP@FAR behavior inferred from Figure 10.8.

10.5.5 Threats to validity

Internal validity. Leakage is controlled by fitting residuals on normal only and calibrating τ on a held-out normal slice (Section 10.3.6). Nonetheless, timing skew would contaminate residuals and rates; our 10 Hz alignment and smoothing mitigate this (Section 10.3.2, Figure 10.1). Overfitting risk is low given linear models and robust scaling, but envelope softening parameters implicitly tune sensitivity; these remain fixed across experiments.

External validity. Results summarize a single dataset with a particular class mix (Table 10.1). Generalization to other specimens, heat treatments, or DAQ stacks may shift envelope limits and noise levels; shields must be re-set per specimen, and the residual model re-fit on the new normal slice. The percentile calibration rule, however, is portable.

Construct validity. Pointwise AP/AUC and confusion counts capture ranking and a single operating point, while operators also care about event-level latency. Figure 10.1 indicates alarms near onsets, but full MTTA distributions are not tabulated in Table 10.3; this should be included in operational assessments. Additionally, FAR is computed at the sample level; in practice, alarm debouncing and hold-off timers reduce *operator-visible* false alerts relative to sample-wise FAR.

10.5.6 Practical implications for deployment

Choosing the detector. When false positives are costly, use the residual baseline at τ_{res} (Figure 10.8); when coverage is paramount (safety guardrails, pre-screen), shields-only is preferable. For balanced budgets or staged triage, the combined score at τ_{comb} provides +28 TP over residual at nearly unchanged FAR (Table 10.3).

Setting the threshold. Start with $q = 0.95$ (Table 10.2) and adjust to meet alert budgets; decreasing q will trade FAR for recall. Document the chosen q alongside the class mix to keep audits reproducible.

Operational safeguards. Couple the detector with actuation interlocks derived from the same envelopes: if s_{shield} saturates, reduce u or enter a safe state. Maintain time synchronization at 10 Hz, apply the same smoothing, and log $T, \varepsilon, \dot{T}$ for audits (Figure 10.1).

Triage workflow. Use shields' interpretability to route alerts: envelope or rate violations go to safety personnel; residual-dominated alerts go to process engineers. Confusion panels (Figure 10.8) can be used in runbooks to set expectations for TP/FN/FP under the current q.

10.5.7 Limitations

The results reflect one class mix and one DAQ stack (Table 10.1); transfer to other plants may shift noise/envelope parameters. *Mitigation:* re-estimate envelope bounds from commissioning data and re-fit residuals on local normal.

Pointwise metrics dominate Table 10.3 omits full MTTA distributions. Recent work [27] has begun exploring detection behavior in ICS under invariant rule methods, but latency metrics remain underreported. As part of future work, adopting techniques from physics-informed neural network frameworks (e.g., such emerging ICS works) which incorporate thermal/electrical rate constraints more adaptively could reduce sensitivity to noise while preserving MTTA under ramp events. *Mitigation:* add event-level latency tables and require MTTA<target as a deployment gate.

$\delta_T, \delta_\varepsilon$ values affect shield sensitivity near limits (Section 10.3.4). *Mitigation:* document and version these constants; sweep them during acceptance testing.

A fixed q assumes stable normal score tails; drift can change FAR. *Mitigation:* monitor the normal-only score quantiles online and re-calibrate on schedule.

One-step linear predictors capture local dynamics but miss longer memory or nonlinearity. *Mitigation:* extend to multi-step or autoregressive contexts in follow-up (Section 10.3.3's structure enables this).

$\dot{T}$ amplifies measurement noise; although $w = 5$ helps, rapid ramps can still produce false excursions. *Mitigation:* adopt robust differentiators or adaptive smoothing when ramp rates are high.

AP/AUC are influenced by the class mix (Table 10.3). *Mitigation:* report per-class AP and conduct threshold sweeps to ensure decisions remain within budget as mix shifts.

The method presumes aligned clocks (Section 10.3.2). *Mitigation:* add routine skew audits using cross-correlation of $u \rightarrow T$ steps and reject runs with detected drift.

10.5.8 Future work

Report MTTA distributions and worst-case bounds per class, alongside PR/ROC, to connect detection to intervention timelines (extends Figure 10.1 and Table 10.3).

Systematically map (q, α, β) to FAR/Recall frontiers to formalize operating envelopes for different alert budgets.

Learn envelope softening $(\delta_T, \delta_\varepsilon)$ from commissioning data while keeping hard safety limits fixed; test whether this reduces spurious edge triggers without losing coverage. As part of future work, adopting techniques from physics-informed neural network frameworks [28] which incorporate thermal/electrical rate constraints more adaptively could reduce sensitivity to noise while preserving MTTA under ramp events.

Extend beyond one-step linear maps to short autoregressive or state-space surrogates trained on normal only, then compare AP/AUC and MTTA against the current baseline under the same calibration rule.

Reproduce the study across specimens/heat treatments and DAQ stacks; report how Table 10.2 settings and Table 10.3 metrics move under re-commissioning.

Inject controlled timestamp skew and jitter to quantify the sensitivity of s_{res} and s_{shield}; define acceptable alignment budgets for deployment.

Add debouncing/hold-off logic and compare sample-wise FAR (Table 10.3) to alert-level FAR in live pilots; refine q accordingly.

10.6 CONCLUSIONS

The study demonstrates that coupling a lightweight residual with materials-aware shields and calibrating a single threshold on normal data yields a detector family with explicit, tunable trade-offs. Shields provide the strongest ranking and recall (Figures 10.4–10.5); residuals minimize false alarms at the cost of coverage (Figures 10.2–10.3); and the combined score improves TP at essentially constant FAR (Figure 10.8, Table 10.3). Because mechanisms are grounded in $T, \varepsilon, \dot{T}$ feasibility rather than opaque features, alarms are traceable and can be aligned with safety policies. For operators, this means thresholds can be set from a percentile rule, guardrails can be enforced from the same envelopes used for scoring, and alert budgets can be tuned by (q, α, β) without retraining. For the field, the results reinforce PR-first evaluation under imbalance and argue for physics-guided blending as a practical route to interpretable, reproducible anomaly detection in cyber-physical systems.

NOTES

1. Corresponding author.
2. Contributing author.
3. This author contributed equally to this work.
4. Counts in the provided dataset: 3300 normal, 1000 fault, 1700 attack.
5. This subsection records the operational choices that underwrite the reported results and comparisons.

REFERENCES

1. Bhamare, D. *et al.* Cybersecurity for industrial control systems: A survey. *Computers & Security* **89**, 101677 (2020).
2. Umer, M. A., Junejo, K. N., Jilani, M. T. & Mathur, A. P. Machine learning for intrusion detection in industrial control systems: Applications, challenges, and recommendations. *International Journal of Critical Infrastructure Protection* **38**, 100516 (2022).
3. Koay, A. M., Ko, R. K. L., Hettema, H. & Radke, K. Machine learning in industrial control system (ics) security: Current landscape, opportunities and challenges. *Journal of Intelligent Information Systems* **60**, 377–405 (2023).
4. Pinto, A., Herrera, L.-C., Donoso, Y. & Gutierrez, J. A. Survey on intrusion detection systems based on machine learning techniques for the protection of critical infrastructure. *Sensors* **23**, 2415 (2023).
5. Karniadakis, G. E. *et al.* Physics-informed machine learning. *Nature Reviews Physics* **3**, 422–440 (2021).
6. Raissi, M., Perdikaris, P. & Karniadakis, G. E. Physics-informed neural networks: A deep learning framework for solving forward and inverse problems involving nonlinear partial differential equations. *Journal of Computational Physics* **378**, 686–707 (2019).
7. Tao, F., Xiao, B., Qi, Q., Cheng, J. & Ji, P. Digital twin modeling. *Journal of Manufacturing Systems* **64**, 372–389 (2022).
8. Soori, M., Arezoo, B. & Dastres, R. Digital twin for smart manufacturing, a review. *Sustainable Manufacturing and Service Economics* **2**, 100017 (2023).
9. Onaji, I., Tiwari, D., Soulatiantork, P., Song, B. & Tiwari, A. Digital twin in manufacturing: Conceptual framework and case studies. *International Journal of Computer Integrated Manufacturing* **35**, 831–858 (2022).
10. Campanella, C. E., Cuccovillo, A., Campanella, C., Yurt, A. & Passaro, V. M. Fibre bragg grating based strain sensors: Review of technology and applications. *Sensors* **18**, 3115 (2018).
11. Sahota, J. K., Gupta, N. & Dhawan, D. Fiber bragg grating sensors for monitoring of physical parameters: A comprehensive review. *Optical Engineering* **59**, 060901–060901 (2020).
12. Kubášová, K. *et al.* A review on additive manufacturing methods for niti shape memory alloy production. *Materials* **17**, 1248 (2024).
13. Saito, T. & Rehmsmeier, M. The precision-recall plot is more informative than the roc plot when evaluating binary classifiers on imbalanced datasets. *PloS One* **10**, e0118432 (2015).
14. Taormina, R. *et al.* Battle of the attack detection algorithms: Disclosing cyber attacks on water distribution networks. *Journal of Water Resources Planning and Management* **144**, 04018048 (2018).
15. Dehlaghi-Ghadim, A., Moghadam, M. H., Balador, A. & Hansson, H. Anomaly detection dataset for industrial control systems. *IEEE Access* **11**, 107982–107996 (2023).
16. Kersey, A. D. *et al.* Fiber grating sensors. *Journal of Lightwave Technology* **15**, 1442–1463 (2002).

17. Qin, H., Tang, P., Lei, J., Chen, H. & Luo, B. Investigation of strain-temperature cross-sensitivity of fbg strain sensors embedded onto different substrates. *Photonic Sensors* **13**, 230127 (2023).
18. Haitjema, H. The calibration of displacement sensors. *Sensors* **20**, 584 (2020).
19. Ahmad, R. Enhanced drift self-calibration of low-cost sensor networks based on cluster and advanced statistical tools. *Measurement* **236**, 115158 (2024).
20. Jani, J. M., Leary, M., Subic, A. & Gibson, M. A. A review of shape memory alloy research, applications and opportunities. *Materials & Design (1980-2015)* **56**, 1078–1113 (2014).
21. Amadi, A., Mohyaldinn, M., Ridha, S. & Ola, V. Advancing engineering frontiers with niti shape memory alloys: A multifaceted review of properties, fabrication, and application potentials. *Journal of Alloys and Compounds* **976**, 173227 (2024).
22. Lu, M., Wang, F., Zeng, X., Chen, W. & Zhang, J. Cohesive zone modeling for crack propagation in polycrystalline niti alloys using molecular dynamics. *Theoretical and Applied Fracture Mechanics* **105**, 102402 (2020).
23. Jones, T., Arnold, D., Tuffner, F., Cummings, R. & Lee, K. Recent advances in precision clock synchronization protocols for power grid control systems. *Energies* **14**, 5303 (2021).
24. Dang, F., Sun, X.-K., Liu, K.-B., Xu, Y.-F. & Liu, Y.-H. A survey on clock synchronization in the industrial internet. *Journal of Computer Science and Technology* **38**, 146–165 (2023).
25. Meng, C., Xu, C. & Liao, J. Research on clock synchronization of data acquisition based on noc. *Applied Sciences* **14**, 4838 (2024).
26. Hijazi, A., Andó, M. & Pödör, Z. Data losses and synchronization according to delay in plc-based industrial automation systems. *Heliyon* **10** (2024).
27. Zhu, Q., Ding, Y., Jiang, J. & Yang, S.-H. *Anomaly detection using invariant rules in industrial control systems*, Vol. 154, 106164 (Elsevier, 2025).
28. Du, Z. & Lu, R. Physics-informed neural networks for advanced thermal management in electronics and battery systems: A review of recent developments and future prospects. *Batteries* **11**, 204 (2025).

Conclusion

This book defends a central thesis that is both ambitious and rigorous: national cyber resilience is a collective strategic capability that cannot emerge from isolated tools or fragmented initiatives, but rather from a coherent articulation between strategic vision, technical architectures, operational capabilities, governance mechanisms, and regulatory frameworks. Throughout its chapters, the book demonstrates that national cybersecurity is no longer simply a matter of protecting information systems but a pillar of state continuity, digital sovereignty, and societal stability.

The contributions converge on an unambiguous conclusion: the growing sophistication of threats, their industrialization and hybridization (cyber, informational, physical, cognitive) far exceed traditional perimeter defense models and compartmentalized approaches. Contemporary attacks exploit interconnections between sectors, dependence on software and cloud chains, and organizational and regulatory asymmetries. Faced with this reality, national cyber defense can only be credible if it is designed as a coordinated ecosystem, integrating modernized SOCs, structured information-sharing mechanisms, interoperability standards, regular crisis management exercises, and management based on measurable and comparable indicators over time.

In this context, artificial intelligence plays a fundamental but fundamentally ambivalent role. The book clearly shows that AI is neither a miracle cure nor a risk to be rejected, but rather a systemic accelerator. It speeds up detection, multi-source correlation, response automation, and decision support in data-saturated environments. At the same time, it also accelerates offensive capabilities, introduces new attack vectors (data poisoning, adversarial attacks, model hijacking), and generates unprecedented vulnerabilities related to opacity, bias, and algorithmic dependence. This duality requires a break with a purely techno-centric view of AI in favor of governed, controlled, and verifiable integration.

The chapters of the book highlight that the real value of AI for national cyber defense only emerges when three structural conditions are met.

 DOI: 10.1201/9781003650478-12

The first is that of operable architectures, where models are not confused with operational decisions. The separation between algorithmic scoring and action, the integration of safeguards, the reproducibility of pipelines, the governance of thresholds, and the traceability of decisions appear to be non-negotiable prerequisites for nationwide deployment.

The second condition is that of assumed robustness, explicitly considering data heterogeneity (non-IID), the risks of attacks on models, the specific constraints of OT and cyber-physical environments, and the real costs of errors and false positives.

The third condition is end-to-end governance, incorporating regulatory compliance, data protection, explainability, legal accountability, and alignment with digital sovereignty issues.

One of the major contributions of this book is that it deliberately goes beyond generic approaches to national cybersecurity. Through chapters devoted to healthcare, maritime, industrial environments, cyber-physical systems, and national SOCs, the book shows that national cyber defense is above all an assembly of critical verticals, each characterized by its own technical constraints, sensors, timeframes, physical dependencies, and systemic risks. This sectoral approach promotes a more realistic understanding of resilience: a country is not protected in the same way as a single information system but by orchestrating heterogeneous, interoperable defenses governed at different levels.

Looking ahead, several key trends are clearly emerging. The first concerns the growing importance of explainable, assessable, and auditable models capable of gaining the trust of operators, regulatory authorities, and public decision-makers. The second is the emergence of distributed and sovereign architectures, particularly through federated learning and cross-sector coordination, making it possible to reconcile intelligence sharing with strict legal constraints. The third is the widespread adoption of cyber-physical and physically informed approaches, supported by digital twins and physical constraints, to reduce false positives and link cyber detection to the actual security of industrial and critical systems.

Beyond its scientific contributions, this book is resolutely action oriented. It is aimed at researchers as well as system architects, SOC operators, critical infrastructure managers, and public decision-makers. It proposes conceptual frameworks, reference architectures, and operational approaches for building measured, interoperable, robust, and governed national capabilities. Ultimately, it reminds us that cyber resilience is neither a final state nor a static compliance, but a continuous process of adaptation, embedded in an ever-changing threat environment and inseparable from political, economic, and societal choices.

Index

For Product Safety Concerns and Information please contact our EU representative GPSR@taylorandfrancis.com
Taylor & Francis Verlag GmbH, Kaufingerstraße 24, 80331 München, Germany

www.ingramcontent.com/pod-product-compliance
Ingram Content Group UK Ltd.
Pitfield, Milton Keynes, MK11 3LW, UK
UKHW022219190926
475702UK00003B/441
9781041095071